ANTISEMITISM: THE GENERIC HATRED

Antisemitism:
The Generic Hatred

Essays in Memory of Simon Wiesenthal

Editors
MICHAEL FINEBERG
SHIMON SAMUELS
MARK WEITZMAN

United Nations Educational
Scientific and Cultural Organization

Centre
Simon
Wiesenthal

VERBE ET LUMIÈRE
VIGILANCE   www.verbelumiere.org

VALLENTINE MITCHELL
LONDON • PORTLAND, OR

First published in 2007 in Great Britain by
VALLENTINE MITCHELL
Suite 314, Premier House, 112–114 Station Road,
Edgware, Middlesex HA8 7BJ

and in the United States of America by
VALLENTINE MITCHELL
c/o ISBS, 920 NE 58th Avenue, Suite 300
Portland, OR 97213-3786

www.vmbooks.com

British Library Cataloguing in Publication Data
Antisemitism : the generic hatred : essays in memory of
Simon Wiesenthal
1. Wiesenthal, Simon 2. Antisemitism 3. Prejudices
I. Wiesenthal, Simon II. Fineberg, Michael III. Samuels,
Shimon IV. Weitzman, Mark
305.8 '924

ISBN 978 0 85303 745 3 (cloth)
ISBN 978 0 85303 746 0 (paper)

Library of Congress Cataloging-in-Publication Data
A catalog record has bee applied for

The editors can be contacted via email: csweurope@compuserve.com.

The authors are responsible for the choice and presentation of the facts
contained in this book and for the opinions expressed therein, which are
not necessarily those of UNESCO, the Simon Wiesenthal Centre, or Verbe
et Lumière-Vigilance, and do not commit any of these three organizations.

Printed in Great Britain by Antony Rowe Ltd,
Chippenham, Wilts.

Contents

Preface

This book was to have been a 'Festschrift' tribute to Simon Wiesenthal in his lifetime. With his passing at the age of 96 in September 2005, it has become a celebration of his memory. Though he had outlived his enemies and vindicated his life through knowing his great-grandchildren born in Israel, Simon died a disappointed man. He never believed that he would live to see a resurgence of global antisemitism only sixty years after the Holocaust.

This volume emerged from the idea of publishing the proceedings of two international conferences on 'Education for Tolerance – The Case of Resurgent Antisemitism', co-organized by the Simon Wiesenthal Centre and UNESCO in Paris in 1992 and 2003. It became rapidly apparent that, though path-breaking, those interventions did not cover what has been called 'the new antisemitism', nor the perceptions of Simon's work as a paradigm for other victimologies.

It is important to stress that although the Wiesenthal Centre/ UNESCO 1992 conference on antisemitism was the UN acknowledgement that the term refers to hatred exclusively targeting Jews, its propriety is still questioned. A concerted campaign persists – from a Moscow trial on the *Protocols of the Elders of Zion*, to the Durban conference – to de-Judaize 'anti-Semitism' and redefine it as a form of 'Arabophobia', in view of Arab 'Semitic' ancestry. To combat the political ramifications of this semantic theft and reassert the Jewish 'copyright' to the intent of the man who created the term, Wilhelm Marr, the Wiesenthal Centre does not hyphenate 'antisemitism'.

Simon gave his name to our Centre on condition that its work be proactive, universal and contemporary. He would have approved our affiliated French educational foundation – Verbe et Lumière – when, in 2007, it focused on the 70th anniversary of the so-called 'euthanasia programme' (in cooperation with Olokaustos Society in Italy), in which the Nazis exterminated over 100,000 mentally and physically handicapped Germans. Their medical assassins moved on to Auschwitz, proving Simon's maxim that, when a society holds its most vulnerable sectors in contempt (its handicapped, its aged, its minorities), the society itself is at the abyss.

The hatemonger must be made to understand that he cannot act with impunity. We work to impose upon all who incite, perpetrate or glorify bigotry and violence an appropriate moral, legal or material penalty. Whether a Danish radio station calling for the death of Muslims, gas chambers in North Korea, genocide in Rwanda and now in Darfur, or nuclear threats in Iran, the lessons of the Holocaust provide an early-warning system. Our imperative is Simon's first lesson: 'What starts with the Jews never ends with the Jews.' They are the first target of a generic hatred that inevitably menaces the human condition.

The privilege of twenty-five years of working with Simon Wiesenthal has taught me that these challenges must be confronted, in his words, by 'seriosity tempered with humour'. UNESCO Director-General Koichiro Matsuura, in his guardianship of 'intangible heritage', like Wiesenthal, has emphasized justice, tradition and memory. His support for the cause of human rights has been conducted in the spirit of his native Japan's stoic positivism: '*ame futte ji katamaru*' ('after the rain, the earth shall solidify').

Rabbi Marvin Hier, our Centre's Founder and President, is the visionary who brought technology to the twenty-first century battlefield against racism and antisemitism. With his Associate Dean, Rabbi Abraham Cooper, I have shared eighteen years on the frontline of this unrelenting conflict. As the Talmud acknowledges, 'From all my teachers have I gleaned wisdom.'

Special thanks to Michael Phillips, President of l'Association Verbe et Lumière-Vigilance, and his Trustees, to my brother Graham Morris, Chair of the Simon Wiesenthal Centre – United Kingdom, and his Trustees; to my friend Richard Odier, President of Centre Simon Wiesenthal – France, and his Trustees; to L'Oréal for its support; to a distinguished donor in France who, though totally dedicated to this book, has preferred the modesty of anonymity; and to the French Ministry of Foreign Affairs which has endorsed the publication by ordering 527 copies of the French edition for all its embassies and cultural centres.

Our gratitude to Jane Smith and Boris Hoffman, our literary agents; to Frank Cass and Mark Anstee of Vallentine Mitchell Publishers for their guidance and celerity, and to their copyeditor, Heather Marchant; to Michael Fineberg, our editor who came to this project from the Office of the Director-General of UNESCO – this adventure has underscored how Jewish values infuse his ardent universalism; to my colleague and our co-editor, Mark Weitzman, the first Director of our New York Tolerance Center and the Wiesenthal Centre's Taskforce against Hate; Simon's family: Paulinka and Gerard Kreisberg, their children Racheli, Joeri, Danny and their grandchildren; to our Paris office: Marilyn de Saqui de Sannes, Irène Lurçat and Anke Zeugner; and to Rosemary Wiltshire-Romero of UNESCO for her translations. Finally, my thanks to my life partner, Dr Graciela Vaserman Samuels, without whom this book would not have been possible.

The publication of this book marks our fortieth anniversary. Its birth adds a sibling to Davina, Michal, Yardena, Ori and our first grandson, Gil. May his generation heed the lessons in this book, to build a world in which 'antisemite', 'racist' and 'bigot' are epithets of contempt; where, to paraphrase Simon, 'an assault upon any one faith or ethnic community will be deemed an assault upon us all'.

Shimon Samuels
Director for International Relations
Simon Wiesenthal Centre
Paris
January 2007

Acknowledgements

This volume was originally conceived as a Festschrift, a volume in honour of Simon Wiesenthal. While such volumes are ordinarily issued in honour of prominent academics, the idea to create one for Simon was extremely appropriate. Although he never held an academic position, he frequently described himself as a researcher, and his intellectual interests extended as far as Christopher Columbus (about whom he published a book examining the Jewish roots of Columbus' voyage). And, given the immense influence his work had in so many areas of modern life, although he did not have any formal pupils, it is clear that he served as a mentor to many. Although this tribute volume has unfortunately turned into a memorial volume, it has still been both a privilege and a pleasure to work on it, alongside Michael Fineberg and Shimon Samuels, Rabbis Marvin Hier and Abraham Cooper have taken up Simon Wiesenthal's mission and built it into an organization that carries on his work; I am grateful for their vision and encouragement. Martin Rosen and Martin Mendelsohn, Simon's closest friends and advisors, helped bring me into closer contact with him, and gave me an opportunity to know him that I might not have otherwise had, as did my long-standing friend Racheli Kreisberg Zakarin, Simon's granddaughter. Mark Anstee of Valentine Mitchell kept the editorial process moving smoothly, despite the multiplicity of contacts involved – without his persistence this book might still not be published. My sons, Yaron and Ilan, both grew up hearing about Simon; I hope this volume will keep those memories and lessons alive not only for those of us who knew him, but also for the their generation and beyond. And, finally, to my wife Elaine, who accepted the demands of this work with love and encouragement, and who shares our commitment to building a vibrant and safe Jewish future, and a more tolerant world in general, my gratitude and love.

Mark Weitzman
March 2007

UNESCO/Simon Wiesenthal Centre/ Verbe et Lumière-Vigilance Cooperation 1992–2007

UNESCO
The United Nations Educational, Scientific and Cultural Organization (UNESCO) was set up in the wake of the Second World War in order to 'build the defences of peace in the minds of men'. Some of its efforts to this end include the promotion of tolerance and interfaith dialogue. A specialized agency of the United Nations, with headquarters in Paris, it functions as a standard setter and a laboratory of ideas, while advancing international cooperation among its 192 member states in the fields of education, science, culture and communication.

Simon Wiesenthal Centre
The Simon Wiesenthal Centre is an international Jewish human rights organization with a worldwide membership of 440,000. Established in 1977, with headquarters in Los Angeles, it draws the lessons of the Holocaust to the analysis of contemporary issues of prejudice and discrimination. The Centre is an NGO in consultative status to the United Nations, UNESCO, the OSCE, the Organization of American States and the Council of Europe.

Verbe et Lumière-Vigilance
Verbe et Lumière-Vigilance is a French Association, founded in 2002 under the auspices of the Simon Wiesenthal Centre – Europe, to encourage research into the Holocaust in France, and the contemporary application of its lessons.

- 1992 – first international conference on 'Educating for Tolerance: The Case of Resurgent Antisemitism' in Paris.

- 1993 – participation of UNESCO in the inauguration of the Museum of Tolerance in Los Angeles.
- 1995 – UNESCO, Wiesenthal Centre and European Parliament essay contest on 'World War Two: The Lessons 50 Years Later'. The thirty laureates (two from each EU member-state) were received by the Director-General in Paris.
- 1996 – Paris seminar on 'From Xenophobia to Tolerance: Jews and Muslims in Europe and Beyond'.
- 1998 – London seminar on 'The Opening of Archives: Shattered National Myths and Dissonant Collective Memories'.
- 1999 – Moscow conference with the Russian UNESCO National Commission on 'Tolerance-Building for Civic Society: National and Religious Extremism, Xenophobia and Antisemitism'.
- 1999 – Vienna seminar in honour of Simon Wiesenthal's 90th birthday held in conjunction with UNESCO and the Austrian Diplomatic Academy, on 'Confronting Crimes Against Humanity: From Human Rights to International Responsibilities'.
- 2000 – seminar in conjunction with the German National Commission for UNESCO at the Free University of Berlin on 'Conspiracy Theories: Genesis, Dissemination and Deconstruction'.
- 2003 – seminar at UNESCO's Venice Office on 'The Centenary of the Protocols of Zion: A Paradigm for Contemporary Hate Literature'.
- 2003 – Second International Conference in Paris on 'Educating for Tolerance: The Case of Resurgent Antisemitism', at which Director-General Koichiro Matsuura received the Centre's 2003 Humanitarian Award.
- 2003 – visit of the Director-General to Los Angeles to mark the 10th Anniversary of the Museum of Tolerance.
- 2004 – Honourable Mention of Simon Wiesenthal and the Wiesenthal Centre as laureates of the UNESCO-Madanjeet Singh Prize for the Promotion of Tolerance and Non-Violence.
- 2005 – UNESCO commemoration of the 'Sixtieth Anniversary of the Liberation of the Nazi Death Camps' held in Paris.
- 2005 – Sardinia colloquium under the patronage of the President of Italy on 'Building Peace from Below'.
- Regular meetings in Paris of the UNESCO/Simon Wiesenthal Centre/Verbe et Lumière Consultative Committee on Education for Tolerance.

Foreword

MICHAEL FINEBERG

I know how much the background against which a person grows up can mould him. I know how – especially in Austria – people who have probably never seen a Jew, let alone come to know him more closely, have grown up with antisemitism as with the Ten Commandments [...] No one can be blamed for having grown up as an antisemite: the question is whether, faced with SS men loading Jews onto lorries or crowding them into cattle trucks, he remains one.

Anyone siding with us only as long as we play the part of victim has, in a different way, remained the same old antisemite.

To call Jews 'Fascist' is a double advantage: for one thing it helps to make Nazi Fascism seem more harmless (since evidently all nations, including the Jews, incline towards Fascism), and on the other it helps to execrate the Jews (after all, how evil a nation must be to apply Fascist practices when it has experienced them itself).[1]

In the summer of 2004, when this book was just beginning to be prepared, an incident occurred in France that captured the attention of the mass media for several days. It was reported that a young woman travelling with her baby in a suburban Paris train had been the victim of a violent antisemitic assault. She claimed that her assailants – two Arabs and one black – mistakenly believing her to be Jewish, had torn her clothes, marked her belly with a swastika and physically abused her and her child. She also alleged that numerous bystanders had passively witnessed the attack, making no attempt to come to her defence. Following considerable public outcry, it transpired that the story was a pure fabrication, invented by a young woman with psychiatric problems.

Nearly two years later, in the same country, a 23-year-old Sephardic Jew, Ilan Halimi, was lured by a young woman to a meeting place where he was kidnapped and held for ransom. Over a period of twenty-four days, during which the ransom demands dropped from 40,000 euros to 5,000 euros, he was subjected to increasingly vicious torture until finally, naked, covered in burns and knife wounds, he was left to die an atrocious death. In the subsequent investigation, it became clear that the self-styled 'gang of Barbarians' who had abducted him had targeted him because he was a Jew. The staging of the photo taken of him in captivity and sent to his family mimicked the photos taken of hostages in Iraq; when the young man's torturers learned that his family could not raise the ransom money, they pushed him to get it from his synagogue.

Two stories, one distressing, the other horrific, heart-rending, linked by a stereotype: the Jew as an object of hate, the Jew as a chosen victim. It is perhaps not insignificant that the country where they both occurred is the country of the Dreyfus Affair, which, as George Whyte reminds us, turned around issues that still touch us today. But it could have been anywhere. Just recently the Chief Rabbi of Poland was attacked in the streets of Warsaw, to the cry of Poland for the Poles, a cry that goes on echoing all around the world, adapted to each country, against the 'outsider', whether Jew, Gypsy, Kurd or Armenian, whoever fits the bill.

What is most striking about the first story is not just that it was a fabrication but that, despite a few doubts not voiced at the time, it was immediately believed by all those who chose to comment on it. As for the second story, it is all too sadly just one more instance of antisemitic infamy, one more hate crime against a particular group in the person of some hapless individual.

A stereotype, a pattern: for two thousand years people have been persecuted and killed for being Jews and, while on occasion a minority of non-Jews have gone so far as to raise their voices in protest or indeed, more rarely, to defend the victims, this tradition of persecution has been paralleled by a tradition of ignoring, condoning or justifying its perpetrators.

It is for this reason that all civilized people, all who are attached to human rights, owe a debt to Simon Wiesenthal, for he took it upon himself, at first almost single-handedly and then with increasing support from likeminded others, to challenge that tradition and, in the name of all victims of collective discrimination, as noted by Michael Berenbaum, to demand not vengeance but justice. From his example has grown a vast movement to hold war criminals guilty for their crimes, a continuing battle whose significance is discussed by Efraïm

Zuroff. Wiesenthal's belief that 'law and justice must be the cornerstone of society' is also the principle at the heart of all the international war crimes tribunals that the world has seen since Nuremberg. Such tribunals have played and continue to play an essential role in rebuilding nations torn apart by genocide and in halting the cycle of violence.

It can never be enough, however, to track down and bring to trial individual criminals, as indispensable as that is. So long as the Jewish stereotype seems vested with legitimacy, the fight against antisemitism can never be fully won. It is a stereotype that has been reinforced by a long history of intolerance, discrimination, persecution and pogroms. No matter that, culminating as it did in the Shoah, this tradition has finally been divested of its false legitimacy, it has also shown itself capable of again winning acceptance, by assuming the mask of anti-Zionism. Chesler and Rahola respectively argue that some feminists and left-wing intellectuals, in taking up the cause of the Palestinian victims of the complex situation known as the Middle East conflict, seem to have all too readily banished from their discourse a universal concept of human rights, as though they in turn have been contaminated by a hatred institutionalized as state policy in many parts of the Arab world, particularly those where the human rights of ordinary people can hardly be said to count as a major concern.

Rabbi Sacks along with many others speaks of antisemitism as a virus, ever susceptible to mutation. Referring to Robert Wistrich's description of it as 'the longest hatred', he defines it as the paradigm case of the hatred of difference. This is contrasted, or perhaps one should say complemented, by Jerrold Post's view that antisemitism is directed against Jews as a concept or symbol, even by people who have no contact with Jews. He cites the case of Polish communities that have recreated the old scapegoat of the Jew, even in the absence of real living Jews. Steven Baum makes a similar point, noting that people do not hate actual Jews but rather the mythical or imaginary Jew, stressing that it is this that makes antisemitic myths so lethal – the fact that there is no reality to them. No matter how many millions of Jews are killed, the Jew is thus able to serve as an ever-renewable target of hatred. They are hated because they are rich, they are hated because they are poor; they are hated because they stand out or because, on the contrary, they have become as Jews virtually invisible, thus giving grist to the mill of the supporters of conspiracy theories. Some writers emphasize the cultural character of antisemitism, its

transmission from generation to generation, as part of a general outlook on life and society, grounded now in the demonization of the
Jew as the Antichrist, now in the function of Jews as the 'familiar enemies' that some people sadly seem to need for their own self-
definition. They can be used as scapegoats even when they themselves are victims, a recent striking example being the recurring accusation in the wake of 9/11 that the attacks on the twin towers had
been masterminded by Jews. Any study of the history of antisemitism
brings out the awful truth that, as Morad El-Hattab, puts it, 'antisemitism needs no reason, because every reason fits'. What counts,
according to Paul Weller, is the proper dosage of fact and fiction,
which he calls the 'plausibility structure'. Thus, so long as there are
some elements of truth in the vilifications, people will always be
ready to give credence to any trumped-up nonsense being propounded, such as the claim that the blood of Christian babies is used
in the making or matzoth or that there is a Jewish conspiracy to rule
the world. Nonsense, but when it is taken up and repeated enough
times, as for instance through the dissemination of the bogus
Protocols of the Elders of Zion, it provides what Norman Cohn has
called a 'warrant for genocide',[2] and becomes ideologically versatile,
as shown by Mark Weitzman, and globalized, as Ronald Eissens
demonstrates, via the Internet.

Many of the essays in this book reflect an awareness that if we are
to attack the roots of antisemitism we must deconstruct the stereotype of the Jew. Günther Jikeli offers us several useful pointers in this
direction, through the Kreuzberg Initiative, designed to promote personal, human interactions with Jewish individuals and to encourage
people to look beyond stereotypes. Yaakov Kirschen, like Wiesenthal,
believes in the power of humour to diffuse hatred. Pastor Weber gives
a very personal account of his interaction with German neo-Nazis,
while the efficacy of Holocaust education is described by Gert
Weisskirchen. However, the process will be long and can be expected to be affected by political developments worldwide, particularly in
the Middle East.

One may wonder in this connection whether the State of Israel
will ever be able to be viewed as that, as a state, and not as a kind of
reified Jew and/or Western presence in the heart of Islam, fuelling the
hatreds of antisemites and anti-globalists of every stripe, even, as
described by Geoffrey Short, on the university campus. This question, which keeps cropping up in one form or another, raises in turn

another question, analysed by Dina Porat, which is that of anti-semitism as a determinant of Jewish identity.

Irwin Cotler, Shimon Samuels, Goetz Nordbruch and Rachid Kaci have addressed the shift from the Arab–Israeli conflict to a Muslim–Jewish confrontation as 'the new antisemitism' and, indeed, its link to international terrorism. Franklin Littell has characterized the lessons of such shifts, among the proponents of antisemitism, as an 'early warning system' for other targeted groups, or even for genocide, as illustrated by Steven Jacobs. Giovanni de Martis, Assumpta Mugiraneza, Richard English and Xu Xin adapt the paradigm to other victimologies.

We have dedicated this book to the memory of Simon Wiesenthal, the 'conscience of the Holocaust'. Yes, he was concerned about justice, but that was not all. He also gave much thought to the question of whether the perpetrators of genocide could be forgiven, which was the subject of one of his most important works, *The Sunflower*. This is a question that perhaps only the victims can answer, or indeed not even them. John Roth and, indirectly, John Pawlikowski, take up this question again and ask what a post-Holocaust understanding and practice of forgiveness can be. They thus bring us back to the core values of our common humanity in whose name we fight anti-semitism, intolerance and other forms of xenophobia. It is our hope that this book will be a contribution to that fight.

Note

1. Simon Wiesenthal, *Justice not Vengeance* (London: Weidenfeld and Nicolson, 1989), pp.146, 225.
2. Norman Cohn, *Warrant for Genocide: The Myth of the Jewish World Conspiracy and the Protocols of the Elders of Zion* (Harmondsworth: Pelican, 1970).

Tribute

KOICHIRO MATSUURA
Director-General, UNESCO

UNESCO is proud to honour the memory of Simon Wiesenthal, rightly described as the conscience of the Holocaust. The Organization has been actively cooperating with the Centre that bears his name since 1992, when it hosted a major conference on antisemitism. Since that first joint undertaking our two institutions have, in cooperation with other international and national bodies, held a number of other meetings on the role of education and cultural dialogue in the fight against antisemitism and other forms of intolerance.

In 2002, Simon Wiesenthal and the Simon Wiesenthal Centre were awarded an honourable mention of the UNESCO-Madanjeet Singh Prize for Tolerance and Non-Violence 'for their denunciation of the crimes committed by the Nazis during the Second World War and their work in education for tolerance and non-violence'.

In 2003, UNESCO hosted the second major conference on antisemitism organized by the Wiesenthal Centre. I was happy to participate in the press conference that preceded the opening of that event and to pay tribute on that occasion to Mr Wiesenthal, who devoted his life to safeguarding the memory of the Holocaust and fighting impunity for its perpetrators. In the name not of vengeance but of justice, he spent more than fifty years hunting Nazi war criminals, speaking against neo-Nazism and racism and remembering the Jewish experience as a lesson for humanity. His belief that law and justice must be the cornerstone of society is the pillar on which war tribunals stand, helping to rebuild societies torn apart by genocide and averting the cycle of violence. He wanted the world to learn from the tragedy of the Holocaust.

That terrible period of our recent history was preceded by an exacerbation of nationalist sentiments, a rising tide of intolerance and the entrenchment of racism and antisemitism. It was made possible by a denial of human rights and an attitude of superiority or fear in the face of other cultures. In more recent times, such forms of intolerance have led to ethnic and religious cleansing in Bosnia, Kosovo, East Timor, Rwanda and Afghanistan. It is a terrible truth that the Holocaust, the Shoah, cannot but be seen as the defining event of the last century. Its horrendously large number of victims – Jews, but also Roma and members of other minorities – and the ideologies that inspired it must be remembered, not only by historians but by all of us, and especially our young people.

In October 2002, UNESCO attended in Strasbourg the Council of Europe's special session at which the Ministers of Education of forty-eight countries proclaimed a 'Day of Remembrance of the Holocaust and for the Prevention of Crimes against Humanity', to be observed in all European schools. For UNESCO it was an ethical duty to associate itself with that historic moment. We likewise welcomed the decision taken by the General Assembly of the United Nations, in September 2005, to designate 27 January, the anniversary date of the liberation of Auschwitz-Birkenau, as Holocaust Remembrance Day.

The present compilation has been conceived in a similar spirit. Where, however, the purpose of such commemorations is to keep alive the memory of the Holocaust, to honour its victims and to prevent the recurrence of genocide, this book seeks to offer guidance both in understanding the phenomena of racism and antisemitism and in developing ways and means of countering and containing them. For UNESCO, unbiased history teaching and revision of textbooks are a key element. Working at national and regional levels, the Organization has helped its member states to revise school textbooks, improve teaching methods and, within their curricula, to introduce education for religious, ethnic and racial tolerance. It also, as part of its mandate, promotes cultural diversity and intercultural dialogue, seeking better mutual knowledge and appreciation of the values and cultures of different nations, peoples and communities. The Simon Wiesenthal Centre, for its part, in addition to preserving the memory of the Holocaust and seeking justice for its victims, acts as an observatory and warning mechanism. It alerts the world to all manifestations of antisemitism and promotes good practices.

It is therefore fitting that UNESCO should join with the Wiesenthal Centre in bringing out this book, which also benefits from the support of the Ministry of Foreign Affairs of France, our host country. It is our hope that it will be useful to individuals, institutions and states in eliminating the scourge of antisemitism and other forms of racism, xenophobia and intolerance that have left their terrible imprint on all too many pages of the history of humanity.

Introduction

RABBI MARVIN HIER
Dean and Founder, Simon Wiesenthal Centre

In the last few days of the Third Reich, in a bunker beneath the Chancellery, Adolf Hitler began writing his final will and testament. In it, he made this chilling prediction: 'Centuries will pass, but out of the ruins of our towns and cultural centres, the hatred will renew itself against those ultimately responsible ... international Jewry'.

Hitler was wrong, it didn't take centuries; it took sixty years for antisemitism to once again find a welcome mat in Europe and the Middle East. From the burning of synagogues, the desecration of cemeteries, to Jews being beaten on the streets of Paris, Antwerp, London, antisemitism has become a daily occurrence in our lives.

Who would have believed, for example, that it would take only sixty years for a president of a member state of the United Nations to have the audacity to call the Holocaust a myth, to deny the horrors of Auschwitz and Majdanek and even encourage his country to host an exhibition on Holocaust denial? Worse, that President Ahmadinejad could do all this without suffering any consequences – that he could stand at the podium of the General Assembly without any fear that his address would be boycotted.

The Islamic fundamentalists who are largely responsible for the new worldwide antisemitic attacks have a broader agenda than just the Jews. Their real objective is the end of Western civilization. What should concern all of us is that for the first time in history these fanatics will soon have the potential to unleash a 'nuclear antisemitism', leading to a nuclear Holocaust.

Even more troubling, is that these jihadists and suicide bombers have introduced a philosophy unheard of during the dark days of the Third Reich. Namely, a culture of death, that prefers the next world to life on earth. For sure, the Nazis were the quintessential murderers of all time. But even the most sadistic Nazi killers did everything possible to preserve their own lives. For example, Adolf Eichmann, who directed Hitler's Final Solution against the Jews, escaped to Argentina after the war and lived a life of an ordinary labourer. The infamous 'Angel of Death', Dr Joseph Mengele, lived in dingy apartments in Brazil in a desperate attempt to prolong his life. Franz Stangl, the commandant of Treblinka, lived from hand to mouth and regularly changed locations just to avoid the hangman's noose.

But, today's terrorists and jihadists can't wait to blow up a plane, which they perceive as their guarantee to a place of honour at God's table in paradise. Imagine the threat to mankind when these martyrdom seekers gain access to advanced chemical and biological weapons. What is there to say to those who claim they are of the Abrahamic faith yet desecrate God's command to Abraham when he was led to believe that it was God's will to sacrifice his son, Isaac. God said, 'Abraham, Abraham, do not stretch out your hand against the lad nor do anything to him.'

Moderate Muslim leaders throughout the world are well aware of the danger of terrorism that claims for itself the name of Islam. In 2005, when we presented King Abdullah II of Jordan with the Centre's Museum of Tolerance Peace Award, the King pointed out that the reason he had created a special programme, the Amman Initiative, was to reach out to take back Islam from those who have stolen it and abandoned its principles.

Which brings me to Simon Wiesenthal, who many regard as the conscience of the Holocaust. Simon lost eighty-nine members of his family, many of them in Hitler's gas chambers. When he barely walked out of the Mauthausen concentration camp, he weighed less than ninety pounds (forty-one kilos). He had a lot to be angry about, but he refused to embark on the path of vengeance and retribution. Rather, he sought the higher calling of bringing to justice the perpetrators in the hope that mankind would learn its lesson and build a better future.

Simon spent his whole life fighting bigotry and speaking for tolerance and human dignity. May his legacy be a world that realizes that nothing enduring was ever built by hate; that no God is ever honoured by bloodshed and that the only gateway to the next world is a life of human dignity in this world.

A Daughter's Memories

PAULINKA WIESENTHAL KREISBERG

I was born in September 1946 in Bindermichl, a camp for displaced persons, which was located outside Linz/a.d. Donau in Upper Austria, not very far from the concentration camp Mauthausen, from which my father had been liberated. In 1947 we moved to Linz where my father, together with a group of volunteers, had established a documentation centre.

My mother perceived the outside world as hostile and antisemitic; and she shielded me from it by keeping me at home as much as possible. I do not recall that my parents had any social contacts with non-Jews.

When I started elementary school I was suddenly exposed to an environment that seemed alien and threatening. My mother took me to register at the local school and to this day I remember the astonishment of the headmistress when she heard that we were Jewish. 'I can't believe it.' I still hear her saying, 'I thought that there were none left, that all had been killed.'

Was she an antisemite? I do not know. But I do know that going to school felt like running the gauntlet. In no time it was common knowledge that I was Jewish: small stars of David were etched into my wooden school desk. I was asked weird questions. (Did I have a tail?) I was made fun of, singled out and, as a consequence, I felt embarrassed, helpless.

Who were those parents who planted the seeds of antisemitism in their six-year-old children? I do not know. But I do know that my mother told me to keep to myself, not to react, and to come home directly from school. I was allowed to play with the neighbours' children, as long as my mother or our housekeeper was close at hand. I was permitted to invite friends to our apartment, but not to visit them.

It took only a short while until I became an outsider. Even though

I could not figure out why I was different, what constituted my otherness, it was clear to me that there was something about me, something weird, something unhealthy. Instinctively I knew that no matter what, I would never be able to rid myself of my strangeness and therefore would never be accepted as one of them.

Over the course of the years I became more and more exposed to stereotypes about Jews – dishonest, dominant, money-minded. 'You', they said, as opposed to 'us'. I understood that they did not necessarily mean that I personally had all these disgusting traits, but that I was a member of this detested group.

Drop by poisonous drop I felt their hatred enter me; I started asking myself whether they might have a point somewhere, or whether this aggression could be totally unjustified. Maybe, I thought, they were right, maybe there was something about the Jews that warranted this attitude of rejection.

Pleasing them, turning the other cheek did not improve things. On the contrary, they said: 'Look what a coward she is! She cannot even stand up for herself.' When I retreated into myself, they said: 'She thinks she is superior to us, just like all the Jews.'

When I was older, in my teens, I started to provoke the children around me and without fail drew their undiluted aggression, 'You Jews,' they said, 'you do not belong here, go to Palestine.'

In the end I gave up, it was a battle that I could not win. Not being able to defend myself or my group, I wanted the Jews to be invisible, and if already identified then only on their best behaviour, clean smelling, properly dressed, speaking without a trace of an accent.

It took me many years until I rid myself of the antisemitic stereotypes that I had somehow internalized. I came to understand that either the non-Jews had a problem they could not solve, or they felt comfortable with their racism.

My father dealt with antisemitism on a day-to-day basis in his own indomitable way. Even though he was a relentlessly attacked target – letters addressed to the 'Jewish Pig Wiesenthal, Austria' were duly delivered by the Postal Service; he received threatening phone calls late in the evening or in the middle of the night; the home of my parents was fire-bombed in 1982 – it did not seem to faze him unduly. He perceived it as an incentive to continue with his work and he kept saying that it only reinforced his conviction that he had to proceed.

I do not know how my father felt growing up as a Jew, or in his words as 'a second-rate citizen', in Poland. He experienced antisemitism in all its shapes and forms, which culminated in the hell of the Holocaust. It did not break him; he stood his ground; did not cower or hesitate to take any action that he believed necessary to expose the evil of antisemitism. Even though he was surrounded by prejudice he did not generalize, he did not believe that every non-Jew was a potential antisemite nor did he perceive every unpleasant expression as antisemitic.

My father was convinced that the Jews should not claim the monopoly of being a persecuted minority. Without denying the uniqueness of the Holocaust, he was able to focus on crimes against other people and he spoke up for them. Instead of singling out the Jews by stressing their exclusive plight of antisemitism, he defined it as one of the many forms of racism. Having established this common denominator he advocated forging alliances with others to form a strong base to combat racism in all its guises and disguises.

In Memory of Simon Wiesenthal, a Combatant for Memory, Justice and Tolerance

SIMONE VEIL

I wish to salute the courage and moral conscience of Simon Wiesenthal who, from 1945 onwards, worked indefatigably to render justice to the victims of the Shoah. He thus contributed to establishing and acknowledging the responsibility of the Nazi criminals and their accomplices in the extermination machine, that they might not escape justice.

By creating the Jewish Documentation Centre, not only to track Nazi war criminals, but also to research the activities of neo-Nazi groups, Simon Wiesenthal equally led a frontline combat against neo-Nazi resurgence, Holocaust denial and antisemitism.

His example led to the creation in 1977 of the international centre that carries his name and plays a very important role in the preservation of the memory of the Shoah's victims and as a vigilant monitor of antisemitic incidents around the world.

I wish to salute the Centre's action which, beyond community defence, ensures a better knowledge of history, promotes tolerance and dialogue between different cultures and religions and advances the struggle for human rights.

For us, the survivors of the death camps, twice murdered by the extermination of our dear ones and the attempts to efface the crime by the executioners themselves, the work of Simon Wiesenthal – begun in almost total solitude – symbolized the battle so that memory may endure and that the crime will not remain unpunished.

The best homage that one can render to Simon Wiesenthal is to carry on his combat against racism and antisemitism.

Created in 2000, the Foundation for the Memory of the Shoah

has the mission to perpetuate the Shoah's memory. Research, the dissemination of its findings and solidarity with the victims of the Shoah are its major programmatic axes.

In Tribute to Simon Wiesenthal

SHIMON PERES

Several decades after the Holocaust, Simon Wiesenthal put down his pen, metaphorically speaking, and declared: 'My work is done.' Yet sixty years after the Holocaust, the spectre of antisemitism has raised its head once again and Iran is threatening Israel with annihilation.

The incredible is happening. Simon Wiesenthal had devoted his life to relentlessly tracking down Nazi criminals and bringing them to justice, in an effort to initiate a real healing process that would enable the dark days of the Nazi era to be stored in an attic of history, where it could be put aside, but never forgotten. Persistently, diligently, slowly but surely, he gathered every scrap of information that would help uncover the hiding places of the fugitive Nazis and bring them to trial for crimes against humanity. A lesser task would have been daunting to others, but not to Simon. 'I am seeking justice,' he said, 'not revenge.' And he continued towards his goal uncompromisingly, when the interest of the international community had waned, for he understood that unless the cause of the innocent men, women and children, who were murdered for the only reason that they were Jewish, was not fought to the last criminal, their souls would not rest and neither should the conscience of any moral person on the globe.

Silence is what distinguished the pre-Nazi period. The evil Nazi machine moved inexorably forward, not stopped when there was still time, and six million Jews were killed in consequence. The déjà vu situation we are witnessing is chilling. Hopefully the free nations of the world will in this case wake up in time, and justice will be done, so that another Simon Wiesenthal will not have to rise up and right a terrible wrong.

I hope that Simon Wiesenthal has really finished his work, and that he may rest in peace.

8 November 2006

Tribute

NICOLAS SARKOZY

My message is in memory of Simon Wiesenthal and also a testimony to the close ties between the Ministry of the Interior and the Simon Wiesenthal Centre.

Most honoured and profoundly touched by the esteem you have shown me, I thank you warmly and wish every success for this work dedicated to Simon Wiesenthal.

An exceptional man, determined to bring the Nazis to justice, the perpetrators of the greatest crime ever committed in history, Simon Wiesenthal turned his life into a struggle for truth and justice.

His name echoes in our memories, awakens our consciences and incites new generations to reflect on the acts committed against humanity, in order to prevent their recurrence.

Whatever the capacity in which I am called on to serve, you may rest assured of my firm intention to continue the action I have undertaken to combat all forms of racism and antisemitism.

[Nicolas Sarkozy, who has recently been elected President of France, was the recipient of the Simon Wiesenthal Centre's 2003 Annual Award, together with Koichiro Matsuura, at the UNESCO/Simon Wiesenthal Centre's International Conference on Resurgent Antisemitism.]

Tribute to Simon Wiesenthal – The Conscience of the Holocaust

RABBI ABRAHAM COOPER

In our time it is impossible to appreciate the full measure of Simon Wiesenthal's contribution to the Jewish people and to the world. This is not just because of his longevity, which meant that at 96 he had outlived most of the perpetrators of the Nazi Holocaust he doggedly hunted.

The fact is that in our time, where memory of the Holocaust is so central a societal theme – with Holocaust Remembrance Days, museums, films and websites – it may not be within our grasp to fathom the loneliness and aloneness of the path he embarked on sixty years ago as he stumbled out, a skeletal ghost, into the hands of American liberators at Mauthausen.

Make no mistake: Wiesenthal was virtually alone in his quest for justice for the six million Jews murdered in the Final Solution. After the Nuremberg War Crimes Tribunals, the victorious alliance morphed into the bitter confrontation of the Cold War. As far as the Soviets, Americans and British were concerned, dossiers of ex-Nazis were to be scoured, not for evidence of crimes against humanity, but for their potential in abetting their respective intelligence, military or strategic goals.

Wiesenthal also had to face the brutal reality that many post-war Jewish leaders could not fathom the utility of 'dredging up' difficult memories and generating needless confrontation with politicians about 'the past'. In the 1950s, 1960s and into the 1970s prominent and influential Jews would admonish Simon: 'Forget about your Don Quixote quest; it's time to Forgive and Forget!'

For his base of operation Wiesenthal chose Austria. After a brief stint in Linz he would move to a nondescript office in Vienna – 100 yards from the site of Gestapo headquarters. Every day as he strode among the largely apathetic populace, he was an unmistakable, if unwelcome, reminder of the ghosts of genocide that no one wanted to confront. Vienna yielded leads, increasing threats from unrepentant Nazis, and later, after Adolf Eichmann's capture, death threats against his family. When his embattled wife begged Wiesenthal to move to Israel, he sent his daughter, but would not, and could not, close the Documentation Centre. Not even a neo-Nazi bomb that blew apart their apartment would succeed in breaking Wiesenthal's bond with his mission.

What drove Wiesenthal? There's no doubt that like many Holocaust survivors he sought meaning and purpose in the unfathomable fact that he, rather than his mother or eighty-eight other members of his extended family, had survived the Nazi onslaught. He simply could not walk away from the past. But from the outset his pursuit of Nazi War Criminals precluded any cooperation with ex-partisans seeking to dispatch murderers with a righteous bullet. Wiesenthal saw his mission as utilizing the very concepts of law and rights that the Nazis had laid waste to during their Blitzkrieg across Europe. It would turn out that the only rebuilding project this architect would ever undertake was to re-lay the foundations, legal brick by brick, of the fundamentals of justice and human rights that Hitler and his followers strove to obliterate. Each arrest and every trial was not only a token to the families of the victims of Nazi terror. It was in Wiesenthal's words 'an inoculation against hate and a warning to tomorrow's potential mass murderers that they would be held accountable for their deeds'. It meant that Wiesenthal's commitment to bring Nazi mass murderers to justice extended beyond Jewish victims to include the Gypsies and other targeted victims. It slowly but inevitably also brought him into contact with contemporary challenges to fundamental human rights. It accounted for his speaking out on such diverse issues from threatened indigenous tribes in the Americas to helping to lead the campaign to save Andrei Sakharov during his pivotal and historic confrontation with the Soviet Empire.

In the end Wiesenthal told me he took a measure of solace from the fact that he had lived long enough to see presidents and prime ministers stirred occasionally to action when new genocides loomed on the horizon. But alas, from Rwanda to Darfur to North Korea, humankind's record is spotty at best, for we have failed, as yet, to fully embrace Wiesenthal's vision of 'Never Again'. Wiesenthal also said that he was shocked that he lived long enough to witness the re-emergence of violent antisemitism in Europe. Mr Wiesenthal's gritty tenacity in pursuing justice through the rule of law that could not be extinguished, neither by perpetrators of genocide nor by the apathy of governments, should serve as source of inspiration to all who serve the cause of human rights in halls of power and diplomacy.

Mr Wiesenthal's legacy also speaks to today's morally confused times. As a victim of, and witness to, humankind's worst crime, Wiesenthal's choice of Justice over Vengeance and his embrace of life-affirming values stands in stark contrast to leaders who bestow moral legitimacy on those who promote or embrace terrorism's culture of death.

And finally: what of his six million constituents?

Wiesenthal told of a Sabbath meal in Italy in the late 1940s. His friends were urging him to pick up the threads of his life and start building the houses he had been trained to design. His response, as he looked into the twinkling candles: 'Like all of you I believe in the World to Come, and I can safely say that in this world, you the jeweller, the doctor, the businessman will become rich, and I will have to struggle. But when we die we will have to pass before the six million and only I among you will be able to declare: "I never forgot you". In that world I will be the richest amongst us.'

Rest in peace, Simon, and God bless.

Searching for Simon

HANNAH HEER

A famous saying goes, as long as we think of someone who died, this person is still alive and in our midst. Simon Wiesenthal, who was described as one of the most important Jewish men of the twentieth century at the Memorial Service that took place in New York on 27 September 2005, surely will be remembered for a very long time. But I think it is even more important that we who knew him and who shared in his passion for justice continue to bear witness to his life-work in an honest way and help to set the record straight on some of the myths surrounding Simon.

My partner and husband, Werner Schmiedel, and I directed and produced the feature-length documentary film on Simon Wiesenthal, 'The Art of Remembrance', between the years 1986 and 1995. In the mid-1980s we were troubled by the recurrences of antisemitic attitudes and slogans on both sides of the Atlantic. It took us considerable effort and energy to get Simon Wiesenthal committed to our film project and even more time and persistence to secure some funding for it. Once Simon realized how determined we were to bring our film project to fruition, he was very cooperative.

We were sitting in Simon Wiesenthal's modest office in the Salztorgasse in the first district in Vienna, as always when we visited him, in the same chairs covered with dark ruby velvet that was worn down from harbouring visitors for several decades. Werner and I had prepared a simple agreement based on our previous discussions with Simon Wiesenthal that we all three signed. We as the producers/directors wanted him to commit to a certain amount of shooting-days so that we could conclude filming interviews with Simon and follow his actions. For the record, Simon Wiesenthal did not have any editorial control over our project, nor did he ever ask for any.

As soon as Werner and I started to work on the film, we were confronted conspicuously and constantly with 'stories' that tried to distort, diminish or slander Simon Wiesenthal's groundbreaking achievements. The most significant topic that comes to mind is Simon Wiesenthal's role in locating Adolf Eichmann, the Gestapo officer who was largely responsible for organizing the devastating fate of the Jews during the National Socialist regime. A brief encounter at the Jerusalem Film Festival in 1992, where we were invited to present our previous film, 'The Other Eye', summarizes the problem perfectly. When we mentioned the subject of our work-in-progress, an Israeli film curator interjected sharply, 'Wiesenthal didn't catch Eichmann, we did it!' End of discussion.

Well, Wiesenthal never claimed that he 'caught' Eichmann.

Growing up in Vienna, my parents strongly believed in the importance of Simon Wiesenthal's work. In the 1960s, my father, the historian Friedrich Heer, worked closely with Simon Wiesenthal in an effort to establish a Holocaust and Antisemitism Research Institute in Vienna, but the Austrian authorities had no interest in supporting such an institution.

Although Werner and I both trusted Simon Wiesenthal's rendering of his experiences, we also felt the need for our film work to be grounded in serious research. Therefore, any time an expression of mistrust or doubt towards any of Wiesenthal's actions was brought to our attention, we extended our scope of research once more in order to double check the respective facts-in-question.

We spent many hours and long days in Simon Wiesenthal's Documentation Centre of Jewish Victims of the Nazi Regime in Vienna and at the office of Zentralstelle der Landesjustizverwaltungen zur Aufklaerung von NS-Verbrechen in Ludwigsburg, Germany, where we interviewed several prosecutors who were still actively working at the time. As we continued to familiarize ourselves with segments of the vast correspondence in Simon Wiesenthal's archives, we had to realize again and again that very, very few people were committed to bringing Nazi criminals to justice after the Second World War. It seemed that most Jews and non-Jews alike wanted to close this most infamous chapter in history, and escape any lessons and responsibilities that could be learned or taken on. And as if it were not enough that the silent majority made no effort to contribute to the fight towards justice, either financially or through action, they often blamed Simon Wiesenthal for not being 'successful enough', for not having found Mengele or for not getting this or that perpetrator behind bars. For us it was annoying and intensely time-consuming to provide facts to people who consistently refused to acknowledge the sad truth that Simon

Wiesenthal largely had to work on his own, with *resistance* (to use the Freudian terminology) on all levels, not only from governments and organizations, but also from most individuals.

Maybe it is helpful to reflect for a moment on the role the media played in representing and forming Simon Wiesenthal's public image. Over several decades, in numerous articles and headlines, if not in most, Simon Wiesenthal was portrayed as a 'Nazi-Hunter' which clearly evokes images of the central character out of a James Bond movie. Precisely this misleading imagery of an icon of popular culture made it difficult for the majority to understand that Simon was far from that. The fabricated legend of Simon as a famous powerful 'hunter' might have served to allow editors of all media to devote many an article to his agenda and thus made him a famous and a sought-after figure. Consequently, those citizens around the world who wanted to see the perpetrators of Nazi crimes behind bars were eager to contact Wiesenthal and to confide to him about any whereabouts of Nazi suspects. Perhaps the symbol of Simon Wiesenthal as a 'Jewish James Bond' even helped to instil fear in many of the Nazi criminals with false identities, who didn't want their shameful histories to be disclosed in order to avoid being put on trial and subsequently sent to jail.

So there was some merit to the fictitious image of Simon Wiesenthal as a forceful secret agent who flew around the world. But the misleading image of Simon as a powerful superhero prevented serious insight into his accomplishments and undermined a possible understanding of how he worked. Simon Wiesenthal was involved in the continuous pursuit of painstaking detail-oriented efforts to locate Nazi criminals and to then ask the appropriate court to put them on trial. Equally important was his tireless work first to locate and then to convince 'victims' of the Nazi regime that they are also 'witnesses' and needed to appear in this capacity in court.

Today we might say Simon Wiesenthal was a dedicated grass-roots activist, a strategic worker, a detective, who drew both on his intellectual and intuitive abilities. The historian Raul Hilberg described Wiesenthal as an important 'collector of information and archivist', when we interviewed him for our documentary. Further, Simon Wiesenthal was engaged in the pursuit of human rights, he stood up for diverse groups, such as the Roma, the Native Americans and the Bosnians.

We all are embedded in a set of values, whether we are conscious of them or not. When you had the opportunity to speak to Simon

Wiesenthal and to read parts of his comprehensive correspondence in his archive, you found yourself in the presence of a very knowledgeable and careful thinker, a repository of vast data systems, whose judgments and whose life were informed by the guidance of the ten commandments as they are read in the Torah portion every year by observant Jews on the holiday of Shavuot. Once he told us his grandmother was a very religious woman who often took him as a small child to visit a 'Wunderrabbi' in Czortkow, Galicia. I then asked whether he considered himself a religious Jew, and Simon answered with a clear and firm 'Yes'. It was within this ethical and religious framework that Simon believed in the responsibility of the individual; he abhorred the concept of 'collective guilt'; his agenda was to repair the world, '*tikkun olam*', in Hebrew.

Returning to the 'Eichmann Case', Simon Wiesenthal wrote in his published memoir that he knew already in 1954 – thus six years before Eichmann was captured – that Eichmann lived in Argentina under the name 'Klement'. He informed both Nahum Goldmann, who was at the time President of the World Jewish Congress, and the Israeli Consul in Vienna about Eichmann's whereabouts, but nobody seemed concerned to act upon his information. When Werner and I worked on our documentary, we searched and discovered the four-page letter Wiesenthal had sent to the World Jewish Congress together with their reply, and included images of both letters in our film as proof of Wiesenthal's original discovery and action. But even now the Israeli journalist Tom Segev seemed impressed when he finally saw those letters himself during his research in Wiesenthal's former office about a dozen years later, in the spring of 2006. Maybe it is hard for people to understand that one person alone can be so dedicated and persistent. If Simon Wiesenthal hadn't been so consequential in his search for Eichmann, that man would have been officially 'declared dead' several years before he escaped to Argentina. Eichmann's wife, Veronika Liebl, tried to obtain a death certificate for Eichmann by an Austrian Court in Bad Ischl in 1947. Simon Wiesenthal successfully brought to light that the family could not provide any proof of Eichmann's death. Had Adolf Eichmann been declared dead like other high-ranking Nazi officers, nobody would have continued to search for Eichmann and thus he would have probably lived happily ever after in Argentina or elsewhere.

Werner and I filmed in eight countries for 'The Art of Remembrance'; the journey to the Ukraine, where Simon Wiesenthal was born and spent many years before the Second World War, we saved for the end of our filming period. We invited Simon to join us, but anticipated that he would decline our invitation, which he did. He had never returned to the places of his youth in Eastern Europe. After extensive preparations for our journey, Werner and I boarded the train to Lemberg (L'viv or Lvov) on a warm summer evening in Vienna. It was in July 1994. We had packed food and water in a container as though we were embarking on a major excursion. It was the first trip to the Ukraine for both of us and we had heard wild stories about robberies and violence, especially on trains and airplanes. The train rolled gently up and down through green hills in Slovakia, the large windows presenting peaceful moving images of families enjoying barbecues in their gardens. After a good night's sleep we arrived in Lemberg around noon. Our interpreter and driver met us on time at the station. The purpose of this trip was to see and film places of Simon Wiesenthal's childhood and youth, and perhaps to discover one or two of the buildings he had built as a young architect.

During our first hour in Lemberg, while driving to the hotel, we immediately noticed that the architecture of the old city of Lemberg bore a striking resemblance to old Vienna. But the people walked differently in Lemberg: everyone seemed to move in slow-motion and appeared to gaze at some distant empty space. Our interpreter explained that most people were still in a state of hypnosis from years of communism and dictatorship.

Simon Wiesenthal had given us some vague addresses and on one piece of paper he even drew two lines that symbolized a street, where he was born and lived as a child. But the names of all the streets had changed several times within the last century. With the help of our translator, we located a street named Szumlanschi in Lemberg, where according to Simon he had lived as a young man with his wife Cyla and his mother, in a small room, before he was deported to the Ghetto. We went to the building No.5 and walked into the inner courtyard, where we saw a woman hanging up white bridal gowns on high ropes that spanned one corner of the yard to the other. It turned out she was a dressmaker. Her activities would have made a beautiful image in our documentary, but, no, unfortunately, she had never heard of Simon Wiesenthal, as she had moved into this building much later. After asking every single person in the building that we could find, someone suggested we should also try the building across the street, as it was inhabited by people who had lived there for much longer. Unfortunately nobody opened the door.

Returning on another day, we finally met someone on the second floor who remembered Simon Wiesenthal. His name was Roman, and he was 8 years old when Wiesenthal lived there. He said that Simon Wiesenthal was always 'so nice to the children'. Roman led us into a small room of approximately six by twelve square feet in which Simon had lived. At the time of our visit the room had been transformed into a kitchen. As a sort of proof, Roman pulled out some architectural magazines with German titles, such as *Die Baukunst* from 1930, which belonged to Simon; Roman had saved the journals for Simon all those years. He asked us to take the magazines back to Simon as a form of greeting, a task which we were happy to do; and upon our return to Vienna, we delivered the magazines to Simon Wiesenthal. But before, on that hot summer day in Lemberg, Werner and I felt our journey to Galicia was touched by a rare magical moment.

Tribute

MARTIN ROSEN

In my forty-year relationship with Simon Wiesenthal, the most unusual and memorable event occurred at our first meeting.

In 1965, when most of the world did not care about apprehending Nazis, Simon was alone and virtually without funds. The closure of his bank in Austria had caused him to lose his money. He visited the United States to solicit financial aid from survivors. Even though some had become fairly rich, they turned him down, except for small donations. He then decided to terminate his work and move to Israel. An article appeared in an English-speaking newspaper in Tokyo which was read by my good friend and client, Herman Katz, of New York. Herman was a hunter, not of Nazis, but of lions and tigers. He was a very successful businessman in the ladies apparel business. He did not know Simon, but on reading this article he called him and asked why he was closing his office. Simon responded 'because there is no money and no one cares', whereupon Herman said, 'I care.' Arrangements were made for Katz to fly to Vienna and meet with Simon and provide him with funds. Herman asked me, as his lawyer, what more we could do to help. We then founded the Jewish Documentation Centre, a tax-exempt foundation which supported Simon for many years. The foundation was not terminated until last year, after Simon's death.

Some of this money was used to provide Simon with the $7,000 that he needed for the arrest of Franz Stangl, the Commandant of Treblinka. For the next twelve to thirteen years, prior to the advent of the Wiesenthal Centre, and until Herman's death in 1977, the three of us were very close and met on many occasions in the United States and overseas. Simon's most successful cases in apprehending Nazis took place during that period.

Herman Katz's dying wish was to take care of Simon. Simon flew in from Vienna and delivered the eulogy for Katz, and on the way to the cemetery we made a commitment to support his work for the balance of his years.

The other memorable event for me was my role in bringing Simon's work to the attention of President Clinton who forwarded to Simon a glowing and laudatory letter for his work. This resulted in President Clinton awarding Simon the Presidential Medal of Freedom.

Tribute

MARTIN MENDELSOHN

In September 2005 I buried an old friend in Israel. As I shovelled the earth over the shrouded body I thought about the man I had known for almost thirty years.

In 1977 I was appointed by the US Attorney General to create and lead what is now known as the Office of Special Investigations in the Department of Justice. The United States government had finally become serious about prosecuting accused Nazi war criminals who were living illegally in this country. One of the first cases that I personally prosecuted was against Boleslaw Maikovskis, accused of being a police chief in Riga, Latvia, who had been complicit in crimes against the Jews in Latvia, in collaboration with members of the Waffen SS. As Maikovskis was not a US citizen, the hearing was to determine whether he should be deported from the US since, when he had applied for a visa to come to this country, he had concealed the crimes that he had committed. The hearing was presided over by Immigration Judge Francis Lyons. It was the first case to be handled by our new unit and there was a lot of public interest. The hearing was held in a nondescript hearing room, with limited seating for the public, in the Federal building in downtown New York City, at 26 Federal Plaza. We wanted the public to attend so all could see the seriousness of our resolve to do justice. One of the people in the audience was Simon Wiesenthal, whom I had heard of but never met. Judge Lyons, afraid of losing control over the hearing because of the presence of Simon Wiesenthal, ordered the hearing room cleared of spectators. The government protested. After a meeting in the Judge's chambers, the hearing room was re-opened and Simon Wiesenthal, among others, was admitted. During the break we introduced ourselves to one another and thus began our relationship which blossomed into friendship and lasted until his death in 2005.

I knew him as a kindly and thoughtful man, very different from the distorted picture painted by some. His accomplishments were legion yet he always operated within the civilized system of law that exists in the countries of the West. Simon's path was not the path of violence or vengeance. His view was that justice and humanity were served by the judicial process. He wanted to educate the people of the world about the horror that man can do to man.

Simon sought a peaceful solution to the most horrific of crimes: genocide. At the end of the Second World War, first as an employee of the US Army and then as an independent operative, he dedicated himself to seeking out of those who had killed Jews and others considered 'undesirable' by the Nazis. He wanted those who committed crimes too awful to be believed to be brought to justice and appropriately punished.

Simon was concerned about the Jewish people and proud to be Jewish. An attack on any Jew because he was Jewish brought Simon to full vigour and fury. He would not back away from a fight. Through the years he brought many libel suits, including at least one in this country against a prominent newspaper, and never lost one. He believed that truth would bring justice and that justice would bring peace, the possibility of 'closure'.

He was not, however, concerned only about Jews. He was mindful of all humanity and all who were threatened with harm or extermination because who they were made them somehow different. He helped Gypsies, Armenians, Tibetans – all who were persecuted because of their perceived differences.

Simon understood the value of alliances to build strength. Through the years he developed close working relationships with government officials and prosecutors in countries throughout the world. He was honoured in places as diverse as the Netherlands and Israel. His cooperative working arrangement with the German government and the Central Office for the Prosecution of War Criminals in Ludwigsberg in Germany resulted in untold numbers of arrests and prosecutions. We worked together in a case against Josef Schwammberger. First he sent me to Argentina where I worked with German and Argentine prosecutors to secure Schwammberger's extradition to Germany. Then I went off to Stuttgart where I was appointed by the Court to represent the victims at the trial. Simon Wiesenthal was a regular observer at the proceedings.

In his later years he welcomed the opportunity to see and teach young people. Not that he had mellowed much. He was already at an advanced age when he developed information that he thought might lead to the discovery of his mother's killer. He asked me to go to Ukraine where, with the help of the KGB we interrogated a number of people in a small, primitive village. We were too late. As was later confirmed, the suspect had died less than two months before my arrival.

It is hard for me to fully come to terms with this loss. Simon Wiesenthal was a symbol of resolution and strength as he sought justice. He knew that whatever form it assumed, justice would be imperfect, but he felt an obligation to the survivors who idolized him because they knew, as the Jewish 'establishment' eventually realized, that not only was he one of them, but that he represented their desire to impose some form of justice and to keep alive the memory of their experience.

The funeral was held just before the celebration of the Jewish New Year, Rosh Hashanah, where Jews pray for the gates of heaven to be opened. I was reminded of the time Simon and I went to see the Israeli Ambassador in Washington. The Israeli Embassy is a model of security with photo checks on doors and gates that only open electronically after the previous one has been shut: the closest thing to James Bond gadgetry imaginable. As we walked into the secure area outside the main building, every barrier swung open. When I expressed surprise to the guards, one said to me: 'This is our *malach* ('angel' in Hebrew); he will protect us; we don't have to protect him and we know we have nothing to fear from him.'

I know the heavenly gates have opened for Simon.

Simon Wiesenthal and the Romanies

IAN HANCOCK

The Romani people lost a mighty champion with the passing of Simon Wiesenthal in 2005. He was the driving force in getting the first Romani representative appointed to the United States Holocaust Memorial Council, and for that he will always be remembered.

He was always keenly aware of the fate of the Romanies in Hitler's Third Reich, summarized by Miriam Novitch of the Ghetto Fighters' House in Israel: 'The motives invoked to justify the death of the Gypsies were the same as those ordering the murder of the Jews, and the methods employed for the one were identical with those employed for the other.'

Wiesenthal was the first to enunciate our victimology, two decades before Germany's official admission of guilt by Federal President Roman Herzog, on 16 March 1997:

> The genocide of the Sinti and Roma was carried out from the same motive of racial mania, with the same premeditation, with the same wish for the systematic and total extermination as the genocide of the Jews. Complete families from the very young to the very old were systematically murdered within the entire sphere of influence of the National Socialists.

O Simon Wiesenthal, you have left us. But the histories of both our peoples and the situations each has had to confront and deal with merely to continue to exist, are almost too tightly intertwined to separate. We have very many Jewish friends and supporters, but Simon Wiesenthal's name stands highest among them.

[Te na andjas o Simon Wiesenthal kado džanglipe la lumjake, ke gonisarde sas e Rrom, čivar avelas amende skamin ande'l Porrajmaske Kanseloste kaj beljam de deuduj bera. Si amende but amala thaj ankerarja bibolde, ale pnda si o bareder o Simon Wiesenthal. Te del o Del les pča and'o rrjo. Či bisterasa tut.]

Tribute

RICHARD ODIER

It is October 2006 at Saint-Vallier de Thiey near Nice. The first public school to bear the name of Simon Wiesenthal is inaugurated. The ceremony takes place before a French minister of state, local officials, teachers, but above all, the pupils, representatives of the Wiesenthal Centre and the honouree's granddaughter Racheli.

On 23 September 2005, the yet unnamed junior high school at Saint-Vallier de Thiey began its first academic year with 400 pupils. That same day, Simon Wiesenthal was buried in Herzliya, Israel. The funeral was attended by over a thousand Holocaust survivors and mourners. They recall Simon's imperative to them, his fellow deportees: 'Never Forget, survival carries an obligation to track down the criminals and bring them to justice!'

Sixty years earlier, Primo Levi wrote the first line of his epic: 'If This Is a Man, never forget what was, no, never forget, engrave these words on your heart ... repeat them to your children'.

Sixty years ago Wiesenthal began, from Austria, the research that would lead to the arrest of over 1,100 perpetrators of the Final Solution. In October 1946, the first sentences of the Nuremberg Military Tribunal were brought against the former Nazi leadership. 1946 also marked the first steps to the reconstruction of life, the birth of Paulinka, daughter to Simon and Cyla. At the same time, in Kielce, Poland, there was a post-war pogrom of Jewish survivor returnees to their hometown.

Sixty years. A symbolic transmission to French high-school students of the lessons of this story. They will be the vectors of memory, the vicarious witnesses of a commitment to life. They will carry with them a hatred of prejudice and a vigilance against hatemongers. These children of the French Republic will understand that hate, intolerance and fanaticism can spring forth anew.

Each day of class, these pupils will pass between two plaques at the entry to their school, which we hope they will absorb and transmit to their peers:

on one side of the door, the plaque to 'Simon Wiesenthal', on the other, the inscription 'Liberty, Equality, Fraternity'.

Tribute

MARY ROBINSON

Simon Wiesenthal's lifetime commitment to documenting the crimes of the Holocaust and bringing to justice its perpetrators stands as a shining example of the power of truth and the importance of individual action in defending human rights.

But Simon Wiesenthal's work is also a reminder, and a warning for our times. As he put it, 'The history of man is the history of crimes, and history can repeat.' Tragically, the horror of the crimes committed against the Jews were not the last case of systematic murder, rape and displacement.

Cambodians, Bosnians, Rwandans, suffered unspeakable violence as well. Today, we watch again as the people of Darfur are the victims of genocide. Where is the Simon Wiesenthal of today? Who will do something now?

Jewish–Muslim Harmony:
A Time for Reflection among Jewish and Muslim Communities in Europe

BASHARAT (BASHY) TAHIR QURAISHY

ENAR (European Network Against Racism), with its more than 600 NGO members, is the largest network of NGOs working for human rights and against ethnic and religious discrimination in the EU. Over the years, ENAR has become specifically worried about the increasing antisemitism and Islamophobia in many European societies. In the last fifteen years or so, the whole public and official debate in Europe has shifted from one about the question of biological or ethnic racism, to one about cultural and now increasingly religious discrimination.

Since Jewish and Muslim communities are two major victims of this hate manifestation, they have a common cause to join forces. I know this is not a traditional logic but in the struggle for a discrimination-free society, we do have a common destiny.

It has always been my personal understanding and conviction that without concrete cooperation with Jewish communities in Europe, Muslim groups will have difficulty in tackling Islamophobia. Both Jewish and Muslim people have to grasp the fact that antisemitism and Islamophobia are two sides of the same coin. We needed to study, analyse and eradicate these two sicknesses at the same time and with the help of each other.

But since this noble thought required gigantic efforts on the part of both religious and secular forces among Jewish and Muslim communities in Europe, an opening was needed. And luckily, it came at the right moment in 2001. Soon after my election as president of ENAR, I met two very dedicated anti-racist personalities involved in the struggle against antisemitism in Europe: Shimon Samuels from the Simon Wiesenthal Centre in Paris and Pascale Charhon from the Brussels-based Jewish Information Centre. Even though I have been closely involved in human rights and anti-discrimination work in Europe for the last 20 years, listening to their untiring efforts, I came to realise how little I knew about contemporary European anti-semitism – verbal and physical.

This awareness fired my determination that a large network like ours should not only work proactively to correct the situation but also voice our strong opposition to antisemitism and Islamophobia whenever and wherever it raises its ugly head. As a start, in 2001 ENAR's Board not only passed a resolution 'to maintain the solidarity of Muslims and Jews in Europe against all acts of antisemitism and Islamophobia' but also pledged that we were against 'any division between these two communities in Europe, which can only serve the forces of hate of which both communities were targets'. This Resolution was also signed by forty-three Muslim and three Jewish members of the 2001 ENAR General Assembly. This spirit of cooperation has been in action ever since, both at various national levels and on the European scene.

The most memorable moment came when I was asked by Shimon to speak at a UNESCO International Conference, 'Educating for Tolerance – The Case of Resurgent Antisemitism', in 2003 in Paris, in front of hundreds of delegates from all over the globe. There I truly felt that everyone among Jewish and Muslim communities has a personal responsibility to help to build a foundation of trust for the other. Dealing with one's own prejudices will give a clearer sense of identity and cultural awareness.

An examination of self will make it easier to confront the societal prejudices, lay a framework for social action and open the doors of respect. During that conference, I also visited a synagogue in suburban Paris, which had been the victim of an antisemitic assault. This proved once again the importance of our common mission. While standing in the synagogue, I felt among brothers and sisters. My eyes were full of tears and I had to struggle to keep myself from choking with emotion.

I am very thankful that, since that time, the cooperation between Shimon and myself, through our personal relationship and professional assistance, has blossomed to a higher stage. He personally intervened with the Danish authorities to suspend the Islamophobic *Radio Holger*, has taken a stand in France on freedom of choice in wearing the *hijab*, and has campaigned consistently in support of Turkey's entry into the European Union. ENAR has also regularly taken up the issue of antisemitism and Islamophobia in its publications and press releases, and through its participation in a number of international conferences.

My dream of a Jewish–Muslim Dialogue Forum is progressing smoothly. I have spoken at many conferences on the issue of cooperation and now I know that antisemitism and Islamophobia can be dealt with and that this can give our two communities some form of safety net. It is also important to mention that this common cause will transform Europe into a true multi-faith continent, where an individual's loyalty would not be measured by colour, creed, culture or religion, but by the contribution that a person makes to society.

On a recent visit to Pakistan, Karen Armstrong, eminent British scholar and author of many critically acclaimed books on Islam and Judaism, said, 'There is much in common between different faiths especially Abrahamic religions. We should pay greater heed to that.' We can only say Amen.

The Mighty Wiesenthal

GREVILLE JANNER
(Lord Janner of Braunstone, QC)

Simon Wiesenthal was my hero. He escaped death by miracles and bravely spent much of the rest of his life in hunting down Nazi killers. I knew of him when in 1947 I became the youngest War Crimes Investigator in the British Army of the Rhine, and in the 1950s he became my friend.

I first met Wiesenthal in Vienna. I asked him how he coped with his memories of his sufferings at the hands of the Nazis. 'Look forward, not back,' he replied.

'But why do you live in Vienna, of all places?' I asked him.

'Because this is a great centre for anti-Nazi activity.'

'But they all know you here. Isn't that dangerous?'

'It has its advantages,' he said. 'For instance, I never have trouble getting a table in a restaurant. All I have to do is to telephone and ask them to page Simon Wiesenthal, and when they do that, the place empties!' It was, indeed, his sense of humour that was one major key to his survival.

I tried to visit him at least once a year in Vienna, and occasionally in London. The last time we had a real chat was twelve months before he died. I said to him: 'Can you sum up your wisdom in a sentence or two for me?'

'No problem,' he replied. 'Know your enemies – and cultivate your friends.' I asked him to write this out for me and he did so, on his office notepaper, dated and signed. It remains framed by the entrance to my home, a daily reminder of one of the world's bravest, wisest and most wonderful of human beings. I still miss him.

Tribute

BEATE and SERGE KLARSFELD

Up until 1955, while simple prisoners of war were still rotting in the Soviet Union, major Nazi criminals were continuing to avoid prosecution, the death penalty or long prison sentences, thanks to the Cold War. Each side was then courting its own Germany and being very careful not to offend the susceptibilities of Germans, either in the East or in the West. In those days when any concern to punish Nazi criminals was fading, Simon Wiesenthal was alone in not giving up the judicial fight and in continuing to demand justice in the name of the victims.

He did not accomplish his mission with hatred in his heart towards Germans and Austrians, amongst whom he lived and acted. He only targeted the guilty, both leaders and the perpetrators of criminal acts.

Without the permanence of this quest for justice that he embodied, without the repeated reminders that he issued to leaders of the Diaspora and to the Israeli authorities, would Eichmann have been kidnapped by Mossad and tried in Jerusalem? Probably not.

Simon Wiesenthal persisted until every last crime of the Nazis had been judged. His longevity took him, still active, into the twenty-first century and his passing coincided with that of the remaining executioners. After him there will no longer be any major Nazi trials.

During the Holocaust, his life hung by a thread, but it was his lot to live on for another sixty years, years that he devoted to the Holocaust, that disaster he investigated so thoroughly and of which he is one of the principal documentalists.

In the camps, Simon Wiesenthal had the courage and faith to refuse to believe what a cynical SS told him: 'If you live to tell it, no one will believe you.' Simon Wiesenthal lived and told, in the face of all disbelief, while maintaining his own courage and his faith in man.

Tribute

BARON DAVID DE ROTHSCHILD

My generation, born during the war, was marked by antisemitic persecutions that did not spare my own family. For us, Simon Wiesenthal, in dedicating his life to combating the impunity of the Nazi criminals in the name of the six million victims of the Shoah, represents a model of tenacity, courage, but also of unshakeable faith in human justice.

We, who escaped the persecutions, are troubled by the question: how did the survivors find the courage to survive? How did they find the energy to fight? Simon Wiesenthal responded, not by long speeches, but by the force of his own struggle.

The struggle of a man who overcame the loss of dozens of family members and the horror of four years in the Nazi camps, and, with the Second World War hardly over, began his battle that justice be done.

A combat first undertaken alone, and then with the Centre that bears his name, to which I have always lent my support.

For almost half a century, the Centre has strived to promote better mutual understanding between communities and, through its constant vigilance, to alert world public opinion against antisemitic and racist words and deeds from wherever they might come.

All, and among them I include myself, who are attached to preserving the memory of the Shoah, cannot but pay homage to the work of Simon Wiesenthal and to the actions of those who follow in his steps.

To be faithful to his memory is to continue to defend the values of justice, courage and fraternity that never ceased to guide him.

Tribute

BARON ERIC DE ROTHSCHILD

On the occasion of the publication of this volume to the memory of Simon Wiesenthal, I wish to add my admiration for his work.

Throughout the years, Simon Wiesenthal strived indefatigably, as much to perpetuate and defend the memory of the Shoah, as also to bring to justice the perpetrators of crimes not barred by a statute of limitation.

We pay sincere homage to all his deeds.

Tribute

Remarks by
HIS MAJESTY KING HUSSEIN,
the Hashemite Kingdom of Jordan, to the Museum of
Tolerance (Simon Weisenthal Centre), 24 March 1995

Mr President, Distinguished Guests,

It is a great privilege for me to be the guest of the museum of peace and tolerance, in this international year of tolerance. I am especially happy to be with you only a few months after the Hashemite Kingdom of Jordan and the State of Israel finally closed the tragic chapter of forty years of conflict, to begin a new era, where the enemies of yesterday become the good neighbours of today and the friends of tomorrow.

You have honoured many heads of state and individuals who have left their mark on human history. Many among them are esteemed personal friends who have contributed greatly to the cause of peace in the Middle East and in the whole world. I am very proud to be in their midst. It is my great privilege to receive this award in the name of all those in the Middle East who stood and sacrificed in the quest for peace, and it has been my duty and honour to have contributed to this cause.

The museum for peace and tolerance is a haunting reminder to all mankind of man's inexplicable cruelty towards his fellow man – and of the tragedy that is a result of illogical and blind hatred. We must all continue to strive to rid our world of such inhumane aberrations. We all know we must build and protect world peace, where disputes cede to dialogue, and conflict is replaced by cooperation.

But let us now speak of hope and progress. At long last the efforts of Jordan and Israel to achieve a just and peaceful settlement of their conflict have been blessed with success. Now work must continue and intensify to achieve a comprehensive settlement of all dimensions of the conflict, because we believe that a balanced and comprehensive peace is the only peace that will endure, and release the energies of all our peoples in the region to build a better future. For our part, we consider our accomplishment to be just the beginning. We have completed the era of peace making. Now we embark on a new era of peace building.

The Christian-Islamic tradition of tolerance and coexistence in mutual respect has happily survived in the Middle East despite the events and attempts that have threatened, even sought, to undermine it. As we consolidate and develop this tradition, we shall now work to revive the equally noble Judeo-Islamic tradition, which also endured for centuries, though it was temporarily overshadowed by the Arab–Israeli conflict. This cultural interchange made great contributions to the progress of mankind in philosophy, literature, science and the arts in the Middle East, and later it played an important role in the flourishing of the European renaissance.

We look forward with confidence to a future, when the words Arab–Israeli no longer evoke images of strife. We hope to see the Middle East evoke, as in the past, images of human accomplishments in science, technology, medicine, industry and the arts. As much as our goals are ambitious, to struggle to achieve them has always been challenging. To achieve our objectives, we must produce deep transformations in our societies. Our economies must be converted from war economies to peace economies. Our private sectors must be freed to make their contributions to the prosperity of the region. Our administrative systems must be restructured to create an investment-friendly environment. These transformations cannot be produced on order, they can only come about as a result of a concerted effort. We hope that our friends will continue to stand by us as we embark on this new era in the history of the Middle East.

For our part, we shall continue to work for the new dawn when all the children of Abraham and their descendents are living together in the birthplace of their three great monotheistic religions, a life free from fear, a life free from want – a life in peace.

Thank you and god bless you all.

Tribute

HUBERT G. LOCKE

I only met Simon Wiesenthal on two occasions – once at the 1992 UNESCO-Simon Wiesenthal Centre Conference, 'Educating for Tolerance: The Case of Resurgent Antisemitism', and earlier, when he spoke at the University of Washington some two or three decades ago. I think I recall having the honour of introducing him that evening, although age and the passing of the years make that memory less certain. What I do recall – and with clarity – was Mr Wiesenthal's expressed delight at meeting an American of African descent who was introduced to him as a 'Holocaust scholar'.

My delight was, by far, the greater – for the privilege of meeting the legendary pursuer of Nazi war criminals whose tireless efforts as a private citizen exemplify the enormous truth of Gunter Grass's observation:

> I think the Weimar Republic collapsed
> and the Nazis took over because there
> were not enough citizens. That is the lesson
> I have learned. Citizens cannot leave politics
> Just to politicians.

Thankfully, Mr Wiesenthal did not leave the task of bringing Nazi perpetrators to account for their crimes to the vagaries of post-Second World War politics. The priorities of the superpowers quickly shifted after the war's end and, once a series of show trials were concluded, the attention of the Allies turned to Cold War considerations that dominated the world stage for another half-century. Citizen Wiesenthal's work, through his Jewish Historical Documentation Centre in Vienna, saw to it that more than eleven hundred Nazi criminals were brought to justice who might otherwise have escaped detection completely.

But his relentless pursuit of war criminals is only one side of the Wiesenthal story. I am certain there are multiple other 'sides'; the one most poignant for me is revealed in the little volume, *The Sunflower*, first published in English over thirty years ago. Its story is well known: Wiesenthal gives a personal account of an incident that occurred in a concentration camp when he was taken to the bedside of a dying SS officer who, haunted by the crimes in which he had participated, wanted to confess his deeds to one who would have been among his victims. Wiesenthal asks his readers: what would you have done?

The answers given by many voices over the years that have appeared in several editions of *The Sunflower* reflect the immense moral dilemma that the incident poses. But the incident itself, and the fact that Mr Wiesenthal recounts it so clearly and compellingly, leaves us with the memory of a man of uncommon moral sensibility whose efforts were not undertaken in any self-righteous sense of vengeance or retribution but rather with a quiet, persistent passion for justice.

May his memory be a blessing!

Quotes about Simon Wiesenthal

'Mr Wiesenthal has been untiring in his service to the Jewish communities in the UK and elsewhere by helping to right at least some of the awful wrongs of the Holocaust. If there is one name which symbolizes the vital coming to terms with the past, it is Simon Wiesenthal.'

> British Foreign Secretary Jack Straw on announcing
> Simon Wiesenthal's honorary knighthood
> by Her Majesty the Queen, 2004

'From the unimaginable horrors of the Holocaust, only a few voices survived, to bear witness, to hold the guilty accountable, to honor the memory of those who were killed. Only if we heed these brave voices can we build a bulwark of humanity against the hatred and indifference that is still all too prevalent in this world ... We thank Simon Wiesenthal for a lifetime of service and example and reminder, and for the astonishing work of the Wiesenthal Center...'

> President Bill Clinton in remarks at the White House when Simon
> Wiesenthal received the Medal of Freedom, 2000

'As one of the greatest nightmares of all time, the Holocaust prompted humanity to demand justice for those barbarous acts. [Simon Wiesenthal] answered that call with a vision of justice that has transcended the decades and continues to inspire each of us, and the achievements of the Simon Wiesenthal Center heighten our awareness of the events that led to the Holocaust and renew our commitment to the moral values that will never permit such atrocities again.'

> Ronald Reagan, President of the United States, 1981–89

'He has received many tributes ... but the Center for Holocaust Studies bearing [his] name is the most eloquent statement of the world's respect for [him] as a person and for the successes [he] has achieved.'

Gerald R. Ford, President of the United States, 1974–77

'Your selfless dedication to the victims of the Holocaust, your relentless pursuit of justice for the perpetrators and the atrocities of the Third Reich, leave all of mankind in your debt ... [Simon Wiesenthal] has demonstrated how an individual, armed only with dedication and faith, can change the world. He is a living embodiment of mankind's unquenchable spirit and a reminder to all of us that the struggle between freedom and totalitarianism has not ended.'

Henry A. Kissinger, US Secretary of State, 1973–77

'Simon Wiesenthal has reminded us time and again that the statistics of a millionfold suffering and death must not make us blind to the individual victim ... He is a champion of humanity. The assertion of justice against injustice, of morality against barbarism, characterizes his life-work ... In this endeavour, in the quest for a better future, we need the example and testimony of people like Simon Wiesenthal.'

German Chancellor Helmut Kohl, 1980

'He is an extraordinary man who exemplifies respect for human dignity and the inalienable rights of the individual. Throughout his life he has maintained his passion for justice ... Individual responsibility for upholding and defending human rights is something that Simon Wiesenthal has always emphasized. His life and works remind us that we should always be aware of our own human rights and respect those of our fellow human beings and that anyone who violates the rights of another demeans humanity.'

United Nations Secretary General Perez de Cuellar, 1982–91

'We lift our hearts in gratitude for your heroic work, which permits us to seek a world free of fear, a world where justice will prevail, a world capable of protecting all its citizens from the oppression of tyrants.'

Declaration of the Franklin and Eleanor Roosevelt Institute upon awarding Simon Wiesenthal the Four Freedoms Medal, 19 May 1990

'This man has dedicated all his life to uprooting the evil of our times, the Nazi war criminals who have inflicted a severe damage on the moral fibre of mankind. The victims cannot be brought to life but the perpetrators can be brought to trial. Wiesenthal works and lives for them.'

Gideon Hausner, former Israeli Attorney General and Prosecutor of Adolf Eichmann

'Your work, your achievements, and your vision are an inspiration to all who seek justice, cherish truth, and love freedom.'

Refusenik Natan Sharansky, 1988

'There are few people in this world to whom the title 'humanitarian' applies as appropriately as to Simon Wiesenthal. The work he has done has been in the name of justice and humanity, and his selfless devotion has been an example to many others, young and old alike.'

Teddy Kollek, Mayor of Jerusalem, 1965–93

Editorial Comment

We consider criticism of Israeli policy – as, indeed, that of any United Nations member state – as quite legitimate.

When criticism, however, degenerates into the demonisation of the Jewish State and the delegitimisation of Jewish sovereignty, such expression is commonly denoted 'anti-Zionism'.

Denial of self-determination to the Jewish people only is a discrimination that we construe as an extreme form of antisemitism. This is even more patent when calls to 'wipe Israel off the map' are heard in conjunction with denial of the Holocaust.

Language or caricatures that cast Israel in the imagery of the Holocaust we likewise deem as antisemitic.

This interpretation is consonant with the OSCE and EU international instruments, cited below, in their consideration that anti-Israelism and anti-Zionism are often pretexts for antisemitism.

Several of the essays in this volume describe the impact of such positions upon the security of Jews in the Diaspora, and upon inter-community relations within their respective countries.

We wish to emphasize, that not all who express 'antisemitism' may be considered 'antisemites'. The test is intent. It is hoped that this volume may assist those who are ignorant of the consequences of their words. Indeed, this is a rule for all expressions of racism.

In so sensitising the unwitting carriers of the bigotry virus, the pedagogy of 'antisemitism' may truly serve as a generic hatred.

Shimon Samuels
May 2007

European Union Monitoring Centre on Racism and Xenophobia (EUMC) Working Definition of Anti-Semitism, disseminated in March 2004

The purpose of this document is to provide a practical guide for identifying incidents, collecting data, and supporting the implementation and enforcement of legislation dealing with anti-Semitism.

Working definition: 'Antisemitism is a certain perception of Jews, which may be expressed as hatred toward Jews. Rhetorical and physical manifestations of antisemitism are directed toward Jewish or non-Jewish individuals and/or their property, toward Jewish community institutions and religious facilities.'

In addition, such manifestations could also target the State of Israel, conceived as a Jewish collectivity. Anti-Semitism frequently charges Jews with conspiring to harm humanity, and it is often used to blame Jews for 'why things go wrong'. It is expressed in speech, writing, visual forms and action, and employs sinister stereotypes and negative character traits.

Contemporary examples of anti-Semitism in public life, the media, schools, the workplace, and in the religious sphere could, taking into account the overall context, include, but are not limited to:

- Calling for, aiding, or justifying the killing or harming of Jews in the name of a radical ideology or an extremist view of religion.
- Making mendacious, dehumanizing, demonizing, or stereotypical allegations about Jews as such or the power of Jews as collective – such as, especially but not exclusively, the myth about a world Jewish conspiracy or of Jews controlling the media, economy, government or other societal institutions.
- Accusing Jews as a people of being responsible for real or imagined wrongdoing committed by a single Jewish person or group, or even for acts committed by non-Jews.
- Denying the fact, scope, mechanisms (e.g. gas chambers) or intentionality of the genocide of the Jewish people at the hands of National Socialist Germany and its supporters and accomplices during World War II (the Holocaust).
- Accusing the Jews as a people, or Israel as a state, of inventing or exaggerating the Holocaust.

- Accusing Jewish citizens of being more loyal to Israel, or to the alleged priorities of Jews worldwide, than to the interests of their own nations.

Examples of the ways in which anti-Semitism manifests itself with regard to the state of Israel taking into account the overall context could include:

- Denying the Jewish people their right to self-determination, e.g., by claiming that the existence of a State of Israel is a racist endeavour.
- Applying double standards by requiring of it a behaviour not expected or demanded of any other democratic nation.
- Using the symbols and images associated with classic anti-Semitism (e.g., claims of Jews killing Jesus or blood libel) to characterize Israel or Israelis.
- Drawing comparisons of contemporary Israeli policy to that of the Nazis.
- Holding Jews collectively responsible for actions of the State of Israel.

However, criticism of Israel similar to that levelled against any other country cannot be regarded as anti-Semitic.

Anti-Semitic acts are criminal when they are so defined by law (for example, denial of the Holocaust or distribution of anti-Semitic materials in some countries).

Criminal acts are anti-Semitic when the targets of attacks, whether they are people or property – such as buildings, schools, places of worship and cemeteries – are selected because they are, or are perceived to be, Jewish or linked to Jews.

Anti-Semitic discrimination is the denial to Jews of opportunities or services available to others and is illegal in many countries

Organization for Security and Cooperation in Europe (OSCE – 55 states), Berlin Declaration on Anti-Semitism, 29 April 2004

Bulgarian Chairmanship

The Chairman-in-Office

Distinguished delegates,

Let me sum up the proceedings of this Conference in what I would like to call 'Berlin Declaration'. Based on consultations I conclude that OSCE participating States, Reaffirming the Universal Declaration on Human Rights, which proclaims that everyone is entitled to all the rights and freedoms set forth therein, without distinction of any kind, such as race, religion or other status, Recalling that Article 18 of the Universal Declaration on Human Rights and Article 18 of the International Covenant on Civil and Political Rights state that everyone has the right to freedom of thought, conscience and religion, Recalling also the decisions of the OSCE Ministerial Councils at Porto and Maastricht, as well as previous decisions and documents, and committing ourselves to intensify efforts to combat anti-Semitism in all its manifestations and to promote and strengthen tolerance and non-discrimination, Recognizing that anti-Semitism, following its most devastating manifestation during the Holocaust, has assumed new forms and expressions, which, along with other forms of intolerance, pose a threat to democracy, the values of civilization and, therefore, to overall security in the OSCE region and beyond, Concerned in particular that this hostility toward Jews – as individuals or collectively – on racial, social, and/or religious grounds, has manifested itself in verbal and physical attacks and in the desecration of synagogues and cemeteries,

1. Condemn without reserve all manifestations of anti-Semitism, and all other acts of intolerance, incitement, harassment or violence against persons or communities based on ethnic origin or religious belief, wherever they occur;
2. Also condemn all attacks motivated by anti-Semitism or by any other forms of religious or racial hatred or intolerance, including attacks against synagogues and other religious places, sites and shrines;
3. Declare unambiguously that international developments or political issues, including those in Israel or elsewhere in the Middle East, never justify anti-Semitism.

1 Lessons of the Holocaust: The Early Warning System

FRANKLIN H. LITTELL

Since the infamous attack on the Twin Towers in New York City, several colleagues have asked me about my 'Early Warning System' (EWS). I have lectured on campuses and in conferences on this theme for more than thirty years, and the 'EWS' seems even more relevant today than it did when I began.

I pirated the concept from the 'DEW' (Distant Early Warning) surveillance that the US Air Force ran out of Omaha, Nebraska and Great Falls, Montana during the Cold War period. The idea of applying the term to political developments came to me on a trip to Japan. The US Air Force Chaplains had invited me to lecture in Tokyo on the Church Struggle with Nazism and Communism. The thought came to me that it was profoundly unsatisfactory only to lecture about disastrous situations in the past: there were, as a matter of fact, clear signs that made disaster predictable – unless decisive pre-emptive action was taken.

My Early Warning System is a scientific template ('grid') that does three things. One, it makes it possible to identify potentially genocidal movements before they come to power. Two, the basic template signals when a legitimate government is 'losing it', as the Weimar Republic did in 1931–33 – through infiltration and subversion of the instruments of government, by measures inadequate to deal with a major economic crisis, followed by a military coup. Three, the 'grid' identifies regimes (dictatorships, incipient or finalized), for which destruction of unwanted internal minorities and aggression toward outside 'enemies' (real or fictitious) is endemic.

Such regimes – among other crimes against humanity – also sponsor terrorist nets operating across borders, and give them safe haven training bases.

My Early Warning System has been discussed for nearly three decades in seminars and conferences – for instance, in international conferences at Tel Aviv 1981, Oxford 1988, Berlin 1994 and Stockholm 2000. After the 11 September attack it was also the topic of a session at the 32nd Annual Scholars' Conference (ACS) on the Holocaust and the Churches. Before, during and after the Second World War we have seen clear demonstrations of the high costs of ignoring the Early Warning signs. We should have learned by now the frightful cost of political appeasement and economic expediency. EWS provides an analytical tool for bringing the oratory exercised on 'terrorism' down to the concrete challenge of identifying potentially genocidal movements and suppressing them in time.

Seventy-four years ago a 'terrorist' incident occurred that served as an excuse for bringing the last agonies of the German Weimar Republic to a visible end. Hitler, whom the old President, General von Hindenburg, referred to as 'that Austrian corporal', had been named Reichskanzler. His National Socialist Party (NSDAP), although still well below 50 per cent of the electorate, was the single strongest parliamentary bloc. Naive apparatchiks in the conservative parties thought they could get him in harness and control him. That was 30 January 1933, and the republic had already had two and a half years of government by executive decree, under the *Notfallsklause* – the emergency paragraph in the Constitution. During this interim of political expediency, made desperate by the suffering of millions thrown out of work in the Great Depression, the robust give-and-take of democratic government had withered and the violent climate of public terror had gained ascendancy.

Less than a month later, on 27 February, came 'the Reichstag fire'. The story remains obscure to this day. Was the minor figure who was reported to have set such a fire a publicity-seeker? Was he a set-up by the Nazis? The only point about which agreement has been reached is the judgment that he was 'not too bright', perhaps even mentally retarded. In any case, the following day the parliament rushed through an emergency ordinance to save the country from 'Communist terrorism'.

Three weeks later, with the Communists prevented from sitting in the session and only the Socialists voting against, the Reichstag shouted out the Enabling Act (*Ermächtigungsgesetz*). This suicidal act of 23 March 1933 was the concluding outward display of even the formalities of German self-government until after the Second World War. The substance of democratic self-government already had been eaten away by violence in the streets, by the assassination of key political leaders who opposed the Nazi machine, and by the soulless manipulations of political and clerical intrigants who had substituted secretive backroom deals in place of public policy based on open and informed debate.

The overwhelming conviction that emerges from review of this record of the decline of a people's self-respect into the disaster of dictatorship is this: it didn't have to happen. There were warning signs, which we can now itemize in an Early Warning System, as to when a free government is losing it, when violent men are rising to the top of the turmoil. Parallel to this perception is another aspect of Early Warning now susceptible to scientific analysis: the precise identification of a 'fifth column' that only puts on the mask of a legitimate political party, while in structure and programme it undermines the self-governing of a free people.

Item: by 1923, the NSDAP was already a 'fifth column', a potentially genocidal movement. All it lacked was the hand on the throttle of power. In ten years (by public violence and the quiet subversion of centres of authority, for example, the universities, the churches, the professions, etc), the NSDAP had successfully infiltrated and gutted both the political and the non-governmental centres of power. Many general histories refer to the 'Nazi victory' in the last elections, to the Nazi assumption of power 'by parliamentary means', to the Nazi 'take-over'. That language is misleading: on the contrary, by external violence and internal penetration during the previous decade the Nazis had already set up a parallel regime within the hollow shell of the formalities of the dying Weimar Republic.

Lesson Number Two: it is not only important to act as responsible and self-respecting citizens when a free government is losing its way, it is also imperative to identify and suppress organizations that by their actions and structures show they are disloyal and potentially genocidal. There are those of our friends who say, from time to time, that the Nazi genocide of the Jews was a 'dark hole' in the universe of understanding, that nothing can be generalized or learned from it. This is poetic language, and has the merit of warning us to tread softly on sacred ground. However, there are also, as it were, sacred lessons, lessons to be written on our hearts and brains in indelible ink.

On the Second Lesson, the importance of suppressing 'fifth columns' in time: bizarre opinions may in America receive First Amendment protection; aggressive and violent actions and structures are not so entitled, even if they are temporarily being held on a tight leash. If you will forgive the comment, it is a rampant bad habit of us teachers and preachers, not to mention lawyers, to fail to distinguish between opinions and actions. This bad habit is as dangerous as the equally rampant failure to distinguish between unlimited individual freedom and responsible political and religious liberty. Or, to take another example of rampant failure to make essential distinctions: *The Christian Century*, a prominent 'liberal' Protestant journal, indulges in what our colleague Deborah Lipstadt has identified as the fallacy of equivalence. In the 1930s, the *Century* even-handedly criticized both the British Empire and the new German Empire for exploitation of peoples; today the *Century* continues to draw equivalence, this time between Israel's defence actions and Palestinian terrorism. Both are violent, but very different.

Nevertheless there is a profound difference, although the ideologues and the space walkers deny it, between the clash of opinions in open forum and the mobilization of terrorist violence against non-military targets. We have in hand, after a century of genocide, the scientific analysis by which a potentially genocidal movement can be identified in time. (1933 was too late. 1938 was much too late. The time to act decisively was 1923, when the opinions that had been trumpeted freely in the 1920 Nazi Party Programme were translated into concrete, violent and treasonous action against the Weimar Republic.) Faulty ideas can be preached against. Erroneous opinions can be refuted in public debate. But the deliberate mobilization of violent assaults on our liberties as democratic peoples, privileged to live in republics or constitutional monarchies, must be defeated by resolute, timely, prophylactic action at law.

Now, on a matter of clarity and definition: we hear and read a great deal these days about something called 'terrorism'. With the spectacular incidents of 11 September, which yanked our happy island back to the mainland of civil conflict and violence in public affairs, 'terrorism' comes naturally to the lips. Billions of dollars are committed in Washington, DC to set up bureaus to fight 'terrorism'. The American president condemns 'terrorism' and 'terrorist' regimes. In response, of course, the extremists in Baghdad and Damascus and Tehran condemn the US for 'terrorism'. To go to what some – not of this company of readers, of course – take to be the highest authority: the *Reader's Digest* recently dedicated a most unusual volume of print to an issue with presentations on 'terrorism'.

In point of fact, Brian Jenkins of the Rand Corporation published a splendid analysis of 'terrorism' in September of 1982 in *The Annals of the American Academy* to which little has needed to be added in two decades.

For our purpose, the noun 'terrorism', with its several derivatives, has little use in designing action to prevent evil. In fact, on closer inspection, the popular information on 'terrorism' deals neither with infiltration and subversion nor with the shape and style of potentially genocidal movements. The topic is the nature of modern war. Civilians bear the brunt of the assault. As our colleague at the University of Hawaii, R.J. Rummel, has demonstrated,[1] in modern war – as during the Age of Genocide – the losses in civilian lives are far greater than the losses in uniformed personnel. To be blunt, if you want to survive a modern war, get into uniform.

Here, in retrospect, the historical record does show a connection between something loosely called 'terrorism' and the defined crime of genocide: the heavy costs are paid by non-combatants, by innocent children, women and the elderly. In their inherently violent structure and style, on their way to power, potentially genocidal movements ('fifth columns') are destructive of healthy political development; when they are in control, they are genocidal toward internal, targeted unwanted minorities – counted among the 'surplus populations' that Richard Rubenstein discusses,[2] and also aggressive toward external 'enemies'.

The implementation of an Early Warning System, for which I have been arguing since the 1960s, is overdue. The structural 'grid' that identifies a potentially genocidal movement, in time, is known. The template for effective interception is available. To continue a political posture of moralizing generalities, without dedicated attention to the precise measures necessary to neuter the internal enemies, parallel to the reasonable measures to frustrate external enemies, is irresponsible bordering on the criminal.

Thinking only in the old categories, we are trapped in a dead-end street. While aggressive regimes are a constant military threat to their neighbours, the record shows that the free peoples cannot be brought even to self-defence until all other escapes are closed. That is assuredly one of the 'lessons' of the Second World War. The mounting of an Early Warning System on potentially genocidal movements, paralleled by the development and vigorous support of an international police agency, can provide the fresh moral and political initiatives the free world so urgently needs.

The 'grid' defining a potentially genocidal movement numbers fifteen points:

1. Antisemitism, usually the first and always the most virulent form of racism.
2. Ideological politics – decisions based on ultimates rather than on practical, prudential considerations.
3. The politics of polarization: destruction of the idea and practice of loyal opposition, contempt for intelligent compromise, infusion of the religious spirit of the Last Things into the political arena.
4. The reconstruction of sacral society: against modern and scientific thought, and in hostility to religious and cultural pluralism, the forceful, reactionary effort to return to a mythical golden age of uniformity.
5. A new periodization of history: the new 'elite' or 'vanguard' carry history; history is dated from the ideological party's accession to power.
6. A new anthropology: idealization of the New Man (revolutionary activist, 'Aryan'), against lesser persons and races.
7. Formation of an elite with secret discipline, arcane signals and tattoos.
8. The cult of violence: the 'unbelievers' are to be swept from the pages of history, first by the Big Lie and then physically.
9. The inducement of social aphasia: the forceful creation of those conditions of terror that make open debate and free communication of ideas impossible.
10. The police state: police and the military independent of civilian control; a time of lawless policemen, disloyal generals and public adulation of those administering violence.
11. Monolithic party and/or state: the model for society is the wheel, in which all the spokes are locked in the hub.
12. The beautiful state. Political exposition has lost awareness of 'the doubtfulness things are involved in', policy decisions fly into ultimate solutions, and associations below the state are either absorbed or crushed.
13. False picture of political agreement. Instead of the consensus produced by free and informed discussion, a uniformity of slogans and demonstrations is demanded.
14. Reversion to reliance upon the oral tradition – what 'everybody knows', what the party or ruling clique puts out – as against carefully sifted evidence, critically appraised facts.
15. Determinism. The agony of real choice is lifted from the individual by deference to 'economic determinism' or religious fiat.

The major forum for developing and circulating the Early Warning System has been for more than three decades the Annual Scholars' Conferences. Participants have studied the problems of modern society, assessed the human cost of religious apostasy, and studied how men and women of many nations, religions and educational disciplines can study and work together to affirm life.

We know the terrible loss of life that comes when the barriers fall and the flood waters cover the earth. The old rabbis taught mourning for the fall of the Temple – the beacon to monotheism in the midst of a lascivious, brutal, corrupt, exploitative empire. We who are products of the *universitas magistrorum et scholarium* need to learn and master creative mourning for the fall of the higher learning from service to the human being to fealty to the forces of self-serving and destruction.

In the name of the six million victims of intelligent, modern, calculated and technically competent Evil, and not forgetting the guilt of the complicit bystanders as well as the cunning of the perpetrators, the time has come for us to here and now renew our pledge to work from here on out: to affirm life – and not to serve death, to breathe hope – and not to counsel despair, to block violence – and to bless compassion.

A Selection of Franklin Littell's Writings on his 'Early Warning System'

Wild Tongues (New York: Macmillan Co., 1969). The application of a 'grid' or 'template' to distinguish a terrorist movement from a legitimate participant in debate in the public forum and in the quest for power in the free society.

'Early Warning: An Essay', *Holocaust and Genocide Studies*, III, 4 (1988), pp.483–90.

'Early Warning: Identifying Potentially Genocidal Political Movements', *Jerusalem Letter/Viewpoints* (1 Dec. 1989), pp.1–6.

'Early Warning: Detecting Potentially Genocidal Movements', in Peter Hays (ed.), *Lessons and Legacies: The Meaning of the Holocaust in a Changing World* (Evanston, IL: Northwestern University Press, 1991), pp.305–15.

'Creating an Early Warning System', a lecture at a conference in New York City, 5 April 1995, discussing the twentieth century confrontation with genocidal ('terrorist') movements and proposing an 'Early Warning System' (privately printed in pamphlet form, eight pages).

'Creating an Early Warning System: The 20th Century Confrontation with Terrorist Movements', the Annual Ida E. King Lecture at the Richard Stockton College of New Jersey, 7 November 1996; privately published in bound form, twenty-four pages mimeographed.

'Early Warning System', in Israel W. Charny (ed.), *Encyclopedia of Genocide* (Santa Barbara, CA: ABC CLIO, 1999), Vol.I, pp.261–5, with a section by the Editor on 'Franklin Littell's Writings on Early Warnings of Genocide', p.262.

NOTES

1. R.J. Rummel, *Death by Government* (New York: Transaction, 1994).
2. Richard Rubenstein, *The Age of Triage* (New York: Beacon, 1983).

2 Anti-Zionism and Antisemitism

ROBERT S. WISTRICH

My first really serious conversation with Simon Wiesenthal took place in the cafeteria of the Hebrew University Faculty Club in 1985. We had already been in correspondence and spoken on the phone seven or eight years earlier after I had published a number of articles in the British and American press on the Kreisky–Wiesenthal Affair. Wiesenthal, who could be unforgiving in his dislikes, also never forgot a good turn. He vividly remembered that I had strongly defended him between 1975 and 1979, at the lowest ebb in his career as an investigator of Nazi war crimes, when the popular Austrian Chancellor Bruno Kreisky threatened to close down his Vienna Documentation Centre, branding it a festering irritant from a bygone age. Kreisky, taking advantage of Wiesenthal's unpopularity at that time in an Austria all too eager to cover up its Nazi past, accused him of being a former 'Gestapo collaborator', a 'Jewish fascist', an 'agent of Zionism' and other ridiculous libels – for which eventually he would pay in an Austrian law-court. Bruno Kreisky, himself a Jew and a militant socialist ever since his youth, not only sought to whitewash Nazi crimes after he came to power in 1970, he was also a radical anti-Zionist – vilifying the very idea of Jewish peoplehood as a fundamentally 'racist' philosophy. A fully-fledged assimilationist, he had little tolerance for 'Galician Jews' like Simon Wiesenthal. In a notorious interview with *Der Spiegel* in 1975, the Austrian Chancellor actually said 'the man must disappear' (meaning Wiesenthal), adding that 'if the Jews are a people, then they are a repulsive people'.

Our discussion in Jerusalem twenty years ago revolved around the need for a comprehensive scientific study of the connection between antisemitism and anti-Zionism, something Wiesenthal keenly urged me to pursue. The truth is that I needed little persuasion and a few years later, I produced a book entitled *Antisemitism: The Longest Hatred*,[1] and a PBS documentary film of nearly three hours, that addressed this subject. That was only the beginning of what is turning out to be an unending project. The passion and intensity of Simon Wiesenthal's commitment to this topic did undoubtedly leave its mark on me. He was one of those 'voices of conscience' one can never escape from, even if at times one disagrees with their views on a particular topic.

The emergence of new forms of 'anti-Zionist' antisemitism in recent years has only underlined the prescience of Wiesenthal's vision, which lay at the basis of our subsequent relationship. In February 2006 when I addressed the Inter-Parliamentary Committee on Antisemitism in the British House of Commons, this was the first order of business. Surely, the British MPs wanted to know, criticism of Zionism or alarm at Israel's policies must be distinguished from loathing towards Jews? Was it not true that antisemitism was frequently confused with 'anti-Sharonism', as *The Guardian* newspaper liked to claim? Did not Jews themselves often engage in the fiercest opposition to Israeli government policy without being accused of antisemitism? Finally, exaggerated use of the Judeophobic charge, it was suggested, raised the suspicion that Israel's leaders might be seeking to deflect or even silence justified criticism.

My answer to these objections was to argue that anti-Zionism and antisemitism were two distinct ideologies which over time (especially since 1948) have tended to converge without necessarily undergoing a full merger. But, during the past thirty years, anti-Zionism has undoubtedly become the most dangerous and effective form of antisemitism, through its systematic delegitimization, defamation and demonization of Israel. Although not *a priori* antisemitic, the calls to dismantle the Jewish state, whether they come from radical Muslims, Palestinian nationalists, the left, or the radical right, often rely on an antisemitic stereotypization of classic themes, such as the manipulative 'Jewish lobby', the Jewish/Zionist 'world conspiracy', and Jewish/Israeli 'warmongers'. One major driving force of this anti-Zionism/antisemitism convergence is the transformation of the Palestinian cause into a 'holy war'; another source is anti-Americanism linked with fundamentalist Islamism. In the current context, classic conspiracy theories, such as the *Protocols of the Elders of Zion*, are enjoying a spectacular revival. The common denominator of the new anti-Zionism has been the systematic effort by pro-Palestinian propaganda to criminalize Israeli and Jewish behaviour, so as to place it beyond the pale of civilized and acceptable conduct.

I believe that the more radical forms of anti-Zionism which have emerged with renewed force in recent years do display unmistakable analogies to European antisemitism immediately preceding the Holocaust. One of the more striking symptoms has been the call for a scientific, cultural and economic boycott of Israel which arouses some grim associations and memories among Jews of the Nazi boycott that began in 1933. The recent decision of British academic unions to boycott Israeli academics is a symptom of the new discriminatory policies. There are other highly visible manifestations. For example, the systematic manner in which Israel has been harassed at international forums such as the UN, where the Arab states have for decades pursued a policy of isolating the Jewish state and turning it into a pariah. An offshoot of this campaign was the hate-fest at the UN-sponsored Durban Conference against racism of September 2001, which denounced Zionism as a 'genocidal' movement, practising 'ethnic cleansing' against Palestinians. In these and similar public forums, as well as in much of the Western mainstream media, Zionism and the Jewish people have been demonized in ways that are virtually identical to the methods, arguments and techniques of racist antisemitism. Even though the current banner may be 'antiracist' and the defamation is being carried out today in the name of human rights, all the red lines have clearly been crossed. Can there be serious doubt, that 'anti-Zionists' who insist on comparing Zionism and the Jews with Hitler and the Third Reich, are de facto antisemites, even if they vehemently deny the fact! Those who engage in this ugly game are well aware that Nazism today is perceived as the defining ideology of 'absolute evil' which has to be destroyed. The fact that there are Jews (including some Israelis) who participate in this masquerade requires a psychopathological, rather than a political, analysis.

Israel today is the only state on the face of this planet which such a large number of disparate forces wish to see disappear – itself a chilling reminder of Nazi propaganda in the 1930s. The most virulent expressions of this 'exterminationist' or genocidal anti-Zionism have come from the Arab-Muslim world which has become the historical heir of the earlier twentieth-century forms of totalitarian antisemitism in Hitler's Germany and the Soviet Union. The most publicized examples have been the chilling declarations of Iranian President Ahmadinejad denying the Holocaust and threatening to 'wipe out Israel'. But even 'moderate' Muslim statesmen like former Malaysian leader Mahathir Mohammad have publicly repeated the classic antisemitic belief that 'Jews rule the world' while eliciting virtually no objections in the Islamic world. Radical Islamists from al-Qaeda to the Palestinian Hamas go much further since they fuse indiscriminate terror, suicide bombings and a *Protocols of Zion* style of antisemitism with the ideology of jihad. In this case, the so-called 'war against Zionism' unmistakably embraces the total demonization of the 'Jewish other'. Zionists are supposedly the 'enemy of mankind', deadly poisonous snakes, barbarian 'Nazis' *and* 'Holocaust manipulators', who control America and the Western mass media, while they busily instigate wars and revolutions to achieve world domination. Such conspiracy theories sailing under 'anti-Zionist' colours are part of a highly toxic, murderous world-view closely linked to religious fanaticism and a global revolutionary agenda. The same demonizing stereotypes can however be found in 'moderate' pro-Western Egypt (home to the *Protocols*-based antisemitic soap opera *Knight Without a Horse*), secular Baathist Syria, conservative Wahhabite Saudi Arabia and the Shiite fundamentalist Iran of the Ayatollahs. This is an ideological anti-Zionism that seeks both the annihilation of Israel and a world 'liberated from the Jews' – in other words it is a *totalist* form of antisemitism.

'Annihilationalist' anti-Zionism, under the guise of anti-Israelism, has spread to Western Europe, America and parts of the Developing World. It has found grassroots support in the Muslim Diaspora among radicalized youth and more than an echo among anti-globalists, Trotskyists, and far-right groups not to mention parts of the 'liberal' media. There is a loose and shifting coalition of red-brown-green bigotry focused against both America and Israel. Osama bin Laden is a hero not only to those who wish to restore Islam's global hegemony but also for some of those neo-Marxist or neo-fascist ideologues who still believe in the 'world revolution' of the proletarian masses or the demise of 'Judeo-American' domination.

Much of the mobilizing power of 'anti-Zionism' derives from its link to the Palestinian cause. The Palestinian Authority has frequently combined antisemitic motifs – including Holocaust denial, updated blood libels and Jewish conspiracy themes – with its general incitement to violence. Not only that, but some Palestinian Christians have developed a 'theology of liberation' that plays on older antisemitic efforts to de-Judaise the Christian tradition which finds a surprisingly sympathetic echo in some Western churches. As for the Islamic groups among the Palestinians, they openly see themselves as engaged in 'a war against the Jews'. Hamas, which today rules the Palestinian Authority, has embraced a fully-fledged Islamicized vision of the 'Jewish Peril' derived from the *Protocols of the Elders of Zion*, ever since its foundation.

Palestinian suffering and Arab 'anti-Zionism' have helped to infect Europe with an old-new version of antisemitism in which Jews have been transmuted into rapacious, blood-sucking colonialists. The fashionable narrative in educated Western circles today is that Jews are alien, rootless and imperialist invaders, who came to Palestine to conquer the land by brute force, to expel or 'cleanse' it of its natives. They are the modern 'Crusaders' with no legitimate rights to the soil – an alien transplant, absolutely foreign to the region. They allegedly succeeded only because of a gigantic occult conspiracy in which the Zionists (that is, the Jews) manipulated Great Britain and afterwards America. This is an antisemitic narrative of which Hitler might have approved!

The popularity of the *Protocols* is a telling symptom of the growing merger between antisemitism and anti-Zionism. Israel is increasingly depicted in mainstream media as being 'criminal' in its essence as well as in its behaviour – a systematic violator of human rights and international law. This flows from the left-wing mantra that brands Israel as a racist, apartheid, colonialist and imperialist state. Its military actions offer all too many Europeans the tantalizing prospect of saying 'the victims of yesterday have become the [Nazi] perpetrators of today'; and/or the opportunity to present Zionism as heir to the darkest pages of Western colonial history – that is, Algeria, Vietnam or South Africa. Such aspersions by virtue of endless repetition become the ideological rationalization for dismantling Israel.

For the past three decades, anti-Zionism has used a discourse and stereotypes concerning the 'Jewish/Zionist lobby', Israeli/Jewish 'criminality', 'state terrorism' and 'warmongering' which are fundamentally manipulative and antisemitic. This has penetrated the mainstream debate to the point where 60 per cent of all Europeans regard tiny Israel as the greatest threat to world peace; where over a third of those surveyed in Europe and America regularly attribute to Jews excessive power and influence; where Jews are suspected of dual loyalties by ever greater numbers of non-Jews; and where 'anti-Zionist' attacks on Jewish institutions and targets show that we are talking about a distinction without a difference. Anti-Zionism is not only the historic heir of earlier forms of antisemitism. It has become the lowest common denominator and the bridge between the left, the right and the militant Muslims, between the elites (including the media) and the masses; between the churches and the mosques; between an increasingly anti-American Europe and an endemically anti-Western Arab-Muslim Middle East; a connecting link between conservatives and radicals who have lost their ideological moorings. Most disturbing of all, in the hands of the Iranian leadership and radical Islamists, across the Muslim world, it has become an 'exterminationist' pseudo-redemptive ideology with unmistakably genocidal implications.

NOTES

1.   Robert Wistrich, *Antisemitism: The Longest Hatred* (New York: Pantheon Books, 1992).

3 The New Antisemitism: An Assault on Human Rights

IRWIN COTLER

INTRODUCTION: ANTISEMITISM OLD AND NEW – DEFINITION AND DISTINCTION

What we are witnessing today – and which has been developing incrementally, sometimes imperceptibly, and even indulgently, for some thirty-five years now – is a new, sophisticated, virulent, globalizing and even lethal anti-Jewishness, reminiscent of the atmospherics of the 1930s, and without parallel or precedent since the end of the Second World War. This new anti-Jewishness overlaps with classical antisemitism, but is distinguishable from it; it found early juridical, and even institutional, expression in the United Nations' 'Zionism is Racism' resolution but has gone dramatically beyond it; a new anti-Jewishness which almost requires a new vocabulary to define it – but which can best be defined, using a rights-based juridical perspective, as discrimination against, denial of, or assault upon, the right of Israel and the Jewish people to live as an equal member of the family of nations – of the emergence of Israel in a metaphorical but real sense as the collective and targeted Jew among the nations.

Accordingly, I propose a set of indices organized around a juridical framework, a rights-based inquiry that draws upon principles of anti-discrimination law and equality rights as they find expression in both domestic and international law. There are twelve indices that may assist us in identifying this new anti-Jewishness.

Two important caveats underpin the entire analysis: first, none of the indicators is intended to suggest that Israel is somehow above the law, or that Israel is not to be held accountable for any violations of law. On the contrary – Israel is accountable for any violations of international law or human rights like any other state; and the Jewish people are not entitled to any privileged protection or preference because of the particularity of Jewish suffering.

Second, I am not referring to critiques, even serious critiques, of Israeli policy or Zionist ideology, however distasteful or offensive some of these critiques might sometimes be. But the converse is also true. Antisemitic critiques cannot mask themselves under the exculpatory disclaimer that 'If I criticize Israel, they will say I am antisemitic'. In the words of *New York Times* commentator Thomas Friedman: 'Criticizing Israel is not antisemitic, and saying so is vile. But singling out Israel for opprobrium and international sanctions – out of all proportion to any other party in the Middle East – is antisemitic, and not saying so is dishonest.'[1]

THE NEW ANTI-JEWISHNESS: INDICES OF IDENTIFICATION

1. Genocidal Antisemitism

I am referring here to what is described in the International Convention on the Prevention and Punishment of Genocide as 'direct and public incitement' to genocide, in this case to the destruction of Israel and the killing of Jews wherever they may be.

It has three manifestations. The first is the state-sanctioned, indeed state-orchestrated, genocidal antisemitism of Ahmadinejad's Iran – the toxic mix of advocacy of the most horrific of crimes – genocide – with the most enduring of hatreds – antisemitism – propelled by the clear intent to acquire nuclear weapons for this purpose. Indeed, this intent is further dramatized by the parading in the streets of Tehran of a Shihab-3 missile draped in the emblem of 'Wipe Israel off the Map', while demonizing both the State of Israel as a 'cancerous tumour' and the Jewish people as 'evil incarnate', the whole inspired by an eschatological religious fanaticism that sees the 'Death of Israel' as the apocalyptic precursor to the return of the twelfth Imam Mahdi.

A second manifestation of this genocidal antisemitism is in the covenants and charters, platforms and policies of such terrorist movements and militias as Hamas, Islamic Jihad, Hezbollah and al-Qaeda, which not only call for the destruction of Israel and the killing of Jews wherever they may be, but also for the perpetration of acts of terror in furtherance of that objective.

Hezbollah leader Hassan Nasrallah not only speaks of Israel's 'disappearance', but has said that 'If all the Jews were gathered in Israel it would be easier to kill them all at the same time.' In a lesser known, but no less defamatory and incendiary expression, Nasrallah has said that, 'if we searched the entire world for a person more cowardly, despicable, weak and feeble in psyche, mind, ideology and religion, we would not find anyone like the Jew. Notice, I do not say the Israeli'.[2] Shi'ite scholar Amal Saad-Ghorayeb, author of the book, *Hezbollah: Politics and Religion*, says this statement 'provides moral justification and ideological justification for dehumanizing the Jews'. In this view, she went on, 'the Israeli Jew becomes a legitimate target for extermination and it also legitimizes attacks on non-Israeli Jews'.[3]

The third manifestation of this genocidal antisemitism is in the religious *fatwas* or execution writs, where these genocidal calls are held out as religious obligations – and where Jews and Judaism are characterized as the perfidious enemy of Islam.

Israel emerges here not only as the collective Jew among the nations, but as the Salman Rushdie among the nations. Yet there is a difference: when Iran issued a *fatwa* against this distinguished writer, the entire European community and others sought to impose sanctions against Iran. But with respect to Israel and Jews, we have *fatwas* not only from Iran, but *fatwas* issued by radical clerics throughout the Muslim and Arab world. And – with bitter irony – rather than the European community threatening sanctions against those who issue *fatwas* against an entire state and people, we see Israel threatened by sanctions for their response to the anti-Jewish terror mandated by such *fatwas*.

In a word, Israel is the only state in the world today – and the Jews the only people in the world today – that is constantly threatened by governmental, religious and terrorist bodies seeking their destruction. And what is most disturbing is the seeming indifference, sometimes even indulgence, in the face of such genocidal antisemitism.

2. Political Antisemitism

If genocidal antisemitism is a public call for or incitement to the destruction of Israel, political antisemitism is the denial of Israel's right to exist to begin with, or the denial of the Jewish people's right to self-determination, if not their very denial as a people. There are four manifestations of this phenomenon.

The first is the discrimination against, or denial of, the Jewish people's right to self-determination, the only right enshrined in both the International Covenant on Civil and Political Rights and the International Covenant on Economic, Social and Cultural Rights, and a right accorded to all other peoples. The Jewish people, then, is singled out and discriminated against with respect to its right to self-determination, which, as Martin Luther King, Jr. put it, 'is the denial to the Jews of the same right, the right to self-determination, that we accord to African nations and all other peoples of the globe. In short, it is antisemitism'.[4] And more: to the extent that Israel has emerged as the organizing idiom of Jewish self-determination, this new anti-semitism, sometimes coded as 'anti-Zionism', is an assault per se, in contemporary terms, on the religious, cultural, national and juridical sensibility of the Jewish people. Indeed, I suspect that it is this con-fluence that led Martin Luther King, Jr. to equate anti-Zionism with antisemitism. When a student attacked Zionism, King responded by stating that attacks on Zionists were often a cover for attacking Jews. As he put it: 'When you're attacking Zionism, you're talking anti-semitism.'

This segues into the second feature of political antisemitism, which involves the discrimination against, or denial of, the legitima-cy, if not existence, of the State of Israel. Indeed, it may be regarded as the contemporary analogue of classical or theological anti-semitism, which discriminated against, or denied the very legitimacy of, the Jewish religion. In other words, if classical antisemitism was anchored in discrimination against the Jewish religion, the new anti-Jewishness is anchored in discrimination against the Jews as a people and a nation – and the embodiment of that expression in Israel. In each instance, then, the essence of antisemitism is the same – an assault upon whatever is the core of Jewish self-definition at any given moment in time, be it the Jewish religion at the time of classi-cal antisemitism, or the State of Israel as the 'civil religion' or juridi-cal expression of the Jewish people under this indicator.

A third variant is the denial of any historical connection between the Jewish people and the State of Israel, a form of Middle East revi-sionism or 'memory cleansing' that seeks to extinguish or erase the Jewish people's relationship to Israel, while Palestinizing or Islamicizing the Arab and Muslim exclusivist claim.

If 'Holocaust Revisionism' is an assault on Jewish memory and historical experience – including a criminal conspiracy to excoriate the Jewish victims while whitewashing the Nazi perpetrators – 'Middle East Revisionism' constitutes no less an assault on Jewish memory and historical experience, erasing or excoriating the Jews while inverting the historical narrative.

Under this revisionist and exclusionary narrative, Jews are said to have no connection or claim to an historical Arab and Muslim land called Palestine. They have no historical link or claim to Jerusalem, nor any historical link or claim to the Temple Mount, nor even a claim to be a people. Jews are, as it were, erased from history.

Accordingly, Israel is an 'original sin', an 'alien' and 'colonial implant' that 'usurped' the Palestinian homeland, and its inhabitants, a 'criminal' group of 'ruthless' nomadic Jews whose very presence 'defiles' Islam, and must therefore be expurgated.

It is not surprising that this revisionist Middle East narrative – cleansing the Jews from any connection to the land of Israel – should lead inexorably to yet another and fourth variant of political antisemitism. I am referring here to the 'demonizing' of Israel – the attribution to Israel of all the evils of the world, the portrayal of Israel as the enemy of all that is good, and the repository of all that is evil. This is the contemporary analogue to the medieval indictment of the Jew as the 'poisoner of the wells'. In other words, in a world in which human rights has emerged as the new secular religion of our time, the portrayal of Israel as *the* metaphor for a human rights violator is an indictment of Israel as the 'new antichrist' – as the 'poisoner of the international wells' with no right to exist – with all the 'teaching of contempt' for this 'Jew among the Nations' that this new antisemitism implies.

Anthony Julius, the distinguished British jurist – often understated in his characterization and critique of antisemitism – summed it up well as follows:

> to maintain that the very existence of Israel is without legitimacy, and to contemplate with equanimity the certain catastrophe of its dismantling, [...] is to embrace – however unintentionally, and notwithstanding all protestations to the contrary – a kind of anti-Semitism indistinguishable in its compass and its consequences from practically any that has yet been inflicted on Jews.[5]

3. Ideological Antisemitism

If the first two indicators – genocidal antisemitism and political antisemitism – are overt, public and clearly demonstrable, ideological antisemitism is a much more sophisticated and arguably more pernicious expression of the new antisemitism. Indeed, it may even serve as an 'ideological' support system for the first two phenomena, though these are prejudicial and pernicious enough in themselves.

For here, ideological antisemitism finds expression not in any genocidal incitement against Jews and Israel, or overt racist denial of the Jewish people and Israel's right to be; rather, ideological anti-semitism disguises itself as part of the struggle *against* racism. Indeed, it marches under the banner of anti-racism, and under the protective cover of the United Nations and the international struggle against racism.

The first manifestation of this ideological antisemitism was its institutional and juridical anchorage in the 'Zionism is racism' reso-lution at the United Nations, a resolution that, as Senator Daniel Moynihan said, gave the abomination of antisemitism the appearance of international legal sanction. But we have gone beyond the notion of Zionism as racism, notwithstanding the fact that there was a for-mal repeal of this resolution at the United Nations. Indeed, 'Zionism as racism' is alive and well in the international arena, particularly in the campus cultures in North America and Europe, as the recent British All-Party Parliamentary Inquiry into Antisemitism reported. But there are two additional manifestations of this ideological anti-semitism that bear appreciation.

The second manifestation is the indictment of Israel as an apartheid state. This involves more than the simple, though serious enough, indictment of Israel as an apartheid state; it also involves, as evidenced by the events at the UN World Conference against Racism in Durban, the call for the *dismantling* of Israel as an apartheid state. This indictment is not limited to talk about divestment – it is about the actual dismantling of Israel based upon the notion of apartheid as a crime against humanity.

Moreover, and this is the third manifestation of ideological anti-semitism, we are not only witnessing the characterization of Israel as an apartheid state – and one that must be dismantled as part of the struggle against racism – but this is now joined by the 'nazification' of Israel. And so it is then that Israel is delegitimized – if not demo-nized – by the ascription to it of the two most scurrilous indictments of twentieth-century racism – Nazism and apartheid – the embodi-ment of all evil.

Indeed, these very labels of Zionism and Israel as 'racist, apartheid and Nazi' supply the criminal indictment. No further debate is required. The conviction has been secured. And if any further debate is required, it is only to pronounce the sentence: that the conver-gence of these three labels – this 'triple racism' – now warrants the dismantling of Israel as a moral obligation for us all. Such a state, as the discourse puts it, does not really have any right to exist – and who would deny that a 'racist, apartheid, Nazi' state should not have any right to exist today? What is more, this characterization allows for terrorist 'resistance' to this Nazi apartheid state to be deemed justifiable – after all, such a situation is portrayed as nothing other than *occupation et résistance*, where 'resistance' against a racist, apartheid, Nazi occupying state is legitimate, if not mandatory.

What is so disturbing about this ideological antisemitism – and indeed what makes it antisemitic – is not simply the defamatory and delegitimating labels that impugn Zionism as the raison d'être for a Jewish state – or delegitimate the Jewish state itself – but the use of these defamatory and delegitimating indictments to call for the dismantling of the Jewish state itself. And more: disingenuously to mask this ideological antisemitism as if it were part of the struggle against racism, if not also the struggle against apartheid and Nazism, and thereby transform what is, in effect, an antisemitic indictment, that is, to dismember the only Jewish state, into a moral imperative; and to seek to give it the imprimatur of the United Nations and international law.

4. 'Legalized Antisemitism': Discriminatory Treatment in the International Arena

If ideological antisemitism is as prejudicial and pernicious as it is set forth above – in seeking to mask itself under the banner of anti-racism – this fourth indicator of the new anti-Jewishness, legalized antisemitism, is even more sophisticated and insidious, and no less prejudicial and pernicious. For here antisemitism seeks, at one and the same time, to mask itself under the banner of human rights, to invoke the authority of international law, and to operate under the protective cover of the United Nations, the linchpin of international human rights law. In a word – and in an Orwellian inversion of human rights, language and law – the singling out of Israel and the Jewish people for differential and discriminatory treatment in the international arena is 'legalized'. From a juridical human rights perspective, I shall set forth here a series of examples of this 'legalized' antisemitism.

The first is the 2001 UN World Conference against Racism in Durban, which became the 'tipping point' for the emergence of a new anti-Jewishness. It should have been otherwise. Indeed, when the UN World Conference against Racism was first proposed some ten years ago, I was among those who greeted it with anticipation, if not excitement. This was to be the first world conference on human rights in the twenty-first century. Anti-racism was finally going to be a priority on the international human rights agenda. The underrepresented human rights cases and causes would now have a platform and presence. The choice of Durban as host was to commemorate the dismantling of South Africa as an apartheid state, a watershed event in the international struggle against racism.

But what happened at Durban was truly Orwellian. A World Conference against Racism turned into a conference of racism against Israel and the Jewish people. A conference intended to commemorate the dismantling of South Africa as an apartheid state resonated with the call for the dismantling of Israel as an apartheid state. A conference dedicated to the promotion of human rights as the new secular religion of our time increasingly singled out Israel as the meta-human rights violator of our day, indeed as the new antichrist of our time. A conference that was to speak in the name of humanity ended up as a metaphor for hate and inhumanity.

The second example of this Orwellian anti-Jewishness marching under the banner of human rights took place annually for over 35 years at the United Nations Commission on Human Rights. The importance of the Commission's work resides in the fact that not only has the UN emerged as the linchpin of international human rights law today, but that, in all its configurations, it exerts an enormous influence on the large class of UN civil servants; on governments and Members of Parliament around the world, for whom the UN is an ongoing idiom of their foreign policy; on the critical mass of people who are exposed to, and influenced by, UN human rights decision-making internationally; on students and scholars all over the world who learn the 'jurisprudence' of the UN Commission on Human Rights as part of their learning and part of their intellectual experience; and on the media who report it, and civil society, which is influenced by it.

But what happened at the UN Commission on Human Rights was that the annual session would begin with Israel being the only country singled out for a country-specific indictment even before the deliberations began – in breach of the UN's own procedures and principles – an 'Alice in Wonderland' situation where the conviction and sentence are pronounced even before the hearing begins.

Moreover, some 30 per cent of all the resolutions passed at the UN Commission on Human Rights over the past 35 years were indictments of Israel. Among the resolutions adopted, as in the 2002 session which convened at the zenith of anti-Jewish terror, were resolutions that indicted Israel for war crimes, crimes against humanity, and genocide – language right out of the Nuremberg indictments for the very victims of Nuremberg. And while Israel has annually been the target of some five indictments, no other state has been the object of more than one resolution or indictment, while the major human rights violators – Iran, China, Sudan – enjoy exculpatory immunity.

In the anti-terrorism debate that took place at the UN in the immediate aftermath of 9/11, Arab states and their supporters opposed any attempt to classify 'resistance' as terrorism, thereby appropriating the Durban rhetoric of the de-legitimization of Israel, on the one hand, and the legitimization of terrorism as 'resistance' against Israel, on the other. Yet, in a not-so-subtle reference to Israel, the UN Commission on Human Rights astonishingly passed a resolution in 2002 justifying the use of 'resistance by all available means' in instances of colonialism, foreign occupation and the like, which has been taken to validate anti-Jewish terror against Israeli civilians.

Accordingly, it was a hopeful sign when a reform panel of eminent persons appointed by the Secretary-General referred to the Commission's 'eroding credibility and professionalism', going on to note that 'the Commission on Human Rights suffers from a legitimacy deficit that casts doubts on the overall reputation of the United Nations'.[6] The Commission was replaced in June 2006 by the newly created UN Human Rights Council, heralded as 'the dawn of a new era'. But as UN Watch Executive Director Hillel Neuer put it, 'The Council [...] devoted one hundred percent of its country-specific resolutions, two special sessions, one fact-finding mission, and a "high level commission of inquiry" to one single purpose: the demonization of Israel.'[7] A third case study of this 'legalized' antisemitism is even more compelling. This one did not have as much public resonance as the others, but it remains disturbing in its discriminatory application to Israel as the Jew among the nations. In December 2001 the High Contracting Parties to the Fourth Geneva Convention were convened. The Fourth Geneva Convention was passed, in the aftermath of the Holocaust, as a regime of international humanitarian law to protect civilians in armed conflict. For 52 years after its adoption in 1949, the contracting parties of the Geneva Convention never met – notwithstanding the genocide in Cambodia, the ethnic cleansing and genocide in the Balkans, the unspeakable and preventable genocide in Rwanda, and the killing fields in Sudan and Sierra Leone. The first time – and the only time– that the contracting parties of the Geneva Convention came together to put a country in the dock was in December 2001, and the country put in the dock was Israel. This discriminatory treatment is an issue not only for Israel – it stands as an assault upon the international human rights order, undermining the whole regime of international humanitarian law. These three cases are not the only examples of the international 'legal' character of the new antisemitism. The fact is that there have been more resolutions adopted, more committees formed, more deliberations held, more speeches made and more resources expended in the condemnation of Israel then on any other state, or combination of states.

5. European Antisemitism

The documentary record in Europe since the dawn of the new millennium – and particularly, ironically enough, in the post-9/11 universe – and in the aftermath of the most horrific acts of anti-Jewish terror in Israel that reached a zenith in March 2002 (when 126 Israelis were murdered in a single month) – suggest that antisemitism in Europe is finding continuing and growing expression.

Indeed, we are witnessing an explosion of antisemitism in Europe almost without parallel or precedent since the Second World War. In the words of Per Ahlmark, former leader of the Swedish Liberal Party and Deputy Prime Minister of Sweden:

> Compared to most previous anti-Jewish outbreaks, this one is often less directed against individual Jews. It attacks primarily the collective Jew, the State of Israel. And then such attacks start a chain reaction of assaults on individual Jews and Jewish institutions ... In the past, the most dangerous antisemites were those who wanted to make the world *Judenrein*, 'free of Jews'. Today, the most dangerous antisemites might be those who want to make the world *Judenstaatrein*, 'free of a Jewish state'.[8]

6. Radical Muslim and Arab Antisemitism

The sixth indicator of the new anti-Jewishness is what may be termed the radical, globalizing, totalitarian Arab and Muslim antisemitism. Again, as with European antisemitism, an important caveat is required. None of this is intended to suggest – nor should it be inferred – that Islam is antisemitic, or that any Muslim country is antisemitic. Only that there is an extremist genre of radical Islam that is antisemitic, and it would be patronizing – and dangerous – not to identify and combat it, as many Muslims and Arabs are doing. Moreover, totalitarian antisemitism is not new: it found expression in Nazism and communism, the ideological forerunners of this new totalitarian Islamic antisemitism. Similarly, Arab antisemitism is not new; it even preceded the establishment of the State of Israel. What is new, however, is the totalitarian and radical character of this Arab and Islamist antisemitism, its intensity, virulence and fanaticism.

7. Theological Antisemitism

I am referring here to the convergence of state-sanctioned Islamic antisemitism characterizing Jews and Judaism as the perfidious enemy of Islam; and which finds expression in the proclamations from Islamic pulpits – and broadcast on Palestine state television – such as the words of the Palestinian Authority-appointed and funded Imam, Ahmed Abu Halabiya: 'The Jews must be butchered and tortured: Allah will torture them with your hands. Have no mercy on the Jews ... wherever you meet them ... kill them.'[9] And the doctrine of Christian replacement theology which holds that the Jews have been replaced by the Church in God's favour, so that all of God's promises to the Jews, including the land of Israel, have been inherited by Christianity because of the perfidy of the Jews. Accordingly, an illegitimate Israel has usurped and betrayed Christian theology.

8. Cultural Innuendo that smacks of Antisemitism, According to the 2004 Working Definition of the European Union Monitoring Centre on Racism and Xenophobia

I am alluding here to the *mélange* of attitudes, sentiments, innuendo and the like – in academia, in Parliaments, among the literati, public intellectuals and the human rights movement – the discourse of the 'chattering classes' and enlightened elites in the democracies – in a word, *la trahison des clercs*, which has found expression as follows:

- The reported, though never admitted, remarks of a French Ambassador to Britain to the effect that why should the world risk another world war because of 'that shitty little country Israel'; or as Petronella Wyatt put it, 'antisemitism has become respectable once more, not just in Germany or Catholic-central Europe, but at London dinner tables'.[10]
- British novelist A.N. Wilson allegedly accused the Israeli army of 'the poisoning of water supplies'; Tom Paulin, Oxford professor and poet, wrote of a Palestinian boy 'gunned down by the Zionist SS', and stated, in an interview with the Egyptian *al-Ahram Weekly*, that 'I never believed that Israel had the right to exist at

all' – which he is entitled to believe – but then goes on to say, in incendiary rhetoric, that Brooklyn-born Jews who have settled in the West Bank 'are Nazis, racist ... they should be shot dead. I feel nothing but hatred for them'; Peter Hain, a former minister in the British Foreign Office, reportedly stated that the present Zionist state is by definition racist and will have to be dismantled.[11]

- In Germany, Jürgen Möllemann, an official of the Free Democrats, defended Palestinian terrorism against Jews, causing a commentator in the *Suddeutsche Zeitung* to write: 'It's been a long time since the hatred of Jews – once disguised as antisemitism – has been socially acceptable in Germany as it is today.'[12]
- In Italy, in the liberal daily *La Stampa*, a cartoon showed the infant Jesus looking up from his manger at an Israeli tank and pleading, 'don't tell me they want to kill me again'.
- José Saramago, a Nobel Laureate in literature, wrote that 'we can compare what is happening in the Palestinian territories with Auschwitz';[13] Professor Michael L. Sinnot called Israel the 'mirror image of Nazism', stating that 'uniformed Israeli troops murder and mutilate Palestinian children', that there was 'a real Zionist conspiracy' worldwide. He has since apologised for this statement.

In summary, antisemitism appears to be 'the right and only word', in the words of Gabriel Schoenfeld, for a cultural antisemitism 'so one-sided, so eager to indict Israel while exculpating Israel's adversaries, so shamefully adroit in the use of moral double standards, so quick to issue false and baseless accusations and so disposed to invert the language of the Holocaust and to paint Israelis and Jews as evil incarnate'.[14]

9. Holocaust Denial

The cutting edge of this new antisemitism is Holocaust Denial, which moves inexorably from denying the Holocaust, to accusing Jews of fabricating the 'hoax' of the Holocaust, to indicting Jews for extorting false reparations from the innocent German people, to the building of their 'illegal' State of Israel on the backs of the real indigenous owners, the Palestinians. Let there be no doubt about it: those who would seek to deny the Jewish people their past are the same people who, if given the chance, would deny the Jewish people their future.

10. Economic Antisemitism

There are two manifestations of economic antisemitism. The first refers to the economic coercion and discrimination practised through the Arab boycott that emerges as the contemporary economic analogue of classical economic antisemitism. In a word, classical economic antisemitism involved discrimination against Jews in housing, education and employment; the new economic antisemitism involves the extra-territorial application by Arab countries of an international restrictive covenant against corporations, conditioning their trade contracts on their undertaking not to do business with Israel (secondary boycott); or not doing business with another corporation which may be doing business with Israel (tertiary boycott); or even, in certain instances, conditioning the trade on such corporations neither hiring nor promoting Jews amongst them.

Second, the incidence of academic, university, trade union and related boycotts and divestments – whose effects in practice, if not intent in principle – is the singling out of Israel, Israeli Jews and supporters of Israel for selective opprobrium and exclusion. As the UK All-Parliamentary Inquiry into Antisemitism recently reported:

- 'We received evidence regarding the attitudes of a small number of academics whose critical views of Israel have adversely affected their relations with Jewish students.'
- 'At its annual conference in 2005 the Association of University Teachers (AUT) passed a motion boycotting two Israeli universities, Haifa and Bar Ilan.'
- '... though the motivations of the boycotters may not in themselves be antisemitic, the effect of their actions would be to cause difficulties for Jewish academics and students. The majority of those who have institutional affiliations to Israeli universities are Jewish, and thus the consequences of a boycott would be to exclude Jews from academic life. A boycott would have a detrimental effect on Jewish studies departments in the UK leaving them potentially unable to continue teaching.'
- 'The singling out of Israel is also of concern. Boycotts have not been suggested against other countries. Also of particular concern to witnesses was the concept of a "loyalty test" for Israeli Jews, described by some as "McCarthyite", signifying as it does the assumption of collective responsibility and collective guilt.'
- 'The discourse around the boycott debate gave cause for concern,

as it moved beyond reasonable criticism into antisemitic demonisation of Israel.'

- 'A side-effect of the attempt to boycott Israeli universities is that it has the effect of closing down debate on Israel within the Jewish community. British Jews can feel under siege and this leads to a desire among many to show a united front and defend Israel in the face of demonisation.'

The UK All-Parliamentary Inquiry concluded that 'calls to boycott contact with academics working in Israel are an assault on academic freedom and intellectual exchange. We recommend that lecturers in the new University and College Lecturers Union are given every support to combat such selective boycotts that are anti-Jewish in practice.'

11. Racist Terrorism against Jews

This refers to the state-orchestrated incitement to violence and terrorism against Jews, including the singling out of Israeli Jews and Jewish nationals as targets of international terrorism. Indeed, the anti-Jewish attacks in Israel – apart from terror attacks on Jews outside Israel – in the year before 9/11, targeting Jewish schools, synagogues, neighbourhoods, buses and restaurants, were the equivalent in proportional population terms to a half a dozen 9/11s; yet, for the most part, these anti-Jewish terror attacks went unacknowledged outside Israel until 9/11.

This left the disturbing inference that somehow acts of terror against Jews are not considered to be terrorism, or that Jewish victims of acts of terror are somehow not victims. Indeed, the 'inventory' of targets of terrorism in the post 9/11 universe – Bali, Madrid, London – and the 'inventory' of victims of terror, tended to gloss over, if not ignore, the specific dimension of anti-Jewish terror. Moreover, the terrorist targeting of Jews, which has continued unabated, is marked by five disturbing characteristics of an antisemitic nature.

First, terrorist targets in Israel are expressly and explicitly anti-Jewish – designed not only to kill and maim as many Israeli Jews as possible, but to terrorize Jewish neighbourhoods, synagogues, schools, buses, the core symbols and expressions of Jewish life and living. In the words of Muslim cleric Sheikh Ibrahim Mahdi, repeated endlessly on Palestinian Authority television: 'All weapons must be aimed at the Jews, at the enemies of Allah, the cursed nation in the Qur'an, whom the Qur'an describes as monkeys and pigs ... We will blow them up in Hadera, we will blow them up in Tel Aviv and in Netanya ... we bless all those who educate their children to jihad and to martyrdom'.

Second, the terrorist targets are not only Jewish targets in Israel, but Jews and Jewish targets outside of Israel. The phenomenon of home-grown or extremist terrorism in Europe and North America only exacerbate this threat.

Third, the terrorist threat has included what were meant to be alarming cases of 'mega' or 'catastrophic' terrorism, which were thwarted at the last moment, but which, if they had succeeded, would be horrific. I am referring to attempts literally to incinerate thousands of Israelis through the blowing up of fuel and gas storage facilities in the Herzliya area; the blowing up of the Azrieli office towers in Tel Aviv, and of residential areas in Haifa; the attempted blowing up of residential apartment areas in Haifa; and the recent disclosure of Hezbollah- and al-Qaeda-connected plans to target Israeli institutions and Jewish nationals in the Western hemisphere.

Fourth, these terrorist attacks are often religiously inspired or ordered, such that anti-Jewish terrorism is considered obligatory, the terrorists are regarded as 'martyrs', and the Jewish victims as an evil abstraction.

Fifth, anti-Jewish terror is the product of a state-orchestrated, state-sanctioned culture of hate – integrating both old and new forms of anti-Jewishness – that finds increasing expression in the incitement to hatred in state-controlled mosques, media, schools and so on, including such recent examples as the broadcasting of the *Protocols of the Elders of Zion*, the blood libel, and the appropriation of symbols and motifs from classical antisemitism to demonize Israel and the Jewish people today. In the words of Professor Fouad Ajami,

> The suicide bomber of the Passover massacre did not descend from the sky; he walked straight out of the culture of incitement let loose on the land, a menace hovering over Israel, a great Palestinian and Arab refusal to let that country be, to cede it a place among the nations, he partook of the culture all around him – the glee that greets those brutal deeds of terror, the cult that rises around the martyrs and their families.

Indeed, the recent finding by Argentine Special Prosecutors that the bombing of the Jewish Cultural Centre (AMIA) in 1994 was conceived, planned and ordered by the Iranian government at the highest levels; that the Iranian President at the time was Akbar Rafsanjani, who in 2001 called also for the destruction of Israel; that it was executed by Hezbollah; that, as the Argentine Report put it, it was not a random case of indiscriminate terrorism, but a specific act of terror directed against the Jews; that the issuance of the Report calling for the arrest of former President Rafsanjani and other Iranian officials responsible for the most shameful act of anti-Jewish terror since the Second World War – issued fortuitously on the same day that the Iranian President Mahmoud Ahmadinejad called yet again for the destruction of Israel – chillingly recalled Norman Cohn's warrant for genocide.[15]

12. The Old/New Protocols of the Elders of Zion

For over one hundred years, the world has been suffused with the most pervasive, persistent and pernicious group libel in history, the *Protocols of the Elders of Zion* – the tsarist forgery proclaiming an 'international Jewish conspiracy' bent on 'world domination', and responsible for all the evils in the world; that ignited the anti-Jewish pogroms in Russia at the turn of the twentieth century; that underpinned *Mein Kampf*, which served as the linchpin of the Nazi 'conspiracy theory' as justification for their war against the Jews, and for the demonization of the Jew as a prologue to genocide.

Today, more than one hundred years later, the 'lie that wouldn't die' now underpins the most outrageous of international conspiracy thinking and incitement, including:

- That the Jews – Israel – were responsible for 9/11. Evidence: Only the Jews' were capable of orchestrating a macabre deed of such magnitude and complexity; or that Jewish workers were forewarned about the attacks, and therefore did not go to work on 9/11; or that New York rabbis were also forewarned, and urged to withdraw money from the stock markets; or that Mossad actually carried out this horrific act.
- Israel and the Jews are held responsible for a series of 'new protocols', including that the Jews are behind the spread of AIDS, Avian flu, the destruction of the space shuttle Columbia, the Danish cartoons blaspheming the Prophet Mohammed, the Pope's defaming Islam, or the war in Iraq and so on.

But it is not long before the same libellous inheritance from the Jews is transferred to the Jews of Israel – to the international Zionist conspiracy – bringing together the old and new protocols in a conceptual and linguistic cemetery.

In the last few months, Israel, world Jewry or the 'Zionists' have been blamed for fabricating the 'genocide' in Darfur, with Sudanese President Omar el-Bashir referring to it as a 'Zionist plot'; for conniving with the US to initiate the war against Hezbollah; and for being behind the Argentine Special Prosecutors' indictment of Iranian leaders for the bombing of the Jewish Community Centre in Argentina.

But it is in the Arab and Muslim world that the *Protocols* have taken hold, not unlike the incitement of the anti-Jewish pogroms in tsarist Russia, or the Nazi murders of the Third Reich. As Justice Hadassa Ben-Itto has written, they are propagated in the mosques, taught in the schools, published by the state, sold in bookstores and book fairs, serialized in state newspapers with Struemer-like cartoons, and, most compellingly, have secured a captive audience through the daily broadcasting on Egyptian television during the month of Ramadan of a 41-episode series titled *Knight Without a Horse*, which depicts how Jews connive to dominate the whole Muslim world, how the conspiracy influences all major events in history, and how the Jewish serpent is winding its way to one country after another, in its journey of evil.

CONCLUSION

As I said at the outset, none of this is intended to suggest that Israel is somehow above the law, or that it is not to be held accountable for any violations of law. On the contrary – Israel is accountable for any violations of international law or human rights like any other state; and the Jewish people are not entitled to any privileged protection or preference because of the particularity of Jewish suffering.

The problem is that Israel has been systematically denied equality before the law; the human rights of Israel have not been respected; human rights standards have not been applied equally to anyone else.

In a word, Israel and the Jewish people have been singled out for differential and discriminatory treatment in the international arena and, worst of all, have been singled out for genocidal assault and terrorist attack.

The time has come to sound the alarm – not only for Israel and the Jewish people whose safety and security is under existential threat and attack – but for the world community and the human condition as a whole.

NOTES

1. Thomas L. Friedman, 'Campus Hypocrisy', *New York Times*, 16 October 2002.
2. Speech quoted in Amal Ghorayeb Saad, *Hisbu'llah: Politics and Religion* (London: Pluto Press, 2001).
3. Jeffrey Goldberg, 'In the Party of God: Are Terrorists in Lebanon Preparing for a Larger War?' *New Yorker*, 14 and 21 October 2002.
4. Martin Luther King, Jr., quoted in Seymour Martin Lipset, 'The Socialism of Fools: The Left, the Jews and Israel', *Encounter* (December 1969), p.24; see also John Lewis, 'I Have a Dream for Peace in the Middle East: Martin Luther King, Jr.'s Special Bond with Israel', *San Francisco Chronicle*, 21 January 2002.
5. Anthony Julius, 'Don't Panic', *Guardian*, 1 February 2002.
6. *A More Secure World: Our Shared Responsibility*, report of the High-Level Panel on Threats, Challenges and Change (New York: United Nations, 2004).
7. Hillel C. Neuer, Statement at a Hearing before the Subcommittee on Africa, Global Human Rights and International Operations of the Committee on International Relations – House of Representatives, Serial No.109-221, 6 September 2006.
8. Per Ahlmark, 'Combating Old-New Anti-Semitism', Yad Vashem, 11 April 2002, see www.yad-vashem.org.il.
9. From a sermon delivered on 13 October 2000, in the Sheikh Zayed ibn Sultan Al-Nahyan Mosque in Gaza, broadcast on PA Television.
10. Petronella Wyatt, 'Poisonous Prejudice', *Spectator*, 8 December 2001.
11. A.N. Wilson, 'A demo we can't afford to ignore', *Evening Standard*, 15 April 2002; Tom Paulin, 'Killed in Crossfire', *Observer*, 18 February 2001; Tom Paulin interviewed by Omayama Abdel-Latif, 'That Weasel Word', *al-Ahram Weekly*, No.580, 4–10 April 2002.
12. Quoted in Gabriel Schoenfeld, 'Israel and the Anti-Semites', *Commentary*, June 2002.
13. ADL-online, 26 March 2002; Spanish site of BBC: Interview with Saramago, 'Palestina es como Auschwitz'; in the London Arabic daily *al-Hayat* the commentator praised Saramago's courage to compare Auschwitz with the 'massacres against the Palestinian people'. MEMRI, special dispatch, 5 April 2002.
14. Quoted in Schoenfeld, 'Israel and the Anti-Semites'.
15. Norman Cohn, *Warrant for Genocide: The Myth of the Jewish World Conspiracy and the Protocols of Zion* (London: Chatto Heinemann, 1967).

4 The Durban Protocols: Globalization of the New Antisemitism

SHIMON SAMUELS

The Haggadah (the Passover supper reading) recounts that the Lord brought us out of bondage in Egypt '*Beyad chazaka*' (with a strong hand) and '*Uvezroah netuya*' (with an outstretched arm). In today's parlance, the Haggadah would speak of the stick and the carrot as instruments of diplomacy.

ROLE OF THE NON-GOVERNMENTAL ORGANIZATION ON THE POLITICAL SCENE

Over the last three decades, traditional international and intergovernmental relations have been supplemented by the contribution of civil society through an increasingly vocal actor on the political scene: the non-governmental organization (NGO). The numbers of NGOs are growing exponentially, reflecting every imaginable interest, agenda and ideology.

The largest NGOs have memberships in the millions, budgets greater than those of several sovereign states, and acknowledged consultative status in the United Nations, its specialized agencies and other such regional organizations as the Council of Europe, the African Union or the Organization of American States. The Boards of such NGOs glitter with celebrities, their consultants are former diplomats and political and ecclesiastical leaders, and their top officials have access to the corridors of power.

Beyond the UN system, it is the World Social Forum (WSF), founded in Porto Alegre, Brazil, and its regional satellites that provide a global apparatus for recruitment, opinion-moulding, agenda-setting, resource-seeking and image-building. The World Social Forum is deliberately held simultaneously to the Davos World Economic Forum (WEF) of global corporate and political movers and shakers.

The WEF seeks the human factor through NGO input (what it calls CSOs – Civil Society Organizations). The WSF is aware that the most outspoken of its NGO actors can eventually be guests at Davos. To keep their 'victim of globalization' credibility, some of these NGOs send bifurcated delegations to both Porto Alegre and Davos. In January 2006 this resulted in an antisemitic article being infiltrated into the WEF's online and print journal. Klaus Schwab, WEF Founder and Executive Chairman, took immediate measures to apologize and close down the publication. The NGO arena should be considered a vital space, at once a battlefield and a network. To quit the field leaves a vacuum for adversaries to occupy and to hold; absence from the start grants them a victory by default.

In November 2001, at the UN Human Rights Commission Special Conference on Religious Discrimination held in Madrid, I was shocked by the statement of the Syrian Ambassador: 'There are present, in this hall, representatives of an arrogant self-elected faith that defines itself as divinely chosen. They have no place here!' 'His Excellency' was mistaken; there was only one such representative present. I turned to other human rights NGOs and appealed to them to respond to such hatred by leaving the hall with me. They refused, so I walked out – noisily and demonstratively. I then waited three minutes and strode back in, because I could not leave them to their victory, or miss the game.

THE NEW ANTISEMITISM

This essay will address the new antisemitism born of Durban,[1] its globalization (with a focus on the role of Europe), and the anthropologization of the Holocaust as a contributing factor, and, finally, will return to the NGOs when seeking to modulate 'the strong hand' to 'the outstretched arm'.

Only seven years ago, in the millennium spirit of soaring stock markets and hopeful peace processes, the Jewish condition seemed almost messianic, a normalized welcome into the community of nations, equal status in international bodies for the Jewish state, and an '*Am Levadad Yishkon*' ('a people that shall dwell alone') that could emerge as an '*Or La Goyim*' ('a light unto the nations'). Then came the Intifada, Durban and a new global threat both to Jewish survival and to the human condition.

It was at the UN World Conference on Racism (WCAR), in September 2001, that antisemitic propaganda reached its post-Holocaust peak. Durban, in fact, became the new baseline for the metastasis of antisemitic malignancy throughout the global organism. In Durban, terms such as 'genocide', 'Holocaust', 'ethnic cleansing' and even 'antisemitism' itself were distorted and turned against their Jewish victims.

Having been elected to the WCAR NGO Forum International Steering Committee, I had participated in all the Preparatory Committees – Geneva, Strasbourg, Warsaw, Santiago – where we contributed language on Holocaust education and revisionist denial to the draft documents. Denied a visa to the last PrepCom held in Tehran, I arrived in Durban to find that there were now the three holocausts:

- the twin holocausts of slavery in the Americas
- the continuing trans-Atlantic slave trade
- the holocaust visited by Israel upon the Palestinians, i.e., the 'naqba' catastrophe to be undone by the elimination of the Jewish state (Ahmadinejad before his time!)

meaning there was never a Holocaust of the Jews.

There were now two antisemitisms: Professor Hadi Adham of Tehran was quoted as stating: 'antisemitism until 1945 was indeed directed against the stereotype of the Western Jewish banker and the Eastern Jewish communist. With the victory of Zionism, since 1948, antisemitism targets the Arab oil-sheikh or Islamic terrorist. Therefore antisemitism today is Arabophobia and, hence, Zionism is antisemitism.'

The Friday night closing march against racism, due to end at Durban town hall, in fact, surrounded the synagogue in the tiny Jewish Club. Protected by South African police, thousands of demonstrators waved 'Mein Kampf' banners, chanting 'Hitler was right', 'Allahu Akhbar, Death to Israel, Death to the Jews'. That night, the fine distinctions between antisemitism and anti-Zionism died, as was finally acknowledged in the 2004 Organization for Security and Cooperation in Europe (OSCE) Berlin Declaration and the European Monitoring Centre's Working Definition of Antisemitism, which viewed the demonization/delegitimization of Israel as pretexts for antisemitism.

After the Durban conference, a ten-year programme, ostensibly distilled from the Durban Plan of Action was presented at the first meeting of the International Steering Committee. The first five years (2001–06) of this programme were to be an eight-point plan to isolate Israel as 'the last bastion of apartheid'. The solidarity movement of the 1960s, 1970s and 1980s against South Africa was to be reconstituted for educational campaigns, legal suits employed for crimes against humanity, a Law of Return for all Palestinian refugees, an economic boycott, sports/telecommunications/academic/scientific/cultural/tourism embargoes, the rupture of diplomatic relations, and measures against states that would refuse to ostracize Israel totally.[3] The campaign included a focused involvement of the churches, universities, the Internet, NGOs and all United Nations agencies.

During the second five years (2006–11), ostensibly with a Palestine state in place, the focus would shift, in the language of the Iranian ayatollahs, from the 'little devil' (Israel) to the 'great Satan' (the United States) for a campaign against its crimes of globalization and reparations for slavery. This would climax in the, yet to be confirmed, Durban WCAR II – now apparently planned for 2009.

The eight-point plan was next invoked at the World Summit on Sustainable Development in Johannesburg in August 2002. Before arriving, the Wiesenthal Centre tried to contain the damage by contacting 180 Green NGO participants and urging them 'to address the issues of the summit – water, health, agriculture, biodiversity and poverty – rather than lose the occasion to political extremism and distortion that would serve unrelated agendas'.[4] There were over two dozen supportive responses from Burundi to Brazil, from Hungary to Nigeria, but denigration of the United States and representatives of the Jewish National Fund (responsible for afforestation, the reversal of desertification, desalination and water projects in Israel and in the developing world) remained the subtext of the conference.

ANTISEMITISM AND THE WORLD SOCIAL FORUM

The antisemitic expressions that now permeate international NGO gatherings became histrionic at the third annual World Social Forum on the evils of globalization that took place in Porto Alegre in January 2003. Of the 70,000 accredited representatives of 5,500 NGOs from 126 countries, many had been active in Durban. At the opening rally, groups with diverse agendas and grievances carried banners that read: 'Nazis, Yankees, and Jews – No More Chosen Peoples!'

Antisemitic imagery and language were pervasive. At a session on 'Fundamentalism and Intolerance', Jews were labelled as 'the true fundamentalists who control US capitalism and the Iraq war agenda' and 'responsible for the 9/11 attacks', and that 'the American Jew, Robert Zoellick, now in Mauritius for the Africa Growth and Opportunity Act, is an agent of US infiltration for the re-colonization of Africa to support Jewish fundamentalists in Israel and the US'.

José Bové, the French farmers' union militant, reportedly sent a message from his stay with Arafat in Ramallah, allegedly stating: 'Israel is a *reductio ad Hitlerum*, so Jews can be accused of being racists if they support the Jewish state ... Indeed, Israelis are perpetrating antisemitic acts in France, as it is they who profit from the crime.' This type of invective was the backdrop to a physical assault on some twenty local Jewish students holding banners declaring: 'Two Peoples – Two States: Peace in the Middle East.'

The Wiesenthal Centre lodged a protest with the WSF Secretary-General and the Mayor that a flood of posters at the airport and around the city presented as 'a Jewish soldier shooting Arab women and children' created an atmosphere that endangered Porto Alegre's small Jewish community. In the stadium over 50,000 young people from some 120 countries screamed 'Viva the Global Intifada!' A prominent wire agency reporter contended that this was not a story for him, as Jews should know, *a priori*, that the WSF is inherently 'not Jew-friendly'.

Some of the WSF grievances are clearly legitimate, but many of its acolytes are simply provocateurs. WSF-style antisemitism is not new, but it has become refined as the focal point of a political incest whereby extreme right, extreme left, post-communists, ecologists, church 'liberationists', trade unionists, misguided human rights activists and indigenous campaigners, Islamic militants and traditional antisemites converge, especially in Europe, seeking the legitimization of certain governments, legislatures, intellectuals, the campus and the media.

Strange bedfellows march together: atheist Trotskyites and anti-McDonalds pyromaniacs alongside Hezbollah flag-bearers screaming 'Allahu Akbar', 'Death to the Jews', and 'Paperless immigrants [that is, undocumented asylum-seekers] for a paperless nation [that is, Palestinians], the same victims, the same struggle'.

This is opportunistically compounded through the link between anti-Americanism and antisemitism. This nexus is represented in slogans twinning 'two Chosen Peoples' who aim to dominate and exploit the world in the spirit of the *Protocols of the Elders of Zion*; two vampires sucking the life-blood of their victims. The result is contempt and the legitimization of a hatemongering long considered distasteful, if not criminal. The American and the Jew are thereby linked in a shared pariah status.

The World Social Forum coordinates satellite gatherings on every continent. At the 2006 European Social Forum in Athens, the Greek neo-Nazi magazine, Golden Dawn, was freely distributed. This edition was devoted to 'the glorious Arab–Nazi partnership under Hitler and their common anti-Jewish agenda today'. Alongside them, German Communists sold *Young Struggle*, its cover emblazoned '*Solidarität mit Frankreich – Von Frankreich Siegen Lernen*' (Solidarity with France – From France We Should Learn to Win). The picture showed Franco-Arab demonstrators masked in kaffiyehs as 'the Intifada took the Paris barricades in autumn 2005' – a disconcerting message to Jewish victims of antisemitic assault in France. The campaign for 'BDS' – Boycott, Divestment, Sanctions⁵ – against the State of Israel is taken straight out of the aforementioned Durban NGO Forum 'Five Year Plan'. Its planners convene annually at WSF/ESF gatherings. The language in which this campaign is couched and the planned climactic global mobilization for May 2008 to mark Israel's sixtieth anniversary as 'the Year of the Naqba', is almost certain to trigger antisemitic assaults on Jewish communities worldwide. The language is redolent of Hitler's boycott campaign, '*Kaufen Nicht Bei Juden*' (buy not from the Jews), which was the prelude to the Holocaust.

In Athens, a misguided young Belgian Jew was explaining his support activity for the boycott campaign. This author overheard two young Palestinians discussing the speaker in animated Arabic. One asked, 'Why is this Jew talking this way?' His companion responded, 'he is a good Jew who believes in our struggle'. The first rejoined laughingly '*Yitbach al-Yahud*' (slaughter the Jews), as they both had a good chuckle.

ANTECEDENTS TO 'THE NEW ANTISEMITISM'

The 1989 fall of the Berlin Wall and the end of the Soviet empire had released the pent-up ghosts of classical antisemitism in countries where the Holocaust had succeeded, i.e., 'an antisemitism without Jews' or 'a phantom pain syndrome' (the limb had been amputated but the body still sought to scratch it). The last vestiges of the ravaged communities of Eastern Europe became the scapegoats for the pain of withdrawal from the central economy and the transition to market capitalism.

Yet East European antisemitism had less to do with 'genetic Jews' than with the abstract image of 'the generic Jew' – a euphemism or code-word for 'imported', 'foreign', 'Western', etc. For instance, the International Monetary Fund, the scapegoat for unemployment and inflation, was portrayed by ultranationalists as the tool of a Jewish plot manipulated by both Washington, DC and Tel Aviv. The *Protocols of the Elders of Zion* resurfaced in every post-communist country, feeding a persistent disposition to hate that which is most feared – the unknown! To make sense of it, a conspiracy theory of invisible enemies of the nation is the line of least resistance. Thus, antisemitism in almost *Judenrein* post-Holocaust Eastern Europe could serve as a diagnostic code to undemocratic conditions and behaviour and a threat for all minorities

The word 'Jew' represented anything alien to the *Volk*, from Western media to pop music, human rights to technology. Ignorance, frustration, envy, rancour, fear of the new and the different were the bases for the conspiracy theory building blocks of xenophobia. Post-Kosovo Serbs explained their situation as the result of American/NATO interventionism, German revanchism, Islamic fundamentalism, the Vatican and even Zionism. The Croatian narrative drops German revanchism and the Vatican, but retains the antisemitism. The litany had its variants throughout Eastern and Central Europe. There may have been no Jewish presence, but the default page for each conspiracy was still the *Protocols of the Elders of Zion* in every vernacular.

In Western Europe, there remains a psychological trauma which bears conscience pangs and an obsessive guilt, too painful for direct expiation, for its two historic crimes: colonialism and complicity in the Holocaust.

Relief became available for both perpetrator and bystander nations via a projection mechanism of role reversal through the use of Holocaust language to address the Middle East. Its quintessence is the multiple versions of the caricature of the Warsaw Ghetto surrender photo of the child's raised arms under Nazi guns. A 'kaffiyeh' placed on the child's head and Stars of David on the German helmets subliminally Nazifies the Israeli and Judaizes the Palestinian.

The anonymity of Brussels emitting directives to an ever-enlarging European Union exacerbates a crisis of faith and atavistic nostalgia for national expression, militating against the globalized homogenization of the high street, the mall, fast food, music and the Internet. The reactionary becomes more so, as does the radical, as does the stranger in our midst who seeks out the reassurance of his own cuisine, language, dress, religious appurtenances and group solidarity.

The vacuums within the vacuums in the slum peripheries of European cities are the battlegrounds for the venting of frustrations and alienation – the mutual rejection of assimilation by both the host society and by the second-generation immigrant himself. In France, the young North African, untouched by Louis XIV and Napoleon but too Westernized for repatriation to the Maghreb, is an easy recruit to incendiary 'jihadist' prayer halls.

Satellite television and websites inculcate added hate towards the host culture with the authentication/socialization of hi-tech. It is no longer a case of it must be true: 'I saw it in black and white', or 'I saw it in living colour on the television'. Today, access to the Internet has obviated the mosque as a recruitment tool to a new true gospel, the divine cyber-word. There, deracinated Diaspora Muslim youth may buy the twin conspiracy messages of anti-globalization: the crimes of the old rancid capitalist wine in new US multinational bottles, and the ubiquitous and hidden hand out of Zion that manipulates global banking, industry, cinema and media.

While European antisemitism derived from Christian theology of race theory, Arab/Muslim attitudes to Jews were political as a function of the Arab–Israeli conflict. The 'new antisemitism' has been generated by a shift to an Islamist adoption of the Big Lies of European colonialism – the medieval blood libel, the *Protocols of the Elders of Zion* and Holocaust denial – now rationalized by reinterpretations of the Qur'an and the Hadith, and exported back to their European Diaspora via satellite television and the Internet. The Hamas Charter of 1988[6] holds the Jews responsible for the French and Russian revolutions, the First and Second World Wars, Masonry and Rotary.

Hezbollah blurs the lines constantly between Jews, Zionists and Israelis in 'an irreconcilable struggle between Islam and Judaism as between good and evil, truth and falsehood'. The bombing of synagogues and Jewish centres in Istanbul, Djerba and Buenos Aires, together with the murders of wheelchair-bound American Leon Klinghoffer or Daniel Pearl *qua* 'Jews', have nothing to do with the Arab–Israeli conflict.[7]

In strategic geopolitical terms, this can be seen in the emerging threat to global stability of Iranian nuclear National Islamism. Reflected ominously are features of German National Socialism – a cataclysmic ideology, mistreatment of minorities, repression of women, a revolutionary youth movement, state-sponsored terrorism, aspirations for regional dominance.

Indeed, a jihadist-fascist regime seeking nuclear weapons should sound the sirens for every Western and Muslim state potentially in its missile sights. Yet, when seen in the light of Franklin Littell's early-warning system matrix, the motor of National Islamism is, like its National Socialism template, the poison of antisemitism.

The final solution of the Jewish problem was the Nazi key to an antisemitic alliance of collaborator satellites that facilitated its *Lebensraum* imperial expansion. Likewise, the Jew is again the ready means for Shi'ite revanchism on the road to a Sunnite caliphate. Iran's

Su-Shi engagement policy is evident in its patronage of Sunni Hamas and Shia Hezbollah terrorism against Jews in Israel and the Diaspora.

Hezbollah's Sheikh Fadlallah pointedly noted that 'attacking Israel saves going after Jews worldwide', while a British Islamist clarified at the 2004 World Social Forum in Mumbai, that 'it would change nothing if Israel were transplanted to the other side of the Mediterranean, our global conflict against Zionism is eternal'. The Middle East blowback of this incitement on social cohesion in Europe, and markedly in French suburbs where North African Jews and Muslims live cheek by jowl, has become lethal. Our Centre co-founded a twenty-four-hour hotline for victims of antisemitism which is a barometer of such impact. Five to six calls on normal days will jump to fifty with the capture of Saddam Hussein or a libellous Ramadan movie on Jewish infanticide of Muslim children for blood rituals on *al-Manar* Hezbollah television. We had noted the presence of some black converts to Islam in attacks on Jewish individuals, despite very close relations between the Jewish and African immigrant community in France. This came to a head with the 2006 kidnapping, mutilation and murder of Ilan Halimi by a group inspired by the US Nation of Islam leader, Louis Farrakhan. This was followed by a pogrom-style assault on the Paris Jewish quarter by a black gang, calling itself 'Tribe K'. As a result, though still marginal, French-Jewish emigration has grown under the slogan '*la valise ou le cercueil*' (the suitcase or the coffin).

What has broken the taboos on such blatant expression of hate? The Middle East on real-time TV and the Internet? The globalization of the anti-Israel campaign (from sporadic to well-coordinated and well-financed)? The growth and radicalization of immigrant communities? The internalization of Jewish leadership and incestuous closing of community ranks to demonstrate inner solidarity? Palestine-chic as opposed to Jew-fatigue? Holocaust-overdose or hearing enough of Jewish suffering? A heightened need for an all-purpose scapegoat? Vested interests of bystanders seeking Arab patronage, business, votes and investments (versus Jews as liabilities = boycott)? Intimidation of people not ready to stand up and be counted?

Herein lies an information paradox: despite the voluminous information sources, knowledge of history is down. Is this a rejection due to mass media surfeit and the comfort of the superficial, compounded by grandparent-induced memories and parental prejudices? Is it the impact of competitive martyrdoms matched as equal crimes of both sides by a politically-correct-based moral equivalence, as in Germany and Belgium, Turks versus Kurds; in Britain, Turks versus

Greeks, Indians versus Pakistanis; everywhere, Arabs versus Jews? Is the teaching of the Holocaust as an anti-fascist instrument, leading many to fear the de-Judaization of the Holocaust?

ANTISEMITISM AND THE DE-JUDAIZATION OF THE HOLOCAUST

Here are some examples of what I would painfully call the 'anthropologization' of the Holocaust: there are some who prefer to mourn Jews murdered over sixty years ago than those today under assault (here there may be a parallel with Islamophobes using the Palestine cause as an anti-racist figleaf). *Kristallnacht* is marked by anti-racist groups as an icon, but the talk of November 1938 burning synagogues, in the year 2000, included no mention of the more than 100 synagogues attacked that very month. 'Righteous Gentiles' are still honoured by French municipalities but sometimes on condition that no Israeli Embassy or Yad Vashem representative be present. Swedish teacher-training in Russia on the Holocaust did not invite representatives of the local Jewish community. In Archangel, this was justified to me as 'we are teaching the Holocaust, what does that have to do with contemporary Jews?'

On his appointment as President of the Vatican Committee on Relations with Non-Catholic Religions, the eminent German theologian, Cardinal Walter Kaspers, told a Wiesenthal Centre delegation, 'I see as my mission, the unshackling of the chains of the Holocaust from the Catholic–Jewish relationship!' But the Holocaust cannot be uncoupled from Jewish victims of today, for that would be a new form of revisionism, and would create, by attrition, a climate of tolerance for antisemitism. Tolerance of antisemitism is in no nation's self-interest, for 'what starts with the Jews ...'.

If the Holocaust is to become an instrumental pedagogy and is to be used as the touchstone for anti-racist and human rights sensitization, then its commemoration and application must include a deprogramming responsibility by returning to the touchstone itself, that is, antisemitism as the most enduring paradigm.[8]

BACK TO DURBAN

In September 2002, a new High Commissioner for Human Rights, Sergio Vieira de Mello, was appointed by UN Secretary-General Kofi Annan. This High Commission oversees a well-staffed Anti-Discrimination Unit established to implement the Durban Plan of Action of the WCAR intergovernmental conference. The previous High

Commissioner, Mary Robinson, officially rejected the parallel NGO Forum Plan of Action, *inter alia*, for its antisemitic hatemongering.

High Commissioner Vieira de Mello expressed sensitivity to the stigmata of Durban engraved in the memories of Jewish NGOs.[9] At the first of the regional Durban implementation meetings, held for Latin America in Mexico City, the Anti-Discrimination Unit convened a panel of noted experts on racism, rather than states and NGOs who, characteristically, would have politicized and hijacked the proceedings. Absent from the Mexico City conference was the antisemitism that had served as an instrument of discourse and the common denominator for sharply politicised agendas, thus repressing debate on the legitimate grievances of so many parties who find their right to free expression subsumed to the targeting of the Jew. After the murder of Vieira de Mello, I was to discover that he had listed me as Expert Witness on Antisemitism for the 2004 Western States Durban Implementation meeting in Brussels. I took the opportunity to present the racist obscenities of Durban, while acknowledging the PrepCom efforts at building an anti-racist infrastructure by many people of integrity. Vieira de Mello's legacy must be the realization of that work, principally in the National Action Plans, while preventing a repetition of any UN hatefest. Indeed, out of the Brussels meeting came the 2005 UN General Assembly adoption of our proposal for an annual UN Holocaust Commemoration Day. May it be defended from distortion or political hijacking.

THE OUSTRETCHED ARM

In the Talmudic 'Ethics of the Fathers', there is a maxim in three parts:

a) If I am not for myself, who will be for me?

This is tempered by:

b) If I am only for myself, what am I?

And prioritized by:

c) If not now, then when?

Ancillaries of 'the new antisemitism' include hate literature, terrorism, Internet incitement and boycott. The Jew has often served as the hatemonger's visible target, but antisemitism is an all-purpose generic hatred that frequently includes the strategic goal of dismantling democracy itself.

The antidotes must be to seek common ground and third-party endorsement. Just as Jews cannot contain antisemitism without Gentile support, blacks cannot fight discrimination without whites. Women cannot achieve equal rights without men, nor gays without heterosexuals. Here are four examples.

A 2003 UNESCO/Simon Wiesenthal Centre seminar in Venice on 'The Centenary of the Protocols of Zion as a Paradigm for Contemporary Hate Literature' resolved that the 'targeting of any faith or ethnic community must be considered an assault on all faith and ethnic communities'; moreover, 'religious and ethnic leaders must firstly identify, expose and condemn hate literature within their own community'.

ENAR (European Network Against Racism), an umbrella for over 600 anti-racist groups across the European Union, has sought 'to maintain the delicate solidarity of Muslims and Jews in Europe against all acts of antisemitism and Islamophobia. Any division between these two communities in Europe can only serve the forces of hate, of which both are targets'. This resolution was signed by forty-three Muslim and three Jewish members of the 2001 ENAR General Assembly, renewed at the European and national levels several times since that date.[10]

Despite the universal threat of terrorism, there is no international consensus on a definition. The burgeoning number of victim states, in every region, to suicide terrorism had led to a Simon Wiesenthal Centre global campaign to characterize this scourge as a crime against humanity – crimes codified by the 1946 Nuremberg Tribunal as 'acts so egregious that, by their scale or nature, outrage the human conscience'. Blessed by the late Pope John Paul II, our draft convention has been presented to over twenty foreign ministers, the Inter-American Commission on Terrorism and, in October 2006, was adopted by the Australian Parliament. This campaign, which focuses on those who incite to suicide bombings as complicit in the crime, is in the spirit of the conviction of the editors of *Der Stürmer* for facilitating the Holocaust. The UN Arusha Court on Rwanda has, similarly, convicted three radio and print journalists, as complicit in that genocide.

Simon Wiesenthal called the Holocaust 'a meeting point between ideology and technology'. This applies today, to hate and incitement on the Internet. In cyberspace, all are targeted: Jews, Christians, Muslims, blacks, Gypsies, homosexuals, women, children, handicapped – hate becomes indivisible. Our annual CD-Roms based on constant global monitoring of hate sites are an alert for law enforcement, teachers and parents.

CONCLUSION

This battle requires an early warning system to sensitize ourselves and the ears of our neighbours to recognize the sounds of impending danger. Jews have, for 2,000 years, been a lightning rod for social malaise; they should now become a weather vane or wind sleeve together with others, stressing coalition-building with all victims of prejudice.

As victims of conspiracy theories, we must not hold simplistic perceptions of a hidden hand manipulating, 'the new antisemitism'. We must keep ourselves securely placed at the intersection between 'Ostrich Avenue' and 'Paranoia Boulevard'.

Born in the United Kingdom, just after the Second World War, I am acutely sensitive to the power of water. Thirty miles of Channel saved my family from the Holocaust on the continent. Today, thousands of Atlantic or Pacific miles do not insulate nor protect from the globalization of antisemitism or any other form of bigotry.

Survival for us all requires a calculated mix of 'the strong hand' and 'the outstretched arm'.

NOTES

This chapter was originally read out at the World Social Forum 2003 opening rally in Porto Allegre among the greetings sent to the Secretariat, and recorded in the stadium by this author.

1. S.T. Samuels, 'The Road to Durban', *Jerusalem Post*, 17 Aug. 2001.
2. The WCAR NGO Forum International Steering Committee. I was the only Jewish NGO representative elected to the ISC where I was prevented from speaking, misled on meeting times and venues, and ultimately expelled.
3. S.T. Samuels, 'On the Road from Durban – Racism and Terror Converge', *Ha'aretz*, 10 Oct. 2001.
4. 'Antisemitism and Jewish Defence at the United Nations World Summit on Sustainable Development, 2002 – Johannesburg, South Africa', an interview with Shimon Samuels, *Post-Holocaust and Antisemitism*, No. 6, Jerusalem Center for Public Affairs, 2 March 2003.
5. Shimon Samuels, '"BDS" – The New Antisemitism Campaign', *Canadian Jewish News*, 13 July 2006.
6. Simon Wiesenthal Centre translation from the Arabic of the Hamas Charter, 1988.
7. Esther Webman, 'Anti-Semitic Motives in the Ideology of Hezbollah and Hamas', Project for the Study of Anti-Semitism, Tel Aviv University, 1994.
8. 'Off with the Gloves', *Jerusalem Report*, 8 Oct. 2001; and 'Here We Go Again', *Jerusalem Report*, 8 April 2002.
9. In a private conversation with this author in Geneva two weeks after his appointment as High Commissioner for Human Rights, and at the Wiesenthal Centre/UNESCO conference in May 2003. Vieira de Mello was appointed in June as the UN's Special Representative in Iraq. His murder in the August terrorist attack on UN headquarters in Baghdad was a blow for the world in general and for the Jewish world in particular.
10. The author was elected to the Board of ENAR in 1999 and reelected in 2002 and in 2005.

5 Journey to Hell

PILAR RAHOLA

'There was a time when a special place in the depths of hell was reserved for people who intentionally kill children. Nowadays, the intentional killing of Israeli children is legitimized as Palestinian armed conflict' – legitimized and even rewarded, because those who kill children do not go to hell; they are promised paradise instead.

Briggite Gabriel, a Lebanese woman who spent seven years of her life in an underground hideout, eating grass and dodging gunfire to search for water, used these grim words to speak at Duke University, in October 2004, of the self-destructive phenomenon that uses a religion and a faith as an alibi for every form of violence, in an escalation of terror that does not even stop when it comes up against what is most sacred in life. In spite of being 'raised in a spirit of antisemitic hatred', as she put it, the current President and founder of the American Congress for Truth went further in her self-criticism and recalled that in the current scale of things, 'the difference between the Arab world and Israel is a difference in values and nature. It is barbarity versus civilization; democracy versus dictatorship; good versus evil.'[1] Salman Rushdie has described the current degradation of Islam as a process of 'paranoid Islamism' and others, like the Moroccan journalist Ali Lambret, are aware of the significance for millions of Muslims of the disastrous situation of having virtually no democratic point of reference of their own. Yet such commentators, speaking the language of morality and ethics, are all too few and far between; they are like exotic islands in a great ocean of narrow-mindedness, cultural alienation and, more than anything else, institutionalized fanaticism. And it is precisely that which makes them so exceptional and gives us the first key to the serious problem lying in store. So in order to analyse the new global antisemitism, whose many-headed hydra speaks in different accents and uses different language according to where it reveals itself, we must start giving serious thought to the matter because voices such as those I have mentioned are really exceptional. In other words, we need to analyse this narrow-mindedness, this nihilistic, totalitarian way of thinking, which is intent on distilling its pervasive poison in every corner of the Muslim world.

First of all, generic thinking: is there a resurgence of the xenophobic concept, coined by Wilhelm Marr in 1879 – which is when the term 'antisemitic' emerged – that in its most evil manifestation was responsible for the worst atrocity in the history of humanity? There have been so many studies on this issue – including by the European authorities – that it does not need to be demonstrated here. Day in, day out, in comment upon comment, in the media, in discussion groups, in televised debates, in political declarations and in anything that enters into the process of collective thinking, the Jews are there, an awkward, antipathetic presence, and are usually discussed, demonized or directly attacked. There is utter confusion between the words 'Jew' and 'Israeli', to such an extent that the two words are used indiscriminately, but both with negative connotations. Without too much risk of error, we might even go so far as to say that Israel has inherited all the historical demonization of Jews, and has given rise to a more prestigious form of antisemitism, anti-Zionism, and directly to the present-day rabid anti-Israel feeling. To put it another way, just as Jews for centuries were considered to be a pariah people, in the current context Israel is regarded as a pariah state. And of course its prime minister is the pariah prime minister. As I put it at the 2003 UNESCO Conference in my paper entitled 'Jews and flies', 'the umbrella of anti-Zionism is far easier to put up: it keeps off the rain of criticism and provides an intellectually acceptable facade'. That is to say, it is politically correct, which is essential for it to be propounded with ease among gatherings of the intelligentsia, through the pens of well-known writers, and from the mouths of progressive professors. It explains a phenomenon that will be my main focus, namely, the new antisemitism of the left. This is an antisemitism that does not correspond to the classic norms of the extreme right, but rather to modern parameters whose ideology looks to the left, and whose formulation does not rely on xenophobic values but, surprisingly, on those of solidarity. The main type of present-day antisemitism, as it influences the thinking of the masses and as it is reflected in news items, is responsible for the fierce anti-Israel thinking that pervades Western thought; it is imbued with political correctness; it is well thought of, it is leftist and is harnessed to justice, progress and solidarity. That is why it has so much influence and hence, why it is dangerous, elusive and possibly unconscious.

But before going into a more thorough analysis of the phenomenon, I think it necessary to point out the other two major types of antisemitic thinking that influence public opinion to a greater or lesser degree. On the one hand, there is classic antisemitism, perfectly woven into the DNA of collective thought, a by-product of Christianity which, in teaching us to love God, taught us to hate Jews. Since the important *Nostra Aetate* declaration, at the Vatican II Council, the Catholic Church certainly took a big step towards self-criticism and asking for forgiveness but there is also the fact that two thousand years of antisemitic religious culture have left such deeply ingrained prejudice, that it ends up being indelibly printed in everyone's mind. This, combined with the persistence of the concept of a deicide people, helped to spawn Mel Gibson's infamous film *The Passion of the Christ*. Without underrating the tremendous symbolic importance of John Paul II's acts of self-criticism, or the emotional visit of Benedict XVI to a German synagogue, the *mea culpa* of the Catholic Church has been more a catharsis of the leadership than of the people. So we have, then, a historical stigma that continues to flourish. The expansion of Christianity is bound up with the victory of that prejudice and with the signal effectiveness of a process of demonization of an entire people whose object has been to dominate and deceive and, no doubt, breed fanatics. This antisemitism with a religious slant that over the centuries has become a cultural antisemitism, perfectly cemented into people's minds and, hence, unconscious, explains in part the ease with which citizens of the world nowadays accept the clichés, the prejudices and the lies about the Jewish people. And the Jewish people par excellence in contemporary minds are the Israeli people. There is not much difference between the image of the hooked-nose medieval Jew, devious, mysterious and drinker of the blood of Christian children at Pesach, and the powerful Jew with a Star of David on the side of his tank with which, according to televisions the world over, he is systematically killing Palestinian children. If there had not been this building up over centuries of a cultural evil cutting through the cortex of Europe and branding it, to the point where nothing that has happened in European history can be explained without antisemitism, it would not now be so easy to sell Manichaean views of reality, twisted news items, or utter falsehoods of history. This is the basic and often unconscious antisemitism that prevails in the minds of citizens who still maintain that Israel is the world's number one problem; the same approach is taken by journalists whose news items are always written up before they know how the story originated; the same antisemitism that explains how enlightened and theoretically well-read individuals can act towards Israel, like knowledgeable fools. At the conscious level, the antisemitism of the Christian religion has been overcome; but unconscious antisemitism can still detonate the powder keg.

The other major antisemitic phenomenon, highly volatile and far more dangerous, is Islamic antisemitism, a real blemish across the whole of the Muslim world, from one region to another, contaminating not only the minds of the fanatics but also those who want to live in peace. Admittedly, this is not a new kind of antisemitism; it is rooted in the role that some Arab leaders held at the height of Nazism, as witness that pretty song they sang at the end of the 1930s in the Arab world: 'No more Monsieur, no more Mister / Heaven's for Allah, Earth's for Hitler'. Among the pro-Nazis, the prize for Arab antisemitism goes to the former Grand Mufti of Jerusalem, Haj Amin al-Husseini, a personal friend of Ribbentrop, Rosenberg and Himmler, for his leadership role with Palestinian Arabs, his activism and his unvarnished sincerity. Al-Husseini not only gave global currency to his famous phrase – 'Allah has conferred on us the rare privilege of finalizing what Hitler began alone. Let the jihad begin. Kill the Jews. Kill them all' – but he also worked unflaggingly to make it a reality. Pogroms against Jews during the British Mandate, an attempted pro-Nazi *coup d'état* in Iraq, and exile in Germany from 1941, where he lived with every honour and enthusiastically hailed the consecration of Nazism. Among the many pearls that this sinister character bequeathed to the history of ignominy is the pressure he exerted on Hitler to prevent thousands of Hungarian Jews from leaving; and, of course, the most glorious feather in his cap, his direct intervention with Adolf Eichmann, urging him not to agree with the British Government to exchange German prisoners of war for 5,000 Jewish children who were to sail for the Holy Land. The children did not travel to Palestine, but instead were sent to the extermination camps in Poland. It was when travelling to Auschwitz that he reprimanded the guards for being too 'soft' with the Jews. He was also responsible for the 'Hanjar' squadron, the Waffen SS Company of Bosnians who exterminated 90 per cent of the Jews of Bosnia. Heinrich Himmler, in gratitude, created a special school for mullahs in Dresden. One might nonetheless think that al-Husseini does not

represent an Arab, pro-Nazi antisemitism, but merely his own brand
of evil and madness. But that is not the case if one takes into account
that he was a true idol until his death (1974), that he played a significant role in the Arab–Israeli confrontation and that, as a leading
member of the al-Husseini clan (one of whose more modest branches produced another big name in the region, Yassir Arafat), even
today his name inspires respect. That is to say, unlike present-day
Germany which has made peace with its dark past, its guilt and
responsibility, the Arab world has never engaged in any self-criticism
regarding its pro-Nazi leaders, nor does it consider it necessary to
take a hard look at its history. Syria provided a refuge for government
advisor Alois Brunner, Eichmann's right-hand man in the Third
Reich's Office for Jewish Affairs, and the Arab world incorporated as
though it was the most normal thing in the world the tissue of lies
and falsehoods of Goebbels-style propaganda into its system of prejudices.

Nevertheless, if the Islamic brand of antisemitism had been alone
in its historical attachment to Nazism, it would not have become the
huge success it is today. On the contrary, Islamic antisemitism has
managed to combine all the commonplaces of Judaeophobia, from
the religious to the social and political, and thus finds itself in a
happy company that ranges from the infantile myths of medieval
Christian antisemitism, through the socio-political Russian Okhrana
and its *Protocols*, to modern anti-Zionism (understood as a struggle
against 'imperialism') or its own Qur'anic myths. Especially popular
are the Suras devoted to Jews ('The Jews only deserve shame in this
life, and to be banished on the Day of Judgement to the harshest
torment'[2]). As Patricio Brodsky states in his research into the phenomenon: 'anti-Judaism in the Arab world is achieving self-evident
status', 'it holds a central position in the dominant and single strand
of hegemonic thinking in all Arab countries, and, through a state policy of repeating prejudices, it is gradually building the consensus that
Jews are not part of humanity. It thus becomes easy for the masses to
learn the ways of stigma, prejudice and hatred against Jews'.[3]

In most cases, this hatred goes hand in hand with a hatred of
Westerners. After all, is the Jew not the paradigm of Western values?
Films, television series – like the one shown by Egyptian state television during Ramadan – textbooks, classic antisemitic manuals transformed into best-sellers – including the *Protocols* and even *Mein
Kampf* – articles and editorials, religious preaching, and so on, all
reinforce that tendency. Antisemitism underpins current Islamic cul-

ture; it contaminates schools and news reports; it is the engine of political discourse. This is happening in the face of Western indifference, before the traditional, predictable passivity of the United Nations, and with the complicity of intellectuals in the free world. It does not seem to bother us that 1,300 million children in primary school are being taught the hatred that is antisemitism. And let us stress a basic fact here: teaching hatred against Jews is quite simply teaching hatred.

Moreover, this antisemitism not only operates specifically in Islamic societies, but also affects social, civic and religious organizations of an Islamic orientation established in democratic societies. In fact it is practically impossible to find a single Islamic non-governmental organization (NGO) that is not – in its theoretical position – radically antisemitic. Many of these NGOs are invited to congresses, present a united front and have a recognized standing. Some of them were responsible for the antisemitic scandal of the Durban Forum. I saw it at first hand at the last Social Forum in Porto Alegre, where antisemitism was happily slotted in between anti-globalization speeches, pan-Arab epics and revolutionary tub-thumpings. This is not just about verbal antisemitism, since the majority of violent acts of antisemitism that have taken place in Europe recently have been the work of young European Muslims. The philosopher Luc Ferry, former French Minister of Education to Jean-Pierre Raffarin and the instigator of the controversial but effective 'veil law', has stated that '90 per cent of antisemitic acts in France are perpetrated by young Arabs'. He added: 'this is particularly worrying as it allows them to be better tolerated. The left wing feels that it gives antisemitic acts more legitimacy than if they were perpetrated by the extreme right.'

Between classic Christian-style antisemitism and modern Islamic-style antisemitism there is not much space to find protection. If we add modern, self-assured, secular antisemitism, embracing the thinking of the left, we see that the situation is far more serious than we like to admit. It is especially serious because unlike the other types of antisemitism, the antisemitism of the left does not see itself as such, it denies its antisemitism and even considers it an unacceptable offence to be charged with it. If the left is pre-eminently anti-fascist, how can it be branded antisemitic, given that antisemitism is an integral part of fascism? But it can, and the phenomenon that is especially virulent today is neither new nor surprising. In fact, it is rooted in the doctrinal hostility of the Bolsheviks towards Zionism, at the time of pre-revolutionary Russia, despite the enormous number of

Jews who either headed or joined in the Revolution. This is not the place to detail the systematic persecution of Jews in Soviet Russia, but it is clear that Komintern watchwords soon incorporated the language of inveterate Russian Judaeophobia (the driving force of the persecutions that triggered the earliest demands for a Jewish state; the France of Dreyfus did the rest). And very soon they stigmatized Zionism as a counter-revolutionary petty bourgeois movement, a pawn of British imperialism and a bitter enemy of the Soviet Union. It is true that there was a notable parenthesis in the fiercely anti-Jewish slant of Soviet policy, which stands as a historical milestone. I am referring to Andrei Gromyko's speech on 14 May 1947, at United Nations headquarters, proclaiming the Jewish people's right to a state. 'There can be no justification for refusing that right to the Jewish people if we take into account all they suffered during the Second World War', he solemnly concluded. And it was indeed a solemn moment, a prelude to Saturday, 20 November 1947, the day when, at the provisional headquarters of the Flushing Meadows building, in Lake Success, the UN General Assembly voted in favour of the plan for the partition of Palestine by thirty-three votes for, thirteen votes against and ten abstentions. As stated by the renowned historian Joan Culla, 'it is very likely that without Soviet patronage – as important or more important than the North American – the State of Israel would not have seen the light of day'.[4]

But that brief idyll came neither from ideological conviction nor political will, it was perfectly explicable in terms of geostrategic interests: a USSR strengthened since the Second World War, but without any presence in the Middle East; traditionalist Arab societies where communism had made no impression, and were governed by feudal dictatorships backed by Great Britain; ever-increasing pressure on the part of the United States against Soviet expansion (it was the start of the age of the Truman Doctrine); Jewish communities, in Palestine, directly up against British imperialism, and with very many of its members coming from Russia, enthusiastic collective farmers and, for the most part, strong Marxist supporters. With this combination of factors and the certainty that the creation of a Jewish state would be a destabilizing factor in the Arab world that would aggravate hostilities against Britain and the United States (and thus be favourable to Soviet penetration), Stalin momentarily took sides and from 1946 to 1947, the world's champion of the left turned into an 'objective ally' of the Jewish cause in the Holy Land. That did not, however, stop Stalin from pursuing his antisemitic policy inside the

USSR and one only has to remember the assassination of the President of the Jewish Anti-Fascist Committee, the Yiddish Art Theatre playwright Solomon Mikhoels, and the imprisonment of more than 100 Jews on the Committee, accused of being 'rootless cosmopolitans'. That was in 1948, the very same year that the USSR and the brand new State of Israel exchanged ambassadors. There then came one antisemitic trial after another, one of which was marked by the famous blood bath that followed the crazy 'doctors' plot' of 1953, the arrest of all Jewish colonels and generals, the forcing of Vycheslaw Molotov to leave his Jewish wife, and the indiscriminate killing of writers, poets, scientists and political leaders of Jewish origin. In one single night, 217 Yiddish writers, 108 actors, eighty-seven artists and nineteen musicians disappeared into the Siberian gulag. Those killed included the great Yiddish writer Peter Markish, the poet Itzhik Feffer and the writer David Bergelson.

Nonetheless, the overall attitude of the European left, under cover of the attitude held for decades by the Soviet Union with respect to the Arab–Israeli conflict, does not derive from age-old Russian antisemitism perfectly incorporated into the Soviet 'new man', but rather from the foreign policy pursued by Soviet Union almost from the beginning of its relations with Israel. Historians explain the – almost immediate – Soviet 'change of course' in its policy of alliance-building by two basic factors One was domestic, the conviction that Russian Jews were some sort of fifth column in the service of the new state. The enthusiastic welcome Golda Meir received from the Muscovite Jews as the new Ambassador of Israel in Moscow was, in that sense, historic. And from another, geostrategic point of view, it was easily explicable. Stalin's calculations of a kind of 'Jewish Marxist outpost' in the Middle East were proved wrong. Israel, a random product of the Cold War created with the joint support of the Russians and the Americans, needed the delicate balance between the money of the latter (five million North American Jews served as a life insurance) and the susceptibilities of the electorate, with 18 per cent of pro-Soviet Israeli voters. As Culla tells us, 'Non-alignment and a position at an equal distance from Washington and Moscow appeared to be the ideal formula', and one that was adopted by Ben Gurion. Then came the Korean War, the Israeli vote in the Western camp, and the widespread communist paranoia against the Jewish conspiracy, which culminated in the famous Slansky Trial, the first in the history of antisemitism since the Shoah to speak officially of 'an international Jewish conspiracy', prosecuting and condemning several Czech Jews, including the Secretary-General of the Party, Rudolf Slansky, and condemning Israel as 'a spy country'. The proclamation of Zionism as 'enemy number one of the working class', a short time afterwards, fell like ripe fruit from a lengthy, demonizing trial. Upon Stalin's death the Khrushchev policy was to be the definitive policy of the communist bloc and of virtually all left-wing intellectuals worldwide, until the arrival of Gorbachev: wholehearted support for the Arab countries, including massive military aid, opposition against Israel in international organizations, pressure in the satellite countries against Israel, various theatrical severings of diplomatic relations, the stigmatization of Israel as 'a pawn of American imperialism', advocacy of the Arab cause, equated with liberalism and justice, and more or less explicit support for the groups of Palestinian terrorists that were soon to emerge. UN Resolution 3376, approved on 10 November 1975, which condemned Zionism as 'a form of racism and racial discrimination', was to be the high point in a process of slow criminalization, as perfectly explicable in terms of geostrategic interests, as it was unsound in ideological and moral terms. Of course, it was also an expression of the glaring failure of the UN as a champion of fundamental rights – a failure that had begun a few months earlier, when on 13 November 1974, the UN allowed Arafat to speak in the General Assembly, carrying 'a freedom fighter's rifle'. In other words, the UN accepted terrorism as a legitimate means of struggle.

Today, the sources of everything in the press, in the universities and in the intellectual world that informs a powerful current of public opinion that has turned the democratic State of Israel into the most dangerous country in the world; that portrays a democratically elected prime minister, Ariel Sharon, as an evil figure worthy of Nazi comparisons, but never judges any Islamic dictator; that idealizes Palestinian terrorists, but contemptuously disregards Israeli victims; that elevates a corrupt, violent, despotic leader called Arafat to be the champion of romantic heroic struggle (taking the place of Che Guevara on posters of former adolescent revolutionaries, now transformed into honoured intellectuals); that takes as its guru a winner of the Nobel prize for literature whose antisemitism is part and parcel of his dyed-in-the-wool communism, a guru who speaks out against the Israeli security fence, constructed to save lives, but always saw the virtues of the Berlin Wall; the sources of this entire current of politically correct public opinion, cloaked in the rightness of solidarity and justice, lie in that major historical phenomenon that was being spawned during decades of anti-Zionist rhetoric, Jewish demonization and pan-Arab paternalism. Although, as Alain Finkielkraut says, the European left maintained its love affair with Israel for two decades, its attitude changed radically from the late 1960s. First, the Soviet Union's criminalization of Israel gained ascendancy; secondly, between the demonstrations against the war in Vietnam and May 1968, the European left discovered the Third World as the last utopian stronghold against imperialism; and finally, the masses of Auschwitz survivors, would-be socialists and cooperative farmers, had fast become a scientific, technological and military power, and Israel had stopped being David and turned into Goliath. As Culla says, 'from then on, and with the confluence between Third Worldism and classical Communism, there appeared in the West a new mythology, a new symbolic system and a new iconography: alongside the heroic Vietnamese fighters who, wisely led by Uncle Ho and General Giap, defied American imperialism in the jungles of Indochina, there appeared the Palestinian *fedayin* and Arafat, their leader, in an unequal struggle against Israel, Washington's bridgehead in the Middle East'. From then on, in the diplomatic arena, the Communist bloc pitted its weight against Israel. In the military arena, time and again the USSR supplied arms to the enemies of Israel. In the sphere of violent action, extreme-left terrorist groups formed cooperative links with the Organization of Arab Palestine to which it gave logistic support in return for training in its guerrilla camps in Lebanon. It goes without saying that, for example, German Red Army Faction activists participated in some of the most notorious Palestinian plane hijackings; or that France's Action Directe was responsible for attacks against Israel in Paris in 1982; or that the Front for the Liberation of Palestine was in cahoots with the Italian Red Brigade and with Nihon Seki Gunha, the Japanese Red Army group that killed twenty-seven passengers in Lod airport in 1972. Since it could not be otherwise, in the field of ideas there was also a consolidation of the bonds between the left in Western countries and the Palestinian struggle and those bonds, marked, it is true, by ups and downs, still exist today. Communism fell but the demonization of Israel continued.

So despite an obvious change in the factors behind the frontal attacks against Israel by the left, in particular since the collapse of the Communist bloc, not only have the frontal attacks not ceased, but recently they have intensified, attracted greater funding and prestige and have managed to assume a global dimension. It is true that there have been times when there has been less aggression against Israel and that Sharon's coming to power coincided precisely with a peak in the criminalization of Israel; but Sharon was more an excuse than a reason for that criminalization. The left, the same left that enabled 'freedom fighter' dictators to enjoy impunity, that failed to report on repression in the camps of Utopia and went to bed with every kind of monster, that same left never changed its anti-Israel stance. It will be said that, even if the analysis is true, there may be a fierce opposition to Israel, but that is not antisemitism. This may be so, and doubtless there are criticisms of Israel that cannot be said to be antisemitic. But the creation of a body of fiercely militant public opinion turning around a Manichaean view of a conflict (setting the Jew on the side of evil, and the Palestinian on the side of good) and that includes a minimization of terrorism, a selective solidarity and the debasement of news reporting to a point where it becomes the retailing of lies, all amounts to more than just criticizing a government or a state. What is happening with the Arab–Israeli conflict does not happen with any other conflict in the world, no other country is subjected to the brutal pressure that Israel, considered guilty of all sins, has to endure; no other terrorism is viewed with the paternalism that Palestinian terrorism enjoys; and no world news is as twisted and manipulated as the news concerning Israel. Well-known intellectuals, journalists of renown and major media companies lose all rigour and reliability and become muddled when dealing with Israel. The case of Edgar Morin and the conviction for racial defamation of the prestigious newspaper *Le Monde* are notable examples. Some of the world's intellectuals, when talking about Israel, would appear to be speaking not from their brains, but from their stomachs. Antisemitic prejudice? In any case, it reflects a prior demonization whose many roots are unconscious and deeply unjust and reach back far into the past.

Simon Wiesenthal dauntlessly fought against the antisemitism of the extreme right that seared the heart of Europe and wrote the darkest chapter of its history. Yet if some of us, in unison with Elie Wiesel, used to think that antisemitism had died with Auschwitz, we now know that to be untrue. From out-and-out Islamic antisemitism, through the destructive nihilism of fundamentalism, to the educated, enlightened and 'correct' antisemitism of international progressiveness, all the phenomena contribute together to a renewed anti-Jewish stigma. And it does not appear that the world's intellectual elite is bothered by it at all, since many of them are actively creating the stigma or remain indifferent to its materialization. The treachery of intention with regard to the Jewish people is threefold: to divest Zionism of ideological correctness, in such a way as to undermine the very roots of the State of Israel's existence; to expel Israel and its leaders from the concert of legitimate nations so that it loses its moral legitimacy; and thereby to place Jews and not just Israelis outside the orbit of international law. The worst of this attitude is that, while resulting from 'solidarity' with the Palestinian people, it will not help the Palestinians to achieve peace. The main enemy of the Palestinians is the terrorism that kills in their name. And, given the perverse Arab utilization of the Palestinian cause, probably the only friend it can have is Israel. Nevertheless, the left and politically committed thinkers worldwide have been so irresponsible in their uncritical paternalism towards terrorism and so fiercely obsessive in their criticism of Israel, that far from nurturing ways out of the conflict, it has consolidated and nurtured all the dead ends.

Finally, and in line with Briggite Gabriel's words with which I opened, I want to stress the left's glaring irresponsibility in remaining indifferent to the ideological phenomenon of Islamic fundamentalism, preoccupied as it has been by its opposition to America and to Israel. The impunity enjoyed by Islamic nihilism through its emergence, expansion and deployment is due in part to a lack of collective awareness as to the danger it presents. Again, the intellectuals have got it wrong. To show this would take a long time and here is not the place to do so, but it is partly to do with the fact that the left has always been anti-Western, and therefore not so far removed from some of the obsessions of current Islamic fundamentalism. In any case, it has been said that in Israel killings in the name of Islamic nihilism have benefited from increasing impunity, and every Israeli victim that is reviled, ignored or despised by Western intelligentsia, has prepared the way for the killings in Atocha and London. The justification of the ideology, based on a higher cause, has not been for the good of that cause but has contributed to the evilness of the ideology. So this is not just about antisemitism. It is also about irresponsibility.

'Like Faust, I would have sold my soul to make a building. Then I met my Mephistopheles. He did not seem any less overbearing than Goethe's', said the famous architect, Albert Speer, referring to Hitler. Thus was forged the myth of the good Nazi, innocent despite belonging to the dictator's close circle and despite becoming Minister of Armaments and Munitions. 'First and foremost, I was an architect', said Speer over and over again, while he repeatedly stated that he knew nothing of the Holocaust. Years later, Simon Wiesenthal, in a face-to-face conversation, suddenly said: 'if we had known then what we know today, we would have hanged you in Nuremberg in 1946'. Speer kept quiet and Wiesenthal added: 'I always knew I was right'.[5] Today, in a sad coincidence with my writing of these last pages, Simon Wiesenthal has died. His motto, 'there is no freedom without justice', prompted decades of effort, struggle and success. I think it relevant to recall here, in an improvised *in memoriam*, his paper on the identification of Karl Silberbauer, the Gestapo officer responsible for arresting Anne Frank; the detention of the Treblinka commandant Franz Stangl, the identification and detention of Hermine Braunsteiner, happily living as a housewife in the New York borough of Queens and who had supervised the assassination of hundreds of children during the war. And, of course, his outstanding paper on the identification, detention and subsequent trial of the diligent person responsible for carrying out the final solution, Adolf Eichmann. Observing the Eichmann trial in Israel, Hannah Arendt wrote her famous thoughts about the 'banality of evil'; she was struck by the mediocrity and simple-mindedness of that horrendous figure. And on that note I will close, with a tribute to a brave Jewish combatant, who dedicated his life to prosecuting evil; and with a reminder of that banal evil. Antisemitism is the school of intolerance, the prejudice that has so efficiently taught hatred and killing. To encourage it is a crime. To banalize it is complicity. Not to fight it is irresponsibility.

NOTE

1. Taken from a speech given by Briggite Gabriel at Duke University on 14 October 2004, entitled 'Message from a Lebanese woman in support of Israel'.
2. Sura 2, 85.
3. The quotations from Brodsky are from an unpublished essay, communicated privately to the author, under the title 'Essay on the current blindness (on Islamophilia and Judeophobia)'.
4. Joan B. Culla, *La tierra más disputada: El sionismo, Israel y el conflicto de Palestina* (Madrid: Alianza, 2005).
5. From a conversation between Simon Wiesenthal and Speer in the late 1970s, related by Simon Wiesenthal to the historian Gregor Janssen in 1998 and quoted in a German television documentary by Heinrich Brelör entitled 'Speer und Er'.

6 The *Protocols of the Elders of Zion* and the 'Propaganda of Liberalism'

MARK WEITZMAN

I first met Simon Wiesenthal in 1987 when he visited our offices in New York, where upon seeing my cluttered desk, so reminiscent of his own in Vienna, he settled down for a conversation that ripened into a friendship. Our talks ranged over many topics, but one theme that we frequently returned to was the continued presence of antisemitic literature after the Holocaust and the question of freedom of speech. He was always encouraging of my work, and when I sent him a draft of the book I co-authored on the Protocols, *he responded with a note that included the following: 'The refutation of the* Protocols *is very important ... the fact that the entire publication is a falsification needs to be brought to people's minds again and again.'[1] I had very much hoped to see this essay presented to him; and I offer it in memory of a man who was not only a moral inspiration but also a warm and generous friend.*

One of the most surprising elements associated with the *Protocols* is their adaptability. Originally (and still most commonly) associated with the antisemitism of the extreme right, an association derived from their attributed origin in Czarist Okhrana circles[2] and strengthened by their publicized use by the Nazis and their followers, along with antisemites like Henry Ford, the *Protocols* have seen a resurgence in recent years. This revival has been reinforced by the use of the *Protocols* by the Arab states and movements like Hamas that are locked into an implacable hatred of Israel and use the *Protocols'* description of an international conspiracy to justify their enmity.[3] While these traditional users of the *Protocols* have only continued their longstanding reliance on the text, what has been surprising is the growing use of the *Protocols* by those who are not usually thought of as embracing or supporting either of those perspectives. In this essay I would like to briefly illustrate this, as well as to offer some provisional thoughts on the reason for it. Many of the examples that I draw upon are from the Internet which, as I pointed out in *Dismantling the Big Lie: The Protocols of the Elders of Zion* (co-authored with Steven L. Jacobs), is currently the largest distributor of the *Protocols*.[4]

In our book I noted the defence of the *Protocols* by those who defend free speech and oppose censorship.[5] There I cited the case of a website that purports to represent a female perspective on censorship, and which cites the *Protocols* as an example of 'censorship, even of images that offend us, (that) can create profound problems as we fight for our rights – for women or any oppressed minority'.[6] This site cannot by any means be described as fascist or even antisemitic; as a matter of fact one of the authors of the site, identified only by her first name (Alana), writes that 'I wouldn't let a four-year-old child watch an explicit documentary on the Holocaust, but I would definitely want my sixteen-year-old to watch',[7] and on another page they have no hesitation in explicitly describing the *Protocols* (along with *Mein Kampf*) as being 'virulently antisemitic'.[8] Thus there is no reason not to take at face value the website's claim that they are motivated by free speech concerns, and as they explicitly assert:

> We are here because we protest the effect that censorship has on women:
> - We *protest* all the social and legal pressures that leave women and girls thinking that perfectly normal bodily processes are shameful, evil, pornographic, or topics to only be spoken of in embarrassed whispers and euphemisms to the school nurse.
> - We *protest* the laws and customs that have led women into such ignorance and confusion about how their own bodies work.
> - We *protest* the social taboos and governmental laws that have made it difficult for knowledgeable [*sic*] women and mothers to talk to young girls about their growing bodies, and their lives.
> - We *protest* the censorship of women's political, scientific and artistic ideas.[9]

And yet, despite this liberal agenda, we can find the *Protocols* being defended. On the same theme, we can find a discussion thread devoted to celebrating 'Banned Books Week' of 2000 which contains a discussion of 'my favorite often-banned book' (in other words, pointing out the failings of censorship by showing the high quality of books that were banned for various reasons, such as *To Kill a Mockingbird, Flowers for Algernon, Are You There God? It's Me, Margaret, Lord of the Flies, The Adventures of Huckleberry Finn* and *Catcher in the Rye*).[10] Among the books listed were the *Protocols*, with the complaint that 'I've seen too many "anti-censorship" people (even the librarians I've worked with) support removing certain books from shelves ("well, *TKAM* is a great work of art, but the *Protocols of the Elders of Zion* just goes too far so we'll pull it"). It's soured me on the whole thing, because it's so frequently hypocritical.' A similar item can be found in the 2003 listing of acts of censorship that can be found online[11] and that includes this notation about the *Protocols* in Alexandria, Egypt:

> 2003, December 06: *Protocols of the Elders of Zion* By the secret police of Czar Nicolas II. Once again the Library of Alexandria was subject to an attack by the forces of ignorance and censorship. From the left wing, this time, however. Political pressure was brought to bear against the recently re-opened library by the United Nations after complaints in the Middle East press about the display of a volume of the *Protocols of the Elders of Zion*. The book was removed from the display; thereby proving that future burnings of the library's collection can be done by the staff members themselves.

The author of the page has a link to another, more personal page, where he harshly attacks the Wiesenthal Centre for protesting the inclusion of the *Protocols* in the refurbished Library in Alexandria, the action that led to the removal of the book. In his words: 'And to intimate that we can stop the hate by destroying the book? When has that ever worked before?' And, again, the author's rejection of antisemitism is clear: 'It seems that whenever someone needed a people to oppress, it was always the Jewish people who were singled out ... (including) two invasions of Israel just for existing because it's a Jewish state ... I'll admit quite frankly: I just don't get it ... I have absolutely not one tiny glimmer of an idea as to why every raving lunatic turns first to the Jews when selecting an *Enemy of the State*'.[12]

Similarly, we can find the respected professional publication *AB Bookman's Weekly* publishing an article, *Collecting Banned Books* by one Richard Russell that includes the *Protocols* in the category of 'Books Banned on Religious Grounds' and describes the *Protocols* as having 'been banned since the Second World War in many places because it is overtly antisemitic. So Judaism has its modern censorship campaign'. The *Protocols* are accompanied in this category by works of Darwin, Giordano Bruno and even Maimonides![13]

Another example is the appearance of the *Protocols* on Indymedia. Indymedia is a prominent website run by the Independent Media Center (IMC) that describes itself as 'a collective of independent media organizations and hundreds of journalists offering grassroots, non-corporate coverage. Indymedia is a democratic media outlet for the creation of radical, accurate, and passionate tellings of truth'.[14] In 2002 a complaint was lodged about the posting of the *Protocols* on Indymedia, and the following was received as response:

> As you may know, all Indymedia sites use a system of 'open publishing', meaning that any individual is free to post to the site without being subject to prior editorial controls. This innovation has been crucial to our organization's many successes in covering important news around the world. On the other hand, it is a policy which lends itself to abuse, and each IMC including www.indymedia.org has an editorial policy allowing for the removal of certain kinds of posts. Indeed, removing repugnant, antisemitic posts from our site can often be a full-time job for IMC volunteers at many sites, including posts referring to the 'learned elders of Zion'.[15]

The *Protocols* can still be found on Indymedia, at a posting entitled 'The Truth About the *Protocols*'.[16]

Offline, we can find *The Guardian* reporting about appearances of the *Protocols* at conferences organized by the National Union of Students in England, an organization that has espoused many liberal positions, including a code of conduct for student journalists that require a commitment to try and eliminate censorship. In an April 2005 blog discussion, one correspondent wrote that the *Protocols* were on display, despite complaints, due to the NUS policy that applied to all leaflets universally in the interests of free speech. A respondent then raised the point 'Doesn't the NUS have a no-platform-for-racists-and-fascists policy? If so, it can't have a free-speech reason for tolerating a Protocols of Zion leaflet, which is paradigmatically racist.' The blog's author has emailed the National Union of Students for clarification of this issue, but has yet to post any response.[17]

The largest book fair in the world, the Frankfurt Book Fair,

includes freedom of speech as one of the ways that it brings 'a prolif-
erous world of books, information and pictures' to the reader.[18]
Despite their violation of German law, publishers were able to abuse
the loophole for two years, to display the *Protocols* (and other similar
texts such as Henry Ford's *International Jew*). In 2004, as pointed out
by the Wiesenthal Centre, the *Protocols* were overtly displayed by various Arab countries at the Fair, which had chosen the 'Arab World' as
that year's 'Guest of Honour' (an annual designation to a country or
region whose literature is then highlighted at the Fair). Reacting to
criticism, Peter Ripken, director of the Society for the Promotion of
African, Asian and Latin American Literature at the Fair, said 'that he
was bothered not by the Arab literature at the Fair but by repeated
false accusations of antisemitism'. He continued, 'Please define antisemitism. The Fair was attended by 270,000 to 300,000. So who is in
a position to say that it was five percent or ten percent antisemitic –
this is nonsense. The question is not whether there was antisemitism,
but whether antisemitism was the key issue at the Fair.'[19] Thus for
Ripken, the *Protocols* might not even qualify as being antisemitic, but
apparently if they are, antisemitism is quite acceptable, even if publicly
displayed, as long as the matter doesn't become controversial![20] The
controversy of 2004 had little immediate effect on the organizers, as
the 2005 Book Fair also saw the *Protocols* (along with similar materials), still present and visible, with Iran being the biggest offender.
According to the German researcher Matthias Küntzel, the texts were

> brochures that Iran presented here in English – not in order to
> promote the country's own literature, but rather to disseminate
> antisemitism of European and American provenance. There
> was, for instance, under the heading 'Jewish Conspiracy', the
> text that influenced Hitler's antisemitism like no other work:
> the *Protocols of the Elders of Zion*, here in an edition published
> by the 'Islamic Propagation Organization' of the Islamic
> Republic of Iran.[21]

In *Mein Kampf* Hitler wrote about the *Protocols* that 'With positively terrifying certainty they reveal the nature and activity of the Jewish
people ... as well as their ultimate future aims'.[22] The *Protocols*
helped to justify or create the *Weltanschauung* that led to the Third
Reich and the Final Solution; and their reappearance today, as a text
of mass distribution and mainstream public discourse has led to widespread concern about their influence and what to do about it.

Commenting on the historian Peter Pulzer's work on the origins of political antisemitism amidst the rise of liberal democratic societies, Henning Tewes has written that 'Antisemitism as a permanent political feature ... (is) inherently post-liberal' in that it combined pre-liberal ideological 'components with post-liberal political practices'.[23] Tewes is describing how antisemitism can grow in a liberal society, such as Pulzer has observed in his work. Indeed, as Pulzer put it, liberalism failed by being 'slow to recognize that Antisemitism flourished through its own failure to respond to human needs'; among which failures are what Tewes characterizes as 'the gentile liberals' often ambiguous view of Jewish emancipation'.[24] It is this ambiguous relationship with antisemitism that can appear to lie at the core of the defence of the *Protocols* and similar antisemitic propaganda, or that can take other forms, such as the higher standards that Israel is often held to in liberal circles. It is noteworthy that Pulzer acknowledges the threat of the *Protocols* today when he reacted to Tom Paulin's poem 'On Being Dealt the Antisemitic Card', in which Paulin used formulistic denunciations of historical antisemitism and Nazism to deny the possibility of being antisemitic and thus to legitimize his vicious anti-Zionism.[25] Paulin's narrow definition of antisemitism is outside the guidelines of international organisations such as the OSCE and the European Union Monitoring Centre on Racism and Xenophobia.

In his indefatigable pursuit of Nazi war criminals and his fight against antisemitism Simon Wiesenthal forced the liberal democracies of the West to confront some of their ambivalence regarding Jews and antisemitism. His efforts resulted in keeping alive the memory of the victims, in identifying the perpetrators, in establishing where they found shelter and with whose assistance, and in not allowing the victorious West to sweep the question of the Holocaust, its causes and consequences, under the carpet. Although antisemitism persists, there is no question that the efforts of Simon Wiesenthal have in essential ways been responsible for creating a climate where governments have felt themselves required to move against it. This movement has often resulted in a tension between what Kent Greenawalt, in his 1995 book *Fighting Words*, described as the 'value of equality ... and the traditional idea of free speech',[26] a tension that Simon Wiesenthal was certainly sensitive to. Towards the end of his last book, *Justice Not Vengeance*, Wiesenthal, writing as one who had been shaped by the events of the Holocaust, the Cold War, and a post-war life lived in Vienna, commented on the difference between European and US thought on the freedom of speech, calling for legislation to stem neo-Nazi propaganda.[27] In this context the European democracies and Canada have generally been perceived as having taken a more restrictive approach to free speech and the Unites States is seen as having the widest application of protected speech. Greenawalt did foresee that if United States courts and legislatures, for example, begin to move in the direction of consideration of what 'speech does … (and its) harmful effects' then the result might be a more restrictive interpretation of free speech.[28] Nonetheless, if the *Protocols* and such material continue to be disseminated, it might be that this is just a result of one of the choices that members of liberal societies choose to make in defining themselves, and their society. This was, after all, one of the defining themes of the work of one of the most celebrated political thinkers of our time, Isaiah Berlin, and which was described by John Gray in his study of Berlin's political thought as follows: 'Within our own liberal morality, for example, liberty and equality, fairness and welfare are … goods (that) often collide in practice.'[29] Ronald Dworkin takes Berlin's warning that 'One freedom may abort another' as a warning against 'the new acceptance of censorship' by liberals.[30] While that warning is certainly valid, the circumstances that I have outlined above about the defence and dissemination of the *Protocols* are equally serious, and should serve as a warning that liberals need not and absolutely should not become proponents of what Todd Gitlin has called 'the progressivism of fools'.[31] In this effort the life and work of Simon Wiesenthal can continue to be a model for us all.[32]

ACKNOWLEDGEMENTS

My thanks go to Ali Wolfsohn, whose research was invaluable in the preparation of this essay. The phrase 'propaganda of liberalism' is taken from one of the sources that Cesare de Michelis uncovered (see note 2 below). There the phrase was used by a 'mysterious lady' in a note referring to the methods used by Jews to take over the world, as described in the *Protocols*.

NOTES

1.   Simon Wiesenthal, personal communication, 13 June 2001.
2.   The classic study of the *Protocols* is Norman Cohn's *Warrant for Genocide: The Myth of the Jewish World Conspiracy and the Protocols of Zion* (London: Serif, 1996). Cesare de Michelis has recently argued that the text was composed in Russia in reaction to the First Zionist Congress, in de Michelis, *The Non-Existent Manuscript: A Study of the Protocols of the Sages of Zion* (Lincoln, NE: University of Nebraska Press, 2004).
3.   See Hamas' Charter, Article 32 ('Their plan is embodied in the *Protocols of the Elders of Zion*'), online at http://www.yale.edu/lawweb/avalon/mideast/hamas.htm. In Steven L. Jacobs and Mark Weitzman, *Dismantling the Big Lie: The Protocols of the Elders of Zion* (Tel Aviv: Ktav, 2003), I argue that 'scientific' antisemitism was discredited by the Holocaust and 'Christian' antisemitism repudiated by the churches in the post Second World War era, thus leaving conspiratorial (political) antisemitism as the dominant form

of Western antisemitism, and of course the *Protocols* are the foundational document of this antisemitism.

4. Jacobs and Weitzman, *Dismantling the Big* Lie, pp.1–7.
5. Ibid. pp.5–6.
6. Web by Women, for Women – About Censorship, http://www.io.com/~wwwomen/aboutc/. The site dates from 1998 and doesn't appear to have been updated since.
7. http://www.io.com/~wwwomen/about_us/alana.html.
8. http://www.io.com/~wwwomen/aboutc/index.html.
9. http://www.io.com/~wwwomen/index.html.
10. http://www.metafilter.com/comments.mefi/3457.
11. http://www.angelfire.com/scifi/dreamweaver/bannedbks/chrono6b.html.
12. http://www.angelfire.com/scifi/dreamweaver/bannedbks/censoroped035.html.
13. http://abbookman.com/ABBookman_F020204.html.
14. http://www.indymedia.org/en/index.shtml.
15. http://lists.indymedia.org/mailman/public/www-newswire/2002-May/001440.html.
16. http://publish.indymedia.org/en/2004/06/854426.shtml.
17. The journalist's code can be found at http://erictheunred.blogspot.com/2005/04/proto-cols-of-nus.html.
18. Peter Weidhaas, Director of the Frankfurt Book Fair, 1999, http://www.frankfurtmatav.hu/angol/live1.htm.
19. Edwin Black, *The Lingering Taint of Anti-Semitism of the Frankfurt Fair*, hnn.us/articles/8725.html.
20. Ibid.
21. Matthias Küntzel, 'The Protocols of the Elders of Zion' at the Frankfurt Book Fair, http://www.matthiaskuentzel.de/artikel.php?artikelID=96. Since the writing of this article, the situation at the Book Fair has not changed for the better.
22. Adolf Hitler, *Mein Kampf*, translated by Ralph Manheim (New York: Houghton-Mifflin, 1943), p.307.
23. Henning Tewes, 'The Committed Observer of a Janus-faced Century: Peter Pulzer on Liberalism, Anti-Semitism and Democracy', in Fritz Stern, Henning Tewes and Jonathan Wright, *Liberalism, Anti-Semitism and Democracy: Essays in Honour of Peter Pulzer* (New York: Oxford University Press, 2001), p.30.
24. Ibid, p.34.
25. See Pulzer's letter to the editor, 'How to Say It', *London Review of Books*, 23 January 2003. Paulin's poem appeared in the 2 January 2003 edition of the *London Review*.
26. Kent Greenawalt, *Fighting Words* (Princeton, NJ: Princeton University Press, 1995), p.151.
27. Simon Wiesenthal, *Justice Not Vengeance* (New York: Grove Weidenfeld, 1989), p.356.
28. Greenawalt, *Fighting Words*, p.152.
29. John Gray, *Isaiah Berlin* (Princeton, NJ: Princeton University Press, 1996), p.43.
30. Ronald Dworkin, 'Two Concepts of Liberty', in Edna Ullman-Margalit and Avishai Margalit (eds.), *Isaiah Berlin: A Celebration* (Chicago: University of Chicago Press, 1991), pp.102–3.
31. Todd Gitlin, 'The Rough Beast Returns', in Ron Rosenbaum (ed.), *Those Who Forget the Part: The Question of Anti-Semitism* (New York: Random House, 2004), p.265. Gitlin was alluding to August Bebel's famous description of antisemitism as 'the socialism of fools'.
32. Although it appeared after the completion of this article, the recent essay by US academics John Mearsheimer and Stephen Walt, 'Israel Lobby and US Foreign Policy' (Harvard University, Kennedy School of Government, Faculty Research Working Paper Series, no.RWP06-011; an edited version, with the same title, appears in the *London Review of Books*, vol.28, no.6, 23 March 2006), offers another excellent example of how the *Protocols*' theme of allegations that a Jewish cabal is manipulating world events can be introduced into mainstream discourse by writers with respectable academic credentials. Although the authors are not necessarily identified with liberal/left perspectives (being more connected to aspects of international 'realism'), their paper is an attack on neoconservative warmongers whom they identify as Jews. Mearsheimer and Walt have adamantly denied allegations of antisemitism and the use of their thesis for others' antisemitic agenda.

7 Defending Change in Arab Societies: Conspiracy Theories and their Arab Critics

GOETZ NORDBRUCH

1.

'Enough, Egypt, enough!'[1] Such was the furious reaction of columnist Marc Sayegh to news reports about the Egyptian TV series *Knight Without a Horse*. The broadcasting during Ramadan 2002 of this series, in which explicit reference is made to the *Protocols of the Elders of Zion*, attracted wide interest among the Egyptian public; it was later sold to other Arab countries, where it received similar attention. Earlier, in autumn 2001, the terrorist attacks of 11 September were frequently described in Arab media as a Jewish or US conspiracy to push for war. The international tensions triggered by the publication of cartoons depicting the Prophet Muhammad in a Danish newspaper were no less perceived as being part of a global conspiracy against the Arab-Islamic world.

The popularity of conspiracy theories in the Arab world has frequently been commented on in the international press. The evident absurdity of the implied claims and the persistency with which conspiratorial views are promoted have caused concerns about the origins and consequences of such distorted perceptions of society. While in the past, the phenomenon had often been reported in US, British or Israeli media, in the last few years, Arab commentators have increasingly joined in the debate about the implications of conspiratorial thought for the prospects of society. As an obstacle to self-critical assessments of ongoing transformations in the Arab world and as an 'insult to Arab and Islamic rationality and intelligence',[2] as one Arab author put it, such perceptions have a paralysing impact that has been recognized by Arab intellectuals. *Al-Hayat*, a newspaper known for its willingness to publish pluralist voices, including criticism of the policies pursued by Arab leaders and regimes, is one of the media that have allowed the content of such theories to be called into question. On several occasions it has published critical discussions on how to understand and, more importantly, how to oppose conspiratorial formulations in Arab public discourse. *Al-Jazeera*, the Qatar-based TV-network, has done the same by inviting outspoken critics of antisemitic thought to elaborate on the dangers of blaming the Jews for the problems of the Arab world. *Al-Ahram*, Egypt's leading government daily, published an outstanding article by Osama al-Baz, chief advisor to President Hosni Mubarak, rejecting conspiracy theories and expressions of antisemitic thought as harming political culture.

For all that, conspiracy theories continue to be published on a regular basis throughout the Arab media. By pointing at an assumed antagonistic Other who is continuously longing for the destruction of Arab societies, conspiracy theories serve to maintain and strengthen the collective identity of the Arab/Islamic community which has increasingly come under threat. They propose explanations for the far-reaching social, political and economic changes affecting the Arab world today and identify those who are considered responsible. In addition, a second factor contributes to their pervasiveness. By attributing social transformations to the doings of an Other, they make the preservation of the existing order synonymous with the preservation of the community and the protection of its identity. Change, here, tends not only to be explained as negative or undesirable, but as a threat to the very existence of the collective self. By identifying the Other and his aims, interests and deeds, conspiracy theories, by exclusion, provide a definition of oneself.

2.

Following international protests about the above-mentioned Egyptian TV series, dozens of articles and comments were published in local media debating the origins of the *Protocols* and their content. The *Protocols* were not unknown in the Arab world. Available in Arab translations since the early 1920s, they developed in the second half of the century into one of the most frequently cited proofs of a Jewish conspiracy.[3] Various social and political developments have since then been explained as being part of the twenty-four steps laid down in the *Protocols* to achieve world domination by the Jews. According to one editor of a recent Arabic translation of the

Protocols, between 1965 and 1967 alone, more than fifty reproductions or variations of the *Protocols of the Elders of Zion* were published in Arabic.[4] Moreover, the repeated inclusion of excerpts from the *Protocols* in present-day Arab newspapers illustrates their ongoing impact on contemporary Arab discourse.

References to the *Protocols* are not always substantive; indeed the term 'Protocol' has turned into a code word for assumed conspiracies of any kind. 'The Protocols of the Elders of Washington' or 'The Protocols of the Elders of Sharon' are such tropes which are based on a shared public knowledge about the conspiracy theory posited in the book. It is thus not so much the actual book that is important, but the broad public acceptance of conspiratorial approaches to society as such. Not surprisingly, the producer of the Egyptian TV series dismissed doubts about the historical origins of the *Protocols* by claiming that it was of no interest who actually wrote the story; what had to be stressed was that during the last century Zionists had managed to translate it into reality. An editorial in the Egyptian government-controlled daily *al-Akhbar* spells out this argument: 'The most important question is not whether Zionism is behind the publication of the book, but whether Zionism was not really aiming – especially in our generation – to conquer the world, by money, murder, sex and other disgusting means.'[5]

Ongoing processes of social disintegration, changing patterns of identity, transformations of values and norms clearly reverberate in these contemporary Arab interpretations. In 2000, the respected Egyptian editing house Dar al-Shuruq published a book entitled *The Muslims and Globalization*. In this book, Muhammad Qutb analyses the background and consequences of globalization for Islamic societies. The process of globalization, he writes, makes it necessary to renew the warning about the 'domination of devil'[6] – a domination which during the last years has been achieved by international Jewish capital. The history of what he calls Jewish rule over humankind is said to have reached its final phase in our globalizing world. Qutb, then, explicitly links globalization to the threat posed by 'moral corruption, sexual anarchy, heresy, drugs and different forms of insanity'.[7]

The fear of sexual anarchy, which is addressed here by Qutb, is one of the most productive topics in this context. United Nations conferences on population planning and legal initiatives to give women equal rights with men have been described as Zionist or Jewish plots to undermine the traditional Arab family. Prostitution, homosexuality and the increasing use of drugs are similar issues that are linked to the damaging impacts of hidden hands, which are aiming to destroy the community from within. Books that are published under titles like *The War of Prostitutes* or *Prostitution and Spies* offer information about assumed plots to destabilize society. A recent pamphlet which addresses the same topic claims to scrutinize the historical dimension of these plots. Making frequent use of an Arabic translation of the *Protocols*, the author intends to offer 'a complete history of the infiltration of the Arabs by AIDS and sex'.[8] Consequently, one chapter of the book deals extensively with the impact of homosexuality and prostitution in Jewish history. Knowledge of this particular Jewish concept of sexuality, according to the author, allows one to understand the approach of Jews to non-Jewish societies. In the light of the current weak state of Egyptian society a 'door is open for the threat [posed] by the invading children of Zion'.[9]

Other debates in the Arab media likewise reflect such assumed links between social changes and the destructive influences of outside forces. Dana International, the transsexual Israeli singer, who was popular among Egyptian youths in the mid-1990s, has been widely identified as an agent of these powers. Her highly sexualized image, her oriental Jewish background, her modern music have made her the ideal personification of a Western-Jewish cultural threat. In the summer of 1996, a chewing gum sold in thousands of small shops all over Egypt was widely rumoured to be the latest Zionist trap. Then-Prime Minister Yitzak Rabin himself, it was said, was behind the development of this chemical weapon, which first increases men's sexual desire, only to cause impotence shortly afterwards. This, again, was not a marginal debate. The chewing gum threat even became an issue in the Egyptian parliament. Pokemon cards, which became popular among children all over the world in 2001, were another such vehicle of cultural infiltration. The assumed promotion of Zionist values like destruction and domination implicit in the rules of the game, the secret dissemination of Jewish symbols identified in some of the images printed on the cards, were threats linked to the popularity and success this game had achieved amongst children.

These scenarios of outside threats to the authentic identity of the community reflect fears that cultural identity is under constant attack. It is in this context that every so often there are media reports of attempts by Jews or Zionists to gain control over historic sites in the Arab world. Intellectuals and politicians warn against Zionist thefts of symbols of ancient civilization. The pyramids, a central symbol of Egyptian cultural identity, figure high on this list of potential

Jewish targets. The millennium concert given by French musician Jean-Michel Jarre at the pyramids was interpreted as part of such a plot. In the weeks preceding the concert, news reports uncovered the symbolic background of the planned light-show at the Giza Pyramids, which was purported to form part of a Masonic ritual. Jarre was alleged to be a Jewish homosexual to whom the Egyptian cultural authorities had surrendered Egypt's cultural identity.

While the *Protocols of the Elders of Zion* might be the most elaborate expression of conspiratorial approaches to society, Freemasonry and Satanism are among the themes most commonly evoked in connection with the putative agents of these threats. Warnings of Satanism reflect the most complex theories of conspiracies against the community. In the last few years alone, two cases of what was perceived as Satanism attracted attention among the Arab public. In both instances, groups of young people – mostly in their early 20s – were accused of worshipping the devil, propagating apostasy and conspiring against traditional norms and values. In both cases, Judaism was declared to be the historical origin of Satanism, and Jewish philosophy and religion were said to lie at its ideological roots. While in the first case in 1997, most of the accused were students at the American University in Cairo, in the second case in 2001, most of them were homosexuals. While the first group symbolized the Westernized, globalized, non-national Other, the second was identified as a sexual-religious threat for society. It is hardly necessary to mention that in both cases it did not take long until alleged links to Israel, the Israeli ambassador or other Israelis were revealed.

This fear of a loss of cultural identity through conspiracies, such as that thought to be embodied in the *Protocols of the Elders of Zion* and identified with modernization and globalization, is reflected in a concept of a 'culture of resistance', proclaimed by Arab intellectuals of different political and religious allegiances. The rejection of cultural relations with Israel – and increasingly with the West – is connected here with an opposition to globalization, which is similarly regarded as a threat to identity. It is not surprising, then, that it is not Frantz Fanon or Albert Memmi, but the German nationalist philosopher Johann-Gottlieb Fichte who figures high on the list of intellectual references for such critiques of modernity and Western influences in Arab discourse. While Fanon and Memmi were highly critical of the ambivalences of modern Western influences in the context of colonial rule, their theories clearly intended to surpass both local causes of decline and Western cultural domination. Fichte, on the other hand, longed for preservation of identity; he was concerned essentially not with modernization and adaptation to a changing world, but with resisting the forces of cultural dissolution.

In the Arab context, conspiracy theories illustrate the popularity of identifications of the enemy as the 'Jew'. However, while in most cases Jews or Zionists are described as the persons behind the plot, in others, the instigators are defined in no less categorical terms. As a semantic construction of the enemy, the label of 'Jew' is frequently merged with others. 'Satanism', 'Freemasonry', 'homosexuals', 'America', 'the Crusaders' or simply 'the West' are thus often inter-changeably applied to denote the agents of conspiracy.

Most of these views can be traced back to an underlying concept of an authentic community threatened by dissolution. Hence, conspiracy theories and the applied images in the Arab public are in most cases not, as it is often suggested, a superficial means of denouncing a specific Israeli or Western policy. On the contrary, they are part and parcel of ideological perceptions of social and political conflicts unrelated to any concrete confrontation with a Jewish, Israeli or Western Other. While conspiracy theories allow the complex challenges in today's Arab societies to be 'understood', they at the same time provide media discourse with a widely accepted myth that serves to construct and uphold collective identity. In the context of an increasingly complex social reality and a wide range of ongoing social changes and transformations, conspiratorial approaches help to stabilize the community by placing it in an existential confrontation with a hostile Other.

3.

A critique of conspiracy theories cannot be limited to a 'defence of the Jews', to a critique of stereotypical and pejorative depictions of Jews and Judaism in Arab discourse. While conspiratorial views lie at the heart of most violent expressions of present-day antisemitic thinking – as in the case of the Lebanese Hezbollah and the Palestinian Hamas with their strategies of terror – they are no less an obstacle to change in Arab societies themselves. It is this aspect in particular that has increasingly been highlighted by Arab intellectuals of different political and religious outlooks.

Notwithstanding the notable successes of growing radical movements over the past few years in a number of Arab countries, debate about political change and socio-economic progress has all but ceased. The public reaction to the United Nations Human

Development Report on the Arab countries in 2005 was a case in point. The devastating results of the survey, for many, were sufficient reason to engage in critical assessments of local politics and ideological barriers; for them, external factors as much as local obstacles continue to harm social and political development significantly. Relations between state and religion, the urgent need for educational reform, pressing questions of gender relations and personal status and nationality law are topics that have increasingly become the focus of public attention. Being closely linked to questions of culture and community, these questions call mainstream notions of identity directly into question.

In a commentary for *Elaph*, a popular Arab online magazine, Riyad 'Abed exemplarily focuses on this linkage. Under the headline 'Conspiracy theories are a means to avoid facing the facts', 'Abed rhetorically asks:

> Is the backwardness of scientific and cultural research at Arab universities due to an intellectual repressiveness which is a consequence of the absolute rule of religious thought? Is it not that our economic backwardness is a result of the chains which are imposed upon half of society, the women? Do non-Muslims enjoy full citizen rights in Arab countries, and [if not,] what is impeding the granting of these rights? A profound study is required to answer these questions, and hundreds others, and to find possible solutions for them – that is what is needed, and not additional superficial and simplifying theories about imagined conspiracies. To fill the minds of the Arab-Muslim youth with invented scenarios of imaginary enemies [...] means to destroy our civilization and to rob our fortune. Our self-enslavement and the wrecking of our heritage is the main reason for the culture of violence that has spread in these countries.[10]

Following this analysis, theories of conspiracies have been pinpointed by advocates of change as major distractions from most pressing questions that today's Arab societies are facing.

The public standing of such criticism, however, is complicated by the peculiar nature of conspiracy theories: according to these views, all those questioning the underlying outlook tend to be part of the plot. In this context, Arab politicians, academics, journalists and artists who have come out in favour of rational analysis and debate about the current state of Arab affairs have frequently been attacked as agents of foreign powers. While in some cases, such accusations remained limited to radical Islamist or nationalist circles, in others, state repression has followed suit. The arrest of Egyptian academic Sa'ad al-Din Ibrahim in summer 2000 clearly marked a temporary high point of such public campaigns. With both Islamist and nationalist currents attacking the founder of the Ibn Khaldun Centre for Development Studies for his explicit dealings with core issues of social and political reform, government agencies paralleled public pressure with massive intimidations and, ultimately, legal sanction.

While Ibrahim's case has attracted broad international attention, others have not. Charges of *takfir*, of submission to unbelief, are frequently raised by Islamist organizations against Muslim reformists; in nationalist discourse, charges of a betrayal of the nation's cause often echo similar perceptions of dissident voices. Recent campaigns against newspapers, magazines and web blogs, which have given audience to these voices, illustrate the efficacy of such accusations. It is not only the position itself that has come under fire, but its very means of expression.

4.

In view of the mutual dependencies within present-day relations between the Arab countries and the West, change and progress on either side can hardly be achieved unless there is movement on the other. Neither Israel, nor Europe or the US can prove conspiracy theories wrong; as a perception of society that denies reality and facts, the theory of a conspiracy cannot be put into question by changing reality. While this kind of interpretation of society must thus be overcome from within Arab political cultures themselves, Western politics and Western public discourse nevertheless play an important role in advancing self-critical assessments and pluralist political cultures in the Arab world.

The preservation and extension of free media, in this context, are of evident importance. As liberalization of the media and the opening up of public debate are a central part of Arab efforts to achieve political change, it is crucial that they receive international support. From an Arab perspective, however, outside assistance for such endeavours is ambivalent. In fact, Western aid to dissidents in the Arab world has in the past often been selective. Material support and public attention in many cases remained limited to explicitly pro-European or pro-American voices, darkening the image of dissidence in Arab perceptions even further. While the encouragement of self-critical debate and the defence of freedom of opinion are obligations in themselves, Western assistance to individuals and explicit support for certain positions have for that reason rarely contributed to a broadening of political culture. From a local point of view, it was hardly freedom of opinion as a general concept that gained international attention and support; instead, interventions in favour of dissident voices were widely perceived as following Western interests – and Western interests alone.

In the recent past, a new phenomenon emerged in the Arab media that should be considered a starting point for contributions to Arab advocacy of change. In the last few years, Arab media have given considerable attention to controversies that have engaged the European public – and in addressing these European debates numerous Arab commentators have pushed for critical thinking on similar questions related to Arab political cultures. The controversy triggered in the European media by Muslim protests against the publication of cartoons depicting the Prophet is the most recent example of such an effect. While mainstream opinion in Arab media mirrored the anger of Muslims over a perceived attack against Islam, several Arab commentators took the opportunity to analyse in detail the ambivalences of freedom of press and opinion. Although referring to these European debates, these comments and articles were not so much about Europe as about the lack of similar controversies in the Arab world. Europe, here, was a starting point – though a controversial one. In a similar way, recent controversies in France about the showing of religious symbols in schools or about the reform of German immigration laws paved the way for critical assessments of related questions faced by Arab societies themselves. Evidently, controversies about the state of Muslim communities in Europe raise several questions that are neither foreign nor less controversial in the Arab world itself.

Arab proponents of change readily draw on such parallels, pointing not so much to an ideal European or Western model as to conflicts that should be resolved. In this regard, critical debates in Europe and the United States – whether about Western colonial history, traditional concepts of national identity and culture, or about persisting racial and religious discrimination – tend to resonate with the Arab public. Pushing for such controversies in the West will hardly give the lie to the conspiracy theories that continue to shape Arab public discourse to this day. It might, however, improve the standing of those who question those theories.

NOTES

1. *Al-Hayat*, 3 Nov. 2002.
2. Kamaran Karadaghi in a talkshow under the title 'The Protocols of the Elders of Zion', *al-Jazeera*, 19 March 2002.
3. See, for example, Stefan Wild, 'Die arabische Rezeption der "Protokolle der Weisen von Zion"', in Rainer Brunner, Monika Gronke, Jens Laut, Ulrich Rebstock (eds), *Islamstudien ohne Ende. Festschrift für Werner Ende zum 65. Geburtstag* (Würzburg, 2002).
4. Hussein Abd al-Wahid, *The Conspiracy – The Protocols of the Elders of Zion* (in Arabic) (Cairo, 2002), pp.11–12.
5. *Al-Akhbar*, 12 Nov. 2002.
6. Muhammad Qutb, *The Muslims and Globalisation* (in Arabic) (Cairo: Dar al-Shuruq, 2000), p.14.
7. Ibid., p.29.
8. Issam Kamil, *The Nudes of Israel on Arab Pavements* (in Arabic) (Cairo, n.d. [1997?]), p.1.
9. Ibid., p.9.
10. Elaph.com, 1 May 2006.

8 Antisemitism as a Mental Disorder

STEVEN K. BAUM

It didn't start with Hitler, or end there either. Antisemitic beliefs are part of a millennia-long process, part of the social narrative that runs through the heart of society. In general, we know that the least emotionally developed people are the most prejudiced and antisemitic. They are most vulnerable to believing antisemitic myths and indeed all prejudices. And while some people are ardent antisemites and others resistant to those notions, most people, ordinary people, function somewhere between the two poles. This suggests a strong psychological component to understanding the social life of hate.

ORIGINS OF THE ANTISEMITIC NARRATIVE

Antiquity's Emperor Claudius is credited with what may be the first expression of blatant antisemitism. His reference to Jews as 'a great plague throughout the world' stood the test of time and was reactivated by Streicher and the Nazis some two thousand years later. The Greek grammarian Apion penned the blood libel myth 'Jews drink the blood of gentile children', which continues to infest most of the Arab Middle East today. That Jews are about to take over the planet is hardly news either. A Talmud-toting secret sinister group as depicted in the *Protocols of the Elders of Zion* not only makes good reading, but goes along well with the rest of the story.

Everyone seems to know the story, especially the faithful of Islam and Christianity. In case they forget, there are reminders in the form of 450 antisemitic statements throughout the New Testament and 36 in the Qur'an/Hadith. For Christians and Muslims, antisemitism is justified – the story of the Jews as a morality play, a timeless tale of a people who have fallen from grace. Guilty until proven innocent, the Jews are widely believed to have murdered Jesus and even rejected the

Prophet Mohammad. In Islam, a Jewess courtesan poisons the Prophet who dies three years later; in Christianity, a menacing crowd reflecting the Jewish council's wishes calls for Jesus's death. Though the crucifixion is performed by the Romans, Pilate's washing of hands exonerates Rome and Jews are held solely responsible: 'Let his blood be on us and on our children!'[1]

Small wonder that there was a Patron Saint (Simon) of antisemitism until 1966 when an investigation by the Church revealed the story of Simon's ritual murder by the Jews to be a hoax. Small wonder the people believed Hitler when he said, 'By fighting the Jews, I am doing the Lord's work.' Understandable that there are a disproportionate number of hate crimes against Jews that occur throughout the Easter season.

Theologically, the antisemitic narrative also gathers steam by commission. If Jews are not 'for' God, they must be 'opposed' to God, or so the thinking goes. Soon the term Jew was linked to Satan, followed by accusations of practising black magic and witchcraft. From going against God to going against God's Will or Nature, the antisemitic narrative moved from religious to popular culture. Jews as anti-Nature were held to be anti-Volk (the Volk regarded as hard-working, simple, God-fearing Christians); Jews stood in contrast to the natural order, allegedly undoing all that which was normal, good and socially ordered.

The themes in several Grimm Brothers fairy tales are telling. The children's tales portray the Jew as a nefarious, scheming outsider – one whose dealings will eventually result in the victim's undoing. Even Mother Goose rhymes convey the adult message: Jack sold his eggs to a rogue of a Jew who cheated him out of half of his due. 'None of this [antisemitism] would be of significance without the support and preconditioning of popular culture', observed historian George Mosse.[2]

Jews and class themes permeated the anti-Jewish narrative throughout the Middle Ages. As the Church prohibited Jewish guilds and Christian money lending, some Jews entered money lending and collected taxes for the landed gentry. Eventually Christians entered the field and were reputed to be less trustworthy, but by that time the equation of Jew and money was sealed. Forbidden citizenship, blocked from owning land, taxed excessively, Jews still persevered and succeeded but it did not take long for envy and contempt to even out the playing field. By the Industrial Revolution, newfound success reinforced the narrative, fuelling the fantasy of planetary takeover.

Not surprisingly, Darwinian notions of social order placed Jews in the lower social strata. Rumours of physical inferiority (hooked-nosed, frail bodies) and mental inferiority were to follow (insane, weak-willed).[3] However, many of the Jew's alleged deficits were moral, often demonstrated by a lack of (Christian) character perhaps stemming from a stubbornness in refusing to see the light of Christianity. By the nineteenth century, the Jew was transferred from a religious and cultural undermining force with global ambitions to a biological host genetically passing down 'the Jew' in bloodlines. Beginning with the *limpieza de sangre* order of the Spanish Inquisition and its revitalization in the late 1880s, most scholars agreed that a new level of lethality ensued in the form of racial anti-semitism. Depicted in church art and popular folklore as pigs, vermin and well poisoners, the Jew was dirty, reeked of *foetor Judaicus* and transferred diseases like the bubonic plague. Jewish bodies were thought to be different, with a special anatomy. For example, men were believed to menstruate, while women had horizontal vaginas like sows.

There was a medical feel to the racialized aspect of antisemitism. Jews, like disease states within the social body, were to be contained via ghettoization or conversion, expelled or killed off. It was the only reasonable position to take against such an internal enemy – the only problem was that most of what people believed of Jews was based on fantasy.

SOCIAL TRANSMISSION OF THE ANTISEMITIC NARRATIVE

At any given time, about half the planet believed in various antise-mitic myths. With endorsement and direction from the world's two largest religions, there was an authority and legitimacy to antisemit-ic myths unprecedented in the social mind. Antisemitic motifs avail-able via religious iconography now pervaded literature, art, folklore and state public display as well. Israeli writer Amoz Oz recounts that one could not pass through the gates of medieval Frankfurt without first observing the *Judensau* (pig-suckling Jews) on the city plaque – the deplorable image still adorning several European cathedrals today.

With history comes a timeless feel, a solidness surrounding the cultural 'truth'. The advent of new communication technologies such as satellite radio and television, text messaging and the Internet moves the antisemitic narrative into a global network faster and far more extensively than futurologists could have predicted.

The antisemitic narrative continues to be popular because it is transmitted along the same lines as superstitions, rumour and urban legends. Whether superstition or hate, the narrative's message is conveyed and maintained when three conditions are met. The message must be (1) catchy/threatening; (2) able to generate a key emotion such as fear, disgust or anger; and (3) simple and consistent. Most people find Jews a little strange and somewhat threatening, thus fulfilling those criteria all too well. As *Washington Post*'s Charles Krauthammer once quipped, 'Jews are news'.

When a social message is newsworthy or threatening, the message travels faster and endures longer, achieving the status of 'fact' through repetition and distinction. The process is vastly circular. *People believe the rumour because they say it and by saying it come to believe it.* The numbers of those who accept it helps. Once a tipping point is reached, what began as a rumour becomes an established fact. Ask the average person how he or she knows that Jews have all the money, and they will respond that 'everyone knows'. One simply cannot argue with a social truth that has the backing of the masses. 'It must confine itself to a few points and repeat them over and over', observed Hitler in *Mein Kampf*.

New ears are ready to listen to the narrative all the time and whole new cohorts must learn the lessons of their elders. Historian Raul Hilberg has documented how several South American tribes became antisemitic after missionaries told tales from 'the good book' that included antisemitic passages.

The Arab antisemitic narrative owes much of its success to an undereducated, overly politicized conspiracy-prone populace. The message of Israel/Zionism/Jew as illegitimate is energizing and repeated constantly in the media, while no mention is made of the discrimination exercised via dhimmitude, the expelling of 750,000 Jews from Arab lands (post-1948), or the thousands of Jews killed in Arab pogroms prior to the birth of the State of Israel. An exclusive focus on the plight of the Palestinians (and not global Islamic fundamentalism) adds to the message's salience. Linking Arab nationalism and fundamentalist Islam has created a most effective campaign. With calls by a former Malaysian prime minister to 'stop the Jews' and the current president of Iran to have Israel 'wiped off the map', unprecedented levels of anti-Israeli sentiment and antisemitic attacks have occurred.[4]

Even children are affected by the narrative. The results from a Polish potato chip study are telling. In that study, primary school-children were handed one of three bags of potato chips. One bag was labelled as if it was from Holland. A second bag was marked Austria. A third bag was designated Israeli with a large Star of David. The children were asked to rate the taste of the chips and they responded in just that order. Dutch chips tasted best, followed by Austrian chips, while Israeli chips were judged the least tasty. All three bags contained the same chips.[5]

AT WAR WITH THE IMAGINARY JEW

From skinheads in Spokane to the devout in Damascus, far too many people believe in the antisemitic narrative. Survey estimates of antisemitism in democratic nations seem to range between 20 and 35 per cent of the population. Holland is consistently lowest, Spain and Poland highest, with Eastern Europe and Russia even higher. Antisemitism rates among Arab Muslims closer to 50 per cent in North America and 90 per cent in Arab nations.[6] Since September 2000, antisemitic hate crimes are at record highs in Canada, Germany and Australia.

The fact that antisemitism occurs in nations devoid of Jews reflects the power of social myth. People do not hate actual Jews. Rather they hate the mythical or imaginary Jew – the one handed down through history – the undermining dark force that scholars have likened to chimeras, the fire-breathing monster of Greek mythology. The duality is apparent at times. One of the first Jewish mayors in the United States was a German émigré named Julius Houseman (Grand Rapids, MI, 1832–91). He served as state representative and was elected to Congress. He was quite popular and his biographer noted that no one had anything negative to say about him except that he was a Jew. In a recent study, Arab Muslims singled out Jewish traits as 'ambitious, not trustworthy, power-hungry, ethnocentric, religiously lost, smelly, bad', though most had never met an actual Jew.[7]

The figure of the 'imaginary' Jew is even present in Ethiopia. The anthropologist Hagar Solomon has documented how the Jewish tribe Beta Israel (*falasha*) are deemed *buda* (hyenas) because of their special powers to transform themselves by night and wreak havoc on neighbouring Christian tribes. Pre-emptive measures such as the raping of women and children, beatings and ostracism were often taken and spells were cast to ward off the *falasha*'s secret powers.

It is rare, but at times such mythical aspects have worked to Jewish advantage. Oliver Cromwell was said to have made his decision to have Jews return to England based on their 'conversion and the coming of the millennium in the near future'. Japan's Fugu Plan and the Dominican Republic's decision to accept Jewish refugees during the Second World War were based on the perception of 'considerable Jewish resources and financial skill'. Even today, the Christian right's strong support of Israel is based on a belief in the Rapture, namely, the prediction in Revelation chapter 7 that 144,000 Jews must be saved as a precondition for the Second Coming of Christ.

It can be argued that antisemitic myths are more lethal than racist myths against other groups, precisely because there is no reality to them – the lack of grounding offering scope for endless fantasy. It is fantasy and much more. Antisemitic myths contain a negative emotion and a call to action. The imperative is silent but, as Sanford Nevitt reminded us, it offers the public mind what Norman Cohn aptly called a warrant for genocide.[8]

The sanctioning of genocide is retributive justice for excesses of imaginary Jews. 'The Jews damn near owned all of Germany ... that's why he [Hitler] fried six million of those guys ... he sure did clean up a lot', so explained First Nation leader David Ahenakew to Canadian aboriginals.[9] A recent *Der Spiegel* poll reveals the same sentiment, finding that 31 per cent of ordinary Germans agree with the statement 'Jews have too much power'. In democracies, Jews can remain Jews but anything can be used against them in the court of public opinion. 'They aimed at the Jews, but they hit innocent French people', Prime Minister Barre was reported as saying of the 1980 Paris synagogue bombing. Clearly, for him, Parisian Jews are neither French nor innocent. The antisemitic narrative, its fantasies and myths paved the road to Auschwitz. Indeed, only one of the four victims of the bombing was French. The others were a Chinese waiter, a Portuguese postman, an one Jew who was an Israeli tourist.

TOWARDS MATURITY AND MENTAL HEALTH

If the antisemitic narrative is akin to superstition, why consider it mental illness? In a word, because of its lethality. Throughout time, Jews have been subject to imprisonment, forced conversions, relocations, expulsions, attacks on life and limb, property damage, book burnings, persecution and mass killings. When people want to kill actual Jews in order to eradicate the imaginary ones, antisemitism becomes a mental disease. That 400,000 Jews were killed in the run-up to the Holocaust, six million during the Holocaust period (1939–45) and thousands after it, at the hands of ordinary people, suggests that there is really something quite wrong with the minds of the perpetrators.

Surprisingly, you will not get psychiatry to admit that there is something terribly wrong with the minds of racists. The views expressed by UCLA psychiatrist Daniel B. Borenstein reflect the current standard:

> The racism alone doesn't make you mentally ill. Some of the ways in which it manifests itself can be disturbing but prejudice is a normal human tendency. It would be wonderful if we could somehow decrease racism by making it a diagnosis but the diagnostic nomenclature isn't set up to cure social problems; it's set up to diagnose and treat mental disorders.[10]

And while the American Psychiatric Association recognizes coffee and tobacco addiction as a mental health problem, there is no comparable category for skinheads, neo-Nazis and hate-addicted others.

Moreover, if antisemitism were only a social problem, then it should decline with enhanced socio-economic status. Antisemitism is indeed less frequent among better-educated, successful adults. But antisemitism and all forms of prejudice do well in every segment of society. If antisemitism was based on ignorance or *naïveté*, then education should similarly stem its tide. Educated persons tend to be less prejudiced. Yet one has only to remind oneself of the educational level of those who participated in the Wannsee Conference or the 9/11 planning meetings. If antisemitism was a question of morals, then church or mosque attendance should remedy the problem. It does not. In fact, there is research to suggest the opposite. Fundamentalism and authoritarianism in religion and politics are always linked with higher levels of prejudice.

The problem is one of mental health or, more accurately, what the lack of mental health and emotional maturity does to propel hate. Are antisemitic beliefs lessened with treatment? One of the few treatment studies to date, echoed by correlational evidence, noted that the sickest patients were regularly the most antisemitic.[11]

The short answer is that we may never truly know if psychiatric treatment stems prejudice because the psychological state of the nation (and all nations) is so poor. With almost half of the general population having diagnosable mental illnesses, three-quarters received improper or no professional help.[12]

Interestingly, there is some anecdotal evidence regarding skinheads leaving hate groups. Some go on to work for anti-hate groups, but all leave for 'personal' reasons. Those personal reasons have to do with realizing that antisemitism and other forms of hate are emotional dead ends. From an adult development perspective, they move towards the next stage of maturity. And though developmental maturity is not recognized as part of mental health, it should be since mature people and mentally healthy people are the least prejudiced of all groups. Mature and mentally healthy adults are not as vulnerable to the antisemitic myths that pervade a culture. Mature and mentally healthier adults were the ones in the psychology experiments who did not administer what they believed to be electric shock treatment to others when ordered to do so. They are the ones in a genocide situation who rescue others.[13]

SOME TENTATIVE CONCLUSIONS

According to antisemitic narrative, Jews are the killers of Christ and enemies of Mohammad and undermine all that is good; Jews are said to be constitutionally inferior yet are poised for planetary takeover. Despite the contradictions, the antisemitic narrative continues unabated in the social mind. The reality of Jews is never addressed because that is the story of a people who constitute a minute segment of the world population (one twenty-fourth of one per cent; 14 million), have among the highest literacy and lowest crime rates and disproportionately achieve eminence (20 per cent of Nobel prizes in medicine/economics). Instead, the narrative is advanced.

If antisemitism pervades the cultural air of a nation, then efforts to stop the poisoning must be put into place. The fight to stop antisemitism will be an uphill battle to be sure. It is uphill because the three key fantasies of the antisemitic narrative are so ingrained in the social mind. Ordinary people ask – Why help a people who betrayed or killed God? Why help a people who are rich and trying to takeover the planet? Why help people who are lower on the social hierarchy?

Stemming the transmission of the antisemitic narrative is a start. Institutions that teach hate have to be outlawed. Religions that preach hate have to be held accountable. Free speech that hides hate has to be muzzled. At the time of writing the Internet has more than 5,000 hate pages, most of them antisemitic. And while every hate group hides behind freedom of speech, censuring those who are abusive is long overdue. Parenthetically, the precedent has been set. No one but the antisemites seems to miss Hezbollah's *al-Manar* hate transmissions after they were pulled off the air. No one can argue that the world needs more hate.

Antisemitism can also be stopped the old-fashioned way. After Iranian President Mahmoud Ahmadinejad promoted Holocaust denial and called for the destruction of Israel, his remarks were immediately condemned by the Western nations. When tribal leader Ahenakew was stripped of the esteemed Order of Canada award because of his comments about Jews, a clear signal was given that antisemitism would not be tolerated. Clearly, then, the work of the Wiesenthal Centre in monitoring and combating all such expressions of hate remains as essential today as it was when Simon Wiesenthal brought Second World War Nazis to justice.

NOTES

1. Matthew 27:25. See also R.S. Wistrich, *Antisemitism: The Longest Hate* (New York: Schocken Books, 1991); and R.S. Wistrich, 'The Devil, the Jews and Hatred of the "Other"', in idem (ed.), *Demonizing the Other* (Amsterdam: Harwood Academic, 1999), p.2.
2. G.L. Mosse, *Germans and Jews* (New York: F. Grosset & Dunlop, 1970), p.76.
3. S.L. Gilman, 'Jewish self-hatred and the believer', in H. Bean (ed.), *The Believer* (New York: Thunder's Mouth, 2002).
4. EUMC, *Perceptions of Antisemitism in the European Union*. Vienna EUMC, available at www.eumc.eu.int/eumc/index.phpfuseaction=content.dsp_cat_content&catid=3fb38a d3e22bb&contentid=4146a7b291fff.
5. A. Czyzewska, 'The Concept of Human Nature and the Readiness for Anti-Semitic Behaviour', unpublished MA thesis, University of Wroclaw, 1994.
6. S.K. Baum, 'Mythical Aspects of Antisemitism', Paper presented at ASC Holocaust and the Churches, Philadelphia, 2005; for North American rates and 90 per cent in Arab Muslim nations, see Pew Global Attitudes, available at http://pewglobal.org/reports/display.php?ReportID=206.
7. Baum, 'Mythical Aspects of Antisemitism'.

8. S. Nevitt and C. Comstock, *Sanctions for Evil* (San Francisco: Jossey-Bass, 1971); N. Cohn, *Warrant for Genocide* (London: Sherif, 1996).
9. David Ahenakew (2003), available at http://start.shaw.ca/start/enCA/News/National NewsArticlehtm?src= n070753A.xml.
10. D. Borenstein, (1999), available at abcnews.go.com/sections/living/inyourhead/alliny-ourhead_58.html.
11. M. Ostow, *Myth and Madness* (New Brunswick, NJ: Transaction, 1996); W. Bergmann and R. Erb, *Anti-semitism in Germany* (New Brunswick, NJ: Transaction, 1997). See also Baum, 'Mythical Aspects of Antisemitism'.
12. R.C. Kessler, P. Berglund, O. Demler, R. Jin, K.R. Merikangas, E.E. Walters, 'Lifetime Prevalence and Age-of-onset Distributions of DSM IV Disorders in the National Comorbidity Survey Replication', *Archives of General Psychiatry*, 62 (2005), pp.593–602.
13. S.K. Baum, 'A Bell Curve of Hate', *Journal of Genocide Research*, 6 (2004), pp.567–77.

9 The Psycho-Historical Foundations of Antisemitism

JERROLD M. POST

In 1991, during a research trip to Eastern Europe to explore the psychological consequences of the dissolution of the Soviet empire, I visited Auschwitz-Birkenau, major killing camp of the Holocaust. This was an overwhelming experience, a powerful testimony of man's inhumanity to man. Before the war, Poland was the centre of world Judaism, with some three million Jews. About 2.9 million were killed in the Holocaust, to which Auschwitz-Birkenau was a stark memorial. Whereas 30 per cent of the population of Warsaw was Jewish when the Germans invaded, in Poland in 1991, out of a population of 38 million, fewer than 10,000 were Jews, and their average age was 70.

On returning to Warsaw, I was startled to find fresh graffiti on the monument to the ghetto fighters who fought against the Nazis, proclaiming in red letters, 'The only good Jew is a dead Jew.' That afternoon, I had an interview with a prominent Catholic Polish sociologist, Slawomir Nowotny. 'How can it be', I asked, 'that there is such intense antisemitism when the Jewish population was virtually eliminated during the Holocaust?' He responded, 'Oh, we call this platonic antisemitism.' I was perplexed. He went on to explain, 'If platonic love is love without sex, platonic antisemitism is antisemitism without Jews.' He elaborated that the breaching of the Berlin Wall and the end of communist domination did not bring prosperity and the long hoped-for dividends of liberation. Someone must be blamed for the dreadful plight of the Polish citizenry, and the communist masters were no longer present, so their age-old enemy, the Jew, was resurrected. There is a powerful need for enemies, and in this case, when the old enemy disappeared, it was necessary to recreate the old scapegoat of the Jew, even though Jews were virtually absent.

Asked to contribute to this volume a piece on the psychological foundations of antisemitism, a subject with which I have long been fascinated, I have instead taken a more inter-disciplinary perspective, for I am persuaded that analysis of this phenomenon must encompass the perspectives not only of psychodynamic psychology and social psychology, but also of history, economics and culture.

Using Austria as an example, Berend Marin usefully distinguishes among four epochs of antisemitism in European history:

1. The hostility of the Christians towards the followers of their original belief, mainly justified by religion. The hostility towards the faith was not only strongly reciprocated by the Jews, but the existence of an ancient 'anti-Judaism' before the establishment of Christianity and a state religion points towards an underlying, economically motivated antipathy of a mainly agrarian social class towards exponents of a non-agrarian economy as practised by the Jews as an independent 'people-class' or commercial caste.
2. A 'bourgeois antisemitism' that came into existence during the last quarter of the nineteenth century, paralleling the world economic crisis and the appearance of political parties. This was a mass movement of the petit bourgeoisie.
3. A 'fascist antisemitism', quasi-'nationalized' during National Socialism pointedly aimed propagandistically by a totalitarian apparatus of command, which finally led to unequalled genocide. It can be seen as a calculated organization of mass irrationality by the total state. Its most immediate political consequence for the survivors and expatriates was the foundation of a national Jewish state, Israel, in Palestine, which was itself to become a new target of hostility.
4. A 'post-fascist, post-Holocaust antisemitism' after the Second World War and the defeat of Nazism.[1]

The latter is no longer an ideology in the Marxist sense. 'This "ordinary" or *gemutliche,* "everyday" antisemitism of the majority of Austrians is *the typical form of post-war antisemitism*, rather than the doctrinaire, fanatical and militant antisemitism of a minority of former Nazis and neo-fascists.'[2]

This 'antisemitism without Jews' raises important questions about the historical persistence of antisemitism. Aleksander Herz, a Polish social scientist, wrote about this in his 1988 *The Jews in Polish Culture*, observing the 'growing wave of antisemitism' against the remnants of the Holocaust.[3] Given the relative paucity of Jews remaining, he concluded that 'antagonism to certain people is not dependent on their numbers, their objective role, or their "alienness"'. As Ruth Gruber observed in a presentation on 'The New Antisemitism',[4] the hostility is directed against Jews as a concept or symbol by individuals who have had no contact with Jews. Paul Lendvai has eloquently discussed this phenomenon in his definitive study *Antisemitism without Jews*.[5] Nor was the phenomenon confined to Poland.

In the wake of the end of the Cold War, other East European nations – Hungary, Romania and Slovakia – demonstrated the same phenomenon. In Romania, before the Second World War, there were more than one million Jews. More than 400,000 Romanian Jews were killed by German and Romanian security forces. By the mid-1990s, there were only 17,000 Jews remaining, most of them elderly. Yet, intense antisemitism was manifest. Antisemitic articles appeared in newspapers, reviving the antisemitic organization known as the Legion of the Archangel Saint Michel, later renamed the Iron Guard. Their goal, announced in a widely circulated pamphlet, was to restore the 'purity of the Romanian soul which has been poisoned'. The pamphlet ended with the words, 'Our time has finally come. Heil Hitler! We shall be victorious.' There were swastikas in all four corners. When Chaim Herzog, the President of Israel, visited Czechoslovakia, the Slovak fascist party erected a plaque marking the birthplace of Father Tiso, the Catholic priest who was president of Slovakia during the one period of its functioning as an autonomous nation (1930–45). Under Tiso's leadership, Slovakia was allied with Germany and paid the Germans five hundred crowns for each Jewish man, woman and child deported to the death camps.[6] This wasn't what 'the chosen people' was supposed to mean. But indeed that very phrase embodies what some scholars consider to be one aspect of the stereotype of the arrogant, superior Jew who is different, upon whom is projected both envy and anger.

Sander Breiner, a Michigan psychoanalyst who regularly applies a psychoanalytic perspective to historical topics, has conducted a wide-ranging review of the psycho-historical roots of antisemitism.[7] He cites a number of Christian theologians. Reviewing antisemitism embedded in church writings, Reverend Robert Everett observed that 'Masses of people have been so conditioned to identify Jews in the course of centuries of Church-inspired vilification of Judaism and its leaders.' A. Roy Eckerdt in *Your People, My People*[8] went further to observe that the foundation for antisemitism and the responsibility for the Holocaust lie ultimately in the Christian Bible: 'The Church has been a seed bed of anti-Jewish thought for the general populace.' Father Gregory Baum wrote 'the Church made the Jewish problem as a symbol of unredeemed humanity; it painted a picture of the Jew as a blind, stubborn, carnal and perverse people, an image that was fundamental in Hitler's choice of the Jews as a scapegoat'.[9]

Each of the Abrahamic monotheistic religions – Judaism, Christianity and Islam – was fragile at its inception. Christianity at its foundation, a number of scholars suggest, required the image of the Jew as Antichrist. Breiner observes, 'Since the Jews rejected Christ, the Jews are now out of God's grace and are subjected to his anger and punishment, the wrath of God. The Church then says that its response is to act in the role of the hand of God to punish the Jews. The Christians are the basis of bringing the people to God and the Jews are to be rejected and forced to wander in exile and punishment the rest of their days.' In effect, at its fragile beginnings Christianity required Judaism as a counter to justify its own moral superiority, and thus the foundations of antisemitism became enshrined within Christian historical psychology. Indeed, the focused animosity at Judaism preceded the Christian era. The Jewish monotheism and 'differentness' became a motive of hostility during the period of Graeco-Roman civilization. Because of their rejection of infanticide, rejection of the abuse of slaves and of the Greek pantheon of deities, the Jews had threatened the very pillars of Greek society, and accordingly the Greeks held the Jewish people in contempt and ridiculed their religious practices, including the Jewish Sabbath, the dietary code and circumcision.

But the myth of the Jewish deicide was central to the foundations of Christianity. The disavowal of the divinity of Christ by the Jews threatened the consolidation of the fragile emerging religion, and necessitated the demonization of the Jew as the Antichrist. Audrey Droisen went so far as to assert that 'The development of antisemitism as a theory is a consequence of Christianity. Engaged in an early struggle with the Synagogue for converts in the early Christian world, the Church took to equating Jewry with the Satanic influence trying to take over the world and to stress a doctrine which identified Jews as Christ killers.'[10] The early fathers of the Church in effect asserted that since the Jews rejected Christ, the Jews are now out of God's grace and are subject to His anger and punishment of the wrath of God.[11] Breiner goes on to assert that antisemitism, pervasive anti-Jewish hostility, is the requirement of its Christian background. Mathew asserts that the Jews and all their descendants cannot receive the grace of Jesus and any forgiveness. St John Chrysostom said the synagogue was a theatre and a brothel and a place for robbers and filthy beasts and demons.

The blood libel held that Jews killed Christian children to use their blood for rituals. This belief continued into the Middle Ages, and was responsible for the massacres of Jewish communities during the Crusades. In 1348, the Black Death took nearly 50 per cent of the population of Europe. The Jews were held to be the cause of the plague, even though it was also killing Jews.

Unlike Christianity, Islam does not have as a central pillar of the faith the deicide of its founder, and in fact as one of the 'people of the Book', Jews comfortably coexisted with Muslims during the medieval and Ottoman periods, and indeed were treated rather better than Christians. There is, as Bernard Lewis notes, nothing in the history of Islam 'to parallel the Spanish expulsion and Inquisition or the Russian pogroms, let alone the Nazi Holocaust. While prejudice was always present in Islamic lands, it was often muted, rarely violent, and mostly inspired by disdain and contempt, rather than by the explosive mixture of hate, fear and envy that fuelled the antisemitism of Christendom.'[12] It was only after the end of the caliphate that hatred of Jews and intense antisemitism became enshrined within Islamic culture.

The tolerance that had been present during the period of Ottoman domination disappeared as the social structure of Islam collapsed, but the intensity of antisemitism was for the most part muted until the Arab–Israeli War of 1956, and especially after the 1967 Six-Day War. The Israeli victories in both these wars were swift and overwhelming. This, as Lewis observes, was a dilemma for the Arab world, which had depicted the Jews as weak and cowardly. 'The Jew in his very soul and character has not the qualities of a man who bears arms. He is not naturally prepared to sacrifice for anything, not even for his son or his wife.'[13] Following these humiliating defeats, antisemitic literature began to appear, which provided an explanation for how courageous Muslims could be defeated by cowardly Jews. The antisemitic classic, the *Protocols of the Elders of Zion*, is cited with increasing frequency as a definitive authority. In the founding charter of Hamas, for example, the *Protocols* are frequently cited as the basis for their absolutist eliminationist doctrine, even though some Arab writers have called their authenticity into question. As Bernard Lewis notes, they have at various times been cited by Presidents Nasser and Sadat of Egypt, Faysal of Saudi Arabia, and Gadhafi of Libya. Jews were now increasingly cited in a manner which derived from the narrative of the Christian gospels. 'They are depicted as a dark and evil force, conspiring to destroy the Prophet, and continuing as the main danger to Islam.'[14] For the Arab world, going back to the humiliating defeats of the mid-twentieth century, an additional element has become of central importance, namely the fusion of antisemitism with anti-Zionism and opposition to the State of Israel.

Numerous psychodynamic interpretations have been offered for the persistence and intensity of antisemitism. But this preceding review emphasizes the relationship between psychopolitical transitions and the fluctuations in ever-present antisemitism. When the hated communist enemies in Eastern Europe disappeared, and the social and economic crisis was not relieved but worsened, there was a resurgence of antisemitism. The Arab–Israeli conflict has provided further 'evidence' for the purveyors of antisemitism. At times of stress and psychopolitical transition, it is psychologically useful to have identified enemies on whom to blame one's misfortunes. The Jews have played this role since time immemorial.

This emphasizes the value of the 'familiar enemy'. We are comforted by familiarity and others like us. But to maintain the sense of group and self-cohesion, we must differentiate ourselves from strangers. Strangers then are necessary for our process of self-definition. Because enemies are necessary for self-definition, it is necessary to have enemies in our midst. This is the phenomenon of the 'familiar enemy'. The Greeks and Turks have lived near each other for centuries. So have India's Hindus, Sikhs and Muslims; Northern Ireland's Catholics and Protestants; Israel's Arabs and Jews. To one another, these groups remain feared – but familiar – strangers. Maintaining boundaries is the foundation of an integrated psychological, social and economic system that excludes strangers and ensures the continuity of the group. We project into strangers what we disown in ourselves. We end where they begin.[15] Especially at times of social disintegration, we cling all the more tightly to those like us, and fear and hate the stranger all the more. The situation is at its most extreme when major socioeconomic incongruity exists between adjoining groups. In other words, hostility at the boundary is most intense when one group is rich and the other is poor, so that one religious or ethnic group looks upon the other with contempt or envy.

The more different the stranger in our midst, the more readily available he is as a target for externalization. An important aspect of the development of group identity is symbols of difference shared by the other – symbols on which to project hatred. But because it is representations of the self that are being projected, there must be a kinship recognized at an unconscious level. We are bound to those we hate. Nevertheless, there must be a recognizable difference, a distinct gap to facilitate the distinction between 'us' and 'them', qualities that strongly differentiate Jews from Muslims. Those groups from which we most passionately distinguish ourselves are those to which we are most closely bound.

Enemies are therefore to be cherished, cultivated and preserved, for if we lose them, our self-definition is endangered. But this identity-creating process – a psychological necessity – results in a world populated by groups with varying degrees of animosity and fear of others. The Jew and antisemitism provide this valuable function for a spectrum of social groups under stress, and given the major societal stress with which the contemporary world is driven, intense antisemitism, unfortunately, seems guaranteed a long and intense future.

NOTES

1. Berend Marin, 'A Post Holocaust Antisemitism without Antisemites? Austria as a Case in Point', *Political Psychology*, 2, 2 (Summer 1980), p.58.
2. Ibid., p.60.
3. Aleksander Herz, *The Jews in Polish Culture* (Evanston, IL: Northwestern University Press, 1988).
4. Delivered at a conference on 'The New Anti-Semitism', held in Amsterdam on 8 April 2003 (see: http://polish-jewish-heritage.org/Eng/June03/Antisemitism-without-Jews.htm).
5. Paul Lendvai, *Antisemitismus ohne Juden* (Wien: Europaverl, 1972). English translation: *Antisemitism without Jews: Communist Eastern Europe* (New York: Doubleday, 1971).
6. R. Robbins and J. Post, *Political Paranoia: The Psychopolitics of Hatred* (Harvard, CT: Yale University Press, 1997).
7. Sander J. Breiner, 'The Psychohistorical Roots of Anti-Semitism', in Jerry Piven (ed.), *Psychological Undercurrents of History*, Volume IV (Lincoln: Writers Club Press, 2002), pp.181–280.
8. Roy Eckerdt, *Your People, My People: The Meeting of Jews and Christians* (New York: Quadrangle/NY Times).
9. G. Baum, 'Introduction', in R.R. Ruether (ed.), *Faith and Fratricide: The Ideological Roots of Anti-Semitism* (Eugene: Wipf and Stock, 1996), p.7.
10. Audrey Droisen, 'Racism and Anti-Semitism', in Emily Driver and Audrey Droisen (eds.), *Child Sexual Abuse: Feminist Perspectives* (Basingstoke: Palgrave Macmillan, 1989).
11. Breiner, 'The Psychohistorical Roots of Anti-Semitism'.
12. Bernard Lewis, 'The Arab World Discovers Anti-Semitism', *Commentary*, May 1986, p.32.
13. Ibid., p.34.
14. Ibid., p.34.
15. Robbins and Post, *Political Paranoia*, p.91.

10 Humour against Hate

YAAKOV 'DRY BONES' KIRSCHEN

The twenty-first century wave of antisemitism seems to have caught us, or at least the optimists among us, by surprise. I believe that this latest assault on the Jewish people can and must be fought. I am also convinced that humour can be an effective weapon in this war against racist antisemitism. The concept of using humour in this battle requires, first, an objective look at humour itself.

The Dry Bones political comic strip has used humour to comment on Jewish and world affairs for more than thirty years. Like most comedy communications, from comic strips to stand-up comedians, it conveys its messages in what are called 'punch lines'. The term is aggressive and implies a physical blow or punch to the audience. Comedians routinely speak of 'killing' an audience or having knocked them dead or describing them as screaming, or rolling in the aisles. These violent images arise from the true goal of humour and the real purpose of a punch line.

THE MECHANISM OF HUMOUR

The purpose of a punch line is to force an 'unspoken' message into the minds of the audience in a way that will sneak it in under the audience's intellectual or conscious defences. An unspoken message might be that women are bad drivers, that men won't ask for directions, or that TV weather forecasts are unreliable. Street humour often communicates negative stereotypical beliefs about groups; that Poles and the Irish are dumb, Jews and Scotsmen parsimonious, etc. When the newly installed unspoken message matches beliefs already held, an audience enjoys the feeling of 'confirmation', which is expressed by applause or head nodding.

The power of humour is such that even messages an audience intellectually does not want to hear or accept can hit home when communicated through comedy. The unpalatable message that we all fear the inevitable moment of death is true, but an audience recoils from it. Using humour, by contrast, Woody Allen was able to communicate the same message when he wrote, 'I'm not afraid of dying … I just don't want to be there when it happens'.

When the punch works, the hidden and unspoken message is forced into the target's mind as a belief. The successful implanting of such an unspoken belief is signalled in a number of physical ways. Interestingly, these physical signals are similar to signals of pain. Thus the target of a successful punch line will grimace, stretching his or her mouth and eventually baring the teeth. This reflex action is called a 'smile' or a 'grin'. If the instillation has been a particularly surprising one, the target will produce the barking sounds we call laughter, and which, in cases of really successful 'punches', can result in screams, tears and even loss of bladder control. This assault on the target's mind is made easier if it happens in a group setting. Laughter, we recognize, is infectious. A funny movie is that much funnier when it is viewed in a cinema full of laughing patrons. Laugh tracks added to TV sitcoms make the home viewer feel comfortable. It is as if the target finds the implanting of hidden messages more enjoyable if he or she is part of a large group being so targeted. To sum up, humour is an effective way to transmit concepts and ideas while avoiding conscious defences against those concepts and ideas.

THE PLACE WHERE ANTISEMITISM HANGS ITS HAT

Antisemitism, like other irrational loves, hates, beliefs and phobias, lives in the subconscious. If we are to combat antisemitism we need to fight it inside the subconscious, where the ability of humour to instil beliefs makes it an effective weapon.

For example, to assert that the English are prone to antisemitism invites debate. To force that same belief into the mind of a target one only needs to say, 'The English define an antisemite as someone who dislikes Jews more than is necessary'. The target smiles, the belief has been implanted, and the funny, deadpan line defies rebuttal.

The first part of the line leads the target along a predictable path. 'The English define an antisemite as someone who hates Jews'. The unexpected twist, or punch, is 'more than is necessary'. It catches the audience with its defences down. The unspoken belief that is instilled or forced into the brain of the target is 'The English dislike Jews, and consider a degree of Jew hatred to be quite proper and normal'. As usual, the grimace (smile) or bark (laugh) signals the success of the punch. For at least the duration of his or her response, the target has seen the world filtered through the reality of a newly instilled belief. If the one-liner has been heard before, the target will then smile, nod in agreement or even applaud.

With continued bombardment by similar jokes, a population will come to accept and be comfortable with the instilled belief that Poles are dumb, women are bad drivers, etc. Subconsciously, the negative stereotypes and caricatures are accepted as real and true.

Having looked at the mechanism of humour let's now examine the spread of antisemitism. For violent antisemitism to take root in a society, a prior dehumanizing and demonizing of Jews and Jewish institutions is required. The victims-to-be are identified, stereotyped and libelled. In the past, Jews were attacked because of a belief that 'the Jews poison the wells'. Today, Jews are attacked because of repeated stories (that are even reported in the media) about the Jewish state poisoning the Palestinian aquifers, or drugging bottled soft drinks in the Palestinian Authority. In this way twenty-first-century libelling of the Jewish state updates and makes clever use of traditional anti-Jewish libels to pave the way for attacks on Jews anywhere in the world. The spreaders of these age-old lies pose as politically correct and socially acceptable defenders of human rights or merely opponents of Zionism. If we are to combat the growing wave of worldwide antisemitism we need to combat the current politically correct wave of dehumanizing and demonizing the Jewish state in the media, in Western universities, in religious and intellectual circles, and wherever else it attempts to establish a beachhead.

Educators, journalists, politicians and others who are, consciously or otherwise, trying to appease Islamist anti-Jewish and anti-Western animosity, do much of the current, politically correct, demonizing of the Jewish state. In the last century, when faced with similar appeasers, Winston Churchill said 'An appeaser is one who feeds a crocodile – hoping it will eat him last'. In one clever and amusing line he put down the appeasers as cowardly losers rather than as the heroes they believed themselves to be. The question then arises as to how we can successfully fight against today's politically correct demonizers of the Jewish state. The purveyors of anti-Jewish and anti-Israeli libels present themselves and their causes as a natural extension of their yearning for 'Human Rights', their desire to support 'Peace' or their need to seek 'Justice'. The first step should be the correct identification of these urban myth spreaders as all being gullible players in the very same game, interchangeable, wearing the same colours, on the very same side. A tactic that can help us in this is the creation and use of a cartoon image or stereotype.

THE DRY BONES PROJECT

The Dry Bones Project is an NGO established in Israel that uses humour and Dry Bones cartoons to educate and fight against anti-semitism. We at the Project have created such an image. He exudes dopey gullibility. He does not represent evil. He is simply the foolish, pathetic loser who thinks of himself as a hero. In Yiddish he'd be called a shmendrik, and the use of Yiddish in this battle subliminally conveys a funny, familiar, Jewishy, putdown. The term is intentionally not in modern Israeli Hebrew, as this battle is being fought in the Diaspora and not in the Middle East. The use of the shmendrik label conveys a non-Israeli, Diaspora-Jewish feeling, which is strongly sensed by those who may not actually know what the word shmendrik means.

The Dry Bones Project first introduced the shmendrik concept via the Dry Bones Project website (www.drybonesproject.com). The announcement was for a Shmendrik of the Year Award, a competition modelled after the annual Worst Dressed List or the Razzies (the worst movie awards). The competition would hold the nominees and top three 'winners' up to public mockery and expose them as appeasers, rather than heroes. Nominations poured in from places as diverse as Singapore, Sweden, Israel, France, England, Argentina, South Korea and Oklahoma. Winners were chosen from the candidates suggested by the public. A poster of the 'winners' was issued on Purim, the Jewish holiday that celebrates with merry-making and parody the survival of the Jews in ancient Persia.

BEYOND THE SHMENDRIKS

Humour can and should be used to raise awareness of the rise in active antisemitism and to make the general public aware of its presence. As an example, the cartoon entitled 'Speaking Freely' conveys an important truth about a speech and a meeting.

To remain funny and for our humour to get across (and properly convey its messages) we must avoid painting a picture of the situation as dark, dire, grim or threatening.

Sometimes, however, it is our goal to communicate the truth about what we believe to be a grim, dire or frightening situation. The cartoon entitled the Prof Problem is an example of humorously dealing with such a problem: educators banning Jewish students because they are from the Jewish state. The ban, as is usual in these times, was presented as rising from the highest of political motivations.

The techniques we have discussed so far represent the first steps in employing humour in the fight against antisemitism and its spread.

Published in the *Jerusalem Post*, October 2003, and syndicated worldwide.

We have to expand our goals to include making antisemites and anti-semitism itself unacceptable in our societies. Jokes, cartoons, comic books and the Internet can aid in this effort to use humour to push back the Jew-hatred. The cartoon samples are taken from an underground comic book distributed freely on the Internet. One tactic yet to be examined is the creation and distribution of antisemite jokes (as opposed to antisemitic jokes). The antisemite would be the butt of these jokes.

A new and deadly war against the Jewish people has been thrust upon us. Humour is one weapon in our arsenal. Its use should support and compliment ongoing activities by serious workers in the field. If analysis shows Mark Twain to have been correct that anti-semitism is rooted in a fear of Jewish superiority, humour 'proving'

Published in the *Jerusalem Post*, and syndicated worldwide.

the superiority of Jews or the Jewish state could be counter productive. The work done by dedicated organizations and individuals in
analysing antisemitism should be used as a guide in our structuring
and shaping the messages we pack into our punch lines.

11 Antisemitism and Anti-Westernism in the Women's Movement

PHYLLIS CHESLER

Today, the academic postcolonial literature is infected, as with a virus, by an across-the-board view of Palestinians as the symbol of all things noble and the Jews and Israelis as symbols of evil. The Palestinianization of the Western academy began in earnest in the late 1960s or early 1970s. Initially ground-breaking views about gender and racial inequalities became increasingly influenced by Marxist views and gradually came to constitute what is now known as the 'postcolonial' academy. Race replaced both class and gender as primary concerns. European and North American academics, including feminists, actively propagandize students against America and against Israel – which means that in reality they are choosing tyranny and gender apartheid over democracy and human rights for women. Many feminists are not as concerned with the 'occupation' of women's bodies worldwide as they are with the alleged Zionist occupation of Palestinian lands.

For example, according to Professor Emeritus Leila Beckwith, the University of California at Santa Cruz (UCSC) has had a 'steady stream of anti-Israel speakers funded by the university' and sponsored by at least 'ten different university departments'. In 2004 women's studies at UCSC sponsored a talk by International (Palestine) Solidarity Member, Hedy Epstein, who compared Israel to a Nazi state and excused suicide bombings. But they refused to sponsor speakers who wanted to address the lives of women in Muslim countries.

I have previously written about a women's studies conference that took place at the University of New Paltz in 2002. Their keynote speaker was Ruchama Marton, a Jewish Israeli psychiatrist. She likened the Israelis to 'batterers' in a marriage, equating the

Palestinians with 'battered wives'. In so doing, did she intend to misapply hard-won feminist knowledge about battering and also render the specifics of Palestinian and Israeli suffering quite invisible?

Many Developing World academic feminists, such as Bengali-American academic Gayatri Chakravorty Spivak and Palestinian academics Lila Abu-Lughod and Suha Sabbagh, view any feminist who dares criticize Islamic gender apartheid as a colonialist, racist crusader. Sabbagh's 1996 anthology focuses on Palestine far more than it focuses on any other Islamic or Middle Eastern country.[1]

Why is this important? Because when feminists are 'Palestinianized', they tend to ignore the abysmal status of women (and men) in every other Arab and Muslim country.

However, what is just as important as the pro-Palestinian bias of the Sabbagh anthology is its failure to deal with the psychological and economic realities of polygamy, son preference, gender segregation, female genital mutilation, and honour killings; nor does Sabbagh explore the collaborative role that women play in such honour killings.

Western feminist journalists, activists and philanthropists follow suit. The feminist position vis-à-vis the Developing World, the Middle East and Islam began as an essentialist one. All women were sisters who faced a common enemy: men or patriarchy. All women were sisterly, and no one collaborated with patriarchy. All sisters were moral and peace-loving. But as identification with the oppressed and multiculturalism gained more and more influence, feminist essentialism adapted. Thus, while women were still all sisters, some sisters were more equal than others. Formerly colonized women became more equal than Euro-American women.

Another way that Western feminists could properly atone for their culture's racism was to savage Judaism as a religion, Israel and America. For example, Amnesty International, like so many other international and humanitarian agencies, is anti-Israel. In a 2005 report, 'Israel and the Occupied Territories: Conflict, Occupation and Patriarchy. Women Carry the Burden', Amnesty attributes the lion's share of Palestinian female suffering to the Israeli occupation – not to Islamic gender apartheid.[2]

A number of feminists whose work I respect and with whom I have worked have a deeply ambivalent, tortured and ultimately 'cold' relationship to Judaism. Andrea Dworkin (may she rest in peace) is one; Robin Morgan is another. Dworkin understood antisemitism, but then she was highly critical of Zionism and was also anti-religious. In a novel, Dworkin once compared the Jewish God to a Nazi without mercy. In a work of non-fiction, she compared the Jewish state to a 'pimp' and a 'John' and viewed the Palestinians as their 'prostitutes'.

In 1989, Morgan published a book titled *The Demon Lover: The Roots of Terrorism.*[3] It was reprinted again, post-9/11. The book glorifies the Palestinian cause and romanticizes the United Nations Relief and Works Agency for Palestine Refugees (UNRWA).

Morgan profusely thanks seven different UNRWA functionaries for having arranged her trip and guided her through the Palestinian 'camps'. Having UNRWA do this would have been like having the Soviet-era and KGB-controlled Intourist organize your trip to Moscow any time between 1920 and 1980.

Camps? Morgan does not write 'refugee neighbourhoods' or 'Palestinian- and Arab-enforced ghettos'. Rather, she uses the term 'camps'. Is this word chosen to remind one of 'concentration camps' or 'death camps'? In reality most Palestinians live in cities; some live in luxurious villas, others in dreadful poverty. They do not live in tents or cages.

The British-born and American-based feminist journalist Jan Goodwin has written an important book about women in the Muslim world: *Price of Honor: Muslim Women Lift the Veil of Silence on the Islamic World.*[4] Goodwin is not one to hide her prejudices. The revised paperback edition opens with a map of the known Middle Eastern and Muslim world, and Israel is not on it; only Gaza and the West Bank are shown (Muslims also live in Israel).

Goodwin also views most of the grievous problems of Palestinian women as mainly due to the Israeli 'occupation'. She views the suicide terrorism against Israel civilians as 'ultimate acts of political self-sacrifice' and as 'dramatic' expressions of how 'desperate the situation and the polarity between Arab and Jew have become'. In her opinion, this has led 'Palestinians (to become) walking weapons of terror as a means to narrow the military gap'.

Goodwin claims that the Israeli military policies of self-defence have emasculated Palestinian men, who in turn have therefore taken their frustrations out on Palestinian women and children. But here Goodwin was contradicted. In 1992, Jean Sasson published *Princess: A True Story of Life Behind the Veil in Saudi Arabia*. The unnamed al-Saud princess (whose story Sasson tells) describes the typically cruel way in which fathers, brothers and husbands treat their 'womenfolk':

The authority of a Saudi male is unlimited; his wife and children survive only if he desires. In our homes, he is the state ... From an early age, the male child is taught that woman are of little value ... the child witnesses the disdain shown his mother and sisters by his father; this leads to his scorn of all females ... [the] women in my land are ignored by their fathers, scorned by their brothers, and abused by their husbands.[5]

Saudi Arabia has not been 'settled', 'colonized' or 'humiliated' by Israelis. Like many feminists, Goodwin attempts to present the Prophet Muhammad as kinder and fairer to women (or to his own wives) than many of his followers have been – which may actually be true. For example, Goodwin writes that the Prophet married many women in order to forge alliances 'with tribes who had been bitter enemies of Islam'. Her only example given is that Muhammad married a Jew, one Safiya bint Huyay. According to Goodwin, this marriage to the 'daughter of an important Jewish chief, for example, diminished Jewish opposition to the Prophet's mission'.

According to the work of Bat Ye'or, Muhammad systematically attacked, exiled, ransomed or slaughtered those Jews who refused to convert to Islam; he also confiscated their property. In 624, Muhammad did this to the Jews of Medina (the Qaynuqa), and the following year to the Jewish Nadir tribe. In a private conversation in 2003, Bat Ye'or confirmed that Safiya (whom Goodwin refers to) was taken captive by Muhammad after he slaughtered her father, her husband and her entire tribe.

Is marrying the man who has slaughtered your husband and father Goodwin's feminist view of what constitutes peace-oriented marriage? Does her feminist critique of forced marriage apply only to Muslim women and not to Jewish or Christian women?

Columbia University professors Lila Abu-Lughod and Gayatri Spivak, among others, reject the Western feminist 'fixation' on the veil and, in an intellectual and territorial power struggle with Western academic feminists, insist that modern Western feminism is, essentially, 'colonial feminism'.[6] Abu-Lughod and others suggest that Muslim female relatives, including co-wives, may bond, keep each other company, share isolating and repetitive tasks, and so on. Sounds good – but neither research nor personal memoirs supports this theoretical possibility.

Dutch parliamentarian Ayaan Hirsi Ali is a Muslim feminist who has challenged crimes against humanity committed in the name of

Islam. In 2005, left-feminist Deborah Scroggins published an article in *Nation Magazine* entitled 'The Dutch–Muslim Culture War: Ayaan Hirsi Ali has Enraged Muslims with her Attacks on their Sexual Mores'. Scroggins, apparently, does not see Hirsi Ali as a hero but as a reactionary – as part of an anti-immigration, anti-Muslim and anti-Islam faction that includes the assassinated politician and homosexual Pim Fortuyn, and the assassinated filmmaker Theo van Gogh.

In classic left-feminist fashion, Scroggins attacks Hirsi Ali for 'putting all the blame on Islam', instead of blaming 'patriarchal customs; and for failing to focus on the role the West has played and continues to play in assisting the rise of the Islamist movements'.[7] Hirsi Ali's crime is, perhaps, her refusal to rant against the West's history of colonialism and imperialism and against its ongoing racism – as if doing so will somehow lessen or effectively appease the rise of Islamism; or, as if appeasing Islamists as they blow up and behead civilians constitutes a useful action. Scroggins actually views Hirsi Ali's passionate and feminist defence of both Muslim women and European culture as 'contributing' both to the rise of Islamism – and, paradoxically, to anti-Muslim and anti-Islamic sentiment.

In June 2004, I was the first pro-democracy feminist guest on Pacifica's KPFK radio station in Los Angeles. After years of on-air Jew-hatred and Israel-bashing on KPFK, the programme *Feminist Magazine*, run by a feminist collective, had taken a principled position against this unacknowledged form of racism and had invited me to discuss my views on antisemitism, Israel, democracy and Islamic gender apartheid. I said the kinds of things that I am saying in my books *The New Anti-Semitism* and *The Death of Feminism: What's Next in the Struggle for Women's Freedom* – and all hell broke loose. Even while we were still on air, the switchboard lit up with angry feminist listeners. That was only the beginning. Feminist calls mounted for the censure and removal of *Feminist Magazine* from the air or for other feminists to take over the program. An online protest petition was launched against my remarks. A Los Angeles-based group made a bid to take over the collective.

In October 2004, a small group of San Francisco-based feminist activists travelled to Duke University in Raleigh-Durham, North Carolina, to support the Palestine Solidarity Movement Conference that took place there. It would be one thing if such feminists had come to protest Palestinian abuses against women. But they did not have a balanced or particularly feminist agenda. Although many activists were lesbians and/or pro-gay, they had not come to protest the Palestinian persecution of suspected gays in Gaza or the West Bank; nor did they seem to know that Israel has granted political asylum to Palestinian gays, including those who have been tortured and nearly killed by other Palestinians. Instead, these American feminists wore political buttons and T-shirts that read 'We are all Palestinians'.

The cult-like popularity of sacred Palestinian victimhood is very great. It has cast its spell over too many good feminists. The spell has been woven by particularly adept spell-weavers and master linguistic reversalists.

In the decade in which Robin Morgan visited the West Bank and first wrote and published *The Demon Lover* (the 1980s), Palestinian terrorists repeatedly attacked civilians, synagogues, airplanes and cruise ships. Targets spread to Jews and Jewish institutions, as also to Americans worldwide. And then al-Qaeda attacked the World Trade Center and the Pentagon on 11 September 2001.

However, in her post-9/11 afterword, Morgan does not dwell on any of this. Immediately after 9/11, what concerns her and so many other feminists is not America's vulnerability but the vulnerability of Muslims in America. She is worried about the possible lynching of Muslims in America. In the 2001 afterword to her book, Morgan compares the grief and mourning of post-9/11 New Yorkers who are now 'unnerved' by security checkpoints, who feel 'terrified, humiliated, outraged' – to her friends in the refugee camps of Gaza and the West Bank: 'Palestinian women who have lived in precisely that same emotional condition for four generations'.

At the end, Morgan compares herself to a woman named Aziza, in the Gaza Strip. Although oppressed and 'compressed', Aziza still manages to plant flowers. Aziza tells Morgan that the 'soul needs to be fed too'. And in the shadow of the demolished World Trade Center, our American, faux-Palestinian feminist bravely goes out and plants some flowers in Greenwich Village in New York City.

American and Western feminists wear the keffiyah in many ways. It is a way of trying to 'pass' as Developing World hero-victims or at least as champions of Developing World victims. But, in doing so, they are leaving behind any feminist vision of universal human rights for both women and for men.

Abu-Lughod, like her Columbia University colleague, Gayatri Spivak, views a Western-style fight for women's rights in the Muslim world as a dangerous diversion. She recommends that we continue to focus mainly on the 'colonial enterprise'. Why? Perhaps as a way of reminding Western thinkers – heirs to the colonial adventure – that, given their ancestors' past crimes, they dare not feel 'superior' to the Islamic world and above all, dare not intervene to free Muslim prisoners from Muslim jailors, or African slaves and female sex slaves from their tormentors.

I am among a handful of both Western and Eastern feminists who humbly but adamantly question this approach. In fact, let me suggest that the difference between Eastern (or Arab, Muslim or Asian) feminism and Western feminism has become exceedingly vague. For nearly forty years elite Developing World women have mingled with elite Western women at United Nations-sponsored conferences. Pro-Palestinianism and anti-Americanism have become *the* universal point of view for diplomats and for feminist academics and activists everywhere. The uniformity of the politically correct feminist vision and voice represents a great loss – because everyone is speaking the same politically correct universal language from which a universal concept of human rights, even for women, has been utterly banished.

Like men, women also internalize sexist views. Similarly, feminists, both men and women, internalize the left-European view of both Jews and Israel, even though such views contradict feminist principles about human rights, equal rights and democracy. Thus, the failure of feminists to resist Jew-hatred and the demonization of Israel reflects a tragic collective reality that is in no way specific to feminist ideology. However, when the alleged truth-tellers fail the truth; when the alleged independent thinkers spout propaganda and rhetoric, it endangers us all.

NOTES

1. Suha Sabbagh, *Arab Women: Between Defiance and Restraint* (New York: Olive Branch Press, 1996).
2. Amnesty International, 'Israel and the Occupied Territories: Conflict, Occupation and Patriarchy: Women Carry the Burden, March 2005, AI Index: MDE 15/016/2005. Jerusalem Center for Public Affairs.' Amnesty International Exploits Women's Rights, NGO Monitor, distribution@n.g.o.monitor.org, 20 April 2005.
3. Robin Morgan, *The Demon Lover: The Roots of Terrorism* (New York/Washington: Square Press,1989; reissued 4 December 2001 with New Introduction).
4. Jan Goodwin, *Price of Honor: Muslim Women Lift the Veil of Silence on the Islamic World* (New York: Plume, 2002).
    More recently, Human Rights Watch, for the first time, described the rise in violence against women in Gaza and on the West Bank and did *not* attribute it to the Israeli occupation but to the rise of Islamic fundamentalism among the Palestinians. Human Rights Watch, *A Question of Security*, Volume 18, No. 7(E), November 2006, http://hrw.org/reports/2006/opt1106/opt1106webwcover.pdf.
5. Jean Sasson, *Princess: A True Story of Life Behind the Veil in Saudi Arabia* (USA: Sasson Corporation; New York: William Morrow, 1992).
6. Lila Abu Lughod, 'Feminist Longings and Postcolonial Conditions' and 'The Marriage of Feminism and Islamism in Egypt: Selective Repudiation as a Dynamic of Postcolonial

Cultural Politics', both in Lila Abu Lughod (ed.), *Remaking Women: Feminism and Modernity in the Middle East* (Princeton, NJ: Princeton University Press, 1998); Gayatri Chakravorti Spivack, *Outside in the Teaching Machine* (New York: Routledge, 1993); Gayatri Chakravorti Spivack, *In Other Words: Essays in Cultural Politics* (New York: Routledge, 1988); Gayatri Chakravorti Spivak, 'Can the Subaltern Speak?' in Cary Nelson and Lawrence Grossberg (eds), *Marxism and the Interpretation of Culture* (Urbana: University of Illinois Press, 1998), pp.271–313.
7.   Deborah Scroggins, 'The Dutch–Muslim Culture War: Ayaan Hirsi Ali has Enraged Muslims with her Attacks on their Sexual Mores', *The Nation*, 27 June 2005, pp.21–25.

REFERENCES

Bin Laden, Carmen, *Inside the Kingdom: My Life in Saudi Arabia* (New York: Warner Books, 2004).
Goodwin, Jan, *Caught in the Crossfire: The True Story of an American Woman's Secret and Perilous Journey with the Freedom Fighters through War-Torn Afghanistan* (New York: E.P. Dutton, 1987).
Morgan, Robin, *Saturday's Child* (New York: W.W. Norton, 2001).
Morgan, Robin, *Sisterhood Is Global: The International Women's Movement* (New York: Anchor Press/Doubleday, 1984).

12 Common Ground for Hatemongers: Incitement on the Internet

RONALD EISSENS

Remember the first website you ever visited? I do. It was the site of *The Louvre*, one of the first museums that built a website or, as we all called it during those days, a 'home page'. I still vividly remember the small images or 'gifs' on a grey background. Magical. We did not imagine then that this beautiful new tool would also be used for evil. It was 1995 and we'd been on the Internet for a short time, I think from early 1994 on, in a text-only environment provided by the Dutch *Digital City* DDS, which looked very much like the Bulletin Board Systems of old, providing amongst other things a number of thematic newsgroups or discussion groups, on which the users of this first Dutch 'Internet Community' could post news, opinions or just gossip and discuss subjects. Even on this text-only virtual peninsula of the Internet, where progressive *cybernauts* promoted 'changing the world through communication', all was not well. Within a few months after the 'birth' of the *Digital City* old human failures surfaced. This host-site was abused as hate was spread by some of its users, with as its low point the posting of the text of the infamous Nazi anthem, the *Horst Wessel song*. With that, and with the subsequent actions my organization Magenta Foundation took against this, much of the stage was set for things to come on the Internet. I don't think it was the first time that racist or Nazi material was posted on the Net, but it certainly was the first time action was taken to get the material removed or to prosecute an author of online hate speech. Magenta Foundation was by no means the first one working on the issue. Organizations like Nizkor.org and the Simon Wiesenthal Centre were among the pioneers. But Nizkor, based in the then dominant part of the Net, North America, believed foremost in taking action by countering disinformation about the Holocaust and by unmasking neo-Nazi groups. 'Good speech' as an antidote to 'bad speech'. As I said, at that time the Net was predominantly American-based, with which came freedom of speech American-style, annoying to some, a cult to others. For years after, the public debate on the issue of cyber hate would be dominated by those who wanted the Net to be a totally free haven where anything should go which would prove right those who claimed that Auschwitz wasn't built with bricks but with words.

More than ever since the Holocaust, hate and its ideologies are alive and well, giving rise to violence, misery, conflict, murder, genocide and war. Humanity is repeating its historical mistakes, seemingly unable to learn from the past. The political climate in this world is hardening. The contemporary problems are not only antisemitism, racism, Muslim-hate, jihadism, terrorism and other forms of hate, but also the fact that the ideas of citizenship and universal human rights values are by and large being abandoned in favour of ethnic, religious and political agendas, spawning more of the 'us and them' feelings on which extremists and fundamentalists thrive. Moderates on all sides are either not being heard or have to shout so loudly that they are being lumped together with the extremists, the same extremists who use the Internet as their tool of choice for recruitment and propaganda.

The popularity of the Internet with extremists should really be no surprise. It is the biggest information and communication device in the world. Neo-Nazis saw the potential of the Net in its very early stages, using Bulletin Board Systems (BBS) in the pre-world wide web age[1] and moving onto the web in full force from the beginning. By now, the number of extremist websites runs in the tens of thousands. Hate on the Net has become a virtual nursery for real life crime, the 'real life' bit becoming a moot point, since the Internet is an integral part of society, not a separate entity, as some protagonists of 'cyberspace' like to claim. The Internet is just the latest – and possibly the greatest – among communication and dissemination tools which can, like any other tool, be used or abused. Incitement through electronic means is no different from incitement by traditional means, be it a paper pamphlet with the text 'Kill all Jews' being handed out in the streets or a website containing the same message. The end result is the same, violence against Jews. The linkage between racist speech and violations of individual civil liberties is as topical as newspaper headlines.[2] What's more, to some of us it is an everyday reality. Little sparks can kindle big fires, as has been proved time and time again, most recently by all the hate speech and dehumanization that was dished out by the media (including the Internet) during the Balkans war, conditioning the public to support any new conflict,[3] and by radio stations during the Rwanda genocide. I'm afraid that we will find out soon that the same hate-mongering is playing a part in the ongoing genocide in Darfur. To quote Simon Wiesenthal, 'Technology without hatred can be a blessing. Technology with hatred is always a disaster.'

But you don't even have to look at war zones to see the effects of incitement through the Internet. Hit lists targeting groups in society, individuals or organizations, conspiracy theories, defamation, Holocaust denial, it's a long list and the effects can be terrible. Attacks on Jews in Russia and France, firebombing of synagogues, attacks on homosexuals and anti-fascists in Sweden, attacks against Muslims, mosques and anti-fascists in the United Kingdom, jihad-recruitment in the Netherlands, death-threats by e-mail against Asians, racially motivated murders and shooting sprees in the United States – all incited through websites and web forums. Neo-Nazis have been using the Internet from the beginning to spread their hate, but also to recruit, to incite racial violence, to deny the Holocaust, partly in order to make national socialism a 'respectable' option again. They use it also as a means for research into their 'opponents' and for command and control; steering marches and actions, for online *Denial of Service* attacks against websites they hate, racist e-mail spam-actions, concerted efforts to put defamation or misinformation into public discussion forums and last but not least for manipulation of online polls.

Since the rise of Islamism and jihadism there is an increasing over-lap between Islamist and neo-Nazi rhetoric when it comes to anti-semitism and Holocaust denial. Documents such as the *Protocols of the Elders of Zion* or Richard Harwood's *Did Six Million Really Die?* can be found on extreme-right-wing sites but also on Islamist or left-wing websites, uniting natural enemies in their joint struggle against the 'Zionist world conspiracy'. The common ground for online hate-mongers is called Jews. The Internet caters for most of their needs. Antisemitism and Holocaust denial currently account for a large part of all the online hate, a part that is rapidly growing. There are thousands of hate sites and new ones are brought online every day, promoting violence, denying historical facts, poisoning and recruiting. On top of that, a vast amount of hate is being disseminated through discussion forums, peer-to-peer networks, mailing lists and chat boxes. Today's antisemitism has a larger breeding ground, perpetrator group and audience than ever before. That conclusion meets with irritation, resistance, politically correct pussyfooting and sometimes outright denial. Some do not like to hear that others than the extreme right are capable of antisemitism, but the facts speak for themselves. If it isn't a Moroccan web forum screaming that they are really not antisemitic despite all the antisemitism they allow on their site, it is the left-wingers like the Indymedia webforum, who think that antisemitism is really anti-Arabism since, wait for the old canard, 'Arabs are semites'. Anti-racism and human rights have long been left-wing subjects, but antisemitic undertones and at times overtones were never an uncommon thing in the left. Where before you could only find a limited amount of left-wing antisemitism, after the disastrous 2001 World Conference Against Racism (WCAR) in Durban, South Africa, which turned into an antisemitic hate-fest, the masks came off. Blatant antisemitism on left-wing sites is now quite acceptable, of course prudently called 'anti-Zionism'. Some left-wing sites even link to antisemitic content on neo-Nazi sites. Four days after the WCAR another hate-fest took place, 9/11. In my mind those two, the WCAR and 9/11, will always be linked, not in the least because of another vile branch of the antisemitic tree that was created in its wake; 'the Jews are behind 9/11'. By now, five years later, there are thousands of websites claiming this. Don't take my word for it. Just enter 'the Jews are behind 9/11' in Google.

There is a strong tendency to publish or show anything on the Internet, no matter if it is defaming, inciting or racist. The dominant model seems to be hedonistic rather then freedom-loving – anything goes, as was proved a few months back when the gruesome video 'Housewitz', in which the Holocaust is trivialized and ridiculed as a dance-party, was published on a Dutch web forum. The Internet being what it is, the popular Dutch 'schock-log' GeenStijl immediately copied the video clip, after which it spread all over the world. Although the Dutch Complaints Bureau for Discrimination on the Internet (MDI) and other members of the International Network Against Cyber Hate (INACH) got rid of a number of the copies, and the creator of the video, a 22-year-old student, was convicted for racism and defamation, the damage was done.

The Internet is the biggest soapbox in the world. Anyone can use it to publish anything, with the result that people who would not dare air their views in real life find their outlet in publishing them on the Internet, thinking they are totally anonymous. The Internet is also the big recycler. Once something is online, it is quite hard to get rid of it for good. The boost the Internet gave to the *Protocols of the Elders of Zion* is enormous. Created over a century ago by the Czarist secret police to stir up Jew-hatred, the *Protocols*, a so-called 'Zionist plan for world conquest through Jewish world government', has now thanks to the Internet been made readily accessible and become a bible for antisemites. Twenty years ago, virtually nobody had ever heard of the *Protocols*, which at that time had almost disappeared. Now they are back with a vengeance. There's even an Egyptian TV series made based on the *Protocols*, which is a big hit in Arab countries. Hate on the Internet is like a crime that's being committed over and over again.

Not that everybody agrees about the harmfulness of cyber hate – some would like to think that all speech should be freely published, all the more glory to the 'marketplace of ideas'. For me, coming from a continent that survived the Holocaust, this is really out of the question. As the European anti-racist maxim goes, 'Racism is not an opinion, it's a crime', or to quote Sartre on antisemitism, 'it is not an idea as such, it's a passion'.[4] After the 2004 murder of Dutch publicist and filmmaker Theo van Gogh, it was noted belatedly that online incitement and threats against him read as a *chronicle of an announced murder*. On top of that, the murder led to incitement on the Internet to firebomb mosques and kill Muslims, which resulted in a violent wave of arson attacks and attacks on Muslims in the Netherlands. So much for harmless free speech! I do recognize and support free speech as an important value in any democratic society. However, I strongly oppose free speech extremism, the idea that even incitement to violence and murder can be considered free speech. People tend to think that freedom of speech and the prohibition of hate speech is contradictory. It's not. The UN International Covenant on Civil and Political Rights[5] clearly states in its article 20 that:

> any advocacy of national, racial or religious hatred that constitutes incitement to discrimination, hostility or violence shall be prohibited by law;

while article 19 states that:

> everyone shall have the right to hold opinions without interference. Everyone shall have the right to freedom of expression; this right shall include freedom to seek, receive and impart

information and ideas of all kinds, regardless of frontiers, either orally, in writing or in print, in the form of art, or through any other media of his choice. The exercise of the rights provided for in paragraph 2 of this article carries with it special duties and responsibilities. It may therefore be subject to certain restrictions, but these shall only be such as are provided by law and are necessary: (a) For respect of the rights or reputations of others; (b) For the protection of national security or of public order (ordre public), or of public health or morals.

Clearly 143 countries think that those are not opposing or conflicting obligations. In fact, most constitutions of Western states contain an article prohibiting hate speech or discrimination, in close conjunction with one guaranteeing freedom of speech. Even the Constitution of the United States (and for that matter, US jurisprudence), much quoted by freedom of speech advocates, does recognize situations in which hate speech can be harmful and should be illegal, for the simple fact that whereas freedom of speech is a condition for a successful democracy, tolerance is essential for the survival of democracy and social cohesion. As freedom of speech goes hand in hand with the responsibility to have respect for the rights and/or reputations of others, we need to be extremely careful when setting limits on freedom of speech, but we also need to be very careful about giving hate-mongers, extremists and terrorists free rein. History has proven that censorship lurks around the corner but has also proven that free speech without ethics and responsibility can have deadly and devastating consequences. Were we to allow hate speech to run rampant, democracy would ultimately be destroyed and tyranny would result, bringing with it the abolition of free speech.[6]

At the present time, the number of instances of hate speech on the Net is quite staggering. The latest Simon Wiesenthal Centre CD, *Digital Terrorism and Hate 2006,* identifies almost 6,000 'problematic' websites, portals, online games, blogs, forums, etc. The 15-country-strong International Network Against Cyber Hate counted some 12,000 known instances of hate on the Net in 2005, and that is just the tip of the iceberg. A 'normal' popular web forum has 1,000-plus postings per day, of which at least fifty are of a racist or antisemitic nature. There are thousands of web forums like that. If you add the few thousand *extremist* web forums that generate hundreds of hateful expressions *per day*, the total volume of hate on the Net is quite staggering. It really makes you want to unplug and throw your PC out of the window at times, but that might not be such a good idea, as the chances are it will be caught by Nazi skinheads returning from their daily spree of Jew, gay or Muslim-bashing. Yes, the amount of *real life* violence is also getting out of hand in Europe.

Countering hate on (and off) the Net, trying to heal the world, feels like Sisyphus, rolling that rock uphill for eternity. Hate is not something we will ever get rid of, so a long hard battle that may result in a somewhat better world is what we're in for. Sixty years after the Holocaust we have a thriving Holocaust denial industry and the same mistakes are being made again and again. Education is the magic word, but for that to be successful we need to convince politicians that education nowadays is failing. More and more students use unfiltered information from the Internet, not knowing if the information is correct or not, clueless about which sources are legitimate and which are propaganda. A search on Google on 'gas chambers' will lead you to, amongst other sites, the Holocaust-denying Institute for Historical Review. Guidance is called for, either by parents or by teachers. But most teachers are not very Internet-savvy, are overworked, underpaid and interested in just getting through the day. Plus, sixty years after, what do *they* know about the Holocaust? A recent poll in the Netherlands shows that 83 per cent of the Dutch think that the Holocaust was *the cause* of the Second World War! Some teachers are not even willing to talk about the Holocaust in class, for fear of being attacked by students of North African descent, who are not exactly happy with subjects that have 'Jews' written all over them. As for the parents, most of them also lack the knowledge, time and tools to make a difference.

Not all is gloomy. There are lots of excellent projects and initiatives, mostly coming out of the non-governmental sector. Looking at the current Internet cyberscape we see a number of international NGOs dealing with cyber hate. The Simon Wiesenthal Centre, Nizkor, INACH and countless others work hard to monitor and counter online hate, to have it removed from the Net and to educate Internet users. Since 1997 our Dutch Complaints Bureau for Discrimination on the Internet has succeeded in eliminating more than 4,000 instances of hate, some 48 per cent being antisemitism and Holocaust denial. All removal of hate content was on a voluntary basis, meaning that the authors of the material were presented with a choice: either remove the material or face possible legal consequences.

The International Network Against Cyber Hate, of which the

Dutch Complaints Bureau is a member, has secured the removal of more than 9,000 expressions of hate since its founding in 2002, initiated a number of court cases and secured the conviction of more than sixty online antisemites, Holocaust deniers and racists. INACH has members in Denmark, France, The Netherlands, Canada, Germany, Moldova, Poland, Switzerland, Russia, Slovakia, Great Britain, Belgium, Spain, Sweden and the United States. By using the various national and international anti-hate speech legislations, INACH aims to curb the communication of hate speech, thereby preventing the recruitment of others who do not yet hate, and prevent real life hate crime. The issue of free speech versus combating hate speech does not really arise in INACH, which is a practical and flexible network geared towards possibilities rather than debate on seemingly opposed issues.

INACH also concerns itself with education. Young people especially run the risk of being misled, indoctrinated and recruited, thus making educational efforts imperative. As the use of the Internet in schools increases, students seeking information are confronted with racist and antisemitic websites or sites with otherwise discriminatory content. Teachers and parents need help and advice on how best to filter and assess information in order to protect and guide children and students. At the same time educators themselves need a reference guide. To that end, Dutch INACH member Magenta Foundation and German member Jugendschutz.Net have created educational CD-ROMs with practical information on how to recognize and combat racism, antisemitism and discrimination on the Internet. The CDs include teaching modules, explanations of the different kinds of online hatred, manuals on the extreme right, racist symbols and rhetoric commonly used by racists to recruit youngsters, facts about prejudice about minorities, examples of what is happening on the Internet, tips on how to assess websites and what can be done when encountering hate on the Internet. The CDs use a multi-layered approach to make them suitable for use by teachers, parents and (high) school kids.

If you can speak about successes in the daily fight against cyber hate, then INACH network is a success. It is not funded by any European or governmental body, runs virtually on air and owes its success to the commitment and work of its members. INACH activities include: monitoring and removal of hate speech, recruitment and training of new network nodes, development of comparatively-based monitoring and reporting mechanisms, research into specific cyber hate issues, advocacy for codes of conduct for cyberspace, advocacy for (existing) international legislation to combat cyber hate and awareness-raising. If you look at the sheer volume of hate on the Net every successful removal of hate speech is a small victory. But at times you can really 'strike a big blow on the side of the angels' as a Russian colleague likes to say. Such was the case with the shutdown of Front14, an extreme-right 'living room' provider, actually a guy sitting in Alaska, running a server on a private cable connection, hosting hundreds of Nazi sites for groups all over the world. After hammering on his provider for six months, his connection was finally shut down, causing the immediate and simultaneous disappearance of a few hundred Nazi sites. Success like that is much needed, if only to keep up morale.

When the Dutch complaints bureau started in 1997, as the first bureau of its kind in the world it only took a few weeks before the extreme right, the extreme left and anybody just 'extreme' tried to shut us up and shut us down. Assisted by freedom of speech activists, cyber hippies, communication gurus, 'Internet journalists' and some Internet Service Providers they decided that we were trying to 'destroy the Internet', dubbed us 'thought-police' and 'Gedanken Gestapo' and started a harassment and slander campaign which occasionally still flares up. Those working in this field have a high burnout rate, what with all the sheer misery of having to deal with huge amounts of hate every day and with the slander, insults and threats. It's not only successes all the way. Often we just can't get rid of some material, which is extremely frustrating. But Simon Wiesenthal was at it a lot longer than us, against greater odds. That's something we keep in mind.

WHAT IS NEEDED?

Advocacy on all levels, nationally and internationally in bodies like the OSCE, UN, Council of Europe and EU is needed. INACH has already undertaken in some efforts to achieve this and has made some progress, but we need a collaborative endeavour to sensititize politicians, make them aware of the magnitude of the problem; we need training of police forces and justice departments, financial support for NGOs that monitor and combat cyber hate, money for education and educational projects that counter hate; and last but not least, we need to reach out to the Internet industry and work with them in creating codes of conduct. We need to do all that soon; all over the world the forces of intolerance and extremism are marching again, extremist groups and parties are gaining electoral support and the political will to act on hate is rapidly dwindling. Simon Wiesenthal's work was 'a warning for murderers of tomorrow'. Let's try to not need a Simon Wiesenthal again.

NOTES

1. The Germany-based Thule-Netz BBS, which started operations in 1993. IDGR Lexikon Rechtsextremismus, http://lexikon.idgr.de/t/t_h/thule-netz/thule-netz.php.
2. David Matas, *Bloody Words, Hate and Free Speech* (Winnipeg: Bain & Cox, 2000), p.21.
3. Panayote Elias Dimitras, *Hate Speech in the Balkans* (Vienna: International Helsinki Federation for Human Rights, 1998), p.8.
4. Jean-Paul Sartre: 'L'antisémitisme ne rentre pas dans la catégorie de pensées que protège le Droit de libre opinion ... D'ailleurs c'est bien autre chose qu'une opinion. C'est d'abord une passion' [Antisemitism does not fall within the category of ideas protected by the right of free opinion ... it is something quite other than an opinion. It is first and foremost a passion]. *Réflexions sur la question juive* (Paris: Morhion, 1946), Chapter 1, p.10.
5. 1966, signed and ratified by 143 countries. See http://www.unhchr.ch/html/menu3/b/a_ccpr.htm.
6. Matas, *Bloody Words, Hate and Free Speech*, p.38.

13 Antisemitism on Campus: A View from Britain

GEOFFREY SHORT

ORIGINS OF THE CURRENT CONCERN

Following the outbreak of the second intifada in September 2000, antisemitism in Britain's universities became a major concern for Anglo-Jewry.[1] The issue had not previously evoked much interest within the community, despite the Union of Jewish Students (UJS) warning from the mid-1990s about the activities on campus of the fundamentalist Muslim group Hizb ut-Tahrir.[2] Its leadership strenuously denied any suggestion of antisemitism, claiming its comments on Jews related solely to those resident in, or otherwise supporting, Israel. Such denials met with a sceptical response from the UJS whose campaigns organizer at the time was Paul Solomons. In a letter to the *Jewish Chronicle*, he pointed out that:

> In January (1994) at a meeting of the School of Oriental and African Studies a Hizb al-Tahrir activist stated: 'Let's be open about this – the Koran does not mention Zionists, it mentions Jews. They are our enemy and, *insha allah* [God willing] we shall kill them.' And at the City University, one of Hizb al-Tahrir's leaders ... announced to his audience: 'The Holocaust is a fabrication.' In a leaflet distributed on one university campus this year, Jews are referred to as, 'the lowliest people on earth', and in another leaflet Judaism (not Zionism) is called 'a purely racist doctrine'.[3]

In the 1990s the impact on the Jewish community of events of this kind was limited; a reflection, perhaps, of the failure of British society as a whole to recognize the problem of antisemitism in universities. Typifying the general lack of awareness was a comprehensive report commissioned by the Runnymede Trust entitled *A Very Light Sleeper: The Persistence and Dangers of Antisemitism*.[4] While noting the strength of antisemitism among sections of the clergy and its influence on environmental groups and on the New Age movement, the report made no mention of the prevalence of antisemitism on campus. It failed to do so despite acknowledging the malevolent ideology behind Hizb ut-Tahrir.

The second intifada has transformed the situation in the sense that universities in Britain (and in other liberal democracies) are now seen by many commentators as sites of 'the new antisemitism'.[5] In contrast to the classical strain – hostility, bigotry and discrimination directed against Jews *qua* Jews – the new antisemitism refers to criticism of Israel that is illegitimate and intended to demonize the state. In the words of journalist Melanie Phillips:

> Israel's history is routinely denied or ignored, so that the defence against attack that it has been forced to mount since its inception is falsely represented as aggression. Double standards are applied so that Israel is damned for its behaviour while silence is maintained over countries doing far worse. Impossible expectations are made of Israel that are applied to no other country in such circumstances. It is the target of systematic and egregious lies and smears. It is presented in the worst possible light by people who display an eagerness to believe that all its actions are malign, even when the facts clearly refute such assumptions.[6]

In recent years, press coverage of a number of incidents has revealed the diverse nature of the new antisemitism afflicting British universities. Individual academics have articulated criticisms of Israel or taken measures against their Israeli counterparts that are regarded by many within and beyond the Jewish community as unwarranted and unjust. There has been relentless pressure for a boycott of Israel's universities and, latterly, Israeli academics who refuse to criticize the policies of their government have been threatened with international isolation. In addition, Jewish students have been intimidated and generally made to feel insecure in ways explicitly documented in written evidence submitted by the UJS in 2004 to the Parliamentary Select Committee on Home Affairs. Numerous cases of hostility were cited, including messages sent through websites at Birmingham and Lancaster universities warning of violence and possible death. More often than not, the content of these messages was linked to Israel. Elsewhere in its submission the UJS reported 'skullcaps being knocked from people's heads; screwdrivers through letter boxes and knives in doors; anti-Semitic graffiti; verbal abuse (and reports) of students being followed'.[7] Concern was also voiced about what was said to be 'the clearest example of anti-Semitism on campus', namely, motions debated in student unions throughout the country equating Zionism with racism in order to stigmatize and proscribe Jewish societies. 'In most cases, tensions were stirred up ... and a number of anti-Semitic incidents took place'.[8]

The UJS also made plain its unease about 'extremist groups on or around campus who are anti-Semitic, and have a history of anti-Semitic rhetoric and behaviour'. Not surprisingly, its testimony focused in part on Hizb ut-Tahrir, observing that while the movement had been banned by the National Union of Students (NUS) it had reappeared under various guises. Another group causing concern was al-Muhajiroun, led by (the now exiled) Sheik Omar Bakri Mohammed. Thought to be especially active at the universities of Manchester, Nottingham and London, it had held rallies in support of 11 September and its members were alleged to have been involved in the antisemitic attacks surrounding the motions referred to above. The UJS also condemned the activities of the far left, noting its collusion with Islamist extremist groups such as the Muslim Association of Britain.

The NUS itself has not escaped censure. On the contrary, it has been reproached on account of its miscalculating the serious tide of antisemitism on campus. This led to the resignation in 2005 of two Jewish members of the executive, Luciana Berger and Mitch Simmons, and a member of the steering committee, Jonny Warren. To convey their sense of anger and sadness at the union's 'apathy to anti-Semitism', I cite below an abridged version of Berger's final address to conference. At the time, she was the Union's anti-racism convenor.

> Some of you still remember five years ago at my first conference when I stood front and centre as a student having to address the floor after being spat at because I was Jewish. I was unanimously supported and applauded. Not one person stayed seated. I mistakenly believed I had a place in my national union. Some of you may remember five, four, three and two years ago, when Jewish students had to be escorted from the building by the back door for fear of their safety.

I have seen Jews accused of conspiring to write, submit and debate motions we had no part in, by full time members of the National Executive Committee (NEC). This year, I have suffered baseless accusations of NUS being pro-Jewish and therefore biased because I tackled antisemitism where it stood. There was no defence of Jewish students by NEC members who heard those claims. This year, a comment was made in a Student Union meeting saying that burning down a synagogue is a rational act. When asked to comment, NEC members could not even bring themselves to condemn that statement. Over five months ago serious complaints were lodged about antisemitic comments made by an NEC member in a public meeting. There is yet to be any form of official response to these complaints.

When it was rumoured that I, a Jewish student, was standing for the NUS Presidency, whispers of antisemitism were used as a political football. While I accuse no one of antisemitism, this year NUS has been a bystander to Jew-hatred. In the past three days, at the heart of our democratic union, to my horror, I have seen the events of the year replayed. At the beginning of this conference I stood here and warned you against the (British National Party) presence in Blackpool. But it is within these walls I feel most afraid. We have talked for the past three days about NUS' values of equality, diversity and respect. In practice this could not be further from the truth.

... If anyone were to stand up here and allege the Jews are an evil, manipulative people who want to control the world, there would no doubt follow rounds of furious speeches supported by endless clapping. I hold in my hand a leaflet which was readily available on one of the stalls in this building for two days, which alleged just that ... In the past, people have attacked the role of UJS in this national union, alluding to Jewish conspiracies and excessive power ... There was a time when our Jewish societies were banned from campuses around the country to the applause and support of NUS national conferences held in this very hall. It is my sincere hope that the events of this past year, and especially these past few days, do not signal a return to the politics of hate in the broader student movement. UJS will not rest until NUS stops treating antisemitism as second grade racism.

... The leadership of NUS needs to take big decisions and choose whether Jewish students have a place in this national union. It is the leadership of NUS who must decide if they are happy to accommodate NEC members who undermine Jewish colleagues and obstruct conference policy mandating against antisemitism ... Is NUS prepared to demonstrate the leadership required now, which will enable Jewish students to hold NUS positions of responsibility in the future?

... I cannot and will not be a part of a National Executive Committee while some of its members continue to turn a blind eye to Jewish student suffering. I would be betraying those people who elected me to represent them. Therefore I, alongside my Jewish colleagues Mitch Simmons and Jonny Warren of steering, officially resign from our NUS posts.[9]

ACADEMICS AND THE NEW ANTISEMITISM

Media reports over the past few years have exposed the intense antipathy felt by some academics towards Israel and, at the same time, have reinforced Jewish students' sense of insecurity. Press interest focused initially on the activities of Mona Baker, Egyptian-born Professor of Translation Studies at what was then the University of Manchester Institute of Science and Technology (UMIST) and is now part of an enlarged University of Manchester. She had sacked two Israelis, Miriam Schlesinger and Gideon Toury, from the editorial board of a couple of scholarly journals that she owned, apparently on the basis of their nationality. The university investigated the case but took no action against her. She remained on the staff of UMIST alongside a former colleague and sympathizer, Professor Michael Sinnott. He had previously sent an e-mail to a Harvard academic in which he expressed support for Baker and described Israel as the 'mirror image of Nazism', for which he has since apologised.

Another case attracting much publicity involved Andrew Wilkie, Professor of Pathology at Oxford University. In 2003 he was approached by an Israeli student, Amit Duvshani, who enquired about studying for a doctorate. Wilkie refused to consider his application after discovering that he had served in the Israeli army. He sent Duvshani the following email.

Thank you for contacting me, but I don't think this would work. I have a huge problem with the way that the Israelis take the moral high ground from their appalling treatment in the Holocaust, and then inflict gross human rights abuses on the Palestinians because they (the Palestinians) wish to live in their own country.

I am sure that you are perfectly nice at a personal level, but no way would I take on somebody who had served in the Israeli army. As you may be aware, I am not the only UK scientist with these views but I'm sure you will find another suitable lab if you look around.[10]

The response of the university to Wilkie's email was unequivocal. A spokesperson made clear that:

under no circumstances are we prepared to accept or condone conduct that appears to, or does, *discriminate against anyone on grounds of ethnicity or nationality, whether directly or indirectly* [emphasis added]. This candidate is entitled to submit an application and to have it dealt with fairly according to our normal criteria.[11]

Controversy was also provoked at Birmingham University by Sue Blackwell, a militant campaigner for an academic boycott of Israeli academic institutions. The UJS, in its written submission to the Parliamentary Select Committee on Home Affairs, alleged that Ms Blackwell had 'links from her personal Birmingham University page to a website propagating conspiracy theories surrounding the 9/11 attacks, notably that Israel was their true perpetrator' – a claim current on Arab websites and satellite television that wreaked havoc on Muslim–Jewish relations, especially in Europe.[12]

ACADEMIC BOYCOTTS

The first rumblings of an academic boycott surfaced in 2002 when Stephen Rose, Professor of Biology at the Open University, wrote to the *Guardian* newspaper urging a moratorium on European funding of Israeli research. This was followed later in the year by the Association of University Teachers (AUT) passing a motion at its summer conference that instructed its Executive Committee 'to give consideration to the severing of academic links with institutions in Israel if their armed forces ... (in any way) ... disrupt access of (Palestinian) students and staff to their teaching and research'.[13] Support came from Britain's largest lecturers' union, the National Association of Teachers in Further and Higher Education (NATFHE) whose General Secretary stated: 'We have urged all UK Universities and colleagues to review – with a view to severing – their academic links with Israel.'[14] The AUT campaign gathered momentum and at its 2005 conference voted to boycott Bar-Ilan and Haifa universities because of their alleged complicity in the policies of the Israeli government. The move sparked an international outcry and threats of counter-boycotts, as well as much internal dissension. A month later a special conference rescinded the earlier decision.

Recently, NATFHE voted narrowly in favour of boycotting Israeli lecturers who do not publicly dissociate themselves from their government's policies vis-à-vis the Palestinians. Specifically, the motion criticized 'Israeli apartheid policies, including construction of the exclusion wall, and discriminatory educational practices' and invited members to 'consider the appropriateness of a boycott …'.[15]

CROSSING THE LINE?

It is frequently asserted that criticism of Israel is not necessarily anti-semitic. In light of this self-evident truth, the question that needs to be asked is whether the events adumbrated above that have occurred on a number of university campuses in Britain in recent years can fairly be described as antisemitic. In some cases, such as those detailed in Solomons' letter to the *Jewish Chronicle* and in Berger's resignation speech at the NUS conference, there would seem to be little doubt that they can be. Other cases, however, are, *prima facie*, more ambiguous. As Professor Peter Pulzer puts it:

> How can we know when a particular speaker, writer or cartoonist has crossed the line from objective, rationally grounded criticism of Israeli polities to the use of anti-Semitic allusions or codes? This is a question of identifying not the old-fashioned Jew-baiter – we all know what he looks like – but the anti-Semitic wolf in anti-Israeli sheep's clothing.[16]

In answer to his own question, Pulzer recommends the use of a ten-point checklist. Consistent with Phillips' definition of the new antisemitism, he argues that, in the first instance, speakers or writers can be deemed to have crossed the line from anti-Zionism to anti-semitism if, *inter alia*, they 'compare the Sharon government with Nazism and the Israeli army's actions with the SS, genocide and holocaust, or South African apartheid'. Many of Israel's critics fall at this hurdle, for example, Tom Paulin, the Oxford University poet. He wrote about 'another little Palestinian boy gunned down by the

Zionist SS' and went on to accuse Brooklyn-born Jewish settlers in the West Bank of being Nazis.[17] In December 2004 he was a keynote speaker at a conference held at London University's School of Oriental and African Studies (SOAS) entitled 'Resisting Israel Apartheid Strategies and Principles'.

According to Pulzer, writers or speakers are also guilty of anti-semitism if they 'demand boycotts and sanctions exclusively against Israel or Israeli institutions, but not the many more deserving objects of such measures world-wide'.[18] It is this criterion that provides the strongest grounds for condemning the hostility currently shown towards Israel in universities as antisemitic, for the critics are rarely, if ever, heard denouncing the Russian intervention in Chechnya or the Chinese domination of Tibet. Likewise, those who campaign vociferously for Palestinian statehood are silent on the plight of the Basques, the Kurds and the Turkish Armenians. And when it comes to the issue of settlements, they focus obsessively on the West Bank (and previously on Gaza) while ignoring the 1974 Turkish invasion of northern Cyprus, the ethnic cleansing that accompanied it and the replacement of the Greek population over the following quarter of a century by 100,000 Turks (mainly from Anatolia).

Alan Dershowitz, the American academic who has argued passionately for a less jaundiced attitude towards Israel, has compiled his own set of criteria intended to help distinguish antisemitism from anti-Zionism. His list is significantly longer than Pulzer's and, in contrast to the latter, includes as antisemitic any attempt to delegitimate Israel.[19] David Cesarani, among others, has also stressed the importance of this criterion, for in his view, a defining feature of the new antisemitism is 'the unique denial to the Jews of any right to nation-hood'.[20] Prominent academics who have violated this criterion include Tom Paulin, who is on record as saying, 'I never believed that Israel had the right to exist at all. It is an artificial state.'[21] Similarly, Sue Blackwell is reported to have confessed that the academic boycott's true objective is to strike a blow at the 'illegitimate state' of Israel.[22]

ENDNOTE

In the course of this essay I have concentrated on the rise of the new antisemitism in British universities and have discussed and illustrated its various manifestations. While it would be fair to say, at the time of writing, that the new antisemitism has eclipsed the old, it would be a serious misjudgement to regard the latter as having no contemporary relevance. Traditional antisemitism, principally in the form of the British National Party (BNP), remains a potential threat to Jewish students. In November 2004 the BNP was banned from Manchester University after revelations that it was attempting to recruit on campus and, in 2006, a BNP council election candidate was sacked as an assistant warden at a Plymouth University hall of residence because of the racist contents of his weblog. He was found to have posted statements on a student forum denying the Holocaust. More recently Gilad Atzmon addressed a meeting of the Palestinian Society at SOAS. Despite his Jewish heritage and Israeli nationality, Atzmon appears to accept the authenticity of the *Protocols of the Elders of Zion*, for, in 2003, he is reputed to have said, 'We must begin to take the accusation that the Jewish people are trying to control the world very seriously'.[23]

At present, incidents of this kind that are historically associated with right-wing ideologues pose less of a problem for Jewish students than those associated with the far left and with Islamist groups. Nonetheless, they contribute to the atmosphere of intimidation facing Jewish societies and students on campuses throughout Britain and, for this reason alone, should not be lightly dismissed.

NOTES

1. I use the term 'Anglo-Jewry' to refer to the Jewish population of England, Scotland and Wales.
2. *Jewish Chronicle*, 28 Jan. 1994.
3. *Jewish Chronicle*, 12 Aug. 1994.
4. Runnymede Trust, *A Very Light Sleeper: The Persistence and Dangers of Antisemitism* (London: Runnymede Trust, 1994).
5. P. Chesler, *The New Anti-Semitism: The Current Crisis and what we must do about it* (San Francisco: Jossey-Bass, 2003). P. Iganski and B. Kosmin (eds), *A New Antisemitism: Debating Judeophobia in 21st Century Britain* (London: Profile Books, in association with the Institute for Jewish Policy Research, 2003).
6. M. Phillips, 'Christian Theology and the New anti-Semitism', in Iganski and Kosmin (eds.), *A New Antisemitism*, pp.192–212: pp.193–4.
7. House of Commons Home Affairs Committee, *Terrorism and Community Relations* (London: The Stationery Office, 2005).
8. D. Cesarani, 'The Left's anti-Semitism can't go unchallenged', *The Times Higher Education Supplement*, 2 June 2006, p.19.
9. Full text of statement made by Luciana Berger to NUS Annual Conference available online at www.educationet.org/messageboard/posts/47449.html.
10. Available online at www.bmj.com/cgi/content/full/327/7405/12-b?etoc.
11. 'Comments by Professor Andrew Wilkie', University of Oxford Press Office, 27 June 2003.
12. House of Commons Home Affairs Committee, *Terrorism and Community Relations*.
13. P. Curtis, 'Lecturers' Conference opens with an attack on Clarke', Guardian Unlimited, 7 May 2003.

14. J.D.A. Levy, 'The Academic Boycott and anti-Semitism', in Iganski and Kosmin (eds), *A New Antisemitism*, pp.249–57: p.251.
15. P. Baty, 'Natfhe tackles rise of racism', *The Times Higher Education Supplement*, 13 May 2005.
16. P. Pulzer, 'The new anti-Semitism, or when is a taboo not a taboo?', in Iganski and Kosmin (eds), *A New Antisemitism*, p.96.
17. Paulin cited in W. Pickett, 'Nasty or Nazi? The use of anti-Semitic topoi by the left-liberal media', in Iganski and Kosmin (eds), *A New Antisemitism*, pp.155, 156.
18. Ibid., p.96.
19. A. Dershowitz, *The Case for Peace: How the Arab–Israeli Conflict can be Resolved* (New Jersey: John Wiley & Sons, 2005).
20. Cesarani, 'The Left's anti-Semitism can't go unchallenged', p.19.
21. O. Abdel-Latif, 'That Weasel Word', *Al-Ahram Weekly On-Line*, 4–10 April 2002.
22. M. Taylor, P. Curtis and C. Urquart, 'Lecturer defends Israeli boycott plea on eve of vote', *Guardian*, 22 April 2005. J. Pearl, 'Worse then anti-semitism', *Jewish Chronicle*, 3 Nov. 2006, p.35.
23. Cited in D. Aaronovitch, 'How did the far Left manage to slip into bed with the Jew-hating Right?', *The Times*, 28 June 2005, p.18.

14 Admission is not Acceptance: Reflections on the Dreyfus Affair

GEORGE WHYTE

Paris 1789: Declaration of the Rights of Man and the Citizen. Article 10:
No one shall be disquieted on account of his opinions, including his religious views, provided their manifestation does not disturb the public order established by law.

Paris 1894: Conviction of Alfred Dreyfus, a Jewish Officer in the French Army, for a crime of treason of which he was innocent. He was stripped of his rank, publicly degraded and banished to Devil's Island where he was imprisoned under inhumane conditions. The fight for his innocence lasted twelve years. The Affair rocked France, split the country and unleashed racial hatred. Its repercussions were felt worldwide for decades to come and continue to this day.

THE PRICE OF ILLUSION

As Captain Alfred Dreyfus adjusted his uniform every morning, he saw in his mirror the reflection of a proud French Officer. When he arrived at General Staff headquarters, he was perceived as a Jewish officer. He did not see, or want to see, that admission was not acceptance. This was the bitter lesson to be learned from the misfortunes of the assimilationist officer.

Enjoying a successful military career, life still smiled on Alfred Dreyfus in 1894. He had married Lucie Hadamard who bore him two children. At the age of 35, he was a captain in the French Army and, albeit a Jew, posted to a General Staff largely inhabited by a cadre of staunch Jesuit officers. Dreyfus, impervious to the prejudice around him, was soon to pay the price of illusion.

On 15 October 1894 Alfred Dreyfus was arrested, accused of selling military secrets to Germany. He was convicted on false evidence and sentenced to public degradation and lifelong imprisonment on Devil's Island.

'Death to the Jews' drowned the protests of Alfred Dreyfus during his degradation as he was stripped of his rank, his honour and, ironically, the very ideals which had guided his life – love of the army and devotion to the Patrie. His ordeal was to last twelve years and the so-called Dreyfus Affair it precipitated was to become one of the most troubled periods in the history of France, recording for future generations a far-seeing testimony of the social turbulence of the times.

BACKGROUND TO THE AFFAIR

The influx of foreigners and Jews into France met with increasing antagonism from the population. The country was being invaded by 'vagabonds, peddlers and upstarts'. In an atmosphere of growing xenophobia, the people resented this 'pollution' of their land. The theme of *Those without a Country* was to be heard again and again counterpointed with *France for the French.*

Antisemitism, always lurking within a Christian culture, gathered pace when the writer Edouard Drumont, who was to become known as the 'Pope of antisemitism', arrived on the scene. The Catholic Church and its organ *La Croix* had long maintained an anti-Jewish stance and the venom of Drumont would drive their bigotry to fever pitch. 'To be French was to be Catholic'. Protestants, Freemasons and above all, Jews were suspect.

Trading on the Gospels, which had led to the accusation of deicide against the Jewish people, Drumont regurgitated all the groundless calumnies levelled at the Jews over the centuries, from which a stereotype emerged, a Judas figure, increasingly despised and increasingly embedded into the culture of Christian Europe. A professional antisemite, he knew that the Jews, a defenceless minority, were never in a position to challenge these allegations. Unchallenged allegations hardened into fact and the Jew became, by definition, guilty. As in the case of Alfred Dreyfus, evidence never reached the scales of justice but was moulded to corroborate the prejudice.

THE AFFAIR

A deliberate miscarriage of justice, masterminded by the army, condoned by its judiciary, fuelled by racial prejudice, political skulduggery and a nascent press combined to create the Dreyfus Affair. Variously classified as a French affair, a Military affair, a Family affair, a Jewish affair – it was all of these and more.

The Dreyfus Affair went far beyond the confines of France at the turn of the twentieth century, beyond too, the story of the innocent Captain Alfred Dreyfus, the unwanted Jew on the French General Staff. It was a series of events that brought into the spotlight a host of political, social and moral issues. It split France in two, saw the emergence of the intellectual and the engagement of the citizen and paved the way for new forms of civic and political expression. Its repercussions were and remain worldwide. Further afield, the Affair became a crucible for a host of human rights issues such as racism and the rights of the individual against the organs of state. Today, the Affair remains a touchstone for issues of primary importance for our societies.

Above all, the Affair was a warning signal highlighting the fragility of human rights in our most 'developed' societies. Although it is arguable whether antisemitism was the most significant aspect of the Affair, it was this aspect whose significance became paramount in the century that followed, when human rights were desecrated to the point of annihilating a whole people. It is therefore vital to examine the power of prejudice and its mechanism, as revealed in the Dreyfus Affair.

ALFRED DREYFUS

Dreyfus recalls in his diary how, as a young boy, he cried with sadness as he watched the German Army march into his home town Mulhouse during the Franco-Prussian War. He swore to become a soldier and drive the enemy from his country. No longer burdened with the name of Abraham or Israel, like his Orthodox forefathers who had arrived a century earlier from Rixheim to the land of human rights, Alfred kept his promise and began the long march of an assimilationist Jew to become a successful French officer. In so doing, he overstepped the threshold of tolerance in a hostile terrain, which was to lead to his persecution as a Jew.

By misjudging admission as acceptance, Dreyfus became an accomplice to his own martyrdom, prefiguring the fate of many Jews fifty years later who also felt secure in their national aspirations of being German, French or Hungarian.

How often did Dreyfus experience expressions of antisemitism and how often did he ignore its warning in the Jew's desperate attempt to be accepted as an equal? What was the mechanism which blinded his yearning and ambition to the dangers around him? Did he not read Drumont's rantings in his *La France Juive*, a tirade of bigotry and loathing?[1] Was he not aware of the editorials in *La Libre Parole* warning against the admission of Jews into the army? Did he really not realize that he was living in a society in which antisemitism had become part of its fabric? Did he think he was immune from the longest libel in history? Silent, whispered or spoken, the same indelible *J* branded him, just like his forefathers before him and the generations to follow. And, although in a unique moment of history the injustice to one Jew became a world affair, its lessons were to remain, and still remain, unlearned.

VISIONARIES AND FOREBODINGS

The conviction of Alfred Dreyfus left many minds unconvinced. The Jewish thinker, Bernard Lazare, was soon to publish his clandestine pamphlet *L'Erreur Judiciaire* in Belgium, followed by his treatise on antisemitism. He was unequivocal:

> did I not tell you that Captain Dreyfus belonged to a class of pariahs? He was a soldier, but he was a Jew, and it was as a Jew above all that he was prosecuted. Because he was a Jew he was arrested, because he was a Jew he was indicted, because he was a Jew he was convicted, and it is because he is a Jew that the voices of truth and justice cannot be raised on his behalf.[2]

Lucie Dreyfus, the loyal and devoted wife, despairing for the life of her husband, petitioned Pope Leo XIII:

> Lucie Eugénie Dreyfus, prostrate at the feet of your Holiness, most humbly supplicates the mercy and compassion of the Father of the Catholic Church. She declares that her husband is innocent, and the victim of a judicial error. Snatched from all association with humankind as he is, this petition is signed by his grief-stricken wife, who, in tears, looks towards the Vicar of Christ, even as formerly the daughters of Jerusalem turned to Christ Himself.

Lucie's supplication remained without response.

Emile Zola, increasingly convinced that there had been a miscarriage of justice, began to voice his doubts and his articles appeared in rapid succession. He deplored that young minds had already been infected by the poison of antisemitism. He addressed the youth of France

> Oh Youth, youth! I beg you consider the great task which awaits you. You are the architects of the future.
> Youth, youth! Remain always on the side of justice. If the concept of justice were to fade within your soul, you will be open to grave dangers.
> Youth! Youth! Be humane. Be generous.[3]

Zola was to be ridiculed, mocked and caricatured but became the inspired spokesman for the cause of justice:

> Here is the black soul, the abominable figure, the traitor who sells his brothers as Judas sold his God. And, if no reason is found to explain the crime, is it not enough that he is a Jew?[4]

He published his letters to France and addressed the nation:

> France how have your people succumbed to such fear and sunk to such depths of bigotry?
> France, you have allowed the rage of hatred to lash the face of your people, poisoned and fanatic they scream in the streets 'Down with the Jews', 'Death to the Jews'.[5]

Antisemitism was at fever pitch. Zola was relentless:

> A hidden poison has led us to delirium. Hatred for the Jews – there lies the guilt, the daily ritual, recited year in year out in the name of morality, in the name of Christ. Fresh minds infected by this poison declare they will massacre all the Jews.
> What sorrow, what anxiety at the dawn of the twentieth century.[6]

The journalist Theodor Herzl, reporting for the *Neue Freie Presse* in Vienna, was horrified by the mass hysteria at the degradation:

All the unleashed fury has been reserved for Dreyfus. If it had been possible, the rabble would have rolled him in tar, cut him to pieces, committed I know not what torture! And why? They were no longer cries of vengeance for a military treason which normally would barely excite the mob in times of peace. This explosion of anger was of a quite different nature and was like the excesses of a gang of rioters and people in revolt. They took scant account of the accusation. They were not screaming 'Down with Dreyfus!' but 'Down with the Jews!' It was like that from the beginning and so it continued ...

Do people really believe that the devourers of Jews, who have tested their strength on the unfortunate Dreyfus, will be content with a single victim? They have acquired a taste for blood and will ask for more, with all the more assurance and avidity since they have become aware of their own irresistible power.[7]

Herzl's transformation from an assimilationist to a Jewish visionary was eloquently described by Stefan Zweig in his *The World of Yesterday*:

In Paris, Theodor Herzl had had an experience which convulsed his soul, one of those hours that change an entire existence. As a newspaper correspondent he witnessed the public degradation of Alfred Dreyfus, had seen them tear the epaulettes from the pallid man while he cried aloud: 'I am innocent.' At that moment he knew in the depth of his heart that Dreyfus was innocent and that he had brought the horrible suspicion of treason on himself merely by being a Jew.

At the moment of Dreyfus's degradation the thought of the eternal exile of his people entered his breast like the thrust of a dagger ... If we suffer because of our homelessness, then let us build our own homeland! And so he published his pamphlet, 'The Jewish State', in which he proclaimed that all attempts at assimilation and all hope for total tolerance were impossible for the Jewish people.[8]

Paradoxically, it was the interaction of two assimilated Jews, one French the other Austrian, that inspired the manifesto for a Jewish homeland *'Judenstaat'* which was to alter the course of Jewish history. Herzl gave his summary of the Affair:

the importance of the Dreyfus Affair, which has become an abstract symbol representing the Jew in the modern world, who had tried to assimilate into his environment, who speaks its language, approves its ideas, conforms to its spirit and finds himself suddenly exposed to violence. Dreyfus signifies a strategic position which has been fought over, is still fought over, but is already lost ... let us admit it frankly.[9]

But Edouard Drumont had preceded both Zola and Herzl. He was to found the National Antisemitic League of France whose statutes would include:

The National League of Antisemites in France has the purpose of defending the spiritual, economic, industrial and commercial interests of our country with all appropriate means.

Propagating the truth in broad daylight and employing social means, the league will fight the pernicious influence of the financial sway of the Jews whose clandestine and merciless conspiracy jeopardises the welfare, honour, and daily security of France.

Excluded from membership are:

1 Jews

2 Jewish renegades

Drumont railed against the admission of Jews into the Army:

Apart from all religious considerations, amongst the huge majority of soldiers there is an instinctive feeling of repulsion towards the sons of Israel. They see in them the usurer who causes the ruin of the debt-laden officer, the supplier who speculates on a soldier's stomach, the spy who traffics shamelessly in the secrets of national defence.

Already masters of finance and of administration, dictating rulings in the tribunals, they will finally become the masters of France on the day they command the army. Rothschild will have the mobilization plans sent to him, one can well imagine with what aim.

Planting the signpost which would eventually lead to Drancy, France's deportation camp, he predicted with spine-chilling accuracy:

The Jews have to be eternally blind as they have always been not to realize what is awaiting them. They will be taken away as scrap and the people that they oppress so harshly, that they exploit with such ferocity, will dance with joy when they learn that justice has been done.

The leader who will suddenly emerge incarnating the idea of an entire nation will do whatever pleases him. He will have the right of life and death. He will be able to employ any means that suits his purpose. The great organizer, who will unite resentments, anger and suffering, will achieve a result which will resound throughout this universe. He will return to Europe its prestige for 200 years. Who is to say that he is not already at work?

Jews throughout the world mourned the fate of yet one more Jewish martyr while the Jews of France were stunned into silence fearing that the shame of one would be visited on them all. Dreyfus, lingering in his cell on Devil's Island, clutching a small photo of his wife and children, his talisman, ravaged by disease and depression, tortured with double shackles, tried to hold on to life.

J'ACCUSE

Then came the bombshell, the publication of *J'Accuse*. The sham trial and acquittal of the suspected traitor Esterhazy incensed Zola beyond measure. *J'Accuse* roared across the headlines of the newspaper *L'Aurore* on 13 January 1898 to become the watershed of the Dreyfus Affair and history's most famous plea for human rights. The anti-Dreyfusards closed ranks and the knives were out. Zola was indicted and tried. Georges Clemenceau addressed the Jury:

> We stand before you, gentlemen; you will give your verdict shortly. All we ask is that you should demand and uncover the truth. The truth belongs to no party; it is the right of all men. Without the truth, Mr Zola can do nothing. With a grain of truth, he is invincible. Give us, give to the people of France who await it, the truth, the whole truth. France's good reputation in the world demands this.

Foreseeing the emergence of the totalitarian state, he warned:

> When the right of a single individual is injured, the right of all is in peril, the right of the nation itself.

Zola, undaunted by the animosity around him, concluded his testimony:

> Before France, before the whole world I swear that Dreyfus is innocent, and by my forty years of work, by the authority this labour has given me, I swear that Dreyfus is innocent. And by all that I have gained, by the name which I have made for myself, by my work which has helped to enrich French literature I swear that Dreyfus is innocent. May all this crumble, may all my work perish if Dreyfus is not innocent! He is innocent!

Zola would be abused, vilified and stripped of his Légion d'Honneur. He was the friend of a traitor (whom he had never met!), he was a foreigner in the services of an alleged syndicate, he was in the pay of the Jews. Emile Zola, the tireless fighter for justice, was convicted.

The Affair had now reached its explosive phase and would engulf the whole country. Its tremors were to be felt throughout the civilized world. Justice was now on trial on the world stage of human rights. As evidence gathered in favour of Dreyfus, the fight for a retrial was won and the most intensive period of the Affair was unleashed. At Rennes, the site of the second court martial, effigies of Alfred Dreyfus were burnt by uncontrolled mobs. Hatred was mobilized into song with pride of place reserved for the National Hymn converted into *La Marseillaise Antijuive:*

> Take up your arms antisemites! Form your battalions!
> March on! March on!
> Let their tainted blood drench our fields!

Endless caricatures, verses and songs were created in an ever-more vicious circle of abuse. The country was in turmoil, society was divided, families were split. Dreyfusards clashed with anti-Dreyfusards. Violence was in the air. Antisemitic riots ravaged the cities of France. Synagogues were ransacked, shops were pillaged, people attacked. Back in Paris, Jules Guérin, head of the antisemitic League, was roaming the streets with his People's Army. His headquarters at Fort Chabrol churned out the poisoned pen journal *L'Antijuif* and became a veritable factory of venom. A whole catechism of abuse was disgorged by the antisemitic press in a stream of scurrilous texts.

With the innocent officer found guilty again at Rennes, the anti-Dreyfusards were vindicated but world opinion was outraged. Zola was aghast:

I feel terror. The sacred terror of rivers flowing back to their source, of the earth turning without a sun. Never has there been a more detestable monument of human infamy or act of wickedness. It will make future generations shudder.

Dreyfus, convicted a third time by his Presidential pardon, continued the fight until his total exoneration and it is to the everlasting credit of France that justice was finally done. Zola died in suspicious circumstances and was both reviled and honoured in his obituaries. His ashes were eventually transferred to the Pantheon where an attempt was made on the life of Dreyfus. The culprit was acquitted.

The Dreyfus Affair was a turning point in French and European history and triggered many major developments: the strengthening of the Republic; the separation of Church and State; the power of the media and its manipulation of public opinion; Herzl's vision of a Jewish state, which he rightly predicted would be realized within fifty years. It paved the way for the publication of the fraudulent *Protocols of the Elders of Zion*, consolidated anti-Jewish sentiments and laid the groundwork for the excesses of Vichy France, many of whose henchmen were from the ranks of the anti-Dreyfusards.

CONSEQUENCES AND AFTERMATH

Decades of intensive research sadly indicate that little has changed since the Affair erupted. Prejudice, racism and intolerance remain with their powerful roots unweakened by the tragedies of the last century.

Dreyfus, the first Jewish deportee, survived; within fifty years six million others did not. Condemnation of the Jew has blossomed into condemnation of the Jewish state. The former is at the root of the latter, the latter rekindles the former. Convinced that it cannot happen again Diaspora Jews prefer to be complacent and impervious to the signs warning them of all the traditional dangers. Drancy is desecrated, antisemitism is on the increase. What destiny awaits the Jewish people?

The vision of Eduoard Drumont, so valid in its time, begins to haunt many. 'Are the Jews eternally blind, not to realise what is awaiting them? Is there a great leader who is already at work?' Is the power of prejudice invincible? History predicts that the peaceful survival of the Jewish people will remain in doubt, so long as they do not muster a collective and sustained determination to demolish the bastion of prejudice which has led to their persecution throughout the centuries.

History and the passage of time have made the Dreyfus Affair a

Rorschach test for all those who come into contact with it. It exposes bigotry, hypocrisy and guilt with unnerving clarity. Set in a drama where prejudice prevailed over reason, the victory of justice was finally achieved at the price of great personal suffering and national shame. In its struggle for human rights the Affair reached heroic proportions at a time when, in the view of the historian Hannah Arendt, the dramas of twentieth-century France went into rehearsal.[10]

Rumblings of the Affair continued and do so to this day. The first war passed with its horrors, to be surpassed by the second with its atrocities. Members of the Dreyfus family fought valiantly, served in the Resistance and died, other family members were deported to concentration camps where they perished. The venomous 'Death to the Jews' was transformed into reality.

ADMISSION IS NOT ACCEPTANCE

Madeleine, the favourite grandchild of Dreyfus, a young student in Paris in the 1930s, jumped to her feet when her history teacher referred to her grandfather as the Jewish officer Dreyfus. 'No, Monsieur', she asserted proudly, 'the French officer', echoing the same sentiments as her grandfather forty years earlier. Madeleine was destined to pay the ultimate price of illusion.

Transport No.62 left Drancy on 20 November 1943. Its destination Auschwitz. In an act of utter degradation, the cargo manifest lists 300 kilos of margarine, 330 kilos of dried vegetables, 600 kilos of canned vegetables and 1,118 Jews. Amongst them was Madeleine. She was never to return. The signpost to this tragedy was engraved throughout the centuries and unveiled at the time of the Dreyfus Affair. It still stands erect, pointing in the same direction.

NOTES

1. E. Drumont, *La France Juive* (Paris: Flammarion, 1886).
2. B. Lazare, *Une Erreur Judiciaire: La verité sur l'Affaire Dreyfus* (Brussels: Impremerie Veuve Monnom, 1896).
3. E. Zola, *La Verité en Marche* (Paris: Fasquellee, 1901).
4. Ibid.
5. Ibid.
6. Ibid.
7. T. Herzl, *Der Judenstaat. Versach einer modernen Lösung der Judenfrage* (Leipzig: Verlag, 1896).
8. S. Zweig, *The World of Yesterday* (London: Cassell, 1943).
9. Herzl, *Der Judenstaat*.
10. H. Arendt, *The Origins of Totalitarianism* (London: André Deutsch, 1986).

15 The Nazi Extermination of the Disabled as a Prelude to the Holocaust

GIOVANNI DE MARTIS

At the end of April 1945, the US troops occupied Kaufbeuren, a German city less than ninety kilometres west of Munich. A month later, the veterans of the 36th Division celebrated victory on the city's main square. Talking to his men in parade formation, General John Ernest Dahlquist said, 'No nation in the history of the modern world has been so completely defeated. Their entire country is under our complete domination.' Ironic as history can be, Dahlquist was wrong and the proof of his mistake lay a few hundred kilometres from where he was talking to his men. The Kaufbeuren psychiatric clinic – just a few steps away from the US Command – was surrounded by notices warning people to keep away because of an epidemic of infectious diseases; the doctors of the clinic had put them up. No American officer dared to set foot in the clinic for more than two months. Undisturbed, the doctors kept on killing their patients by starving them or injecting lethal substances into their veins. It was not until 2 July 1945 that a group of US officers managed to enter the clinic where they were confronted by corpses scattered around and patients in indescribable conditions. A nurse of the clinic, Sister Wörle, bluntly admitted that she had killed 210 children. For doing so, she had received a salary increase of 35 marks. Evidence of similar acts of atrocity and inhumanity was discovered in the clinic of Irsee, a village only several kilometres away from Kaufbeuren.

If a person travelled today either to Kaufbeuren or to the little village of Irsee looking for traces of the systematic massacre of disabled people at the hands of the Nazis, he would have difficulty in finding any memorial to them. And like General Dahlquist in 1945, the traveller in 2007 would also be hard put to it to imagine that the lovely hotel in Irsee was the setting for the death of 2,000 persons. Just a small monument hidden in a forest nearby serves as a reminder. In Kaufbeuren, the only trace is another small monument hidden in a park out of town, built with the money of the doctors of the clinic. There is no other visible testimony.

The extermination of the disabled under the Nazi regime – better known as Aktion T4 – is distressing in many ways. From the historical point of view, it was brought to light only through investigations conducted by experts with almost no links to the academic world. The first investigation was conducted in 1946 when the German Medical Association entrusted a commission led by Dr Alexander Mitscherlich with the task of reporting on the so-called 'Doctors' Trial' in Nuremberg. The results of the commission's report were never made public. However, the Medical Association believed the atrocities committed to be so repulsive as to undermine for ever the citizens' trust in doctors. For this reason, the massacre of the disabled was hushed up for almost forty years, coming to notice once again around 1980 thanks to Ernst Klee, a journalist and special education teacher. This deliberate forgetfulness should not come as a surprise: it is well known that, after the war, a number of doctors involved in the mass killings went back to their profession and, in many cases, even obtained prestigious professorships. In any case, the sentences passed on the few who were brought to trial were either relatively light or soon followed by acts of clemency.

There is probably yet another reason for the silence surrounding this gruesome massacre: its implications. First and foremost is the fact that the programme of extermination of the disabled represented a sort of 'training ground' for the genocide of the Jews and the elimination of other categories of 'undesirables' in the Nazi extermination camps. Every aspect of the killing system of Auschwitz, Sobibor, Treblinka, Belzec or any other Nazi extermination camp was already present in the 'euthanasia programme'. First of all, its efficacy was based on secrecy: the Aktion T4 members swore never to reveal their activity, their chiefs took up false names and, above all, invented euphemisms to mask what was happening, just as was done later to conceal the truth of genocide. Secondly, all the personnel involved were later employed as operatives in genocide. A striking example was Christian Wirth, who went on from being administrative director of Grafeneck extermination clinic to become the senior officer in charge of extermination in camps such as Treblinka, Sobibor and Belzec and then to die in Istria after creating the only extermination camp on Italian soil, the Risiera di San Sabba. Atkion

T4 solved the main problem of the Nazi leaders: how to kill the highest number of people in one go. The gas-chamber technique was actually invented in the extermination clinics and then applied on a larger scale in the death camps. For the disabled, a more refined approach was adopted: the organization of transports, the practice of involving institutions in the collection of information on the victims, the use of human beings as instruments for scientific research. Moreover, the interests of doctors and pharmaceutical companies were specifically catered for in the Aktion T4 programme.

Between July and August 1941, Bishop Clemens von Galen, speaking from the pulpit of Münster's cathedral, denounced the murder of the weakest and neediest part of the German people. Viktor Brack – one of the Aktion T4 leaders – stated at the Nuremberg trial that the programme had been suspended:

> In 1941 I received an oral order to discontinue the Euthanasia Programme. I received this order from Bouhler as well as from Brandt. In order to preserve the personnel relieved of these duties and to have the opportunity of starting a new Euthanasia Programme after the war, Bouhler requested, I think after a conference with Himmler, that I send this personnel to Lublin and put it at the disposal of SS Brigadefuehrer Globocnik. I then had the impression that these people were to be used in the extensive Jewish labour camps run by Globocnik. Later, however, at the end of 1942 or the beginning of 1943, I found out that they were used to assist in the mass extermination of the Jews which was then already common knowledge in higher party circles.[1]

In 1941 it was known to most Germans that a systematic operation of extermination was being carried out. Secrecy had not been upheld as strictly as had been wished. In several German cities there were even occasional public demonstrations against the operation.[2] Von Galen's sermons were published and started to circulate throughout Germany. On 24 August, Hitler ordered the suspension of Aktion T4 as secretly as he had ordered its beginning.[3] Did the reaction of German public opinion and von Galen's sermons determine the suspension of the extermination of the disabled? Apparently so, since the operation came to an end and the extermination clinics were closed. However, Aktion T4 was replaced by the administration of death to patients directly by health professionals. That is what became known as 'wild euthanasia', namely the autonomous management of massacre through the use of lethal injections and starvation. It is reckoned that Aktion T4 led to the murder of 70,000 persons whereas 'wild euthanasia' was responsible for the death of more than 140,000 patients.

If Aktion T4 can be considered the 'training ground' for the extermination camps, one may well wonder about the effect that might have been produced by such a clear and unambiguous stand by German public opinion and the Church in relation to the killing of the Jews. As with the elimination of the disabled, the genocide of the Jews was known to the German people and the ecclesiastical authorities. Would the death machine have stopped if both had firmly and clearly condemned it? If at the beginning of the genocide, in 1942, public opinion had clearly denounced it, it would in any case have been too late for the Polish Jews. Still, a clear sign that the extermination was public knowledge would have very probably turned active collaborationist governments (such as those of Vichy and Hungary) into less willing ones. As a matter of fact, the collaboration of local police was decisive in the extermination, above all in Western Europe. The Nazis would have never managed to complete deportations without the prompt help of their local collaborators. An example is Denmark where the local population refused to collaborate and thereby managed to save the Danish Jews. Almost seventy years later, there is a lesson to be drawn from the history of Aktion T4: no matter how harsh and repressive a dictatorship can be, actions undertaken by ordinary citizens – if sufficiently numerous and determined – can have a decisive effect. The idea that a dictatorship can crush any form of dissent is an alibi for those who elect to remain helpless and passive 'onlookers and bystanders' in the face of morally intolerable decisions. There is, however, another more chilling aspect. The so-called 'wild euthanasia' was not carried out by the Nazi apparatus. It was health professionals who spontaneously took up the task of perpetrating the crime initiated by the authorities. This fact has huge relevance when one realizes that doctors in any organized society represent a sort of elite trusted by the rest of the population. In taking a stand for or against certain initiatives, elites shape public opinion among their own people. Through their actions, they justify political choices by backing them. What German doctors implicitly condoned was the idea that mass murder could be taken as a kind of 'therapy' for those who were regarded as a problem. It must be stressed that genocide or any kind of extermination project can be carried out only if there are people in society who are willing to turn into actual murderers and also if an elite is ready to rationalize, justify and legitimize the act of killing. There has to be a tiger to kill as well as somebody willing to open its cage.

Under Nazism, the work of justifying and rationalizing the massacre of the disabled first and of the Jews shortly after was delegated to doctors and experts in jurisprudence. Medicine and jurisprudence somehow worked as 'alibi givers' for the rest of the population in Germany as much as in all those European countries under Nazi influence. Any violent action can be taken against a minority when it has legal and scientific backing. This is absolutely pivotal not only in turning the masses into indifferent spectators of the events but also in ensuring that the executioners – the murderers – are as efficacious and efficient as possible. For violent action against a community to be successful, it is vital that the murderers be able to develop a split morality, that is, to build in themselves a dual track moral system. Among the many examples that could be given to explain what I mean by a 'split morality', the most eloquent is that offered by the letters that Friedrich Mennecke wrote to his wife while working as a murderer. Mennecke was 40 years old, had a degree in medicine, had been a member of the Nazi Party and of the SS from 1932 and became part of Aktion T4 in 1940. His task was visiting German psychiatric hospitals to select patients to be sent to the death clinics. Later on, when Aktion T4 was suspended, Mennecke was chosen for 'Operation 14 f 13', which consisted in weeding out the diseased, those unfit to work and the 'pathological rebels' at Dachau, Buchenwald, Ravensbrück and Auschwitz. During his time as a 'counsellor', Mennecke was in the habit of writing several letters a day to Eva, his wife.

> Wednesday, 26 November 1941, 7 a.m.: Brring-brring-brring: seven o'clock!! Wake up! A healthy good morning, Mommy!!! Kissy! Still snoozing, eh? Now up, shave! Ahoy!!! ... 7.50 p.m.: Home again, my little mouse!! My first day at work in Buchenwald is over. We went out early this morning at 8:30 ... first there were some 40 forms still to complete on the first portion of Aryans, which my other colleagues had already worked on yesterday. Of these 40, I worked on around 15 ... we were not finished with this until noon, for our two colleagues only worked theoretically yesterday; so I re-examined those that Schmalenbach (and myself this morning) had prepared ... at noon we took a break and ate in the officers' mess (first class! Soup, boiled beef, red cabbage, boiled potatoes, apple compote

– for 1.50 marks!), no ration coupons ... after that we did examinations until around 4:00; I did 105 pats., Mueller 78 pats. so that in the end our first share of 183 forms was completed. The second portion followed, a total of 1,200 Jews, none of whom are even examined; it is enough to take the reason for the arrest (often very comprehensive!) from the file and enter it on the form ... At exactly 5:00 p.m. we 'threw in the towel' and went to dinner: a cold plate of salami (nine large slices), butter, bread, and a helping of coffee! Cost: 0.80 marks without coupons! ... Tomorrow I expect your (third) letter. So my dearest Mommy, once again you get sooooooo many loving kisses, and I hug you very, very tightly in joyful expectation of your coming, you leetle mouse, from your faithful Pa.[4]

With the same casualness as he writes endearingly to his wife or talks about what he had to eat, Mennecke reports on his work of selection, which translates, for that very same day, into the death of tens if not hundreds of persons. Undoubtedly Mennecke was a loving husband, a dear neighbour, a well-mannered and kind person, very respectful of the laws. But this was just one of the two moral tracks his daily life was travelling on. The other track was the one characterized by absolute indifference to the fate of those he 'selected'. It is for this reason – the split moral tracks – that he manages to describe in the same letter the cold cuts he ate and his job as a murderer. This is a phenomenon well described, under the name of 'doubling', by Robert Jay Lifton.[5] Mennecke was authorized by the context he lived in, he was justified and legitimized *a priori*. For the same reason Mennecke as well as many other murderers whose activities are known to us were perfect fathers, loving husbands, caring and appreciated friends. This has nothing to do with what Hannah Arendt defined as 'the banality of evil' because it goes well beyond both banality and evil: backed by their entire world, Mennecke and the many Menneckes who acted first against the disabled and then against the Jews had dismissed the victims as objects animated by a 'life not worth living' and, as such, so easily exterminable that they would not be troubled in any way by their death.

What lesson is there then to be drawn for the future from the memory of the massacre of the German disabled? I believe that it offers us a key to what must be done to prevent it from happening again. Every citizen has the political duty to be vigilant and be alert, with no distractions. We must always be ready to raise our voice whenever we witness even the slightest form of discrimination. Our daily attention is the most direct and efficient message to the ones trying to breed divisions and hatred based on ethnic, religious or political differences. Attention is like a dam; its absence gives free rein to those who seek to stir up hatred against minorities. However, being alert and willing to speak out is at times not enough. One has to subject to critical scrutiny the pronouncements of the elites and withhold political trust from anyone who justifies, relativises or legitimizes any legal, moral or political inequality among human beings and any form of terrorism for any reason or in the name of any cause. There is no cause that can justify the murder of even one single person. Hatred comes to the surface and transforms itself into active violence only with the complicity and forbearance of the bystanders. Any act of justified violence generates other violent acts because, once the dehumanization of a group of people is legitimized, hatred and aggression against them are authorized. The massacre of the disabled in Germany was a prelude to the genocide of the European Jews, not only technically and chronologically but morally as well.[6] There was no social dam to its development so it was able to overrun all sense of justice and humanity. Acceptance of the killing of the weakest and neediest of the German people paved the way for the infamy of Auschwitz.

NOTES

1. Affidavit of Viktor Brack, 14 October 1946, Document NO-426.
2. E. Klee, *'Euthanasie' im NS-Staat : die 'Vernichtung lebensunwerten Lebens* (Frankfurt am Main: S. Fischer, 1983), pp.324–5.
3. Ibid., p.339.
4. G. Aly, P. Chroust and C. Pross, *Cleansing the Fatherland: Nazi Medicine and Racial Hygiene* (Baltimore: Johns Hopkins University Press, 1994), pp.254–5.
5. R. J. Lifton, *The Nazi Doctors: Medical Killing and the Psychology of Genocide* (New York: Basic Books, 1986).
6. See Henry Freelander, *The Origins of Nazi Genocide: From Euthanasia to the Final Solution* (Chapel Hill, NC: University of North Carolina Press, 1977).

16 The Importance of Prosecuting Nazi War Criminals in Post-Communist Europe

EFRAÏM ZUROFF

One of the most famous cases of Simon Wiesenthal's career was that of Karl Silberbauer, the Gestapo operative who arrested Anne Frank, her family, and the other Jews who were hiding together in the secret annex in Amsterdam. As the Viennese Nazi-hunter explained in his book *Justice Not Vengeance*, his primary motivation in the case was to disprove the claims of Holocaust deniers that Anne Frank's diary was a forgery and that the Holocaust was a hoax. (He had encountered such demonstrators at the performance of a play based on the diary.) In that respect, Wiesenthal fully understood and appreciated the extra-legal dimensions of the prosecution of Nazi war criminals, and especially the important role they can play in preserving the accuracy of the historical record and assisting in the ongoing efforts to combat antisemitism.

In recent years, the degree to which these three issues are intertwined can be clearly seen in Eastern Europe, where in the wake of the dismemberment of the Soviet Union and the fall of communism, the countries of the region were forced to confront six practical issues relating to their histories during the Holocaust, as well as an increase in antisemitic manifestations directly related to the handling (or mishandling) of these matters. The issues in question were acknowledgement of guilt, commemoration of the victims, prosecution of the perpetrators, documentation, education and restitution. Given the fact that members of the local population in practically every single one of these countries actively participated in the persecution, if not mass murder, of their Jewish fellow citizens and/or Jews from other countries as well, these issues, which were never dealt with honestly and freely during the Soviet/Communist era, became important tests of these fledgling democracies. To what extent would the new democracies be able to confront the complicity of their own citizens in the mass murder of the Jews? Would they be able to bring the guilty to trial or would they seek to evade that important, but ever-so-painful, responsibility?

An important corollary of these questions related to the deep-seated antisemitic traditions in these countries, which played an extremely significant role in spawning local collaboration with the Nazis and encouraging widespread participation in the implementation of the Final Solution. In theory, the transition to democracy was supposed to relegate such prejudices to the dustbin of history, but would that indeed be the case? It was clear from the beginning, however, that the institution of a democratic regime in a country with little or no democratic history or tradition would not automatically ensure that antisemitism, racism and other religious or ethnic prejudices would quickly and automatically disappear.

Indeed, this understanding was, I believe, one of the most important reasons that during the past decade and a half, practical issues related to the Holocaust have gained growing significance as barometers of moral and democratic behaviour in post-communist Europe. That being said, it is clear that some of these issues offer greater potential than others for combating prejudices such as antisemitism, because of a combination of content and technical considerations. Thus, for example, I believe that it is fair to say that the successful conviction of a Nazi war criminal, following a properly-conducted trial of several months' duration, if fairly and extensively covered by the local (and international) media, will have a greater impact than an hour-long commemorative ceremony to honour Holocaust victims. (In this context, it is also important to note that unlike all the other Holocaust-related practical issues currently on the agenda, except that of restitution to the direct victims as opposed to their families, the prosecution of Nazi perpetrators is the only one which is severely time-limited and therefore cannot be postponed. If commemoration, documentation or education, for example, are delayed, that is regrettable, but they can always be undertaken at a later date, which is categorically not true as far as the prosecution of Holocaust criminals is concerned, a factor which adds to the urgency of the task.)

For these reasons, it is particularly unfortunate that during the years 1990–2005 with the exception of two cases – one in Croatia – of Jasenovac commandant Dinko Sakic, which received extensive coverage and therefore had a significant impact – and one in Poland

– of Chelmno operative Henryk Mania, which was underreported and therefore had almost no impact whatsoever – there have not been any significant trials of local Nazi war criminals in post-communist Europe. In this context, it is imperative to note two highly significant facts that directly relate to this situation. The first is that there were numerous Nazi war criminals who could have been prosecuted in practically every single one of these countries, including several relatively prominent Nazi collaborators who played significant roles in the persecution and murder of the Jews. The second is that during the same period, numerous communist criminals were prosecuted in these countries. The unfavourable comparison between the ostensibly concurrent efforts to bring the two types of criminals to justice is perhaps the most telling indication of why the trials of Nazi war criminals in these countries were (or would have been) important.

If we take the Baltics as an example, we see noteworthy efforts being made by local prosecutors to bring communist criminals to justice, at least a dozen in Latvia alone, but little or no serious attempts being made to prosecute local Nazi war criminals. Thus not a single Lithuanian, Latvian or Estonian Holocaust perpetrator has ever been incarcerated for even a minute, since these countries have regained their independence. In Lithuania, leading Nazi war criminals such as Saugumas (Lithuanian Security Police), Aleksandras Lileikis, commander of the Vilnius district, and his deputy Kazys Gimzauskas were only indicted after they were medically unfit to stand trial and not one of them was ever obliged to appear in court. (Thus, although the latter was actually convicted by a Lithuanian court, the verdict had virtually no public impact since the defendant did not appear at a single session and was not punished for his crimes.)

Other Nazi war criminals, including members of the infamous Twelfth Lithuanian Auxiliary Police Battalion which murdered many thousands of Jews in Lithuania and Belarus, were ignored even after several of its members who had escaped to the United States after the Second World War were stripped of their American citizenship and returned to Lithuania. Latvia failed to prosecute Arajs Kommando officers Konrad Kalejs and Harijs Svikeris, and Estonia never brought charges against local Nazi collaborators such as Evald Mikson, Harry Mannil and Michael Gorshkow, all of whom should have been convicted years ago. (Kalejs, Svikeris and Mikson have already died without ever being held accountable for their crimes.)

The tragedy of this situation, it must be noted, is seriously compounded by the fact that the efforts to bring these Holocaust perpetrators to justice have been received very negatively by significant portions of the local population in these countries. The reactions in the local media, and especially on the Internet, to the demands that Lithuania, Latvia and/or Estonian Nazi war criminals be brought to justice in these countries found few local supporters, and aroused considerable opposition, much of it antisemitic. Demands for retaliation by the prosecution of Jewish communists, believed to be responsible for crimes against Balts, were among the more mild expressions of anti-Jewish sentiment, which included calls for the murder of the present author. Under such circumstances, the most effective means of persuading the public of the importance of conducting such trials would have been legal proceedings against Holocaust perpetrators, which could have revealed the scope and enormity of local criminality and collaboration with the Nazis. Held in local courts, before local judges, and conducted in the local languages, such trials could have been extremely powerful educational tools in the fight against antisemitism, as well as in the efforts to help local societies confront their complicity in Holocaust crimes. In countries where much of what was written about the Holocaust was regarded as propaganda and many of those prosecuted for Nazi crimes were regarded as Soviet victims of communism rather than as the genocidists which they were, such trials could have had enormous judicial, educational, moral, historical and public significance. The failure to bring these criminals to justice is, therefore, not only a stain on the history of these countries, but a tragedy for these local societies, which squandered a unique opportunity not only to confront their bloody histories in a meaningful way, but also to finally help bury the scourge of antisemitism which has plagued their societies for generations.

Seen in this light, Mr Wiesenthal's life mission and efforts take on increased significance and added meaning. And his unqualified support and endorsement of the Centre's decision in 2002 to launch its 'Operation: Last Chance' project, which offers financial rewards for information which will facilitate the prosecution and punishment of Nazi war criminals, in the Baltics, reinforces the need for such trials in post-communist Eastern Europe.

'Operation: Last Chance' was conceived by Aryeh Rubin, the founder and president of the Targum Shlishi Foundation of Miami, Florida, who over the past fifteen years has actively supported and assisted the Simon Wiesenthal Centre's efforts to bring Nazi war criminals to justice. With time running out on these endeavours, however, he believed that a more proactive approach should be attempted and guaranteed a generous contribution to undertake the project as a joint programme of Targum Shlishi and the Wiesenthal Centre, whose Jerusalem Office was entrusted with its implementation and coordination. It was officially launched in July 2002 in Lithuania (8 July), Estonia (10 July) and Latvia (11 July). There were several reasons for starting the project in the Baltics. One was the extensive role played by the local population in the murders and the extremely high victim rate in all three countries. (Over 95 per cent of the Jews who were living under the Nazi occupation in Lithuania, Latvia and Estonia were murdered.) The fact that practically all the Jews killed were murdered near their homes (rather than in the death camps in Poland) increased the likelihood of being able to obtain information regarding the identity of the killers. In addition, we assumed that the relatively large number of local Nazi war criminals who had been convicted by the Soviets after the Second World War and had already served their sentences and had returned to their countries of origin might be willing to reveal the identities of their fellow perpetrators in return for a reward. While this possibility certainly raised a daunting moral dilemma, we believe that in numerous instances of mass murder, only perpetrators could possibly identify the killers and they were our only hope of being able to bring some of the guilty to justice.

The project was launched at press conferences held in each of the capitals, which were followed by ads in the local media that deliberately focused on the atrocities committed by the local population. Thus, for example, the illustration used in the ads in Lithuania was of the murder of Jews by Lithuanians in the Lietukis garage in Kovno, a well-known atrocity in which more than fifty Jews were murdered by a gang of Lithuanians wielding crowbars, who shoved fire hoses into the mouths of some of their victims and turned on the water until their stomachs burst. The murders were witnessed by a crowd of men, women and children who cheered as each Jew succumbed, and after all the Jews had been killed, sang the Lithuanian national anthem. The caption of the ad published in the national media noted, 'Lithuanian Jewry did not disappear. They were brutally murdered at Ponar (Vilnius), Fort IX (Kaunas), Kuzai Forest (Siauliai) and over one hundred places of mass murder.' Besides announcing a reward of $10,000, it listed the phone numbers of the local Jewish community, the local special prosecutor for crimes committed by totalitarian regimes (Nazi and Communist), as well as the contact numbers of the Israel office of the SWC.

In Lithuania, we benefited from the help provided by the local Jewish community, headed by Dr Shimon Alperovich, which agreed to serve as our local partner and to record the incoming information. The issue of local partners ultimately turned out to be more complicated than originally anticipated. One might imagine that local Jewish communities would be more than happy to support the project and provide the necessary technical assistance, but that was not the case. In fact, several communities, such as Estonia and Germany, refused outright to cooperate, whereas the Latvian Jewish community was publicly critical of the project even though they had initially agreed to cooperate. A good part of the opposition by these communities undoubtedly stemmed from a fear of an antisemitic backlash. Yet while this concern was shared by all the communities, there were those such as Lithuania and Romania (headed by the late Professor Cajal and Julian Sorin) which chose to provide excellent public support and cooperation, whereas others rushed to join the local critics. In retrospect, the responses of the local Jewish communities were not necessarily a function of their size (Romania has approximately 9,000 Jews and Lithuania 5,000, whereas Germany has over 100,000 Jews and Latvia has 12,000), but rather of the courage of their leaders and their commitment to bringing the murderers to justice. The latter factor was often influenced by whether these leaders' relatives had been murdered in that country during the Shoah.

During its initial year of operation, 'Operation: Last Chance' received the names of well over 200 suspects, mostly from Lithuania. Encouraged by this success, the project was expanded in September 2003 to Poland, Romania and Austria. Our principle in this regard was to focus exclusively on those countries in which the local population and/or its government (Romania for example) played an active role in the murder of its Jewish community and/or other Jews. While this fact was quite well known in the Baltics, the situation in the next three countries was more complex. The Poles, for example, were severely victimized by the Nazis (three million Poles, including a significant percentage of the Polish intelligentsia, were murdered) and were not given an integral role in the implementation of the Final Solution in Poland. Yet, notwithstanding the brave and often successful attempts of Zegota, an underground organization set up in 1942 to aid Jews in occupied Poland, numerous Poles did play a role in the murder of Jews, a fact which many Poles refused to acknowledge, preferring to foster their country's image as a victim of the Nazis.

In Romania, the government's role in the mass murder of Jews in Romania and in the territories it annexed as well as in the Ukraine was largely covered up. In fact, since Romania became a democracy not a single Holocaust perpetrator had been investigated, let alone prosecuted, and rehabilitations had been granted to several Romanian Nazi war criminals.

As far as Austria is concerned, its record on bringing Nazi war criminals to justice has been utterly abysmal, with not a single conviction recorded during the past three decades. This is not that surprising, however, in view of the fact that until about fifteen years ago, Austria touted itself as 'Hitler's first victim', rather than as Germany's zealous partner in crime. (Many of the leading Holocaust perpetrators, such as Adolf Eichmann, Franz Stangl, Artur Seyss-Inquart and Odilo Globocnik were Austrians.)

In the wake of this expansion of 'Operation: Last Chance', we encountered our first legal challenge based on data protection. Questions apparently posed by right-wing nationalist elements prompted inquiries by the Polish Office for Data Protection which questioned the legality of the project and whether the transfer of information regarding Polish citizens to another country (in this case Israel) without their knowledge, was not a violation of Polish law. We later encountered a similar challenge in Hungary. Another worrisome phenomenon, which we encountered at this stage, was a plethora of antisemitic phone calls to our hotline in Austria. Out of approximately one hundred calls, more than ninety were by persons who called to express unequivocally antisemitic (and often anti-American) views. Typical of such calls were those who identified Bush and Sharon as 'the real war criminals' and demanded the financial reward. Others sent copies of the ad we published in the Austrian mass circulation daily *Kronen Zeitung* under the caption 'Der Morder sind unter uns' (The murderers are among us) along with similar comments to our office in Jerusalem. A recurring theme of these calls, letters and emails was when will the Jews stop milking us because of the past?

While we received antisemitic responses in practically every country, it was only in Austria that their number was so large and in direct disproportion to the number of serious leads received. Elsewhere, we received not only hundreds of names of suspects but also expressions of support and information of historical value. In many cases the people who submitted the information stated that they did not want any reward, but felt an obligation to inform us. One such example was the following story received from Lithuania about the fate of the Jewish community of Panemunelis (in Yiddish Panemunok), a *shtetl* with about one hundred Jews, about whose murder during the Shoah no details were hereto known. The informant related that as a young boy, in August 1941, he saw a wagon with ten Jews aboard, five from the Olkin family and five from the Jaffe family, along with four armed Lithuanians whom he named headed in the direction of the nearby town of Rokiskis. Thirty minutes later he heard shots ring out from the nearly Karolishkis Forest and some time after that he saw the same wagon return to the *shtetl* with only the four armed Lithuanians aboard and with a large pile of clothes in the wagon. According to the informant, who began his letter by stating that he did not want any reward, two of the four Lithuanians in question were no longer alive. Unfortunately, as it turned out, all four had already died by the time we received this information. Nonetheless, the information received shed historical light on the cruel fate of this Jewish community.

In the summer of 2004, 'Operation: Last Chance' was expanded to Croatia and Hungary. The launch of the project in the former was unique for three reasons, two of which were excellent, while the third was terrible. The first was that President Mesic himself granted us a meeting on the day of the launch to express his support. The second was the receipt of a complete dossier on former Slavonska Pozega police chief Milivoj Asner, including anti-Jewish and anti-Serb directives he had personally signed into law which clearly proved his complicity in Holocaust crimes. The third were death threats against Croatian Jews (whose community leaders chose to ignore our request for assistance), and the offer of rewards for the murder of the Croatian Justice Minister ($75,000), our local partner (Dr Zorin Pusic of the Civic Committee for Human Rights – $50,000) and myself ($25,000).

In Hungary we were challenged on legal grounds, as noted above, and the project aroused an intense internal polemic regarding its validity in which the critics were led by a well-known Holocaust historian of Jewish origin. Here too, extremely incriminating evidence was submitted, in this case by the brother of a young Jew murdered in Budapest in 1944 by a Hungarian Army officer named Karoly Zentai, who escaped to Australia in 1950 and had never been tried for his crimes. To date Zentai and Asner are the most likely to be brought to trial from among the suspects whose names were received in the framework of 'Operation: Last Chance'.

With our efforts in Germany just beginning, we are hopeful that the project will register its most successful results in the country which was the seat of Nazi power and whose nationals played such an important role in the implementation of the Final Solution. Contrary perhaps to common thinking, many Nazi war criminals have been convicted during the past several years and we are cautiously optimistic that 'Operation: Last Chance' will help increase that significant figure.

That being said, it is now quite clear that any assessment of the project cannot be limited to its concrete judicial results. Besides attempting to facilitate the prosecution and punishment of Nazi war criminals, 'Operation: Last Chance' has played an integral and important role in the struggle for historical truth in post-communist Europe, where new national narratives are being written about the Second World War and the Holocaust and the issue of local complicity in the murder of the Jews remains disputed and painful. Under these circumstances, 'Operation: Last Chance' has a significant role not only in ensuring historical accuracy but also in helping combat contemporary antisemitism and paving the way for better relations between Jews and non-Jews in Europe.

17 How Should the Holocaust be Understood: The Elie Wiesel/Simon Wiesenthal Controversy of the Late 1970s

MICHAEL BERENBAUM

The death of Nazi-hunter Simon Wiesenthal brings to a close a storied career shrouded in achievement, in dazzle and even in mystery. None of us who came of age in the post-Holocaust world could fail to be moved by his passing; all of us were impacted by his life.

Physically, Simon Wiesenthal was a heavyweight; so too spiritually. An architect by training, after the Holocaust he never returned to his profession but found his calling in bringing Nazi war criminals to justice, and in his pursuit of it he was unyielding, tenacious and indefatigable – a stiff-necked man, heir of a stiff-necked people. He represented, he embodied *midat hadin,* the attribute of justice. Wiesenthal insisted that Nazi criminals be brought to justice. He intuited that justice was needed – or at least the attempt albeit at limited, imperfect justice, the façade of justice if not its actuality – if the world was to rebuild itself after the destruction he had witnessed. He did not cooperate with those seeking revenge, even though their path was more certain, more immediate, more passionate and perhaps even more just. Nor would he make accusations without merit. Sometimes, his point was so subtle that neither the media nor the public grasped it. Thus, he knew that Kurt Waldheim was a liar and a German soldier who had served in the vicinity of where atrocities were taking place. He insisted that we did not know – and have not yet proven – that the former UN Secretary-General and the President of Austria was a war criminal, despite his proximity to the crimes.

In the late 1940s and early 1950s, after the first trials and the grand theatre they represented, and the much heralded successor trials were completed, there was much less enthusiasm for facing the past, much more for getting on with the future. Attention had turned to the Cold War and not the World War. The United States was interested in battling communism not Nazism. Wiesenthal pressed on. He opened a documentation centre and started corresponding with survivors all over the world, seeking to identify the perpetrators and to locate them. But in the mid-1950s, his documentation centre was forced to close because of lack of funding and lack of interest in the hunt for Nazi war criminals: Israel was at war; it needed intelligence on the Arabs and not the Germans, and it had strategic interests – basic survival interests – and, soon, important financial and trade interests with Germany. The American Jewish community was not yet prepared to buck American national interests, which were to be found in making friends with Germany and having West Germany join the United States in a common front against the Soviet Union and its Allies. If that meant forgetting the past, so be it for the Americans and even for American Jews, but not for Simon Wiesenthal.

Wiesenthal's cause only began to gain wide support with the capture, trial and execution of Adolf Eichmann in the early 1960s. Contrary to popular perception, Wiesenthal did not capture Eichmann. Israel's Mossad did the work. Wiesenthal's contribution can be described as modest. Still, if his hand in the actual capture has been exaggerated, his role in preparing the world for it cannot be. For years before the nabbing, Wiesenthal had a hunch about the widows of Nazi criminals: he suspected that the men they married during the post-war years were in fact their former husbands with new names and new identities. Eichmann's wife tried to have him declared dead so that she could receive a pension and so that Eichmann's name would disappear from the list of the wanted. She even produced an affidavit 'proving' that Eichmann had died in Prague. But Wiesenthal would not let her get away with it; he produced his own documents declaring that witnesses had seen Eichmann alive after the date of his supposed death. He also alerted Israeli and World Jewish Congress officials to information that Eichmann had escaped to Rome and then had gone to South America – but they were uninterested in pursuing the issue. (Recent documents show that the CIA knew where Eichmann was and even the name – misspelled as it was – which he used as a cover to live among German émigrés in Argentina, but such information was not shared, buried in the vaults of the CIA.) In frustration, he closed his office, shipped off material to Yad Vashem and went through an emotionally tough time.

After Eichmann's capture and the fame brought about by the trial, Wiesenthal was able to reopen his office and greatly increase support for the modest centre. Though the numbers are not precise, it is said that Wiesenthal was involved in bringing 1,100 Nazis to justice. Some were major criminals; others were minor. One, Dr Josef Mengele, eluded him. In fact, Mengele's death in a drowning accident, a simple, swift death without suffering, violated our sense of justice.

I was an observer to Wiesenthal's most well-known philosophical battle, which was with the other iconic survivor of this generation, Elie Wiesel. The two squared off indirectly in the late 1970s over the question of who were the true victims of the Holocaust; that is, was the Holocaust a Jewish event or a universal event? At that time, it seemed as if the two ideas were in conflict, as if the Shoah had to be one and not the other – and certainly not both.

For years Simon Wiesenthal had advanced the notion that the Holocaust was the murder of eleven million people, six million Jews and five million non-Jews. His purposes were utilitarian, not historical, for he was a detective, a pursuer of war criminals and not a scholar. Such a representation of Jews and non-Jews was more faithful to his experience in the camps, where the populations were more mixed, Jews and non-Jews and the environment more multinational and religiously diverse. In contrast Elie Wiesel was deported primarily to Auschwitz as part of the great Hungarian deportations; 437,402 Jews were deported on 147 trains between 15 May and 9 July 1944 – Jews and only Jews, at least by Nazi definitions of the term. For Wiesel the Shoah was solely Jewish metaphysically, historically and experientially; not so for Wiesenthal.

It was also essential for Wiesenthal to enlist the support of non-Jews and of the nations of Europe and South America in the prosecution of Nazi war criminals, and to do so he had to offer them a stake in his efforts. If their own citizens, if fellow Christians, were also regarded as victims of the Nazis, the European nations and their citizens would be more likely to support his efforts, more likely to bring these criminals to justice even as their prosecution would raise uncomfortable issues for the society and shatter the convenient falsehoods that had been the touchstone of Europe's efforts to rebuild.

The world he confronted was one in which:

- West Germany was struggling to think of the Nazis as a few bad apples misled by a cruel totalitarian leader and the German people as essentially good and their culture noble;

- Communist East Germany perceived its leaders – and seemingly therefore its citizens – as victims of Nazi capitalism;
- Austria considered itself as the first of the Nazi victims and that Austrian history ended in March 1938 and resumed in May 1945;
- France spoke of its grand record of resistance and rescue and not of collaboration and betrayal;
- Switzerland spoke of heroic neutrality and not of its economic cooperation with the Third Reich;
- Belgium spoke of the Jews it rescued and not the ones who were murdered;
- The Netherlands publicized its general strike and ignored the role of its police in gathering the Jews for deportation;
- The Vatican portrayed Pope Pius XII (who served until 1958) as protector of the Jews and omitted its own complicity, most especially its role in rescuing Nazi officials and resettling them in Roman Catholic countries of South America;
- Poland depicted the six million dead; 3.1 million Polish Jews and 2.9 million Polish Christians, according to its Jews in death the status denied them so often in life, their respect as Poles, citizens of the state and members of the nation;
- Spain and Sweden proclaimed their neutrality and hence their innocence;
- The Soviet Union did not utter the 'J' word. Its citizens were victimized as citizens of the Soviet Union, not as Jews.

So for Wiesenthal the purpose of defining the Holocaust in more universal terms was essentially utilitarian, a search for potential allies in his quest for justice.

Wiesel argued that the Holocaust was a uniquely Jewish experience. He feared that at first the public would speak of six million Jews and five million non-Jews; later they would remember eleven million victims, Jews among them, and still later the Jewishness of the victims would be obliterated. Prominent Israeli historian Yehuda Bauer accused Wiesenthal of submerging the fate of the Jews. Prior to his acceptance of President Jimmy Carter's appointment in 1978 as Chairman of the President's Commission on the Holocaust, Elie Wiesel had only written of the Jewish experience and he was asked by the President to confront issues that he had not faced. He was asked to speak as an American and to address the American ethos and experience. Still, by then Wiesel, a resident of the United States for almost a quarter of a century and an American citizen for almost

eighteen years, continued to write in French and have his work translated into English; he regarded himself as a Jewish writer and a
French writer even though he lived in New York. He thought he
could settle the role of non-Jews in the Holocaust with the turn of a
phrase: 'While not all victims were Jews, all Jews were victims.'[1] For
him, that served to protect the uniqueness of the Jewish experience
while including non-Jewish victims. Wiesel also sought to move from
the particular to the universal: the Holocaust was Jewish, its implications universal.

Even the definition of the Holocaust that was offered in the
Report to the President, submitted by the President's Commission on
the Holocaust to Jimmy Carter on 27 September 1979, defined the
Holocaust metaphysically, and ahistorically. The *Report* said: The
Holocaust is 'the systematic state-sponsored murder of Six Million
Jews by the Nazis and their collaborators during World War II; as
night descended millions of non-Jews were killed as well.' Contrary
to the historical record, the murder of the Jews was given the appearance of historical primacy in order to protect its metaphysical primacy
as the defining nature of the event. In reality, the concentration
camps were first developed for political prisoners; only in 1938 after
the November pogroms (*Kristallnacht*) throughout Germany, which
had been expanded to include Austria and the arrest of some 30,000
Jewish men aged 16–60, did Jews constitute a majority of its inhabitants. Gas chambers were first developed in the euthanasia programme first as mobile gas vans and later as stationary gassing instal-
lations. This provided what the minutes of the Wannsee Conference
euphemistically terms the practical experience that 'is already being
collected, which is of greatest importance in relation to the future
final solution of the Jewish problem'.[2] There is a direct continuity
between the staffing of the T-4 (Tiergarten 4) Programme and the
Aktion Reinhard Camps of Treblinka, Sobibor and Belzec. So, historically, the murder of non-Jews preceded the Final Solution and paved
the way for it.

Wiesenthal, in contrast, argued that the Holocaust was the death
of eleven million people, six million Jews and five million non-Jews.
The figure, as he later admitted, was invented: if we consider all civilian non-Jewish deaths, then it is too small; if we consider only those
who died at the hands of the Nazi killing apparatus, then it is too
large. But the central point was Wiesenthal's belief that while
the Holocaust was primarily Jewish, it was not exclusively so;
the numbers reflect Jewish primacy, and also an unequal balance in

victimization, more Jews than non-Jews but not overwhelmingly so. The inclusion of non-Jews was essential to his post-war commitment. Nations had to feel that they had lost their own if they were to bring the war criminals to justice. So clear was Wiesenthal's position that he insisted that the Simon Wiesenthal Centre in Los Angeles, which bore his name, reflect his understanding of the meaning of the Holocaust. Thus, the Los Angeles based Centre and the museum that it was to develop were inclusive of non-Jews as victims of the Holocaust *ab initio*.

Wiesenthal's position was supported by President Jimmy Carter, who in the handwritten memo approving the establishment of the United States Holocaust Memorial Council by Presidential Order before Congress approved its creation wrote 'Universalize' and initialled it 'JC'. Ismar Schorsch, the former Chancellor of the Jewish Theological Seminary also supported Wiesenthal's position. He wanted to diminish the role that the Holocaust played in American Jewish identity fearing that it was becoming predominant and furthering the lachrymose sense of Jewish history.

It was ironic that the human rights organization headed by an Orthodox rabbi, Marvin Hier, who was an intense advocate of Jewish interests, was more universalistic in its inception than the US government-sponsored national Holocaust Memorial which was threatened by internal controversy on this issue. Mindful of the dissent that had greeted the issue in Washington, New York's Museum of Jewish Heritage: A Living Memorial to the Holocaust positioned itself exclusively on Jewish victimization by conceiving of itself as a museum of Jewish Heritage even though it received major backing from the City of New York and New York State. Wiesenthal would not budge on this issue and thus over time the Simon Wiesenthal Centre reflected his view and evolved into a double-named institution, the Museum of Tolerance/Beit Hashoah, the House of the Holocaust, pushing to the forefront on the issue of tolerance and opening more modest satellite centres that focus their programmes on tolerance more than the Shoah. This will most likely culminate in the Museum of Tolerance in Jerusalem, which because of its proximity to Yad Vashem, has agreed not to become another Holocaust Museum.

Judging from the content of all three American museums – Los Angeles, Washington and New York – one might not know the depth of this controversy for the content of their exhibitions relating to non-Jewish victims are not dramatically different and even the new exhibition in Yad Vashem, which opened in the autumn of 2004, includes non-Jewish victims of Nazism in a Holocaust museum that centres on the Jews.

Why?

The battle of titans between Wiesel and Wiesenthal was never resolved between the two men. The issue that divided them was resolved, at least as far as presentations within museums is concerned, though the tension as to how to depict the non-Jewish victims of Nazism in a manner respectful of, and proportionate to, their victimization remains.

A focus on history – not ideology – resolved the issue, and the audiences (the plural is deliberate) that visit these museums required that it be resolved. New vocabulary eased some very basic concern, and with new language, a new way of viewing the totality of the Nazi victims.

First to history: the inclusion of non-Jews was mandatory to telling the story of what happened to the Jews. Contrary to the definition offered in the President's Commission on the Holocaust Report, the victimization of the non-Jews preceded the victimization of Jews, chronologically if not metaphysically. Thus, the concentration camps were developed first to house political prisoners and opponents of the regime, trade unionists and dissonants, social democrats and others who opposed Nazi rule. Until 1938 Jews were a minority of the victims of these camps. The apparatus first developed to secure Nazi political dominance such as the Gestapo and the SS later were used to impose Nazi policy on the Jews, but their inception must be seen in the context of the Nazi rise to power and Nazi rule. Gassing was first developed to murder German Aryans deemed by the ideology of the party and the policies of the German state 'life unworthy of living'. Those whose status as German Aryan could not be denied were seen as an embarrassment to the myth of Aryan supremacy because they were retarded or handicapped, emotionally distraught or addicted, and the staff of these T-4 operations were later used in the death camps. They began their careers by killing hundreds and thousands, moving up to tens of thousands and when the thrust of Nazi policy turned against the Jews, these men – successful killers all – used their newly acquired skill to murder hundreds of thousands and millions of Jews.

As these exhibitions developed, the historians and curators came to understand that some were victimized for what they did, some for what they refused to do; some were victimized for what they were and Jews were victimized for the fact that they were. Their elimination was perceived as central to the future of the German nation, essential to its security and the very health of the society.

Let me explain. Trade unionists and social democrats among others were victimized for what they did. Without their doing something, they would not have ended up in incarceration, at least not at the beginning. Jehovah's Witnesses were victimized for what they refused to do; they would not swear allegiance to the state, they would not register for the draft, the words 'Heil Hitler' never passed their lips. They would not stop proselytizing. Even when incarcerated they would not sign a simple document denouncing their faith and thus leaving the camps. Unlike the Jews, they were voluntary victims of the Nazis, they chose their faith; in that sense they were classical martyrs; they chose incarceration rather than conversion or even swearing falsely to a Nazi government unworthy of their allegiance and trust.

German male homosexuals were incarcerated because their sexuality offended the 'manliness' at the core of Nazism. There was no policy of incarcerating lesbians because of their sexual activity. The fate of Roma and Sinti, known as Gypsies, most closely paralleled the fate of the Jews. They were killed in family units, they were gassed as Auschwitz-Birkenau where some 19,000 were killed, yet their murder was not seen as essential to the national salvation of Germany, their presence was not considered a 'cancer' on the health of the society; they played a secondary role in the Nazi policy of genocide, though undoubtedly they were the victims of the genocide.

With the decision to include non-Jews, there also came a change in the language that addressed the problem. For Wiesel and Wiesenthal the victims were divided into Jews and non-Jews. When the proceedings of the conference on the victimization of non-Jews were first published, I deliberately used the term *A Mosaic of Victims* in order to avoid the fault line of Jews and non-Jews.[3] In the US Holocaust Memorial Museum, more historical and less interpretive terms were chosen; thus the non-Jews are referred to as they were considered in Nazi ideology, 'enemies of the state' on the top floor of the exhibition, and 'prisoners of the camps'. Similar terms have been used elsewhere.

Even where museums were not initially willing to be inclusive in their approach, the presence of a potential pluralistic audience imposed such inclusion. Thus, New York's Museum of the Jewish Heritage: A Living Memorial to the Holocaust, which was deliberately named to focus exclusively on the Jewish experience, found itself including the homosexual victims of the Nazis in response to the large homosexual community in New York that were to visit the Museum, and with their inclusion came the requirement for the wider focus on the totality of the Nazis' victims. In the multicultural world and with its many foreign visitors, even Yad Vashem had to include the non-Jewish victims of Nazism for their exclusion would have been noteworthy.

In the almost three decades since this controversy first surfaced much more research has been done on the totality of all the Nazi victims and much greater understanding of the historical issues has been achieved. In turn, this has secured our understanding of the interrelationship between the victimization of the Jews and the diverse victims of Nazi policy, and with each historical understanding came the realization that the Nazi policy against the Jews was distinct and singular – unique.

I think that it fair to say that in the two decades since Wiesel won the Nobel Prize his role too has become more universal. Were he chairman of the US Holocaust Memorial Council, he might take a very different point of view today, as has Yehuda Bauer, who, as the academic advisor of the International Task Force on Holocaust Education, now speaks of the singularity of the Holocaust in an inclusive rather than exclusive manner.

Over time, Wiesenthal's definition of the Holocaust has been rejected by historians and the public alike. But his sense that all the victims of Nazism must be included as a matter of historical truth and sensitivity to the public, and that such inclusion need not detract from a focus on the Jewish tragedy, has been sustained. It is one of his many contributions to Holocaust discourse.

NOTES

1. President's Commission on the Holocaust, *Report to the President*, submitted to Jimmy Carter on 27 September 1979, p.iii.
2. Translation of Document No. Ng-2586, Office of Chief Counsel for War Crimes.
3. Michael Berenbaum (ed.), *A Mosaic of Victims* (New York: New York University Press, 1990).

18 Who Needs Forgiveness? Further Thoughts on the Moral Dilemma Posed by Simon Wiesenthal's *The Sunflower*

JOHN K. ROTH

To forgive means to be merciful, to pardon an offence or an offender, to give up a claim against another individual, to set aside a debt, to relinquish anger or resentment, however justifiable those feelings may be. Thus, *forgiveness* is what I call an *after*-word.

In ways large and small, unintentional as well as intentional, we human beings do harm – often immense harm – to each other. Without such actions, forgiveness would remain an abstract possibility, but once human-made harm has been done – only then, in fact – forgiveness can become real, specific, concrete, important and also problematic.

The frequently devastating circumstances that make *forgiveness* an *after*-word can have numbing effects on our moral and spiritual sensibilities, but it remains plausible to say that few people, if any, have never felt the need for forgiveness, asked to receive it, and found relief when it was granted. It is also true that countless people have granted forgiveness to others who have done wrong, often forgiving even when no petition for forgiveness has been made. In many cases, those who grant forgiveness have found relief in doing so.

None of us is perfect. Thus, one credible answer to the question 'Who needs forgiveness?' is *all of us do*, at least insofar as the phrase 'all of us' refers to men, women and children who can reasonably be judged responsible for their actions. The High Holy Days in Judaism, culminating in Yom Kippur (Day of Atonement), provide a striking example that shows how religious traditions do much to keep this sensibility alive. Secular approaches in ethics, psychology, self-help and politics also stress that human beings fall far short of what is right and good. Wherever steps are advocated and taken to make up for the human deficit between right and wrong, justice and injustice, forgiveness and issues about it will not be far behind.

The question 'Who needs forgiveness?' has more bite and complexity than these preliminary remarks contain. Consider, for example, two particular inflections of the question: '*Who* needs forgiveness?' and 'Who *needs* forgiveness?' They both contain suspicion. The first implies suspicion about the universalizing view that 'all of us' need forgiveness. True though that claim may be, the fact of human history is that some people inflict much more harm than others – Heinrich Himmler, Josef Mengele and their SS brothers during the Holocaust come to mind – and it is important to measure responsibility accurately and to place accountability where it belongs.

The second inflection – 'Who *needs* forgiveness?' – questions the virtue of forgiveness. Far from assuming that forgiveness is simply good, this outlook suspects that forgiveness can become – unwittingly if not expressly – the partner of forgetting, condoning, relativizing and trivializing, all of which sacrifice justice to indifference, to what the theologian Dietrich Bonhoeffer called 'cheap grace'. As the Jewish philosopher Emmanuel Levinas put the point, 'a world where forgiveness is almighty becomes inhuman'.[1]

Such problems suggest that *forgiveness* is not only an *after*-word but also a *wounded*-word. Its wounded status has a long history, but the wounded status of forgiveness is also an effect of recent events, including the Holocaust. Consider some aspects of that history.

At *Berakoth* 7a in the Babylonian Talmud, the rabbis probe a verse from the fifty-sixth chapter of Isaiah: 'I will bring them to My sacred mount / And let them rejoice in My house of prayer.'[2] Interpreting the text literally to read 'And let them rejoice in the house of My prayer', the rabbis indicate that God says prayers. That claim, however, is puzzling: Why, and about what, would God pray? The unfolding inquiry suggests that God prays for his mercy to prevail so that divine anger stops short of what the Talmud calls 'the limit of strict justice'.[3] The implication is that God overrides his anger but not completely, for his attributes include anger rightly aroused by injustice. Even with God, it seems, tension exists between forgiveness and justice.

One question leads to another: even if God suppresses his anger, it remains awesome. Thus, it is important to know the duration of divine anger, especially when Scripture states that each day includes God's indignation.[4] The Talmud indicates that the duration of God's daily anger is 'one moment', but 'how long is one moment?' The answer proposed is so minuscule that it scarcely amounts to a split second: 'One fifty-eight thousand eight hundred and eighty-eighth part of an hour.' The point is that God's anger and his inclination to act according to strict justice remain. Their power is awe-ful (awesome) but far less dominant than God's mercy and forgiveness. If that were not the case, the world could not exist.

In addition to its being a text that reiterates God's imperative to 'observe what is right and do what is just', Isaiah 56 also contains God's promise to remember those who are faithful to his covenant: 'I will give them, in My house / And within My walls, / A monument and a name / Better than sons and daughters. / I will give them an everlasting name / Which shall not perish.'[5] That verse is the source of the name Yad Vashem, meaning a monument and a name or, figuratively, a monument and a memorial, which identifies the distinctive Israeli site of Holocaust remembrance and memorialization in Jerusalem.[6] The Holocaust complicates everything, including forgiveness.

The Holocaust's complications include that event's power to call into question the existence of a just God, let alone one who is merciful and forgiving. If the Holocaust affects people in that way, then the issues surrounding forgiveness are altered accordingly: religiously grounded understandings of, or appeals about, forgiveness will lack credibility. Advocacy for forgiveness, if it continues to exist, would have to come from other sources – ethical or psychological ones, for example. Even for those who find that the Holocaust does not leave religious perspectives utterly ruined, religiously grounded understandings of, or appeals about, forgiveness may still be important, but they are not likely to be unwounded. Some Holocaust-related examples can illustrate these points.

Ever since its publication in 1969, Simon Wiesenthal's book *The Sunflower* continues to provoke serious Holocaust-related reflection and discussion about forgiveness. Its dilemma goes back to a day in 1944 when it became Wiesenthal's fate to hear the deathbed confession of a mortally wounded SS man – Wiesenthal (1908–2005) called him Karl – who had participated in the mass murder of Jews but now wanted forgiveness from a Jew. Wiesenthal listened to the man's confession, found 'true repentance' in it, but left the German's hospital room without saying a word.[7] Puzzled about whether he had done the right thing, Wiesenthal asked others to say what they would have done in his circumstances.

Responses to *The Sunflower* have been as impassioned as they are varied. For example, identifying himself as 'an atheist who is indifferent to and rejecting of any metaphysics of morality', the Auschwitz survivor and philosopher Jean Améry thought that Wiesenthal's anguish was largely irrelevant, except that from a political perspective forgiveness had no place. 'What you and I went through', he wrote to Wiesenthal, 'must *not happen again, never, nowhere*. Therefore ... I refuse any reconciliation with the criminals and with those who only by accident did not happen to commit atrocities, and finally, all those who helped prepare the unspeakable acts with their words.'[8]

In contrast to Améry, Theodore Hesburgh, long-time president of the University of Notre Dame, said that his 'whole instinct is to forgive. Perhaps that is because I am a Catholic priest ... I think of God as the great forgiver of sinful humanity ... If asked to forgive, by anyone for anything, I would forgive because God would forgive.'[9] The Holocaust scholar Lawrence Langer took a very different position. Regarding Wiesenthal's 'What would you have done?' to be an illegitimate question because 'I have no idea what I might have done in Simon Wiesenthal's place', Langer went on to call the Holocaust 'an unforgivable crime'. In his view, the SS man in *The Sunflower* had made killing choices, choices to commit atrocities that cannot be encompassed by conventional moral and religious vocabularies that use words such as 'misdeed' or even 'wrong'. Thus, Langer argued, the SS man's actions had 'permanently cut himself off from the possibility of forgiveness'.[10]

Less certain than Langer, Hubert Locke, a pioneering African-American scholar of the Holocaust and genocide, focused on Wiesenthal's silence. 'There is much that silence might teach us', wrote Locke, 'if we could but learn to listen to it. Not the least of its lessons is that there may well be questions for which there are no answers and other questions for which answers would remove the moral force of the question.'[11] Abraham Joshua Heschel was more direct than Locke but not inconsistent with the latter's ethics: no living person, said Heschel, 'can extend forgiveness for the suffering of any one of the six million people who perished'.[12]

No writer has responded to the Holocaust with greater insight than the Auschwitz survivor Primo Levi. He thought that Wiesenthal correctly refused to pardon the dying man but added that 'it is quite easy to see why you were left with doubts: in a case like this it is impossible to decide categorically between the answers yes and no; there always remains something to be said for the other side'.[13] Levi's insight is important: where forgiveness and the issues surrounding it are concerned, a 'one size fits all' interpretation may rightly elude us. Nevertheless, some basic principles still come into view. Levi and others who have been mentioned bring them into focus.

In another place, Levi said that 'to forgive is not my verb', but he also articulated conditions that might move him to use it. He would be unwilling to forgive any of the Holocaust's culprits

> unless he has shown (with deeds, not words, and not too long afterwards) that he has become conscious of the crimes and errors ... and is determined to condemn them, uproot them, from his conscience and from that of others. Only in this case am I, a non-Christian, prepared to follow the Jewish and Christian precept of forgiving my enemy, because an enemy who sees the error of his ways ceases to be an enemy.[14]

Levi's statement indicates that forgiveness is voluntary. It is a gift, freely given by the victim, not a requirement or an obligation. Furthermore, forgiveness should have conditions; it ought not to be granted too freely. The one who has harmed another should seek forgiveness and approach the wronged person not only with words that ask for forgiveness but also through actions that reveal both deep awareness of, and regret for, the wrong that has been done, plus determination to condemn and uproot attitudes and policies – in oneself and others – that perpetuate such harmdoing. Furthermore, and this condition is of crucial importance, these steps of repentance and atonement must be timely. Where genuine repentance is concerned, the kind that condemns and roots out the wrong one has done and extends those actions in taking responsibility for others, the rule should be 'the quicker the better' as far as any case for forgiveness is concerned.

In addition, Levi implies, forgiveness would be wrong if it tried to speak for others and particularly for the dead. Levi's reflections about forgiveness are focused on what happened to him and on how he should relate to people who affected him directly during the Holocaust. His outlook supports the view of Abraham Joshua Heschel, which is widely shared by the respondents to Wiesenthal's dilemma in *The Sunflower*: 'It is preposterous', said Heschel, 'to assume that anybody alive can extend forgiveness for the suffering of any one of the six million people who perished. According to Jewish tradition, even God Himself can only forgive sins committed against Himself, not against man.'[15]

Clarity about forgiveness requires lucidity about who can forgive whom and for what. I can forgive someone for the wrong they have done to me. You can do likewise for those who have harmed you. The harm that has been done may have been primarily directed at others and caused me or you to suffer for that reason. Your forgiveness or mine can be for the hurt that is ours, but not for the suffering or loss that another has experienced. They, and they alone, have the prerogative to forgive for that. In no case, moreover, is forgiveness something that can be earned. Nor can it rightly be demanded. The perpetrator can ask; the victim can rightly refuse. As the Belgian-Catholic moral theologian Didier Pollefeyt has wisely said, 'Like love, forgiveness must be given freely; otherwise it cannot be real.'[16]

How would that view fit, if it does, with the Jewish tradition that a person who sincerely seeks forgiveness three times should be granted it, or with the Christian tradition, which enjoins forgiveness so intently and frequently that a follower of Jesus seems all but duty-bound to grant it?[17] One sound response is that injunctions to grant forgiveness are important because the absence of forgiveness, when conditions for it have been met, is dangerously close to mercilessness, which is, in turn, a condition that makes the world inhuman. Yet even when one should forgive, the forgiveness can only be real when it is neither coerced, nor done out of duty alone, but instead is freely given.

If the reality of forgiveness depends both on its being freely given and on its being given properly, what does that perspective imply about whether some actions and events, such as the Holocaust, are unforgivable? My response is as follows: strictly speaking, as far as human relationships are concerned, many actions and events are unforgivable. If one person, for instance, has murdered another, the murder is unforgivable in the sense that the basic condition for forgiveness has been abolished. The victim is dead. He or she cannot forgive, no matter how repentant the murderer may turn out to be, and no one can speak for the victim. Others may forgive the repentant murderer for what has been done to them, but the offence remains unforgivable in a basic way. It follows that the Holocaust is unforgivable because, as Heschel pointed out, no living person can speak for the millions of murdered Jews. 'Forgiveness', as Pollefeyt says, 'can only take place between the living.'[18]

What about God's point of view? Is the Holocaust forgivable by God? The answer could be *yes*. Heschel, for instance, holds that God cannot forgive sins committed against man but can forgive those 'committed against Himself'.[19] The Holocaust, of course, was a sin against God or nothing could be. Assuming, and it is a huge but still instructive assumption, that repentant perpetrators stood before God in an afterlife, would God, should God, forgive them for the Holocaust?

Elie Wiesel thought about such questions at Auschwitz in late January 1995. When he spoke at a ceremony commemorating the fiftieth anniversary of that camp's liberation, his remarks included prayerful comments. 'Although we know that God is merciful', said Wiesel, 'please God, do not have mercy on those who created this place. God of forgiveness, do not forgive the murderers of Jewish children here. Do not forgive the murderers and their accomplices ... God, merciful God, do not have mercy on those who had no mercy on Jewish children.'[20] Troubled by Wiesel's statement, the Roman Catholic Holocaust scholar Carol Rittner interviewed him about it in October 1996. Thought-provoking points resulted.

Affirming that God can do what he wants, Wiesel indicated that divine forgiveness for the Holocaust's perpetrators would truly be a cause for protest against God unless two conditions, both unknown to us, have been met. First, it would be obscene for God to show mercy to Holocaust perpetrators if God has not done so for the 1.5 million Jewish children whom they killed during the Holocaust. It is not clear, at least not yet for those of us who still inhabit the earth, that God has been merciful to those girls and boys or to any other Jew murdered by the Germans. Second, Wiesel stressed that forgiveness 'presupposes an admission of guilt, contrition, and remorse. I have not seen', he added, 'the killers express remorse or contrition, much less guilt.'[21]

What if those conditions were met, somehow and somewhere, not in this world but perhaps beyond it? Wiesel did not address that issue in his interview with Rittner, but speculative though it is, the question may be instructive. Even if a Holocaust perpetrator admitted guilt and expressed contrition and remorse in an after-life, God might say, 'Too late.' But given the emphasis that Judaism and Christianity place on God's mercy and love, it seems likely that God would say, 'Better late than never', if the admission of guilt and the expression of contrition and remorse were genuine. It is this possibility, remote though it might be, that gives Wiesel's petition at Auschwitz – 'God of forgiveness, do not forgive' – its jarring quality. God's ways, however, are not for us to decide, although it is important to underscore two more points that are closely related to

Wiesel's prayer at Auschwitz: first, if God forgave even one *repentant* Holocaust perpetrator but did not show mercy to the murdered Jewish children, then there would be additional reasons for protest. Furthermore, if God forgave even one *unrepentant* Holocaust perpetrator, to that extent God would be complicit with that perpetrator, especially if God had not been merciful to the Holocaust's victims. In addition, not even God could rightly grant forgiveness for the entire Holocaust unless all Holocaust perpetrators were genuinely repentant and all Holocaust victims were shown mercy. It is scarcely imaginable that God's mercy after the Holocaust could be sufficient to meet these conditions.

Such judgments, focused as they are on circumstances beyond history, also direct attention back to our present world and God's possible relation to it. Who needs forgiveness? If the answer, in part, is *all of us do*, and, in part, *some of us do more than others*, then God may need forgiveness too, for unless God is either nonexistent or lacking in power, God was not merciful during the Holocaust, at least not sufficiently, or God's anger was unleashed in ways that are truly and hideously beyond understanding.

Forgiveness is an *after*-word and also a *wounded* word. Differences about forgiveness, its value and priority, are to be expected, for there is no 'one size fits all' approach to forgiveness that is likely to be credible. Nevertheless these reflections may have glimpsed some insights that can be shared by people of diverse experiences and traditions. In summary, I offer six of them:

- Human beings do harm, often immense harm, to one another. Therefore, forgiveness is needed because without it too many wounds will fester unnecessarily.
- Although needed, forgiveness is dangerous because it can minimize accountability, trivialize suffering and condone injustice, if only inadvertently.
- To avoid the dangers of forgiveness while undergirding the human need for it, basic conditions for granting forgiveness should be met. First and foremost, repentance is required. It includes heartfelt confession that one has done wrong, contrite determination to do all that one can to set matters right, and timeliness in taking those steps.
- Where forgiveness is concerned, no one alive can speak for anyone else, let alone for everyone and least of all for the dead. Forgiveness is a relationship between specific living persons, one

in which a person can seek or grant forgiveness for particular harm that one person has inflicted on another.

• Many deeds and events, including the Holocaust, are unforgivable, at least in large measure, because they involve persons whose lives have been taken from them, and they are in no position to forgive, at least not in any way of which we have knowledge in our current times and places.

• Forgiveness cannot rightly be demanded or coerced. If and when it is granted, forgiveness is a gift. When genuine repentance exists, however, the reasons *for* bestowing and *against* withholding forgiveness grow more compelling.

Reaching the end of these brief reflections on forgiveness, there is no closure. As we struggle with forgiveness as an *after*-word, as a *wounded* word, the goal is not so much to have the last word but to summon a latent word, to discover anew or for the first time what a post-Holocaust understanding and practice of forgiveness ought to be. Forgiveness, then, is an *after*-word in more ways than one. In exploring forgiveness we are not only trying to discern what it can mean at a time subsequent to, or later than, what came *before*. We are also seeking or questing for something we do not yet have, something we are *after*. In their most fundamental sense, our inquiries about forgiveness are after nothing less than the restoration of a broken human image. Reflections about forgiveness are by no means the only path in that direction, but the quest to recover and deepen our humanity will be impeded and impoverished unless we continue to ask and respond thoughtfully to versions of the question 'Who Needs Forgiveness?'

NOTES

1.   Emmanuel Levinas, *Difficile liberté: Essais sur le judaïsme* (Paris: Albin Michel, 1963), p.37. The translation is Didier Pollefeyt's. For a fuller discussion of the themes and issues discussed in this essay, see my book *Ethics During and After the Holocaust: In the Shadow of Birkenau* (New York: Palgrave Macmillan, 2005), especially the chapter on 'The Ethics of Forgiveness'.

2.   The quotation is from Isaiah 56:7 as found in *Tanakh: The Holy Scriptures* (Philadelphia: Jewish Publication Society, 1988). Citations from the Hebrew Bible refer to this translation and edition.

3.   For this discussion see *Berakoth* 7a, trans. Maurice Simon, in I. Epstein (ed.), *Hebrew-English Edition of the Babylonian Talmud* (London: Soncino Press, 1990).

4.   See Psalms 7:12.

5.   Isaiah 56:5.

6.   See James E. Young, *The Texture of Memory: Holocaust Memorial and Meaning* (New Haven, CT: Yale University Press, 1993), pp.243–60, esp. p.244.

7.   Simon Wiesenthal, *The Sunflower: On the Possibilities of Limits of Forgiveness*, revised and expanded edition (New York: Schocken Books, 1997). All citations are to this edi-

tion, which includes an updated symposium edited by Harry James Cargas and Bonny V. Fetterman.

8. Ibid., p.108.
9. Ibid., pp.163–4.
10. Ibid., pp.177–8.
11. Ibid., p.192.
12. Ibid., pp.165–6.
13. Ibid., p.182.
14. See Giorgio Calcagno's interview with Levi, regarding the latter's 1986 book *The Drowned and the Saved*, in Primo Levi, *The Voice of Memory: Interviews, 1967–1987*, edited by Marco Belpoliti and Robert Gordon; translated by Robert Gordon (New York: The New Press, 2001), p.111. See also Levi, 'Self-Interview', in *The Voice of Memory*, p.186. In the quoted passage, Levi's specification that he is not a Christian is a significant one. As Levi himself would have understood, his Jewish identity is well known. Ordinarily there would have been no need for him to state that he is not a Christian. He did so, I believe, because he was speaking about forgiveness, even suggesting that there might be Holocaust perpetrators who could once have been worthy of it. Conventional wisdom sometimes holds that forgiveness is more a 'Christian' quality than a 'Jewish' one. Levi may have wanted to clarify that his outlook was not buying into a Christian ethic of one kind or another. On the issue of whether the Christian tradition emphasizes forgiveness more or at least differently than Judaism does, a one-size-fits-all resolution is not to be found. It can be said, however, that a position such as the one articulated by Theodore Hesburgh in *The Sunflower*, and noted above, would be consistent neither with Jewish teaching nor even with all forms of Christian theology and ethics.
15. Wiesenthal, *The Sunflower*, pp.165–6.
16. Didier Pollefeyt, 'Forgiveness after the Holocaust', in David Patterson and John K. Roth (eds), *After-Words: Post-Holocaust Struggles with Forgiveness, Reconciliation, Justice* (Seattle: University of Washington Press, 2004), p.61.
17. The Gospels of the Christian New Testament make clear that Jesus expects his followers to be forgiving people. A classic text is Matthew 18:21–2. Peter asks how often one should forgive a person who sins against him. 'As many as seven times?' he wonders. Jesus replies, 'Not seven times,' Jesus replies, 'but, I tell you, seventy-times seven'. The context surrounding this passage is important because it illustrates that Jesus typically insists not that forgiveness should be given no matter what, but that the imperative to forgive is especially strong where the person who has harmed another is repentant toward that individual. It is even important for a community to hold its members accountable, to point out the error of their ways, so that repentance is encouraged. Then, if and whenever repentance is genuine, forgiveness should follow, for that is God's way, and Jesus urges his followers to walk in that path. Indeed, only if Jesus' followers forgive those who have trespassed against them, can they expect God's forgiveness for their own sins.

Jesus also makes clear that timeliness is important. Repentance and forgiveness should come the quicker the better, for God's judgment is at hand. In this context, Matthew 5:23–6 has important light to shed. In that passage, Jesus teaches that repentance before a brother or sister who has 'something against you' takes precedence over making an altar gift to God, the implication being that the gift to God could be neither authentic nor well regarded by God if a person is unrepentant about wrong or harm he or she has done to another. Likewise, Jesus urges his followers to 'come to terms quickly with your accuser'. Here the implication is that the accusation is just, and that one needs to come to terms about it and in a timely manner. If not, says Jesus, 'your accuser may hand you over to the judge, and the judge to the guard, and you will be thrown in prison. Truly I tell you, you will never get out until you have paid the last penny.' Jesus did not dispense 'cheap grace', nor should his followers.

When the Christian emphasis on repentance and judgment gets muted, that tradition is open to the charge that it dispenses 'cheap grace'. Thus, Christians need to be careful about some New Testament texts that seem to make forgiveness imperative even where repentance is not evident. Mark 11:25, for example, might appear to be an unqualified imperative that does not make repentance a condition for forgiveness: 'Whenever you stand praying,' says Jesus, 'forgive, if you have anything against anyone; so that your Father in heaven may also forgive you your trespasses.' This passage should not be regarded as trumping the far more pronounced emphasis that Jesus places on repentance as a condition for forgiveness, but it can and should be read to stress that followers of Jesus are to be predisposed to granting forgiveness. When the right conditions for forgiveness are present, a follower of Jesus will not hold back forgiveness any more than God himself would do so. It is important for Christians to be clear that Christianity is not a religion of 'cheap grace'. It is also important for Christians to be forgiving when repentance is forthcoming.

18. Pollefeyt, 'Forgiveness after the Holocaust', p.64.
19. Wiesenthal, *The Sunflower*, p.166.
20. The quotation from Wiesel is taken from Carol Rittner's important chapter, 'What Can a Christian Say about Forgiveness?' in Carol Rittner and John K. Roth (eds), *'Good News' after Auschwitz? Christian Faith within a Post-Holocaust World* (Macon: Mercer University Press, 2001), p.121. Rittner's careful research about Wiesel's statement is significant. 'Although Wiesel includes a version of this prayer in his memoir, *And the Sea Is Never Full*', says Rittner, 'I have taken the version I am using from the *New York Times*, 27 January 1995. This version is corroborated by what was reported in the *Washington Post*, 27 January 1995, and also by the excerpt of his speech reprinted in *McLean's* (22 February 1995).' The version in Wiesel's memoirs appears to be slightly edited from what appeared in the news media almost immediately following his presentation (pp.121–2, n.17).
21. See Rittner's interview with Wiesel, 'What Can a Christian Say about Forgiveness?' p.125.

19 Forgiveness and Reconciliation after the Shoah

JOHN PAWLIKOWSKI

For the last decade or so I have grappled with trying to understand what forgiveness and reconciliation might mean in the context of the Holocaust for me as a Christian theologian. I have been accompanied in that search by a Jewish colleague and friend, Carolyn Manosevitz, who has struggled with overcoming the pain and suffering after the Holocaust through her art and teaching. For her the search has been a very personal one in view of the impact on her own family of the horrors wrought during the Nazi era. She has taken this search to her art studio and to her classrooms at Austin Presbyterian Seminary as well as Wesley Theological Seminary in Washington. We also pursued this search through dialogical encounters such as the one she organized in Aspen, Colorado, near her home, several summers ago, and her presentation at the 2006 International Annual Conference of Christians and Jews in Vienna.

Manosevitz's goal has always been the same – personal healing. But, while deeply personal for her, she has also sought to share this experience of healing with others. For in the end, she has found healing, as she makes clear in her writings, in the presence of the other. I myself have been an enriched recipient of the fruits of her search through her writings, reflecting on her art and sharing in the Aspen encounter with her.

To a degree, my search has paralleled that of Carolyn Manosevitz. But only to a degree. Mine has been an effort to recover integrity for my religious tradition and my continued participation in it. Hers has been much deeper, for it has involved a healing of soul and spirit. I have tried to articulate my response through speaking and writing. So has she. But she has also expressed the results of her personal search through art, something I cannot ever hope to duplicate. The artist's image and the writer's word are both powerful symbols. But the former carries the greater power to evoke and ultimately to heal the basic depths of one's being.

My more than four decades of involvement in study and reflection on the Shoah as a Christian scholar in dialogue with the Jews, as well as a central participant in the establishment of the United States Holocaust Memorial Museum in Washington, has enabled me to enter the life stories of many different participants in the overall experience of the Shoah – victims, rescuers, military liberators, resistance leaders. I have felt the pain of the victims, the shock of the liberators, the fierce determination of rescuers and resisters, though I have not endured the experience the same way as those directly involved. I have, as a scholar and teacher of the Shoah, been forced to grapple with the challenging reality that many of my brothers and sisters in the Christian faith at the time chose the path of collaborator or bystander rather than rescuer.

On a number of occasions during my academic career, I have been asked to discuss the issue of forgiveness in the context of the Shoah. As I have done so in writings and conference addresses, I have come to realize a considerable distance between Jewish and Christian perspectives. The bone marrow of Christians is filled with words of Jesus urging love for enemies and forgiveness. Some biblical scholars, such as my colleague at Catholic Theological Union Donald Senior and the late Jewish scholar of the New Testament David Flusser, have termed this emphasis on forgiveness as Jesus' most distinctive teaching. As a Christian, one feels almost hardhearted not to consider forgiveness and reconciliation, no matter how heinous the crime. But understanding gained from contact with survivors of the Shoah that I have encountered through my work with the Holocaust Museum in Washington and my teaching at the Holocaust Foundation in the Chicago area has put a large roadblock in my instinctive Christian impulse immediately to argue for forgiveness. The writings and dedicated work of Simon Wiesenthal have also given me pause in this regard. The question that has haunted me as a Christian in such circumstances is whether I can stand in the presence of people who have endured the pain and loss of the Holocaust and immediately proclaim the need for forgiveness and reconciliation. In all honesty, I began to realize that if I were to retain personal integrity I could not.

The question of forgiveness/reconciliation in the context of the Shoah has been with us for a long time. My long-time colleague in the dialogue, Rabbi Leon Klenicki, has addressed it in a number of essays. Klenicki has pressed hard over the years for his fellow Jews to overcome what he terms the 'triumphalism of pain' in terms of contemporary Jewish identity. Yet, despite his call, he too has found it difficult to deal with the question. In an article appearing in *The Catholic Response* Klenicki speaks of the same thought that arises for him every Yom Kippur (Day of Atonement).[1] What would he do as a member of a family that lost loved ones during the Shoah if an SS officer or an Argentine torturer were to ask him for forgiveness? He does not feel that he has an answer that is completely satisfactory. The experience of personal and familial pain cannot determine his response. Yet, can he simply act as an individual in the matter? He thinks not. Rather, primacy must be given in his answer to his situation as a member of the Jewish community. Since he was not personally present in Germany during the Shoah nor in his adopted country of Argentina in the days of governmental terror which took the lives of the *desaparecidos* he does not feel that he has the right to forgive anyone in their name, no matter how sincere the request for such forgiveness. All he can do is urge a perpetrator to repent and atone.

Klenicki believes that the Jewish tradition sustains him in the above approach. While the tradition certainly recognizes the importance and possibility of human forgiveness, in part as a prelude to the forgiveness that ultimately comes from God, such forgiveness can come only after demonstrated atonement through acts of goodness. The community, through witnesses, must attest to the verbal requests for forgiveness and to the performance of good deeds. This has in fact been the position adopted by the Action/Reconciliation movement begun in Germany in the aftermath of the Nazi era. Only in this way can the rupture in the divine covenant caused by the sinful acts of the perpetrators be healed. Since God is integral to the covenant, there must be divine confirmation of the forgiveness initially offered at the human level.

So, for Judaism, forgiveness/reconciliation is considerably more complex than for Christianity. In Christianity, the tendency is far more of an individual–individual process and a God–individual process although one might argue for a communal dimension to the Sacrament of Penance which regrettably has been de-emphasized over the years. The efforts to restore a far more communal approach to the sacrament after Vatican Council II has often met resistance. In Judaism, the role of the community, even if expressed only in symbolic ways (that is, a few witnesses) remains central. This distinction often causes tension within the Jewish–Christian dialogue where Christians want to offer forgiveness rather quickly after a sincere request while Jews are considerably more hesitant. Failure on the part of Christians to understand this distinction sometimes makes the Jews appear 'hardhearted' in contrast to Christians. But, as Klenicki puts it, unless the perpetrators have shown that they have been transformed into 'tools of goodness' on a sustained basis, 'granting a provisory forgiveness without a changing of the heart is essentially an act of forgetting the crime and the criminal'. The Truth and Reconciliation Commission in South Africa took something of this approach.

In the end Klenicki insists he can grant forgiveness only if the rabbinic conditions are met: a change of heart on the part of the perpetrator, a spoken confession of sins, and evidence of a permanent new commitment to virtue and goodness that positively impact the welfare of society. Nothing less will suffice. Klenicki then goes on to add that genuine forgiveness will also affect one's natural resentment in such a situation. We should not pretend that resentment is not part of a full picture in such a context. It is naturally there and it is best to lay it out rather than give the impression of false nobility in this regard. He speaks as follows: 'My forgiveness is also a response to my personal resentment. My forgiveness of the other who has gone through confession and repentance is the beginning of healing, my own personal healing, and hopefully of the one who confessed and repented. Forgiveness, though difficult at times, is a process of overcoming resentment and achieving healing.'[2]

Klenicki's approach parallels that of Simon Wiesenthal to some extent. In his famous volume *The Sunflower*, Wiesenthal took up the issue of the possibilities and limits of forgiveness/reconciliation through a story about a dying Nazi soldier who requests forgiveness from him.[3] Whether an actual or fictional account, the tale has become a classic introduction to the Jewish approach to forgiveness and to the apparent differences between Christianity and Judaism in the matter.

The basics of *The Sunflower* storyline are these. While imprisoned in a Nazi concentration camp, Wiesenthal was taken one day from his work detail to the bedside of a dying member of the SS. Haunted by the crimes in which he had participated, the soldier wanted to confess to, and obtain absolution from, a Jew. Wiesenthal agonized over this man's request which he judged sincere. Many of the questions raised by Klenicki came to his mind as well, with respect to the Jewish tradition on forgiveness/reconciliation. The issue was somewhat more complicated because the soldier sought not so much personal forgiveness from Wiesenthal (with whom he had no prior contact) but rather forgiveness from the Jewish community. In the end, Wiesenthal rejected the soldier's request, feeling, as Klenicki has felt, that he could not offer forgiveness in the name of the Jewish people. But that was in fact not quite the end of the story. For after the soldier dies, Wiesenthal arranges to have the dead soldier's personal effects sent home to the man's mother with a note. One can interpret this gesture in several ways. I prefer to see it as an act resulting from a measure of uncertainty within Wiesenthal. He did what he sincerely believed that Jewish tradition demanded of him. But on a personal level he still wished to respond to the soldier's genuine wish for reconciliation. So the complexity of the forgiveness/reconciliation issue seemed to remain for Wiesenthal. He solved it as best as he could which is perhaps all any of us can do.

In my judgment Wiesenthal was correct in withholding such requested reconciliation, for it would have provided the man with what the theologian Dietrich Bonhoeffer referred to as 'cheap grace'. That Wiesenthal might have said or done something to provide the dying soldier with a limited sense of personal forgiveness is certainly open to discussion, although the fact that the soldier seemed to regard Wiesenthal primarily as a 'Communal symbol' rather than a single human person complicated the matter considerably. If Wiesenthal had unlinked forgiveness from reconciliation, however, he might have found the way to offer the man some sense of forgiveness while making it clear that under the circumstances it was impossible to effect reconciliation with the Jewish victims as a whole. Reconciliation and forgiveness do not always have to be in tandem. One can grant one and not the other. That is the reality of the human situation. If Wiesenthal had taken this last path rather than the one he did, he may have alleviated that burden of uncertainty that appears to hang over him till the very end of the story. He would have responded positively to the sense of human bonding, despite the soldier's terrible crimes, of which he seems terribly aware, while safeguarding against any premature feeling of reconciliation on the part of the soldier.

The other central question with respect to Wiesenthal is his reputation as 'the Nazi hunter' par excellence. This leads us directly into a central point of discussion and controversy in our day: the struggle between the viewpoints represented on the one hand by the people who support the International Criminal Court (ICC) and on the other those who advocate the model of South Africa's Truth and Reconciliation Commission as the preferred way to deal with massive assaults on human dignity whether fully genocidal or not. Wiesenthal clearly represented the mindset behind the first option. I find myself somewhere in the middle. I have supported the establishment of the ICC because I do believe that war criminals need to stand trial and deserve severe punishment if they played a leading role. The purification of society requires this. I think Wiesenthal clearly and correctly understood this in his relentless search for those who masterminded the Shoah. As one committed to my Catholic ethical tradition where the death penalty has been practically eliminated from the canons of acceptable punishment, I would not support implementation of the death sentence. And for those who played a lesser role, I would lean to the methods employed in the Truth and Reconciliation process in South Africa. But we still need additional debate on this question.

In her own struggle to find healing after the Shoah my colleague Carolyn Manosevitz has travelled much of the same road as Klenicki and Wiesenthal. Her present response is not exactly theirs – but this is the nature of such reflection. It will invariably produce differing answers to the same queries. As I have come to understand her current outlook, healing for her has come through personal encounters with the other, particularly with the other in the tradition of many of the perpetrators, that is, Christianity, who have decisively repudiated the church's classic antisemitism which served as a seedbed for the success of Nazism and demonstrated a deep commitment to prevent it from ever walking that path again. She may not have attained a fully satisfactory theology of forgiveness/reconciliation. Nor have I. But she has achieved a measure of healing through this encounter. I have a similar experience not only with regard to the Shoah but also to social and interreligious conflict generally. Such personal healing and reconciliation can overcome conflict and violence at the interpersonal level even if certain conflicts remain at the level of theological theory. We can thus live together in human solidarity as we continue to mourn, to reflect and to dialogue.

NOTES

1. Rabbi Leon Klenicki, 'Forgiveness and Repentance', *The Catholic Response*, Sept.–Oct. 2005.
2. Ibid.
3. Simon Wiesenthal, *The Sunflower: On the Possibilities and Limits of Forgiveness*, with a symposium ed. Harry James Cargas and Bonny V. Fetterman (New York: Schocken, 1997).

20 Conspiracy Theories and the Incitement of Hatred: The Dynamics of Deception, Plausibility and Defamation

PAUL WELLER

Conspiracy theories and the incitement of hatred can exist in systematic and/or arbitrary forms, as substantial components of social and political programmes and/or as individual outbursts. They can both feed upon, and feed into, individual prejudice, leading to direct and indirect discrimination against minorities, and eventually issuing into actions based on hatred and so contributing to a highly combustible social and political cocktail.

In responding to these phenomena it is very important to recognize both the *group-specific* and *generally characteristic* dynamics that are associated with conspiracy theories and the ways in which they incite hatred. For an effective understanding of, and response to, the dynamics of the prejudice, hatred and discrimination that are reflected in, and sustained by, such theories, it is important to delineate aspects of *both* their *specificity* and their *generality*.

Conspiracy theories and the incitement to hatred are just these – whichever group they are directed against, or from whatever background they are produced. In this sense, then, conspiracy theories and the incitement of hatred are a *generic issue* and they have at least some *generic characteristics*. Not to recognize this is to run the risk of being blind to the fact that there is nothing that prevents at least the *possibility*, given certain circumstances, of people from within all groups becoming involved in the creation and spread of conspiracy theories and in the incitement of hatred against another group. It is thus both the responsibility of *all* groups, of good governance in the wider society, and in the ultimate interests of all, to tackle these phenomena *whenever and wherever they appear*.

At the same time, there are also very specific aspects of the dynamics of conspiracy theories and the incitement of hatred that are directed against particular groups. Thus, the classical conspiracy theory publication the *Protocols of the Elders of Zion*, purports to reflect the conspiracy of an international group of Jews to control the world.[1] In the case of the *Protocols*, it has clearly been demonstrated that these were a forgery on the part of the real authors who, by means of this deception, had the intention of stirring up hatred against Jewish people. The broader context of antisemitic thinking and imagery reflected in the *Protocols* persists and is dangerous, still fomenting hatred against Jews and lending itself to the continuing dissemination of the *Protocols* themselves.

There are also specificities in the incitement of hatred that groups other than Jews experience. The particularity of that which is experienced by Muslims is, currently, often denoted by the term 'Islamophobia'. One of the earliest known uses of this word was in the periodical *Insight* of 4 February 1991, where 'Islamophobia' was cited as a substantial reason for the former Soviet Union's reluctance, at the time, to relinquish its position in Afghanistan. In the context of the United Kingdom, a Runnymede Trust report on discrimination against Muslims that used this word in its title brought the terminology into wider public use, with the authors of the report describing the use of this word as follows:

> The word is not ideal, but is recognizably similar to 'xenophobia' and 'europhobia', and is a useful shorthand way of referring to dread or hatred of Islam – and therefore to fear or dislike of all or most Muslims. Such dread and dislike have existed in western countries and cultures for centuries. In the last twenty years, however, the dislike has become more explicit, more extreme and more dangerous. It is an ingredient of all sections of our media, and it is prevalent in all sections of our society. Within Britain it means that Muslims are frequently excluded from the economic, social and public life of the nation ... and are frequently victims of discrimination and harassment.[2]

The Runnymede Trust had, in fact, also published an earlier report on antisemitism that, at the time it was published, received less public attention than the later one on Islamophobia.[3] The report on antisemitism was entitled *A Very Light Sleeper* and it set out some of the specific characteristics of antisemitism as a particular form of discrimination.

However, the subtitles of both these reports are significant for an understanding of the characteristics of conspiracy theories and the incitement of hatred. The subtitle of *A Very Light Sleeper* was *The Persistence and Dangers of Antisemitism*. This highlights, again, that the incitement of hatred has *specific* as well as *generic* dimensions. It is also a reminder that antisemitism is *not*, as some try to suggest, only an historical matter. Like Islamophobia, it exists today and it has specificities as well as characteristics that are shared with other forms of incitement of hatred. The subtitle of the report on *Islamophobia* was *A Challenge for us all*. This is also significant in providing a reminder that both antisemitism and Islamophobia are indeed challenges for us all, whether Christians, Jews, Muslims, people of other religions, or secular humanists – as are conspiracy theories and incitement to hatred that have either an Islamophobic or an antisemitic character.

Antisemitism is, of course, a key starting-point and focus of this memorial volume. In *not* concentrating my own contribution on this *alone* I hope I will not be misunderstood. Since the other contributions focus primarily on antisemitism, most of my chapter will address conspiracy theories and incitement of hatred against groups other than Jews in an effort to better identify some of their generic characteristics, arguing that it is a matter of universal human responsibility to combat them all.

CONSPIRACY THEORIES AND INCITEMENT TO HATRED AGAINST MUSLIMS

While in European experience, antisemitism, conspiracy theories and incitement of hatred against Jews hinge almost completely on pseudo-science, fantasy and fabrication about the supposed power that Jews have never actually wielded in European history, in the case of Islamophobia, the military conflicts between territories associated with the House of Islam and those associated with Christendom, mean that there has been an historical locus connected with Islamophobia that makes its imagery and continuing reality complex to challenge. Even more problematically, of course, aspects of this inheritance have been reinforced in a contemporary locus arising from the recent contemporary experiences of the al-Qaeda 9/11 terror attacks on the World Trade Center, the Madrid train bombing, and the London suicide bombings of the summer of 2005.

Such matters need to be stated carefully in order, as far as possible, to minimize the unfortunately almost inevitable risk of misunderstanding of what is and what is not being said in this – as would also be the case in any noting that, in the current balance of military and political power in the Israel–Palestine conflict, there is a contemporary locus that can inform aspects of current antisemitism among Muslims in the Middle East and beyond. Since acknowledging this fact does not cancel out the threatening existence of antisemitism as manifest in the continuing unrestricted circulation of the fabricated *Protocols* that can be found in many Arab states, or in attempts to turn a conflict between two people's rights to self-determination into a denial of the other's right to exist in peace and security; so, also, the historical and contemporary loci of conflict that can make Islamophobia difficult to challenge do not cancel out the reality of the Srebenica massacres of Muslims during the breakdown of Yugoslavia or the rise in religiously and racially motivated attacks against Muslims in Britain following the London suicide bombings.

As with antisemitism, many of the key images that appear in incitement to hatred against Muslims appear to have developed a life of their own that has been reproduced in a variety of different social, historical and political contexts. Steve Cohen's book *That's Funny, You Don't Look Anti-Semitic* charted the antisemitism that was to be found among the political left.[4] Similarly, Islamophic incitement to hatred is not the preserve of neo-fascist or extreme right-wing populist politics, but can also be found in politically leftist forms. In its production and dissemination, Islamophobic literature of various kinds also draws upon a common store of images. These charge Muhammad with being a liar and a deceiver. They also suggest (due to the permissibility, under certain conditions, of polygamy in Islam) that Muhammad in particular, and Muslim men in general, have insatiable sexual appetites. Finally, these images associated Islam and Muslimism per se with violence and intolerance.

In 1213 Pope Innocent III described Muhammad as 'the Beast of the Apocalpyse' and, as Richard Webster explains, 'In subsequent centuries, the view of Islam as a demonic force, and of Muhammad himself as Antichrist, became deeply established in the Christian imagination.'[5] Today, and especially in the wake of the 11 September attacks on the World Trade Center and the Pentagon and the bombings in Madrid and London, many of these images appear in forms secularized by 'Orientalism'[6] in ways akin to those in which the store of classical antisemitic images also became secularized through the development of pseudo-scientific theories of racial eugenics.

Such images are recycled in crude ways in the propaganda of organizations such as the British National Party which, in recent years in Britain, has particularly targeted Muslims. This has been done by separating out Muslims as a specific category of 'undesirable other' from among other religious and ethnic minority groups, such as the Hindus and the Chinese, who are portrayed as being more acceptable. Thus, in Allen and Nielsen's *Summary Report on Islamophobia in the EU after 11 September 2001*, for the European Monitoring Centre on Racism and Xenophobia, instances were cited with special reference to Britain, where 'anti-Muslim alliances have been formed ... between right-wing groups and immigrant and ethnic minority groups', and in which generally racist agendas appear to have been suspended in favour of a (presumably temporary) alliance with extremist groups of Sikh and Hindu backgrounds.[7]

But the use of Islamophobic imagery is not only a matter of political extremes. It can also be found amongst those who would characterize themselves as political liberals. At the height of *The Satanic Verses* controversy,[8] the Muslim intellectual Shabbir Akhtar wrote an essay published in the *Independent* newspaper entitled 'The Liberal Inquisition'.[9] In its juxtaposition of two key words usually seen as incompatible, the title of this essay reflects what Muslims in Europe often experience as a sneering, ignorant form of journalism that is sometimes practised by those who would otherwise claim to be politically liberal but who nevertheless draw un-self-critically on the store of anti-Islamic imagery that many of them felt was also embodied in Rushdie's book.

Of course, this is not to say that there were no serious issues at stake in *The Satanic Verses* controversy as seen from perspectives other than those of Salman Rushdie's opponents. It is also clear that some Muslims are among people of all groups who are receptive to conspiracy theories and incitement against other groups; that there are also *some* who are active in their promotion; and also *others* who are complicit in not challenging this. In particular, the *Protocols of the Elders of Zion,* which has long been a mainstay of European antisemitism, and was also given credence in some Christian circles, building upon the broader tradition of antisemitic anti-Judaism that affected the development of much of the broader stream of Western Christianity as a whole, were given a new contemporary impetus by dissemination among Muslims. To take just one example of such dissemination, one may mention the Internet website, Radio Islam.[10]

Radio Islam does not represent any Islamic organisation, and it misrepresents the name of the religion. Under the guise of a political anti-Zionism the Radio Islam site has hyperlinks with web pages that attack Jews as such and insinuate that the Holocaust of European Jewry is historically questionable, while making accessible for its readers the original texts of the *Protocols* and of Adolf Hitler's *Mein Kampf.*

In the incitement of hatred to which they are *both* subjected, Muslims as well as Jews have been the target of Internet materials that share one of the key generic features of conspiracy theories, and that is the characteristic of 'deception'. One of the key dimensions of the *Protocols* is that they purport to be what they are not. In view of the commitment to truth-seeking that lies at the heart of the academic endeavour and vocation, such deception is one of the key reasons why academics as academics have a role and a responsibility in combating such literatures and the conspiracy theories that they contain. But compared with other forms of literature that are a pure and unadulterated outpouring of incitement to hatred, what is particularly pernicious about conspiracy theories is that they build upon a *plausibility structure*.

Again, what is and is not being said here should not be misunderstood. Reference to a plausibility structure is not in any way intended to legitimate the validity of the claims reflected in the *Protocols*. But whereas literature that consists of pure outpourings of hatred is dangerous, literature that incites hatred, but does so on the basis of a plausibility structure that *mixes elements of fact with fiction* is arguably even more dangerous. Thus, the *defamation* about a global Jewish conspiracy rests upon the *fact* that the Jewish people have been a people in Diaspora. Were this not so, then claims of a global conspiracy would have lacked any plausibility structure.

With regard also to the incitement of hatred directed against Muslims, arguably the most dangerous literature is not the crude propaganda disseminated by a number of racist and neo-fascist groups but, as with incitement to hatred that is directed against Jews, literature that is based on a *plausibility structure* that mixes the historical *fact* of military conflict along the fault-lines between the House of Islam and the territory historically identified with Christendom, together with the recent terror actions of al-Qaeda, with contemporary *fictions* about Islam as a whole and Muslims per se.

An example of a 'sophisticated deception' of an Islamophobic kind was the Sura Like It website that appeared in 1998, the story of which is outlined in Gary Bunt's book *Virtually Islamic: Computer-Mediated Communication and Cyber Islamic Environments*.[11] The very name of the website itself played on the sections or chapters of the Qur'an known as surahs. It also connected with a specific 'ayah' (or verse) of the Qur'an that stated: 'And if you are in doubt as to what We have revealed from time to time to Our servant then produce a surah like thereunto; and call your witnesses or helpers (if there are any) besides Allah if your (doubts) are true.'

What the website apparently seemed to contain were four surahs. These were entitled Surah al-Iman (Faith); Surah al-Tajassud (the Incarnation); Surah al-Muslimoon (Muslims) and Surah al-Wasya (Commandments). But these were, in fact, not surahs at all and appear to have been constructed in a way informed by aspects of Christian theology but produced in an Arabic style that was intended to evoke the Qur'an and thus to have the effect of deceit about the nature and origins of this material. On 24 June 1998, following complaints from scholars at Al-Azhar University in Cairo, the AOL (America On Line) service provider closed down the Sura Like It site, with an AOL spokesperson stating, 'We have removed that page. Our terms of service are very clear on what we call appropriate content, such as content that is defamatory in nature. This page had that. It was deliberately targeting Islam.' Thus the website was removed from its original location.

However, the site reappeared in other locations and so could still be accessed online, thus bringing out the special challenges presented by the Internet as a medium for the incitement of hatred. The Surah Like It website was dangerous precisely because, while purporting to embody words of the Holy Qur'an, it played on the images of Muhammad as a liar that have been so prevalent in the Islamophobic inheritance. As Bunt put it: 'Logically, to take Surah-Like-It one stage further, the potential exists for the creation of a totally fabricated "Islam" site, containing unauthentic materials and opinions, and claiming to be the "genuine article". The potential also exists for different religious perspectives to "hack" into each other's sites and paste messages representing their own opinions.'[12]

MUSLIMS AND SIKHS

There are, however, also other examples of deception, incitement to hatred and conspiracy theories that emerge from beyond the particular triangular dynamics involved in the relationships between the Abrahamic religious traditions and the societies and civilizations that are related to them.

An example of such conspiracy theories and the incitement of hatred can also be found in the context of Sikh–Muslim and Hindu–Muslim relations in Britain. Muslims constitute the largest religious minority in Britain, with some 1,591,126 people self-identifying as such according to the 2001 decennial Census. Britain is also home to one of the largest Sikh populations outside of India – 336,149 people according to the Census. Although perhaps not so well known except among those most closely engaged in this area, there have, in recent times, been increasing tensions, sometimes spilling over into violence, between Sikh and Muslim youth.

The particular example set out here to illustrate the role that deception can play in conspiracy theories and incitement to hatred is not one, like that of the *Protocols*, that relates to a formal publication, but rather emerges from the category of literature known as ephemera. Ephemera are a type of literature that is often not taken sufficiently seriously in academic study and research – although the growth of the Internet means that the distinction between publication and ephemera is beginning to break down. Even in printed form, among ordinary members of many religious communities, what is written and distributed in newsletters, magazines and leaflets can play as much if not more of a role in the formation of opinion and attitudes than major published works.

While historical analysis can show the *Protocols* to be a forgery, deception is a particularly difficult issue to deal with in the case of ephemera. In the end, the provenance of ephemera might *really* remain unclear, and the uncertainty and mutual suspicion that such literature brings about, regardless of who actually created and circulated it, can very much be a part of the problem that is thereby created and of its effects. The following examples are drawn from the Internet.[13] The first piece appeared under the overall heading 'Conversion Truths' and was entitled 'The Truth about Conversions: 10 Secrets the Muslims Don't Want You to Know'. Although the title of this piece refers to 'the Muslims' in general, much of its content is actually concerned with the radical Islamist group, Hizb ut-Tahrir. This group is known for its activities on university campuses in Britain, targeting especially Jews, Hindus and homosexuals and, as a consequence, have been banned from a number of British universities.

The now-defunct singh.co.uk website had picked up on these activities in featuring unprovenanced leaflets that had circulated in Derby and other cities, as if coming from a Muslim source. In these leaflets, Sikh women were talked about in various crude ways. The centrepiece of one flyer posted ostensibly encouraged Muslims to convert Sikh girls, by taking them to pubs and getting them drunk. The crudity of this leaflet, by focusing on women to impact sharply on the highly emotive issues of family honour that can be found among people of a South Asian cultural background, sent shock waves through local Muslim–Sikh relations.

The second piece on the same website, entitled 'Open Your Eyes', picked up on this, quoting the leaflet entitled *A Message to Muslim Youth* to the effect that, 'It is easy to take the Sikh girls out on a date as they generally like a good drink and from there gradually they can be brought into Islam.' The third piece was a poem entitled *Regrets...I have many*, and which portrayed 'the lifestyle and thoughts of an impressionable young Sikh girl who had been deceived by the false charm of a Muslim boy'. The piece on 'Open Your Eyes' stated that 'This is not a hate campaign against Islam' and that 'We apologise if we have made any errors in this article, or if we have offended anyone.' However, it also stated that 'this is the truth and sometimes the truth hurts'.

The issue of what did and did not actually occur here is very difficult to determine owing to the nature of the literature concerned and the mutual antipathy that exists between parts of both the groups concerned. Once again, there are difficult and sensitive issues involved here that any attempt to highlight can all too easily run the risk of being misunderstood. However, whatever the rights and wrongs of the claims and counter-claims in an example of this kind, what does clearly emerge from this example is that incitement to hatred by targeting particular groups and playing on community fears and vulnerabilities, and/or by the advocating the existence of wider conspiracy theories as held by whole groups can, especially in ephemera literature, contribute to a *general destabilization* in relations between groups.

The practice of using sexual attraction to recruit impressionable young people does exist in other contexts. It is, for example, attested in the so-called 'flirty fishing' for recruitment used by the group (often seen as a Christian-related 'sect' or 'cult') known in the 1970s as the Children of God. In this and other examples, entrapment via the use of sexuality has been used as a means of recruiting others. So, in the case of this particular material relating to the relationships between Muslims and Sikhs a general *plausibility structure* is there. More particularly, the Hizb ut-Tahrir organization *has* been involved in conflictual activities and ephemera literature of the kind referred to in the pieces on 'Open Your Eyes' and 'The Truth about Conversions' *did* exist and *were* circulated.

But the actual provenance of the literature was, at the time, uncertain, and a number of features of the leaflets concerned gave rise to questions about the authenticity of their apparent source. It is also the case that everything is as not always as it might seem at first sight. For example, in the wake of destruction of the mosque at Ayodhya in India, a number of arson attacks occurred on places of Hindu worship throughout Britain, including one in the author's home city of Derby. No doubt some attacks of this kind did occur at the hands of some Muslim youth. But there was also evidence to suggest that others were conducted by external *agents provocateurs* with the specific intention of fomenting inter-community strife. So, it may well be that there are some groups of Muslims who are targeting Sikh girls for conversion and, in the process, were distributing crude literature in ways that that could definitely be seen as inciting hatred.

Sadly, however, it is also possible for responses that seek to highlight such forms of incitement to hatred themselves to also exhibit some of these traits by extrapolating actions claimed to be being undertaken by one, small and extreme faction within a particular group, and applying these to the generality of the group as a whole. Thus the singh.co.uk piece on conversion begins with a prefatory statement that explains: 'All of this can be verified by reading transcripts of the Koran or visiting the Hizb ut-tahrir and Khalifa websites.' However, no specific references are given and the reader is only referred to web search engines. In so doing, the impression is given of the authenticity of the claims but without the provision of any reference that would allow this to be checked. In addition, a formulation of this kind associates the teaching of the Qur'an with the supposed ideological positions of a particular organization such as Hizb ut-Tahrir.

In closing its preface, the singh.co.uk piece on conversion goes on to urge its readers to 'remember that we as a Sikh people have been under attack from the Muslims since the Arabs rose to power in 713AD'. Therefore, whether or not the original leaflet came from Hizb ut-Tahrir or another Muslim source, a website that seeks to warn about this ends up by associating the vast majority of Muslims with something that, if produced by Muslims at all, is likely to have been produced by only a small minority.

PAGANS AND NEW RELIGIOUS MOVEMENTS

Finally, there is incitement of hatred against Pagans and members of New Religious Movements (often popularly referred to as 'sects' or 'cults'). This may be thought by many within 'mainstream' groups as something not to be associated with in any way. But it is important also to take account of this particular form.

Paganism, like other traditions, has itself not always been immune from conspiracy theories and connections with the incitement to hatred of other groups. In this connection there has especially been some use of the so-called 'Northern Traditions'[14] of Paganism among a number of individuals and groups who hold extreme right-wing ideologies and antisemitic views. However, there has been comparatively little attention paid to the Pagan experience of being at the sharp end of conspiracy theories and of the incitement of hatred. But in a project on religious discrimination in England and Wales that the author and other colleagues undertook for the Home Office in 1999–2001, while discrimination against Muslims, Hindus and Sikhs was highlighted and there was also evidence of continuing antisemitism, the stories of incitement to hatred and conspiracy theories as experienced by Pagans made particularly poignant reading.[15]

In the measured language of such reports for government, the summary findings stated that, 'Pagans and people from "New Religious Movements" also complained of open hostility and discrimination, and of being labelled as "child abusers" and "cults", particularly by the media.'[16] And one of the key findings of the report was that: 'Pagans and members of New Religious Movements, in particular, reported a degree of hostility which often seemed to match the experiences of visible minorities, and they also drew attention to stereotyping and sensationalism in the media.'[17]

To give some flavour of the effects of such reporting, the project's final report included a range of short 'sound bites' from responses to the project's questionnaire survey. For Pagans these included: 'fostering made difficult', 'child taken away for being a witch', 'Pagans treated with hostility and mistrust', 'accused of being devil worshipers'.[18] In fact, contemporary Pagans and members of New Religious Movements have to deal with very severe defamation in the popular media, starting with their very characterization as 'sects' and 'cults'.

In the case of Paganism, the contemporary media have linked Paganism so closely with child abuse that many Pagans feel they cannot openly affirm their Pagan identity, especially if they are employed in any job connected with children. Thus our project's report recorded an interview with two Pagans who 'reported that they feel that they have to take measures to keep their religious lives secret while at work. One said that, if confronted about his Pagan identity, he would need to lie. As a consequence, however, they fear they may be perceived as being suspect and dishonest and they were worried that negative stereotypes would be perpetuated if anyone found out.'[19]

To understand at least part of the reason for how such misrepresentation can come about, one has only to consider the way in which early Christians in the Roman Empire were accused of incest and cannibalism. This was, of course, on the basis of a sensationalist and distorted external perception of a small religious minority in which a liturgical 'kiss of peace' took place between male and female Christians who referred to one another within the community of faith as 'brothers' and 'sisters', and in the context of celebrating the eucharist in which bread and wine were shared among the congregation using words that liturgically connected these elements with the body and blood of Jesus.

Richard Webster points out that the European imagination's linkage of Paganism with lurid imagery of sexual abuse is something that has been deeply rooted and developed over centuries. He says,

> It was this vision which was, for some two hundred years, expounded, elaborated, documented or illustrated by some of the most pious and educated minds in Europe. It was by minds such as these, working in a troubled alliance with the popular imagination and including the inquisitors themselves, that the idea of witchcraft as an unclean anti-Christian conspiracy was created and subjected to wholly fantastical elaboration.[20]

Thus the example of Pagans and New Religious Movements is particularly instructive because, in many ways, it is a test case in relation to the generality and specificity of the dynamics of conspiracy theories and of incitement to hatred. Pagans and members of New Religious Movements have often experienced a degree of suspicion and outright hatred that would certainly be deemed unacceptable if directed towards other religious groups and this has even extended to efforts in the European Parliament to have a range of New Religious Movements restricted under European law.[21]

Again, there are sensitive and important issues involved here and what is being said and not said should not be misunderstood. That

there *are* religious groups about which it is right for the wider society to have concerns is clear. But such groups are not the preserve of
any one tradition. They can be found among New Religious
Movements and among Pagans, but they can also be found in all
'mainstream' religions. Therefore the most appropriate way
to respond to such concerns is to focus on unacceptable *activities*
conducted by *any* religious groups – particularly where these, like
conspiracy theories, involve deception and the incitement to hatred
– rather than on the *groups themselves*. Thus the example of Pagans
and members of New Religious Movements is a reminder that, if
incitement to hatred is dangerous and its effects need to be combated,
then this includes incitement to hatred *by all* and *about all*, including
also those that are among the most marginalized.

CONCLUSION

Understanding some of both the specific and general characteristics
of conspiracy theories and the incitement of hatred is not a luxury –
it is a necessity for action in containing and, where possible, rolling
back the threat presented by such phenomena. Such action might
include the following:

- Scientific research work further to develop an understanding of
  both the commonalities and specificities of conspiracy theories
  and incitement to hatred and the environment that informs and
  interacts with these.
- Comparative work with academics, professionals in the judicial
  system, and with people from religious groups, on legal provisions
  and instruments relating to the incitement of hatred.
- Educational programmes to tackle the historical roots and
  contemporary effects of the imagery used in conspiracy and hate
  literature about Jews, Muslims and other groups.
- Work with organized religious and ethnic groups to tackle the dissemination of conspiracy and hate imagery and literature within
  their own religious and ethnic communities.

On a governmental and societal level, preventative and remedial
actions are important in combating conspiracy theories and incitement
to hatred. Statements, guidelines, codes of practice and initiatives in
inter-faith dialogue are also important. However, in the end, it is *also*
crucial to engage with these issues from *within* each particular

religious and ethnic group. Such groups form powerful networks with either a potentially positive or negative role in the wider context of the civil societies in which they play an important part. Since all religious traditions affirm the centrality of truthfulness and integrity, religious leaders in particular have a responsibility actively to intervene when ephemera and other literature that defames those of other traditions goes into circulation – and especially when it circulates among worshippers in churches, mosques, synagogues, *gurdwaras* and *mandirs*, and other places of worship.

As is well known, following 11 September – and at present there is some evidence of this pattern being repeated in Britain in 2005 – many ordinary Muslims in Western societies had good reason to be living in fear. 'Enemy images' of Islam and of Muslims were beginning to develop and be reproduced, associating the entire religion of Islam and all Muslims with the actions of al-Qaeda. The atmosphere of the time is well evoked in the following extracts from Humuyan Ansari's summary in a recent Minority Rights Group International Report on *Muslims in Britain*:

> Muslim adults and children were attacked, physically and ver-
> bally. They were punched, spat at, hit with umbrellas at bus
> stops, publicly doused with alcohol and pelted with fruit and
> vegetables. Dog excrement and fireworks were pushed through
> their letterboxes and bricks through their windows. They were
> called murderers and were excluded from social gatherings ...
> Vandals attacked mosques and Asian-run businesses around the
> country. Nine pigs' heads were dumped outside a mosque in
> Exeter. Many mosques were said not to have reported attacks
> because of fear of reprisals.[22]

Experiences of this kind will also, in other circumstances, be recognized by Jews, Sikhs, Hindus and, in some parts of the world, also by Christians. But while attempting to keep a global perspective, each of us as individuals and groups can only personally act in the specific contexts in which we find ourselves. In the Western world, when modern media images of contemporary terrorist violence mingle with powerful inherited imagery, then such an atmosphere brings with it significant dangers that can affect religious communities as also the wider society. At around the time of 9/11, I happened to have been asked to be responsible for leading a service of evening worship in a Baptist Christian congregation in Derby, of which I am a member. The

Baptist Christian tradition is, in fact, one that has had an honourable tradition of upholding religious liberty and standing against intolerance and persecution on the grounds of religion, and the Baptist founder Thomas Helwys' 1612 pamphlet, *A Short Declaration of the Mystery of Iniquity*, is one of the earliest English language justifications for religious liberty that specifically included Jews, Muslims and heretics within the scope of its arguments in favour of religious freedom.[23]

However, historical positions are no guarantee of contemporary fidelity to such traditions. Basically the members of the congregation of which I am a member are good people. But, in truth, I wasn't sure how they would react to facing issues relating to relationships with Muslims post-9/11 in the context of worship. In the end, I decided that it was not good enough for me to be a Professor of Inter-Religious Relations, to write and publish on inter-faith relations, and to be involved in organizations such as the Wiesenthal Centre's Academic Response to Antisemitism and Racism in Europe, if I did not also try to address these issues in the place where I worshipped.

Although uncertain of how this would be received, I resolved that I should seek the agreement of the church's minister for me to invite a Muslim both to be present and to take an active part in that evening's worship. What I wanted people to do was to meet and hear a real Muslim and not the media images encountered on the TV screen. Agreement was given and I invited the Muslim faith advisor from the University of Derby to attend the evening worship of my church and, as part of the service itself, to be interviewed about what it means to be a Muslim in post-11 September Western societies.

It is an important part of our responsibility to press for national governments and international organizations to accept their public responsibilities in the critically important and necessary part they have to play in containing and rolling back the environments in which conspiracy theories and incitement of hatred can flourish. But in the end it is also important that all of us *individually* accept both the responsibilities and opportunities that we have in the places where we belong and in the groups in which we are active. To adapt an old rabbinic question, it really is a matter of if not me – as an academic, a parent, a citizen and a member of a religious or ethnic group – then who?

NOTES

1. N. Cohn, *Warrant for Genocide: The Myth of the Jewish World Conspiracy and the Protocols of the Learned Elders of Zion* (London: Eyre and Spottiswoode, 1967).
2. Commission on British Muslims and Islamophobia, *Islamophobia: A Challenge for Us All* (London: Runnymede Trust, 1997), p.1.
3. The Runnymede Trust, *A Very Light Sleeper: The Persistence and Dangers of Antisemitism* (London: Runnymede Trust, 1994).
4. S. Cohen, *That's Funny, You Don't Look Antisemitic: An Anti-Racist Analysis of Left Antisemitism* (Leeds: Beyond the Pale Collective, 1984).
5. R. Webster, *A Brief History of Blasphemy: Liberalism, Censorship and 'The Satanic Verses'* (Southwold: Orwell Press, 1990), p.79.
6. E. Said, *Orientalism: Western Conceptions of the Orient* (Harmondsworth: Penguin, 1987).
7. C. Allen and J. Nielsen, *Summary Report on Islamophobia in the EU after 11 September 2001* (Vienna: European Monitoring Centre on Racism and Xenophobia, 2002).
8. S. Rushdie, *The Satanic Verses* (London: Viking Penguin, 1988).
9. S. Akhtar, 'The Liberal Inquisition', *Independent*, 10 Oct. 1989.
10. Created in support of Ahmed Rami, a former army officer from Morocco living in exile in Sweden who established a radio station called 'Radio Islam' that was periodically broadcasting over the past decade and a half, and who has been tried and convicted in Sweden for incitement. Radio Islam (http://www.radioislam.org/islam/english/english.htm) should not be confused with another Internet site that has the similar name of 'Radio al-Islam' (http://www.islam.org/Radio), which is an Internet audio project concerned with recitations of the Qur'an.
11. G. Bunt, *Virtually Islamic: Computer-Mediated Communication and Cyber Islamic Environments* (Cardiff: University of Wales Press, 2002).
12. Ibid., p.130.
13 Accessed at www.singh.co.uk/3453.html and www.singh.co.uk/1154.html and www.singh.co.uk/8825.html on 2 Dec. 2003 and again on 5 Aug. 2005.
14. These traditions are known, according to the emphasis of those within them, as Hutta, Asatru or Odinist. The Hutta tradition focuses on the *Aesir* (culture deities) and the *Vanir* (vitality and fertility deities), while Asatru, means 'trust in deities'. Odinists have a particular affinity with the deity Odin.
15. P. Weller, A. Feldman, K. Purdam *et al.*, *Religious Discrimination in England and Wales: An Interim Report* (Derby: University of Derby, 2001). P. Weller, A. Feldman, K. Purdam *et al.*, 'Religious Discrimination in England and Wales', Home Office Research Study 200, Research Development Statistics Directorate (London: Home Office, 2001).
16. Weller, Feldman and Purdam *et al.*, *Religious Discrimination in England and Wales*, p.viii.
17. Weller, Feldman and Purdam *et al.*, 'Religious Discrimination in England and Wales', pp.117–18.
18. Ibid., p.73.
19. Ibid., p.42.
20. Webster, *A Brief History of Blasphemy*, p.72.
21. R. Cotterell, MEP, 'Interview: Richard Cottrell, MEP', *Update: A Quarterly Journal on New Religious Movements*, 8, 3–4 (1984), pp.30–4.
22. H. Ansari, *Muslims in Britain* (London: Minority Rights Group International, 2002), p.4.
23. R. Groves (ed.), *Thomas Helwys: A Short Declaration of the Mystery of Iniquity* (Macon, GA: Mercer University Press, 1998).

21 The Kreuzberg Initiative against Antisemitism among Youth from Muslim and Non-Muslim Backgrounds in Berlin

GÜNTHER JIKELI

The forms and sources of antisemitism today are diverse. In recent years, antisemitism has often found expression in conspiracy theories and hatred towards the State of Israel. Many forms and sources depend on a national or cultural context. However, antisemitic resentment is common among many groups and is widespread in mainstream society. There is a growing consensus among analysts that in Europe antisemitic manifestations today are a feature of three distinct groups: a minority of people from an Arab/Muslim cultural background; neo-Nazis and fascist groups; and the so-called 'chattering classes', primarily parts of the liberal-leftist intelligentsia and media.[1] Some strategies have already been developed to fight far-right antisemitism. So far, however, there has been a lack of strategies for fighting the antisemitism of the 'chattering classes', the left and people from Muslim backgrounds.

The Kreuzberg Initiative against Antisemitism, founded in 2003, is the result of the commitment of a small group of social workers, residents, students, political activists, researchers and teachers – both migrants and Germans – in Kreuzberg, a district in Berlin. They recognized the increase in antisemitism both globally and in their local area, and chose not to tolerate it. Members of the action group developed strategies to fight antisemitism locally and focused primarily on education. An understanding of current forms of antisemitism and funding for their work were essential in the creation of a local centre for projects against antisemitism. Considerable importance was given to networking with other NGOs, for example, the Antonio-Amadeu-Foundation in Berlin. The Kreuzberg Initiative is not itself a Jewish organization. The commitment of its founders derives from a perception of antisemitism as a threat for Jews and for the development of individual freedom, emancipation and democracy in general. They therefore see it as a serious challenge to civil society.

The forms assumed by antisemitism in Kreuzberg seem to be similar to those in many European cities. The need for an international exchange and for further research has become increasingly evident. In response, members of the Initiative recently founded the International Institute for Education and Research on Antisemitism.[2] I shall seek here to describe the Initiative's approaches and experiences in the hope that some of them will prove helpful and encouraging for others.

ANTISEMITISM IN BERLIN-KREUZBERG

The Berlin district of Kreuzberg has a large population of Muslim origin made up of immigrants, their children and grandchildren. The immigrants originate mainly from Turkey, but also from Bosnia and a number of Arab countries.[3] In many schools, pupils with a migrant family background represent a large majority. Many people in Kreuzberg depend on social welfare. Unemployment is very high, especially among the young. At the same time the district is very popular for its pubs, cafés, galleries and artists. There are many small NGOs, networks and individuals that claim to belong to the political left.

In Kreuzberg, antisemitism is frequently expressed with reference to the Middle East conflict and often in the guise of anti-Zionism. In recent years, young people of Arab/Muslim origin have been identified as responsible for documented assaults on Jews. They are sometimes responsible for verbal antisemitic abuse and often use antisemitic expressions in their language.[4] This appears to be particularly disastrous as antisemitism among young people of Arab/Muslim origin is often excused and tolerated by society. To many, it appears only as a more radicalized 'criticism' of Israel, which many people share.

In the German context, the casting off of guilt, related to so-called secondary antisemitism, is an important motive for antisemitism. In contrast, migrants in Germany do not feel affected by condemnation of the Shoah: their families were not usually involved in its perpetration; they do not consider themselves Germans and therefore do not share Germany's history, even in the third generation. The collective identity of migrants is usually linked to their families' country of origin and, at least often in the case of Muslims, to their religion.

Antisemitic thinking and stereotypes are linked to different contexts within national identities, discourses and cultural and religious backgrounds. Like many others, both the Muslim and the Arab collective identity seem to have specific links to antisemitism. Antisemitism forms part of the ideology of Islamism and Arab-nationalist ideology.[5] It is true that only a small minority of Muslims and Arabs are devoted to these ideologies. Nevertheless, their Manichaean views regarding the community of Muslims (Ummah) or respectively, the community of Arabs and their self-conception, are very influential. A key component of Islamist ideology today is the imagined war on Islam, which calls on every person with ties to Islam to unite against an external threat. Radicals overemphasize ties to a collective identity. Some mechanisms in European societies tend to push (post-)migrants into collective Islamic identities as well. Identification as a Muslim has three dimensions: religious self-description, cultural self-description and attributive self-description. The latter means that society imposes pressure on people with alleged Muslim attributes (for example, name or appearance) to identify themselves as Muslim.[6] Similarly, identification as an Arab consists of a cultural and a national self-description, as well as an attributive self-description.

Numerous media in Arab countries, as well as some in Turkey, have been noted for constant hate-mongering against Jews and Israel. Two examples are the Hezbollah TV channel *al- Manar*, and the Islamic daily newspaper *Vakit* in Turkey. In these media Jews, Zionists and Israelis, often without differentiation, are pictured as the natural enemies of all Muslims. *Al-Manar* and *Vakit* are both known to many young people of Muslim/Arab origin in Kreuzberg. The newspaper *Vakit* was advertised in Kreuzberg and presented at local book fairs before its prohibition in Germany. The newspaper publishes clearly antisemitic caricatures and articles denying the Holocaust.[7] Antisemitic discourse in immigrant families' countries of origin is transmitted mainly by mass media and in some cases by political or religious organizations, but also by friends and relatives. Where the credibility of facts is concerned, young people of Arab origin often state: 'You have your sources and we have ours. The truth can be seen on Arab TV channels.'

Another aspect is identification with the 'Palestinians'. A Palestinian flag has been flying since 2003 on top of a house in the centre of Kreuzberg; in summer 2004 a huge banner spanned Oranien Street for several weeks, stating: 'Solidarity with the resistance in Iraq and in Palestine'. Some young people see parallels between their own marginalized and stigmatized position and the situation of Palestinians. They have a feeling of being victims of an unjust world order or of an imagined war on Islam. In their eyes, Israel and the United States are responsible for this world order. In a Manichaean world view the Palestinians symbolize the oppressed victims and stand for the 'good side', against the Israelis/Jews as perpetrators. It is also based on the incorrect premise that the (apparently) weak position is always right and the strong position is always unjust. These patterns of thinking can be observed among both migrants and Germans – with different references in each case.[8] It often involves self-styling as victims because of an affiliation with a certain culture or religion. In this 'competition of victims' the bogeyman image of Jews is the enemy of the 'community of the oppressed'. An imagined 'war on Islam' and in some aspects the term Islamophobia contribute to an affiliation with the 'community of the oppressed'. The 'competition of victims' can also lead to equating present-day discrimination against minorities with the Shoah.[9] This does not mean that people of Arab or Turkish origin are not victims: in Germany they are indeed often victims of racism. Thus, there are two main difficulties in focusing on anti-semitism among migrants in Germany. The first risk is a heightening of the stigmatization of migrants, and the second is relieving German mainstream society of the burden of German antisemitism.

In addition to the aforementioned manifestations of antisemitism in Kreuzberg, classical antisemitic stereotypes are still alive. They are transmitted both by migrants and Germans, mainly as a heritage of an anti-Jewish tradition in European culture.

The Kreuzberg Initiative against Antisemitism grew out of several events and observations in the neighbourhood. After terrorist attacks on two synagogues in Istanbul in 2003, migrants in Berlin-Kreuzberg organized a memorial demonstration for the victims. The feedback from this memorial showed that people from Turkish communities did not agree with antisemitism and terrorism. On the other hand, antisemitism in Kreuzberg has been on the rise and became obvious to residents who would listen and open their eyes:

- 'Jew' is used as a swear-word and some youths even glorify the terrorists of 9/11 and suicide bombers in Israel. Teachers and social workers report that with some pupils they face serious problems in discussing topics such as the Holocaust, antisemitism and the Middle East conflict.
- Two antisemitic assaults in Kreuzberg have been publicized in

newspapers within a relatively short period of time.

- Antisemitism in Islamist propaganda has become more frequent in Kreuzberg and has been distributed in public places, for example, the German language magazine *Explizit* from the organization Hizb-ut Tahrir. At Turkish book fairs the *Protocols*, *The International Jew* and books denying the Holocaust have been advertised and sold.
- There is a group of young people of German, Turkish and Arab origin, who have been wearing t-shirts labelled 'Anti-Zionist Action Berlin'. Members of this group are responsible for a knife assault on a person who accused them of being antisemitic.[10]
- Antisemitic graffiti, such as 'Death to Israel', appear frequently.
- A local study was published in 2003, warning of the rise of anti-semitism in Kreuzberg.[11]

STRATEGIES IN EDUCATION, LOCAL ADMINISTRATION AND MIGRANT COMMUNITIES

The Kreuzberg Initiative is a very small and young organization with a budget of about €100,000 per annum. Nevertheless, it has at its disposal a large office and seminar rooms in the heart of Kreuzberg. The idea of the Initiative is to work through a variety of methods: education in schools and youth clubs and efforts to influence discourse in communities, for instance through public debate, and the denunciation of antisemitic propaganda and assaults. The project aims to work in conjunction with local government, stakeholders, teachers, schools, migrant associations, youth centres, local politicians, researchers, etc. Joint projects with individuals working in institutions such as schools or youth centres have proved successful. However, the effective impact of the Kreuzberg action group has not yet been fully evaluated.

The first and most important step is to acknowledge the existence of antisemitism, in all of its forms. A public debate together with the monitoring of antisemitic incidents and research on sources of anti-semitism are a precondition for combating antisemitic ideologies and stereotypes in civil society, and for effective educational work. In this respect, the Initiative has helped to achieve some successes. Teachers, social workers and politicians have become more and more inclined to deal with these issues, which they ignored in the past. However, a major problem remains the lack of understanding of contemporary forms of antisemitism, such as the demonization of the State of Israel.[12] For many, antisemitism only exists in neo-Nazi and fascist groups.

Work with Muslim community leaders has proved difficult. Explicitly Muslim organizations tend to adopt a religious perspective as a matter of principle. In the few cases where any action has been taken, their approach towards tackling antisemitism has been inter-religious dialogue, which leaves out many forms of antisemitism. Experience has shown that it is more effective to work with individuals than with 'representatives' of communities. The latter reinforce the pressure for attributed self-identification. Positive results have been achieved through cooperation with secular, progressive organizations with ties to migrant communities. Extremism, reactionism and oppression of women in the name of Islam are seen by many as a threat. There is a common goal in fighting these ideologies.

The most progress has been made in the development of educational tools. Instead of schematic concepts, the people working in the Initiative have offered their experience to teachers and social workers to develop concepts adapted especially to their 'clients'. Another goal in the creation of a visible organization is to help young people become active against antisemitism through their own projects (for example, workshops/debates on antisemitism, homophobia and sexism, projects on the history of the Nazi period, photo/film-projects, and excursions to memorial sites, etc). Considerable success has been achieved through intense work with small groups of pupils over a three-week internship at college. Overall, the impact of the Initiative has been seen only at the individual level. So far there has been no common stand by the whole district against antisemitism and other ideologies.

EDUCATION

At the time when the Initiative was founded, few applicable pedagogic tools were available to tackle antisemitism among specific target groups. There is an even more glaring lack of specific pedagogic tools for young people from migrant family backgrounds.

So-called Holocaust education in schools is not sufficiently effective against contemporary antisemitism.[13] Some teachers have reported that they avoid talking about the Holocaust because they do not know how to handle expressions of antisemitic resentment in the classroom. Contemporary forms of antisemitism are not impeded by knowledge of the Holocaust, as seen in the likening of Israel to Nazi Germany.

Knowledge of the Holocaust and empathy for its victims are no guarantee that Jews will not be collectively portrayed as evil. Israel and the Middle East conflict are often used as socially acceptable projections in this way.[14]

Present-day European societies are woven of heterogeneous identities and family experiences, resulting from differently lived or bequeathed history. It is important to take this into account in pedagogical approaches focusing on identity-related issues, not only for better mutual understanding but also for effective action against antisemitic paradigms. The development of specific tools is necessary because antisemitic resentment originates in part in the specific collective identity and in its ideology. The OSCE Office for Democratic Institutions and Human Rights, which makes recommendations for education to combat antisemitism, notes that 'different antisemitic motifs require different educational programmes'.[15] From a pedagogic point of view it is important to define goals and to find adequate methods to achieve them. Experience shows, not only in Kreuzberg, that the focus of tolerance education and anti-racist education is not sufficiently specific to change antisemitic attitudes and that other approaches have to be adopted.

These pedagogic tools have been applied in several schools and youth centres. They were developed jointly with teachers and social workers especially for their pupils. In Kreuzberg, this has led to the development of concepts involving hands-on elements for culturally mixed groups composed mainly of young people belonging to Muslim families. For practical reasons, only short-term approaches have been adopted. The Initiative has developed new workshops adapted to the situation in Kreuzberg, which last from a few hours to a maximum of two days. These, however, cannot be a substitute for more holistic approaches in education, which help individuals develop a strong personality structure. This is a key factor in determining whether they are susceptible to irrational antisemitic thinking. Since it is clear that antisemitism is bound up with questions of identity and how the world is interpreted, education against antisemitism must incorporate these dimensions. This means more long-term approaches with and by the individuals themselves. The crucial question we have to answer is: can we offer something better than the antisemitic resentments that provide a certain satisfaction, fulfil a desire to personify evil, explain the world, and allow those who harbour them to feel on the right side of a Manichaean universe?

One approach in education against antisemitism is to offer something positive. As we have seen, antisemitism is very often carried by collective identities. People reproduce antisemitism as an act of collective identity in a pattern. It does not necessarily reflect a personal *Weltanschauung*. Didier Lapeyronnie observes such patterns in the language of the ghetto in France.[16] The collective identity provides the individuals with a certain kind of security but prevents them from being themselves. This is where emancipatory education can help. It can open the eyes for individual development based on rational argument, considering individual needs without the restrictions and resentments resulting from indoctrination in the name of tradition, religion and nation. Some modern primary school teaching methods focusing on the individual pupil and its individual needs and desires are promising in this respect.

The experiences in Kreuzberg with young people have shown that they are not very often confronted with contradictory thoughts. Their social environment usually confirms their resentments which, in the worst case, are bolstered by friends, family members, and even social workers and teachers, at least when they take the form of antagonism against Israel.[17]

Current approaches in education are obviously not effective in fighting antisemitic thinking. New efforts in education can only be successful if they are assisted by politics and societal discourse. The basis for education against antisemitism on a larger scale is awareness of problems in institutions of education. This means that advanced training for those working with pupils is absolutely necessary.

Antisemitism on the part of pupils is often ignored, tolerated, or not even perceived as such. Several factors seem to hamper educators in their handling of antisemitic attitudes and statements by their pupils, namely:

- Lack of knowledge and uncertainties regarding the topic of antisemitism;
- Little expertise and experience in handling current antisemitism;
- Lack of reflection on this topic and their own antisemitic feelings;
- Mistaken 'tolerance' for antisemitism if it is expressed by people with a migrant background, because they themselves are victims of racism, and in some cases victims in the conflict between Israel and Palestinians.

Nevertheless, some educators are very committed and do an excellent job. The pupils are usually open to reflecting on these complex topics and even to changing their minds. They are eager to discuss topics dealing with their identities and feelings. The challenge is to establish the right framework, to ask the right questions and to provide knowledge where necessary. Pedagogy against antisemitism does not mean unmasking antisemites – the person is not the target, but rather his or her resentments. This is the point where the limits of education appear. Sanctions and isolation may be appropriate if the resentment is entrenched and if it leads to antisemitic incidents. The goal in pedagogy, however, is to make people think, to change their attitude and free themselves of feelings of resentment. For this, a cognitive approach alone is not efficient, even though knowledge of antisemitic structures is the key to a rational approach.

In education, the Kreuzberg Initiative against Antisemitism is geared to the following principal goals:

1. Enabling pupils to recognize antisemitic stereotypes, resentments and ideologies in contemporary forms;
2. Encouraging them to question Manichaean interpretations of the world as 'good or bad';
3. Stimulating reflection and self-perception as an individual and subject (as opposed to self-perception as an object and as part of an ideologically constructed community);
4. Developing a critical historical consciousness (and deconstructing nationalist and Islamist historical interpretations);
5. Condemning antisemitism through recognition of its anti-human character.

In order to achieve at least part of these goals it is important to deal with individual structures of resentments. Teachers should be capable not only of recognizing the spectrum of antisemitic motives among their students, but also of addressing the various dimensions and specific forms of antisemitism in their target group.[18]

In Kreuzberg, the Turkish context and discourse are important. Educators should know that antisemitic conspiracy theories appear frequently in Turkish discourse. Clearly antisemitic caricatures appear in Islamist and left-wing newspapers. Nationalists also disseminate antisemitic stereotypes. According to a popular antisemitic conspiracy theory, the 'Dönme' are attempting to govern Turkey. The word 'Dönme' means convert and refers to the descendents of Sabbatai Zevi, the 'false Messiah' who converted to Islam under the Sultan 300 years ago. However, the collective Turkish memory also includes the admission of Jews in around 1492 into the Ottoman Empire and a generally positive relationship towards Jews throughout history. Most Turkish people assume (wrongly) that antisemitism does not exist in Turkey. Another important aspect in working with pupils with a Turkish background is the strong secularism in Turkey and its differentiation from Arab states.

Educators from migrant backgrounds are at an advantage in dealing with young people from migrant backgrounds. It would be a mistake to over-emphasize this, however, as it gives added weight to the role of religion and minority group allegiance in identity building and can lend itself to cultural stereotyping through an implicit assumption that only migrants can educate and engage other migrants. Ultimately, such an approach means not taking seriously the individuals concerned, treating migrants as it does simply as representatives of their inherited community. It ends up confining people with a migrant heritage in a permanent role as members of a minority group.

The following are three examples of workshops organized in Kreuzberg.

WORKSHOP ON CONSPIRACY THEORIES[19]

In the first part, a sketch about a conspiracy is presented. The wire-puller of the conspiracy is a community with which the pupils can identify. In such a workshop, where the target group consists of pupils from a Turkish background, 'the Turks' will be portrayed as trying to conquer Europe, with the help of spies wearing hair scarves to cover their microphones with which they record everything and send it directly to Ankara. Obviously, for the pupils this story is nonsense and they can laugh about it. The aim is to use this as a basis for analysing elements of conspiracy theories. The pupils are then invited to invent their own conspiracy theories in groups of three or four. They are given questions as starting points, such as: 'Why do students with the letter "m" in their name achieve better results in school and who is behind it?' or 'Why are mobile phones getting cheaper and cheaper, and who is the leading force behind it?', etc. They learn that 'it is easy to develop weird theories and even to convince others that such theories are right', as one pupil put it. They get the feeling that there is a kind of satisfaction in inventing these theories and in believing them. Then, the pupils analyse the characteristics of conspiracy theories with reference to their own invented theories. In the end, the pupils deconstruct examples of conspiracy theories in contemporary Turkish and Arab media (TV sequences and cartoons in newspapers and books). The pupils learn to recognize conspiracy theories and to analyse the antisemitic elements in them. Moreover, they learn some elements of critical media analysis.

WORKSHOP ON THE FOUNDING OF THE STATE OF ISRAEL

The aim of this workshop is to tackle the antisemitic myth of the creation of the State of Israel as an act of colonialism implemented by the US. It helps to re-evaluate Manichaean views of the Middle East conflict. In a role-playing game the young people play people of different positions at a conference in the year 1947. They represent the interests respectively of the Nashashibi clan, the Al-Husseini clan, the Zionists around Ben Gurion, revisionist Zionists, the King of Egypt or the King of Jordan or Great Britain. In a 'conference' they debate on how to come to a solution, and who should govern Palestine in the future when the British soldiers leave.

The pupils get to know the history and the basic lines of conflicts between Israel and Palestine. They understand the different approaches and interests within 'the Zionists', 'the Palestinians' and 'the Arab countries'. The black-and-white scheme of the Israel–Palestinian conflict doesn't work any more. The pupils experience the following:

1. There are different and divergent interests within the two groups of Palestinians/Arabs and Zionists/Jews/Israelis, previously seen as two blocks.
2. Bargaining between divergent interests is an influenceable, historical process.
3. Antisemitic ideologies are destructive in the Middle East conflict.
4. Palestinian and Arab groups were active players in history (in contrast with their image of being victims).

WORKSHOP ON INDIVIDUAL IDENTITY

This workshop focuses on the conflict between individual desires and the pressure exercised by community-based ideologies, in the name of tradition, religion or nation. Its origins lie in the case of a group of young people who glorified suicide bombings. One of them, a 14-year-old boy, told an educator that in ten years it would be a good time to go to Israel and blow himself up to kill 100 Jews. The boy's fantasy was a complete denial of his individual desires. His literal wish for total self-destruction in order to kill others was fuelled by an abstract hate against Jews. The boy did not know any Jews. It is evident that a workshop alone cannot deconstruct such a way of thinking. However, the incident led to the development of a workshop that is relevant to young people who are not used to rational discussions and the exchange of arguments. In role playing they search and find arguments instead of the more typical behaviour of reproducing masks moulded by a group dynamic. Three topics of conflict are given as initial discussion points:

1. The individual desire of playing football versus having time to meet the cultural or religious expectations of the father.
2. Love between two teenagers, where one is the sister of a friend.
3. Marriage between a Muslim man and a Jewish woman.

The workshop raises the question of the relative importance of collective identity. The prospect of change is able to be considered through the acting of different roles, questionings and the examination of individual interests and desires. The workshop reveals the constraints of collective thinking under the influence of tradition and religion and encourages individuals to think for themselves.

CONCLUSIONS

The example of the Kreuzberg Initiative shows that it is possible to fight antisemitism in civil society at grassroots level. The interlinking of action in education, civil society and politics at local level seems to hold promise, along with international exchange about sources of antisemitism and education against antisemitism.

International research, declarations such as the Berlin Declaration[20] and the EUMC working definition of antisemitism[21] are helpful in convincing others to include in their definition of antisemitism contemporary forms of antisemitism that appear more legitimate. Since antisemitism is condemned by all societal groups, the definition of antisemitism becomes very important. Cooperation with international organizations raises the level of competency in the fight against antisemitism. More teaching materials specifically dealing with contemporary forms of antisemitism should be provided by experts.

I do not know if the Initiative has actually prevented antisemitic incidents. However, it gives yet another signal that antisemitism

cannot be accepted. At the very least, the Initiative provided and generated resources and expertise to become active against antisemitism
at the individual level.

Such undertakings need a supportive framework from national
authorities and international NGOs. National policymakers can be
helpful by expounding the problem of antisemitism and by setting
firm boundaries on the social (and legal) acceptance of antisemitism.
Effective education and a readiness to address the issue in public
discourse must go hand in hand. What is essential is a rational
approach that allows no scope for resentment.

NOTES

1. See, for example, Yehuda Bauer, *The Educational Challenge of European Antisemitism*.
    Speech at the OSCE conference in Cordoba, 8-9 June 2005: www.holocausttaskforce.org/
    feature/bauer.pdf. See also Mike Whine, 'Anti-Semitism on the Streets: Is there a New Anti-
    Semitism in Britain?', in Paul Iganski and Barry Kosmin (eds.), *A New Antisemitism?
    Debating Judeophobia in 21st Century Britain* (London: Profile Books, 2003), pp.31–2;
    www.jpr.uk/reportsCS%20reports/new_antisemitism/main.html. Iganski and Kosmin (eds),
    A New Antisemitism? Stephen Roth Institute, *Anti-Semitism Worldwide 2003/2004*,
    www.tau.ac.il/Anti-Semitism/asw2004/general-analysis.htm. European Monitoring Center
    on Racism and Xenophobia, *Manifestations of Antisemitism in the EU 2002-2003*,
    http://eumc.eu.int/eumc/material/pub/AS/AS-Main-report.pdf. See also Doron Rabinovici,
    Ulrich Speck and Natan Sznaider, *Neuer Antisemitismus? Eine globale Debatte*
    (Frankfurt/M.: Suhrkamp Verlag, 2004).
2. The institute encourages further development in education against antisemitism and relat-
    ed research. See www.IIBSA.org.
3. The number of Muslims can be estimated as the majority of Turkish, Bosnian and Arab
    nationals plus the majority of naturalized Germans with a migrant family background in
    those countries; the latter do not appear in the statistics. Official statistics survey only
    nationality. In the inner Kreuzberg area where the Initiative is based, 39.5 per cent have a
    non-German nationality; 26.5 per cent have a Turkish nationality and 1.9 per cent have an
    Arab nationality. Source: www.friedrichshain-kreuzberg.de/media/de/Sozialraum_III.pdf.
4. Some very aggressive antisemitic statements by young people in Kreuzberg were filmed in
    interviews from Alice Salomon University of Applied Sciences Berlin (ASFH) students.
    These interviews were shown on 1 July 2005 under the headline: 'Hitler gefällt mir' ('I like
    Hitler').
5. See, for example, Jochen Müller (2005), *Ventil und Kitt. Die Funktion von Israel und den
    Juden in der Ideologie des arabischen Nationalismus*. www.memri.de/publikationen/auf-
    saetze/ventil_kitt.html
6. Tietze, Nicola, 'Antisemitische Denkmuster unter Muslimen in Frankreich', *Werkstatt
    Geschichte*, 38, 12 (2004), pp.46-66; p.48.
7. There are no figures available showing scale of distribution in Kreuzberg. However, in our
    workshops some pupils recognized the newspaper as the newspaper their parents read at
    home. To see some of the antisemitic caricatures published in Vakit see www.kiga-
    berlin.org/images/images/Vakit.pdf.
8. In 2004, 68 per cent of the German population agreed with the statement 'Israel leads a
    war of extermination ("Vernichtungskrieg") against the Palestinians'. See Wilhelm (Hg.)
    Heitmeyer, *Deutsche Zustände. Folge 3* (Frankfurt/M.: Suhrkamp Verlag, 2005), p.151.
9. Some seem to see 'Muslims as the Jews of today'. Imam Abduljalil Sajid, said at the OSCE
    conference in Cordoba 2005, 'Islamophobia has replaced antisemitism as the new sharp
    end of racist issues', or in a more sophisticated way: 'L'antijudaïsme ou "judéophobie" n'en
    forme plus, si ce fut jamais le cas, la réalisation unique. Il est devenu l'un des termes d'un
    couple qui reconstitue sur d'autres bases le mythe "sémite" du XIXe siècle, et dont l'arabo-
    phobie ou islamophobie constitue l'autre composante' [The anti-Judaism or 'Judeophobia'

is not any more, if it ever was, the only manifestation. It became one of the terms of a couple which reconstitute on other bases the myth of 'Semite' of the nineteenth century and of which the Arabophobia or Islamophobia is the other component]. Etienne Balibar, 'Un nouvel antisémitisme?' in Etienne Balibar *et al.* (eds.), *Antisémitisme: l'intolérable chantage. Israël-Palestine, une affaire française*, 90 (Paris: La Decouverte, 2003), p.90.

10. For further information see the open letter to local authorities: http://www.hagalil.com/archiv/2004/09/kreuzberg.htm (March 6, 2006). The local authorities have not taken appropriate measures.

11. http://www.mut-gegen-rechte-gewalt.de/files/images/Studie_ZDK_Kreuzberg.PDF.

12. For example, the person responsible for youth, family and sports in the local administration was shown antisemitic caricatures from the Islamist newspaper *Vakit*. Her comment was that one should also show the anti-Palestinian caricatures in Israeli newspapers, otherwise it would be one-sided.

13. See OSCE-ODHIR, *Education on the Holocaust and on Anti-Semitism in the OSCE Region*, http://www.osce.org/documents/odihr/2005/06/14897_en.pdf (2005), p.156. Holocaust education is still very important as such and in education against antisemitism. Nonetheless, it has proved to be an illusion that Holocaust education is a sufficient means of education against contemporary antisemitism.

14. See Werner Bergmann and Wilhelm Heitmeyer, 'Communication Anti-Semitism', in Minerva Institut für deutsche Geschichte, Tel Aviv University, *Tel Aviver Jahrbuch für deutsche Geschichte XXXIII: Antisemitismus - Antizionismus - Israelkritik* (Göttingen: Wallstein, 2005), pp.70-89; p.76 ff.

15. OSCE-ODIHR, *Education on the Holocaust and on Anti-Semitism in the OSCE Region*, p.165.

16. Didier Lapeyronnie, 'La Demande d'Antisémitisme', *Les Etudes Du CRIF*, Paris, 9 (2005). See also Michel Wieviorka (ed.), *La tentation anti-Semite* (Paris: Robert Laffont, 2005).

17. In 2004, I attended a debate in a school about the Middle East conflict. The teacher announced it as a debate to show the pupils the Israeli point of view as well, because an Israeli and a Palestinian (from the same organization) were invited. As it turned out, the entire debate was about the negative effects of 'the wall' for Palestinians. It comforted the resentments of all participants.

18. See OSCE-ODIHR, *Education on the Holocaust and on Anti-Semitism in the OSCE Region*, p.165.

19. The central idea of the workshop is based on ideas from 'Bausteine zur nicht-rassitsischer Bildungsarbeit' (2003), p.181 (www.baustein.dgb-bwt.de).

20. Berlin Declaration, Bulgarian Chairmanship, the Chairman-in-Office, http://www.osce.org/documents/cio/2004/04/2828_en.pdf.

21. 'Working Definition of Antisemitism', *EUMC Discussion Papers - Racism, Xenophobia, Anti-Semitism*, http://eumc.eu.int/eumc/material/pub/AS/AS-WorkingDefinition-draft.pdf.

22 Antisemitism is the Legitimate Child of Islamism: The Real Cancer of Islam

RACHID KACI

Antisemitic remarks and behaviour have been on the increase in France, particularly in the suburbs, for some years now. It is quite right to demand an explanation from the whole country on these anti-Jewish attitudes. Unanimous condemnation on the part of the political community, inter alia, could not be more justified.

However, some people are surprised – and again, rightly so – on the one hand about the lack of reaction on the part of French people of Muslim culture faced with this spread of antisemitism, and on the other hand about the deafening silence surrounding this new kind of antisemitism on the part of French nationals from the North African and African immigrant population.

I most strongly condemn, as do many others, obviously, the physical and verbal aggression to which our Jewish compatriots are subjected, but any condemnation is futile and to no avail unless and until the unspoken, the silence, that has been growing into an infected abscess for some years now, is lanced. Here, as elsewhere, the deep-rooted hatred that some Muslims, or so-called Muslims, feel with regard to Jews cannot be denied. In the housing estates of the Paris suburbs this feeling well and truly exists. It has been there for decades but hidden, masked by a few irresponsible people, in particular members of anti-racist associations who would have had difficulty in putting across young, second-generation North Africans living in France [known as *Beurs*], as victims of Western society – pretext for state subventions – if they were perceived as being antisemitic.

This hatred is fuelled by the rivalries that have traditionally opposed North Africans and Jews, and some residents in the housing estates from other communities have adopted the same stance.

The result is a multiplication of antisemitic acts of violence that worry a large section of the population but end up creating a veritable psychosis within the Jewish community and the population as a whole. Let me remind you of the story in 2004 of a young woman who said she had been a victim of antisemitic aggression on the RER-D line, at Epinay-sur-Seine. She said she had been attacked by some young louts who thought she was Jewish. For several days, the story hit the headlines on television, radio and the daily papers, until it became clear that it was all a hoax. Quite apart from the news item, it should be pointed out that the story appeared utterly credible. It followed a spate of all kinds of acts of dreadful aggression and insults. That just shows you the situation France is in at the moment.

The conflict opposing the communities is therefore both real and dangerous. It affects not only the living but even the dead. For a good fifteen years now, the media has given widespread coverage to the wrecking of Jewish cemeteries. To say the least, what can clearly be described as racial confrontation is now overflowing into a latent war of religion, whose beginnings we already saw during the autumn 2005 riots, when not only synagogues but churches as well were attacked or even burnt.

We have to face facts. The Palestinian 'cause' serves as a pretext for some well-known visionaries to broadcast their antisemitic venom and give free rein to views that have been suppressed for years. It was this aversion to Jews that some people also used in order to put up a so-called 'Euro-Palestine' list at the European electoral ballot in 2004. The 'comedian', now politician, Dieudonné, was one of the spearheads of that initiative. Indeed, in the housing estates of the suburbs he often bases his argument on anti-Zionism.

Names on this list called on French people to choose their political affiliation according to an external conflict. This fanned the flames of ordinary hatred even more, particularly with the *Beurs*. By not making any attempt to ban the list, which had nothing to do with that electoral ballot, our political leaders became complicit in the dislocation of our society and in the community breakdown of our country.

The same political leaders had already agreed to issue credentials to the Muslim Brotherhood, through the Union of Islamic Organizations of France (UOIF) on the spectral French Council of Muslim Worship. Now, of what use is it to condemn anti-Jewish acts if at the same time there is official recognition of structures that develop among young Muslims an anti-Zionism which is only a front for latent antisemitism? The Palestinian cause is often a convenient pretext for getting people 'to swallow the pill', notably to sway opinion with the media and the courts.

And what do you think about our incapacity to enforce the law and to expel undesirable foreigners like the Imam of Vénissieux who, after being deported, returned to France to deride us and exude his fascistic ideology advocating polygamy, vindicating the stoning of women, and often, like his ideological friends, turning hatred of Israel into a conviction?

We saw a blatant demonstration of this apathy, not to say cowardice, a short while ago with the release of those responsible for the attack on the son of the Boulogne-Billancourt rabbi in the Hauts-de-Seine. What a wonderful message this gives to all those budding fascists: 'keep stabbing our Jewish compatriots, and speak out in favour of stoning ... at worst you only risk getting a week's detention'. Obviously, if these young people are constantly represented as being victims of our poor country, former colonizer to boot, it is going to become difficult to punish them.

Furthermore, the concept of Islamophobia – invented by human rights professionals, often with an extreme left background, to make us feel even more guilty – came at just the right time to remove any remaining responsibility. It is, in fact, this very concept that allows all sorts of things to get out of hand and prevents Muslims from working towards a thorough reform of interpretation of the Qur'an, which is so badly needed.

To crown it all, we are now to have positive discrimination. This woolly concept, a downright insult to intelligence, will allow citizens of foreign extraction, mainly African and North African, to get a job not according to their competence but according to their skin colour or their presumed religion.

The time has come for the authorities to put a stop to these kinds of cringing, cowardly, politicking compromises, and remind religious extremists of the actual meaning of the words 'democracy' and 'secularism'.

This abdication on the part of politicians faced with a populist movement, and of the Republic faced with fanaticism, does nothing to serve the interests of an immigrant population whose future would be better insured if it were inscribed in the Republican ideal rather than turned towards Mecca.

In France, the resurgence of antisemitism feeds on that abdication and those compromises, accentuated by the fantasy of millions of Muslim voters who will apparently decide – or so we are told – on the future President of the Republic. And what if, in the end, that really was the explanation for all these problems and particularly for the guilty aberrations of the authorities?

With the development of fundamentalist Islam in those suburbs is a parallel rise in antisemitism, but that, however, was already there. The antisemitic speeches given, for example, at the pro-veil demonstration organized in Paris in 2004, show that the two phenomena are, to say the least, interlinked. For strategic reasons, however, Islamist movements, whether the Muslim Brotherhood of the UOIF or even the Tabligh, at the moment are calling for calm, as could be seen during the Halimi affair. The repercussions of that tragic incident have enabled us to establish the truth about the progress of communitarianism (ethnicity) in our country and assess the growing rift between the communities. A former President of the Representative Council of Jewish Institutions in France (CRIF) was wise in advising prudence.

If we are to believe the Minister of the Interior, there had been several other kidnap victims not all of whom were Jewish. The fact they attacked a Jew was explained by the perpetrators as based on the well-established conviction, in the ethnically volatile tenement slums, that Jews have money – which is a clear indication of antisemitism.

In Bagneux and housing estates elsewhere in the Paris suburbs and even further afield, in this particular affair I noticed the pernicious effects that excessive media coverage gave to the subject of anti-semitism, and the demonstration organized the day following the murder. Residents of those suburbs had the impression society was pointing at them – the society that some see as being hostile and believe is controlled by 'the Jews'.

The condemnation, in itself very legitimate but badly handled, of antisemitism being the prime motive in the murder of Ilan Halimi, provoked a resurgence of antisemitism in the suburbs. And yet anti-semitic acts do not comply with the teaching of Islam. Islam is not antisemitic in its doctrine. This antisemitism represents a real cancer in the body of this religion. Sincere Muslims are thus entangled in the snare of Islamist totalitarianism spreading around the world. Its prime aim is to destroy Israel because that country symbolizes a model of democratic society to be eliminated. That is why there needs to be a thorough debate on Islam with the silent majority of enlightened Muslims. They alone are capable of embarking on a reform whose aim is to integrate this religion into our secular Republic and make it espouse our times.

We must have the courage to overcome our complexes and denounce the incompatibility of some interpretations of the Qur'an with our universal values. We can no longer content ourselves with merely reciting the well-known phrase 'no mixing Islam with Islamism', which tends to be a way of avoiding the debate and evading responsibility. True, our attitude vis-à-vis Muslim immigrant populations has always been ambiguous to say the least. In the name of respect for cultures of origin, we have never demanded that traditions or customs should be abandoned, whether of a religious nature or not, most of them retrograde and imbued with ancient superstitions and at times diametrically opposed to our models of society. On the contrary, we have done everything for them to become a kind of identifier and common denominator. Not demanding the same culture and same civic responsibility of French nationals of foreign extraction as are required of those who are French born and bred, is a pure colonial mentality and shows profound contempt.

The same can be said of Islam and French Muslims. In the country of the Enlightenment and Voltaire, we have been unable to devise a modern, liberal Islam, integrated into the secular structure on the pretext that it does not exist in any Muslim country. That is how we have created French sub-citizens brandishing their Muslim origins like shields of humiliation: a kind of passport for mediocrity if they cannot win social recognition through their individual abilities. The Muslim Brotherhood thrives on frustrations such as these, and on ignorance.

If Islam is to succeed in integrating in France, it has to be a liberal, moderate Islam. The risks of Judaeophobia and antisemitism are too real to let extremists be the only ones to represent the reality of Islam in France. France has to state clearly the route it intends to follow – one of religious openness to a dialogue of religions – a route where their values and demands are neither imposed upon nor opposed to France's humanist values and tolerance. The worldwide image of Islam has been spoiled since September 2001, and all Muslim leaders should strive to rediscover the rich, edifying roots that enlightened Muslim civilization and shone with Averroes and Avicenna.

Today, France is wary and at times afraid of the aggressive, clumsy declarations of some Muslim leaders. And yet there is a liberal current of Islam in France – far stronger than one would think. This current wants to dialogue, to integrate and live its modernity, respecting women's rights and respecting other believers. It is up to France to give it credibility, strength and vitality. However, and this is paradoxical, nowadays it is more difficult to be a moderate Muslim than a radical or extremist Muslim! But in the end this is the current that will make the encounter between France and Islam possible.

The only effective way to combat this new form of antisemitism has to be through the fight against an Islamist, totalitarian, murderous ideology. Clearly, this fight is crucial for Jews, but so it is for Muslims as well. This fight concerns all democrats who care about values of tolerance and fraternity whatever their belief or non-belief. We must never lose sight of the fact that the Jew always represents a kind of barometer. When the target is a Jew, then our common foundation stone and pillar are also in the line of fire. The Jew is always the first victim of totalitarian or fascist ideologies. The Nazis began by massacring Jews before attacking others – gypsies, homosexuals and so many others. Not only is it a religious appurtenance being singled out but also the embodiment of a model of liberal society. When the State of Israel is threatened with destruction, it is democrats like us who should feel very concerned.

I shall end with an anecdote which will support my line of argument: the insult used by fundamentalists to describe enlightened Muslims or simply those who dare to defend the values of equality, secularism, tolerance and freedom – those values so universal and yet so far removed from the ideology of death, is 'dirty Jew'.

Lengthy speeches are sometimes futile.

23 The Absurdity of Antisemitism in the Arab World

MORAD EL-HATTAB EL-IBRAHIMI

> The Prophet Muhammad – may the salutations and blessings of Allah be upon him – said: 'Whoever oppresses a mu'âhid [beneficiaries of the pact between Jews and Christians] or despoils him of a right or charges him with something beyond his ability or takes a thing from him without his consent, I shall be his adversary the day of the Resurrection.'[1]

With the help of modern technology, humanity seems to be returning to primitive forms of confrontation where savagery and brutality dominate. The causes of conflict must not be ignored on some false pretext; pacifistic ingenuousness and utopianism strengthen the hand of the oppressors.

In confronting antisemitism, we have to come to terms with the reality of the problems, seeing aggressions for what they really are and not just random conjecture or whims of fate. It means questioning our mind sets – not because of an inability to understand, but because of a refusal to leave behind long-held views and generally accepted ideas, and because of a submission to the shortest intellectual path or to narrow thinking. Narrow through conformism, fear of complexity and lack of courage.

Any conflict is unfortunately shot through with cut-and-dried theories, pushing back to an unspecified future any hope of harmony and peace and, even worse, making us incapable of considering a different historical viewpoint. That is why I am convinced that to disarm a person one first of all has to disarm his mind.

Stefan Zweig's *The World of Yesterday* reveals a cosmopolitan, peace-loving society; how were concentration camps and the Holocaust conceivably possible in the country of Johann Sebastian

Bach and Immanuel Kant? And yet, Auschwitz is no figment of the imagination, and Buchenwald is just a few kilometres from Weimar where the memory of Goethe still lives on. How can anything be created after Auschwitz? I'm not talking about art or literature; I'm talking about salvation. Does humanity contain within itself the capacity for growth? Contrary to what one may think, Hitler's megalomania was neither irrational nor mad. It was a concentration, rationalization and culmination of scientism.

Primo Levi noted with despondency his early realization that 'our language lacked the words to express the ultimate insult: the degradation of a human being'. The memory of Auschwitz remains the memory of a wound that nothing can heal; the Nazi horror was carried out through hatred of the other, not in defiance of a moral doctrine. The aim of that regime was to divest a people of their humanity and destroy its history. Nazism attacked man's very being; it was the culmination of nihilism, the dehumanization of death itself.

I keep thinking of those women, children and old people removed from the land of the living, and of my Jewish and Gypsy friends, survivors of the camps, and the Nazi barbarity that suddenly deprived them of even their names and their identity as human beings. Utterly dehumanized, waiting for death, they were nothing more than the number tattooed on their arms. Let us not forget that!

That wound on its own would be enough to justify, if it were necessary, the need for a state whose existence would guarantee 'never again'. Thus it was that Elie Wiesel, witness of the horror, and now an activist for peace, could write: 'Jews can live outside Israel, but they could not live without Israel'; Israel, whose friend I am and which legitimately aspires – as do my Palestinian friends and all the people of the region – to live in peace and security, within safe, agreed and recognized borders.

Never since the end of the Second World War has anti-Jewish 'mythology' re-emerged with such virulence and met with so little resistance in both political and intellectual circles. At different stages throughout the history of the Jewish people there has been a 'modern' antisemitism adapted to the circumstances of the time and to the interests of antisemites of every stripe. When Judaism was essentially religious, then antisemitism was also religious. When Jews left the ghetto and acquired financial capacity, then antisemitism became financial. With the creation of the State of Israel, when Jews showed they were able to defend themselves, and the archetype of the spineless, stateless Jew was overturned, there again antisemitism showed a different face – an anti-Zionist and anti-Israeli face. Behind that attitude lies a gradual shift away from a subconscious or repressed antisemitism into a more politically correct anti-Zionism. The fault of the Jews is basically that they have left behind their status as victims and have, after two thousand years, fulfilled the universal aspiration to a democratic nation-state: Israel. Geared to an absolute anti-Zionism and the 'demonization' of Israel, this emergence of a new form of antisemitism, centred around the conflict in the Middle East, has not excluded the resurgence of age-old accusations against the Jewish people, revisited to assume a new meaning under the impact of certain ideological transformations. This 'Judaeophobia' now presents itself as a sort of anti-colonial, anti-American, anti-capitalist 'humanism' and anti-Zionism. This new humanism steeped in 'infinite tolerance', and justifying the unjustifiable is accompanied by a falsification of language which liberates antisemitic expression. Thanks to the 'demonization' of Israel, there are no longer any shamefaced antisemites, there is no longer any censorship.

While the permanent antisemitic frenzy and racist ravings of the extreme right are well known to us, today it is mainly on the left and the extreme left that this 'Judaeophobia' is spreading under the new guise of anti-Zionism. In France, particularly, but also in many other, notably European countries, it is in the name of anti-racism and anti-imperialism, and couched in the rhetoric of 'Human Rights' that Judaeophobia is deployed and legitimized. The equation: Jew = Zionist = colonialist = racist = Nazi, enables the so-called anti-racists and other Third Worldists to take part with no false sense of shame in what we would call the 'Durbanization of minds'.

Because it was in Durban, in September 2001 that, under the aegis of the United Nations, a conference whose official theme was the fight against racism and the denunciation of slavery of the African peoples, turned into a mob attack against 'the Zionist entity' with an anti-Jewish virulence rarely seen since Nazism. A group of disparate non-governmental organizations managed to put together a simplistic argument: 'If Israel did not exist, peace and justice would prevail in the Middle East' without any real protests being raised by any of the democratic countries represented, apart from the United States and Israel which left the conference, and a half-hearted protest from the European Union which stayed! The practical, logical conclusion being: 'Israel is one country too many.' In the recent past, that kind of reasoning has already been tried: 'If Jews did not exist there would be no antisemites'. A prescriptive conclusion which was translated into 'Jews are a people too many'. The final resolution proposed by these NGOs, under cover of the Palestinian cause, revealed a hate-filled, negationist racism against all Jews.

A quick historical reminder: when the State of Israel was founded, philosopher Emmanuel Levinas remarked: 'At a time when Jewish history can also expect to be matched by land, everlasting antisemitism lives on in anti-Zionism.' Some intellectuals of the left and extreme left believed that as 'the Jews do not form a true people, nothing justifies the political or national expression of that non-people'. What lies behind this radical negation of Israel as a state? In the minds of those anti-Zionists, Israel, seen in terms of an extra-national, extra-territorial and hence 'stateless' Judaism, could only be 'an instrument in the hands of the imperialists for pursuing and perpetuating the oppression of the Arab nation'. Such a line of thinking glossed over the deep-seated motives for Zionism which, in the minds of its founders, had been created with the object of normalizing the situation of the Jews and giving it a national dimension, and enabling an oppressed, rejected and massacred people to have a piece of land so as to develop there a normal national life.

What underlies this sectarian attitude on the part of some of the so-called intellectual left, incapable of realizing that the Zionist movement drew the main sources of its theoretical thinking from the French Revolution of 1789? Part of the answer can be found in the words of the chief editor of a French newspaper who, in a wildly anti-Zionist essay, levels his accusations in theological and religious terms: 'Israel embodies a stain, inherited from the original sin that is at the root of its illegal political existence; the State of Israel is intrinsically guilty. The original sin of Israel is its creation.' That says it all.

Being anti-Zionist to avoid being called antisemitic – this is a hypocrisy that in the form of inversions and substitutions constitutes a kind of perverse rhetoric. Back in 1967 Dr Martin Luther King wrote: 'Antisemitism, hatred towards the Jewish people, was and still remains a stain on the soul of humanity. Then know also this: anti-Zionist inherently signifies antisemitic, and it will always be so'; because hatred for Israel is the good conscience trying to confuse the issue. It is an open door for repressed hatreds, as though antisemitism were just an empty space into which can be flung all resentments, fantasies and lies. There is no need to look for the causes or to ponder its resurgence and re-emergence. Antisemitism needs no reason because every reason fits. The only condition needed for it to reappear in all its virulence is the underhand work of disinformation carried out with complete impunity. If the facts belie the thesis being presented, they only need to be silenced, minimized and denied.

The Shoah still weighs heavily on the conscience and subconscious of Europeans. Europe cannot be understood without its Jewish soul but is also to be explained by its hatred for Jews. After the Holocaust – the ultimate stage in the process of destruction of the Jewish soul which has been going on for centuries – can Europe be said to have a guilty conscience? Europe knows it is guilty of silence and pro-bably thinks it will find forgiveness for its guilt in an unconditional defence of the Palestinian cause. How can Europe completely shed its guilt? By shifting onto Jews in general, and Israelis in particular, the responsibility for their misfortunes, by likening them to their Nazi executioners so as to clear their name and cast off all remorse: 'It's plain to see, the Jews are capable of the same atrocities as the Nazis. They are therefore like them!'

Sadly, we find the same equation in the work of such well-known writers as Luis Sepulveda, whose book written in the form of a jour-nal, *Une Sale histoire, Notes d'un carnet de moleskine*, contains the fiction that, just as 'the Nazis tattooed numbers on the skin of the Jews … so now the Jews are marking numbers on the skin of Palestinians. Never mind that an Israeli army officer made it clear that "these numbers can be erased", we are witnessing the same per-version, and nations, particularly Europe, are looking on with the same passivity as they did the Holocaust in the past'. It is therefore important to recall the words of respect and fraternity spoken by writers 'physically' involved in this conflict, for example Edward Said's interview with Joseph Algazy for *Ha'aretz* where he states:

> We must convince the Israelis and the Jews that we are aware of the Holocaust, its horrors and their pain, even though the Holocaust does not justify what Israel has done to the Palestinians. Let me emphasize that it would be obscene to compare the extermination of millions of people with the expulsion of people from their land. The common history of suffering of all human beings must be known in order for them to be able to live alongside one another.

Today we face a threefold phenomenon. First, there is the unde-niable and worrying upsurge of hatred of everything Israeli, which is equated with everything Jewish, a hatred stirred up by Islamic fundamentalists and those nostalgic for the Third Reich, and also trivialized by the Trotskyist and Marxist extreme left, a not insign-ifi-cant section of the so-called traditional, democratic left, and anti-Zionist intellectuals. This mixed but like-minded company main-tains a discourse coloured by anti-capitalism, anti-globalization and anti-Americanism which, through an extraordinary reversal of the just fight against racism, is basically antisemitic.

These distortions, false equations and silences might be seen as no more than fallout from a foreign conflict. But this campaign of anti-Jewish hatred is being pursued with the blessing of supposedly progressive organizations and political parties known for their self-proclaimed 'anti-fascist' stand. The hatred for Israel and Zionism of a small band of Trotskyists and leftists, deprived of their last revolution-ary utopia since the fall of the Berlin Wall, makes them forget all reason. Today it would be easier to vindicate Pol Pot than Israel. Hatred for that country and for Jews is so deep-rooted that all other troubles around the world and their thousands of victims are forgotten.

These troubles are also reflected in a tendency to make light of suicide bombings, hostage taking, the killing of civilians and the staging of gruesome, humiliating scenes. I shall always feel sympathy and compassion for the scores of innocent victims reduced to cinders or shreds in buses or on the underground: for the dozens of children blown to pieces, the mothers and old people wounded by these hor-rendous attacks, who will be disabled or mutilated for the rest of their lives, transforming their days into a slow, irrevocable agony. How can we see it as anything other than the 'conformism of perverted thinking' when terrorists who target civilians and children are called 'resistance fighters'; when the media talks of 'executions' of hostages and not 'assassinations'; when the end justifies the means and horror is explained by despair; when the victim is regarded as guilty and the killer as non-accountable; when we are urged to make concessions to terrorism in order to be spared; when the powers that be do not recognize the contradiction in stating that no cause can justify terrorism but that to combat it we must address its causes.

Terrorism is not an expression of the planet's ills but an extension of them. I think that terrorism must be condemned absolutely, universally and unconditionally, and I go along with Camus when he said: 'Whatever the cause being defended, it will be forever dishon-oured by the blind killing of innocent people when the killer knows in advance that women and children will be among the victims'.

It saddens me to note that this hatred for Jews has spread even to

France, in our suburbs, among a minority of young people of North African origin, many of whom are being indoctrinated by Salafist propagandists. I condemn such intense propaganda in the service of a retrograde, death-dealing, totalitarian ideology because that view of Islam advocates conquest, crushes the individual, fires hatred, martyrdom and murder and transforms human beings into weapons of mass destruction. In 1999, the political scientist Ian Lesser published a premonitory book, *Countering the New Terrorism,* in which he writes that terrorism upheld by religion as an overarching ideology is capable of using unlimited violence and of generating an unlimited cohesion – within set borders. This new terrorism is especially dangerous in that the perpetrators of attacks have no fear of unpopularity since 'they say that they are only accountable to God'. Such people should, in these dreadful times, meditate on the noble lesson of life and respect proclaimed by the Holy Qur'an: 'He who has killed a man who has not killed or who has not committed a violence on this earth, is considered to have killed all men; and he who saves one man is considered to have saved all men.'[2] And also this Hadith of the Prophet Muhammad (peace be upon him): 'The ink of the wise man is more holy than the blood of the martyr.' Indeed, the Qur'an emphasizes the superiority of the *alim,* one who is intelligent and learned. Only 250 verses are devoted to legislation whereas 750 – almost an eighth of the Qur'an – aim 'to cause to take heed' and 'to increase knowledge',[3] and not to produce suicide bombers who kill innocent people.

'The crisis of the human ideal is foreshadowed in antisemitism, which is essentially hatred of the Other'. If these words of Emmanuel Levinas are still meaningful, then it is high time for us to denounce this perversion of the soul that is also sustained by some of our Muslim 'brothers'. This trivialization of ordinary racism, this pernicious ideology that ultimately destroys the fabric of 'living together', is what is also meant by 'anti-Jewish' hatred.

The barbaric violence perpetrated against our Jewish brothers and sisters is reprehensible and has nothing to do with our faith, and the tragedy of it is that instead of accusing the aggressors, Islam is being incriminated. It is an aberration to claim that Islam is a religion of combat, running against the grain of all that might make for universal peace. Islam is a religion of mercy and does not permit terrorism. In the Qur'an it is said that 'God forbids you not respecting those who have not fought against you for religion's sake, and who have not driven you forth from your homes, that you should act righteously and justly towards them. For God loves the just.'[4] The Prophet Muhammad (peace be upon him) ranked murder as the second major sin (related by Sahih Al-Boukhari no.6533 and Sahih Mouslim no.1678) and he even warned people that 'The first cases to be judged among people on the Day of Judgement will be cases of bloodshed.'

My analysis does not claim to be exhaustive, nor do I seek to impose solutions, since vouching for a faith does not mean replacing the critical spirit by a taste for the marvellous. But what does Islam actually say about relations with the Jews?

Admittedly, the Qur'an contains about ten verses which need to be looked at in relation to the circumstances of the time; they should be placed in their historical context, notably that of the beginning of the Muslim era in Medina when the first believers, under the leadership of the Prophet Muhammad (peace be upon him) were under siege by the tribal coalition that wanted to eliminate them. For example, 'You will see that those most hostile to the believers are the Jews and the polytheists. You will see that men closest in friendship are those who say: "Yes, we are Christians" because among them are to be found priests and monks who are not filled with pride.'[5] As Salah Stétié stresses in his book *Le monothéisme: Un Dieu, trois religions*, 'Does that mean that dialogue should be renounced, or that this or that aspect of dialogue should be favoured rather than another, while – regardless of one's inevitably biased, subjective and affective feelings, diplomatically kept secret – looking kindly on one real or prospective partner in dialogue, and holding another up to public obloquy?' The answer's no: that is not the position of Muhammad (peace be upon him); which is in fact diametrically opposed to such sectarianism. Indeed, as the Qur'an discovered its aspiration towards universality and its mission to speak to all human beings so it came to emphasize the need for a plural approach, and the importance of talking to others, as is reflected in the following verse:

> Oh you, the people!
> We have created you from a male and a female,
> We have formed you in peoples and in tribes
> So that you may know one another.[6]

I must stress that the Qur'an does not say that Muslims should forcibly convert Jews – or any other people. For it clearly refers to freedom of religion as a requirement of law: 'There shall be no compulsion in religion.'[7] The Qur'an never says that Muslims should mistreat Jews. Never does the Qur'an say that Jews should be persecuted, destroyed and expelled from the face of the earth because they are Jews. Speaking of the children of Israel, God says: 'They are not all the same; among the followers of the scripture, there are those who are righteous. They recite God's revelations through the night, and they fall prostrate. They believe in God and the Last Day, they advocate righteousness and forbid evil, and they hasten to do righteous works. These are the righteous.'[8]

One day (as related by al-Bukhârî, no.1250 and Muslim, no.961), a funeral procession passed before the Prophet Muhammad (peace be upon him) so out of respect he stood up. Someone said: 'It is the funeral of a Jew!' He replied: 'Is it not a human soul?'

Al-Bukhârî relates that when the Prophet (peace be upon him) died, his shield had been pledged to a Jew in order to cover his household expenses. The Prophet could easily have borrowed from his companions who would not have refused him anything, but he wished simply to set an example to his community.

That attitude was also apparent in his companions' and successors' behaviour towards non-Muslims. Thus Omar ordered that from the Public Treasury of the Muslims a permanent allowance should be made to a Jew and his children. He added: 'The Almighty said: "Charities should go to the poor, the needy, ..." and those are the poor among the people of the Book.'[9]

Likewise, Abdullâh Ibn Amr ordered his servant to give a share of their sacrificed meat to his Jewish neighbour. The astonished servant asked the reason for such kindness towards a Jewish neighbour. Ibn Amr explained: 'The Prophet (peace be upon him) said: "The Angel Gabriel did so insist that I be kind towards my neighbour that I came to think that he was going to grant him a share of heritage."'[10]

It is clear that for a long time Jews have lived largely in peace and security in Muslim lands even though not always without being caused suffering. In his book *Aux origines du conflit israélo-arabe, l'invisible remords de l'Occident*, Bruno Guigue writes:

> The responsibility for antisemitism is far from universal ... The presence of non-Muslims in Islamic lands is expressly provided for by the Qur'an and by tradition, the Sunna ... They are the *dhimmis*, the protected ones ... Their status there is in fact codified by the covenant of *dhimma*, which is a guarantee, a protection and a contract ... Thanks to *dhimma*, strong Christian

and Jewish minorities have long lived in peace and security among Muslims ... Accordingly, there is no equivalent in Islamic culture to the opprobrium heaped on the Jews by the Christian West. Expelled from Spain by the Catholic kings after 1492, the Sephardi Jews found asylum in the Arab world. And until the early twentieth century the Ottoman Empire offered them an irreplaceable refuge.

The followers of the religions of the Book were respected and usually held high-ranking positions within the Muslim state. It may be noted that at the time of the early caliphs, a Syrian Christian, John Damascen, canonized by the Greek Orthodox Church, occupied the position of Grand Vizier. The Jew Don Isaac Abravanel held the same office under the last Emir of Granada in Spain in the fifteenth century, and another outstanding Jewish politician, Don Joseph Nassi, 'Duke of Naxos', was the true architect of the Ottoman Empire's foreign policy in the sixteenth century and the organizer of the alliance between the Sultan Süleyman the Magnificent and the Valois monarchy of northern France.

There doubtless does exist an image of Islam as an enemy, but what is worse is that there exists an Islam that sees itself as an enemy. I think that Muslims should not combat the image of Islam as an enemy but concern themselves with Islam itself, which is often today seen as being aggressive.

'The best jihad', proclaims one hadith, 'is to tell the truth to a tyrannical sovereign.' Considering that the 2004 United Nations Development Programme report on 'Human Development in the Arab World' emphasizes the backwardness of the Arab world, I am astounded by the attitude of some Muslim religious guides and political leaders who deafen us with calls for a holy war against Israel and the United States without ever urging people to conduct the jihad against their own shortcomings. The report makes depressing reading:

- Productivity in the Arab countries has decreased over the past forty years; over the past twenty years there has been zero growth;
- 30 per cent of the Arab population live on less than two dollars a day;
- One in every two Arab women can neither read nor write;
- Access to information technologies is very limited: one per cent of Arabs own a computer.

The Arab League Educational, Scientific and Cultural Organization (ALESCO) has identified several obstacles to cultural development in the Arab world:

- Widespread illiteracy;
- Too much importance given to patriotism;
- Administrative barriers preventing the free circulation of culture between countries;
- Government control over people's minds;
- Power of propaganda.

Neither Israel nor the United States is responsible for this sorry situation in the Arab world. It is regrettable that, while most of the world's nations have managed by and large to become modern democracies, no Arab country is included among the 120 democratic states recognized by Freedom House, a liberal American think-tank. And neither is there any Arab country on the list drawn up by Amnesty International and Reporters Without Frontiers of states that respect press freedom.

In short, these countries now find themselves below the poverty line and above the shame line, for what would have happened if, since 1948, every Arab state had concentrated on building up the country instead of making the Palestinian problem its major concern and constant cause of worry? What would have happened if all Arab countries had dedicated themselves to educating their citizens and improving their standard of living? Why has the Arab League not called an Arab summit to tackle these issues? Why are Arab politicians so slow to protest about the dreadful state of basic utilities in their countries, lacking as they do health, education and social services? How can Israel and the United States be held responsible for this dramatic state of affairs?

In this world there are many things that can be complained about, but in my view true social or philosophical thinking means first and foremost self-criticism. That is our duty. Cultures have always been strong when they have called themselves into question and have accepted external inputs while maintaining a sense of their own particular worth, instead of going to ground or just griping. For centuries, Islam had fascinated many of the most forward-looking European intellectuals and artists. We should acknowledge the contribution made by Muslims to the body of universal knowledge and their share in the heritage of all humanity.

But Islam now seems to have become an object of criticism, even of derision, for many intellectuals, frightened by the fanatical, simplistic character of those who take the words of the Qur'an, the Holy Book, literally, without understanding its symbolism or mysticism, and who come to adopt a clearly absurd and, at times, criminal mode of behaviour. What regression! And how sad for such intellectuals of yesteryear as Henry Corbin, Louis Massignon, Jacques Berque and Paul Balta, who thought that through Islam the West would find a source of spiritual renewal.

Misguided jihadists, paltry preachers and literal-minded Muslims, you are undermining and ruining our culture, denying the mystical and Sufi heritage and preventing men and women who might have believed in our tradition from turning to it. Then afterwards you come tearfully complaining or threatening, as the case may be, saying: 'They are criticizing Islam, they are insulting religion.' Well then, stop making it appear detestable and reactionary!

Do you think you can attract the best people by siding with reactionaries and oppressors? What did your predecessors do to make Islam so alluring and to win over so many distinguished minds? That is the question you should be asking yourselves. If you are really believers, you should fear your God, whoever He is, and instead of playing at politics, oppressing women, trying to find sinister justifications for ignoble practices such as stoning, you should practise a little more contemplation and charity, and become examples for humanity. Through attending to spirituality and radiating goodness, you will attract souls.

But by wreaking terror in Muslim countries and elsewhere, by treating Jews as criminals, by trying to intimidate the most destitute, by seeking to excuse the inexcusable, and by being even less virtuous than non-believers, your only reward will be the failure and rejection of the religion you purport to serve! You prefer to become examples of inhumanity and barbarity rather than supportive friends and brothers, and you oppose the new spirit of freedom for women and men, which lifts them up and transcends them. A harsh malediction is what you should fear at the end of this path. Do not forget: 'you all come from Adam and Adam is of the earth' said the Prophet Muhammad (peace be upon him); and the Qur'an calls for respectful conduct towards others: 'You shall remind, for your mission is to deliver this reminder. You have no power over them'[11] and 'To you is your religion, and to me is my religion.'[12]

The poet Salah Stétié offers us this insight: 'One last hadith serves to guide us and justify our ambition to see Islam find fulfilment in modernity, better than heretofore, by following its own inspiration: "Wisdom is a thing so precious and so sought after, says the Prophet (peace be upon him), that the believer must, if he has lost it, seek it mercilessly wherever it may be". It is that search, lit by an invisible inner light, that must henceforth be the main concern of Islam.' That is why I remain an 'anxious optimist', for though I see in the Arab world a renewal of censorship and inquisitions, the substitution of anathema for argument, and downright murder in the place of discussion, Islam will have to reinterpret its basic legal principles in the light of modernity and scientific evidence in order to adapt to the world of today.

Let me conclude with one last thought, about something no fundamentalist, whether Muslim, Jewish or Christian, can ever understand: the Creator loves freedom, He created free women and men, free to praise Him but also free to err. Religion is not there to rule human life; it sets an example, suggests ways of answering our gravest concerns, inspires deep devotion. But when a religion attempts to impose norms and laws on human beings, it negates the implicit will that we see at work in the Creation. 'Had your Lord willed, all the people on earth would have believed. Do you want to force the people to become believers?'[13] The modern world offers dozens of different religious traditions, atheist and agnostic movements, and the possibility for each individual to decide for himself. This diversity and this choice are clearly willed by the Creator, who, if he had wished to impose a unique, obligatory revelation on everyone, would have arranged the world otherwise. 'If God had so wished, he would have made of you a single community. But he wanted to test you with the gift he gave you. Seek to surpass one another in good deeds. One day you will return to God and then he will enlighten you on the matter of your differences.'[14] So let us then respect the freedom of every woman and every man, it is the only way to conform to the supreme Will!

Let us meditate on these lines of the Muslim mystical poet Ibn Arabi:

> My heart is open to the faith of all men,
> Christian hermitage or temple of icons,
> Table of the Torah or verse of the Qur'an.
> Along whichever path love leads its caravan
> I will follow it: love is the only road of faith.

NOTES

1. Recounted by Abû Dâwûd and Al-Bayhaqî. Cf. As-Sunan Al-Kubrâ, volume 5, p.205.
2. Sura 5, verse 32.
3. Sura 20, verses 113 and 114.
4. Sura 60, verse 8.
5. Sura 5, verse 82.
6. Sura 69, verse 13a.
7. Sura 2, verse 256.
8. Sura 3, verses 113–14.
9. Sura 9, verse 60.
10. Related by Al-Bukhârî, no.128 and Abû Dâoûd, no.5152.
11. Sura 88, verses 21–2.
12. Sura 109, verse 6.
13. Sura 10, verse 99.
14. Sura 5, verse 48.

24 Containing Antisemitism: A Model for Combating Negrophobia

ASSUMPTA MUGIRANEZA

INTRODUCTION

By the word 'model' used in the title, I understand all the human and material means, tools, techniques and theories used to understand how antisemitism operates and to fight it effectively. The parallel suggested in the title, while not predicated on an epistemological definition, reflects certain common realities on the ground.

While it is generally agreed that every form of hatred of others is to be combated resolutely, antisemitism stands out as needing to be particularly fought because of the unique event of the Shoah. The survivors and people of goodwill have thus understood the absolute need to find new ways of effectively combating hatred of the Jews which, in Europe, long predates their genocide. Every field of activity – science, art and literature, justice, memory – has been mined in order to understand and learn from the Shoah, but also to combat antisemitism in all its forms. For, like racism, antisemitism assumes many guises and is propagated in a variety of ways depending on the period and the motive. Much has been achieved by all these means to counter antisemitism, but unfortunately an immense amount still remains to be done.

Efforts to this end must not only be sustained over a long period of time; they must also be constantly adapted to the changing features of the modern world. As an example, we may cite the changes ushered in by the new information technologies and the use to which they are put by fundamentalists of every kind. Antisemitism has thereby found an extraordinary means of attracting new recruits and spreading at an alarming speed. As a result, the fight against antisemitism, while evolving and adapting to globalization, is led towards other battles against other forms of hatred, negrophobia in particular, and to offer them the solid experience that it has gained over so many years and indeed to cooperate with them worldwide. Efforts to contain negrophobia have much to gain by looking to the successes of efforts to contain antisemitism. Indeed the fight against negrophobia, without being an exact replica of the fight against antisemitism, finds therein a set of means, tools and techniques that should enable it to fight effectively against the poison of racial hatred.

THE FIGHT AGAINST NEGROPHOBIA

Since the discovery of the African continent and the slave trade, down through the years of colonization, it has been a long and difficult battle for Blacks to be recognized as being fully human. Because of the widespread acceptance of the idea that black people are inferior to all other human beings, it is no longer felt to be even surprising when basically racist remarks are made or indeed when works are acclaimed whose authors make no secret of their contempt for blacks simply because they are black.[1] Offensive words, clichés and stereotypes are common currency, whether wielded by ordinary citizens, politicians (not necessarily of the far right), journalists, intellectuals, doctors, etc. All these good people make negrophobic remarks, often without being aware of it. Africans, black people, are at best noble savages and at worst terrible barbarians, condemned to remain in a primitive state. This perception colours all interpersonal relations between non-African and African countries. All areas of life are contaminated by this view. The problems of a black African will thus not be analysed according to the same criteria as those of a non-African. In the latter case, explanations will always be found in terms of individual qualities, while in the case of Africans, one can expect explanations that refer more to external qualities, to situations.

Then again, the history of the continent is written elsewhere, published elsewhere and, most of the time, taught by people from elsewhere. To be convinced of this, one has only to consult the school textbooks and curricula of many schools in Africa. The differences that exist between the various groups fighting for the recognition of slavery, the heavy legacy of colonization and other injustices suffered by the black people seem to reveal a lack of coordination and of coherence between each group's perception of its own history. One example of this is the different points of view expressed by black Americans, the descendants of slaves in French overseas territories and departments and blacks in Africa. This lack of coherence, of convergence, this phenomenon that may sometimes suggest a competition between victims, reflects first and foremost a lack of common, objective and impartial culture in respect of a continent which is and which remains the original birthplace of them all.

The Fight against Negrophobia should take Inspiration from the Fight against Antisemitism

No one can be aware of the horror of the Shoah without realizing the full significance of the fight against antisemitism. But how much one knows about the Shoah depends on the means used to make people understand the unprecedented nature of that event – the work done by historians, documentation centres, Shoah memorials, commemorations, conferences and many other events, but especially public court proceedings. All of this contributes to a fuller awareness of the tragedies that may be spawned by hatred of others.

To combat negrophobia, it would be useful to be able to write the history of the black people, in its diversity, in its complexity and in its singularity – a history that would not be exclusively that of the oppressed who accuses or that of the accused who justifies himself. It is true that work has begun along these lines, but polemics abound and significant gaps remain. Historians will need to be trained and teaching courses will need to be introduced, so that the history of Africa assumes its rightful place.

One possible danger is that of an attempt to establish a hierarchy among the victims of crimes perpetrated against the children of Africa. Thus there will be some who will hoist the flag of the slave trade, while others will rally under the banner of the crimes of colonization. What must be learnt, in the light of the example of the fight against antisemitism, is that it is the same crime that continues to be perpetrated and also that the various activist groups complement one another and share the same goals.

Another real danger, which must not be overlooked, which needs to be attended to rapidly and lucidly, is the latent antisemitism being spawned in many black communities. In black Africa for instance, in those places where Christianity has not taught that it was the Jews who killed Jesus, Islam has become implanted, in the fundamentalist version that has been holding sway in recent years. In addition, the media coverage given to the Middle East conflict has only made the situation worse. What with the antisemitism of certain black

American liberation movements and the depiction of Jews as being responsible for the slave trade, there still remains much to be done to open up people's minds, develop awareness, and educate against the germ of antisemitism among blacks generally, and among Africans in particular. Ignorance and a narrow, distorted version of history are often at the root of this regrettable situation. Certain associations and organizations, like the Jewish–black friendship initiative, HEVEL,[2] and others in France, have started up, but a higher level of investment is needed. It would be worthwhile, in fighting this type of anti-semitism, to take the opportunity, at the same time, to develop an effective tool against negrophobia through exchanges between the activists concerned. When the majority of those engaged in the fight against negrophobia have understood the meaning of the fight against antisemitism and what that example can bring to their combat, the world will have benefited doubly. Not only will antisemitism have lost its influence in such communities, but above all, by arming themselves with the weapons offered them by the paradigm of the fight against antisemitism, those bent on combating negrophobia will have found an effective means of pursuing their combat. Notwithstanding the Shoah, many people still remain susceptible to hatred towards others for reasons that have to be fiercely combated, be they fundamentalist religious groups, unscrupulous politicians, youth movements manipulated by troublemakers, etc. Everyone develops a pretext for hatred, not hesitating to draw on Nazi ideology and putting in place a fully fledged programme for exterminating the targets of their hatred. For anyone who is at all mindful of the lesson of the Shoah, it is inconceivable not to do something. But danger lurks in every corner and it is not always easy to act, as we may see with the example of Rwanda.

THE GENOCIDE OF THE TUTSI IN RWANDA IN 1994: A CASE TO MEDITATE ON FOR AFRICA AND FOR THE WORLD

From April to July 1994, in three months, one million Tutsi in Rwanda were killed, slaughtered by their Hutu countrymen simply because they had been born Tutsi. Eventually, the rest of the world woke up to the fact, but soon after the curtain fell on that barbaric and distant crime. Rwanda would have to face up to this unspeakable crime and its consequences, far from the eyes of the civilized world, which did not wish to be disturbed. Had it not proclaimed 'Never again!'? Yet the United Nations recognized that a genocide had been committed and an international tribunal for Rwanda was set up in

Arusha, Tanzania, to try the highest political and military authorities of the genocidal regime.

Since we have been talking about latent antisemitism in Africa, it should be noted that when, in Rwanda, every possible insult had been hurled at the Tutsi, they could still be called Jews or Falasha. This speaks for itself.

The Lessons of the Shoah Applied to the Genocide of the Tutsi in Rwanda

What is comparable is not necessarily the same, but when one knows something about the Shoah and takes a look at what occurred in the small country of Rwanda in 1994, one cannot help seeing parallels. Admittedly, the European Jew of the 1930s is not the Rwandan Tutsi of the 1990s. Admittedly, the extremist Hutu leaders of Rwanda were not the Nazi leaders who terrorized Europe in the first half of the last century. However, there is no lack of similarities both in the organization of the crime and in its execution. This leads us to think that the survivors of the Rwandan genocide and those working alongside them would do well to be guided by what was done in earlier times by the survivors of the Shoah.

It can never be said too often that before being deported to the death camps, before being attacked with knives and clubs, the victims of the Shoah had long ceased to be regarded as human beings. With breathtaking opportunism, taking advantage of the political and economic crisis of the time, the authorities devised their extermination ideology. An unprecedented propaganda machine (political speeches, radio and television broadcasts, print media, arts events, etc) was painstakingly assembled. Everything was done to ensure the 'best' possible accomplishment of the programmed crime. Step by step, the future victims became the target of attacks whose effect was to take away their human status before taking away their lives.

The propaganda developed a referential framework in which two opposing groups were established who could not live together: *us* (the good guys) and *them* (the bad guys). Subsequently we see the emergence of the other, who cannot have the same value as us. He is subhuman, without a homeland, without moral standards. Propaganda succeeds in dehumanizing the other. From being subhuman, without a homeland, he becomes the subject of entomology or even parasitology. Thus, the Jew is not merely a non-Aryan, who doesn't like to work (save to destroy other peoples), without a homeland, simultaneously a capitalist and a communist. He becomes a flea, a germ. Likewise, the Tutsi will not be just a Hamite/Semite come from elsewhere in order to enslave the true Rwandan people, not only does he thirst for the blood of the Hutu, the enemy of Rwanda (inyangarwanda), but also his depravity will go so far as to make of him a cockroach, a vermin, a snake, a virus. It then becomes almost a duty to destroy him, no longer as an act of manslaughter but in a spirit of pest removal. The aim is to protect the health of the people against a biological evil that threatens the whole of society.

It is interesting to compare anti-Tutsi propaganda from before the genocide in 1994[3] with the views expressed by Hitler.[4]

Foreigners, without a Homeland

The Tutsi is a foreigner, without a homeland, thirsting for power:

> We remember them arriving in Rwanda with their herds of cows, searching for grazing land. They came from northern Africa. In Rwanda they found what they needed for their herds and settled. Then they approached the Hutu kings and, with their usual guile, which consisted in offering their cattle and daughters, they overthrew the Hutu, seized power and held onto it until the 1959 revolution. In actual fact, the Tutsi have long been developing an ideology of Hutu domination.

For Hitler, the Jews have never had any country: they have been wandering since the dawn of time, living off other people. 'And besides, Jews were then living like parasites on the body of other peoples and so it had to be; for a people that does not want to work ... work which is so painful for a Jew ... such a people will never found its own State and will always prefer to sponge off another state.'

Evil by Nature, through Tainted Blood

Of impure race, born of incest, the Jew described by Hitler is over-run by evil, from which there is no escaping:

> There too, the Jew stands out. He is of impure race and has practised incest while reproducing on a scale that cannot be equalled. We are witnessing the emergence of a species which, through this incest, bears all the defects for ever inherent in

incest ... And from this peculiarity, which he cannot avoid and which comes from his blood, as he himself admits, there arises for the Jew the need to wreak the destruction of the state. He cannot stop himself, whether or not he wishes to.

The Tutsi described by *Kangura* practises incest and is a cockroach that cannot but produce another cockroach. He has always been wicked, regardless of the circumstances; such is his nature:

> The geneticists tell us that the demographic weaknesses of the Tutsi derives from the fact that they intermarry exclusively. People from the same family marry one another and reproduce. They do not know that if they are not careful, this way of seeking a partner among their own kind may cause them to vanish from the earth. We began by saying that a cockroach cannot give birth to a butterfly, and that is true. A cockroach gives birth to another cockroach. The history of Rwanda clearly shows that the Tutsi have remained true to themselves and have never changed. Their guile and wickedness are familiar to us from the history of our country. If in our language we call them snakes, that is in itself enough. The Tutsi is someone who seduces with words but whose wickedness is immeasurable. The Tutsi is someone whose desire for vengeance is never slaked, someone whose thoughts you cannot know and who laughs in the midst of terrible suffering.

Drawing on its own folk wisdom, *Kangura* describes the Tutsi in offensive terms:

> The following proverbs bear witness to the sadism and natural wickedness of the Tutsi:
> – Tend the sex of the Tutsi, he'll take your wife!
> – Give hospitality to a Tutsi, at nightfall he'll push you out of your bed!
> – A country that does not thrash its dogs will soon see them all frothing at the mouth.
> – In Swahili we say: the young of a snake is a snake!
> The above proverbs show that the wickedness and arrogance of the Tutsi are nothing new but have always existed.

An Imminent Threat that must be Nipped in the Bud

The future victim, who is evil by nature, will find himself accused of a crime of which he has often been a victim in history (pogroms) and of preparing an extermination when he is the one who is due to be exterminated. Is this a pretext for speeding up the preparations for slaughter, rallying the troops, making light of all the massacres already suffered by the future victim, or simply the devising of explanations beforehand? Is it all this is or are there yet other reasons? There can be no clear-cut answer but it may be noted that, in Hitlerian propaganda, Jews are a threat to the Reich and to the entire Aryan race, it is they who make it necessary for others to exterminate them, out of self-defence:

> For millennia the Jew thus fitted into other races and we know perfectly well that whenever he lived somewhere, the first signs of collapse were seen, so that peoples had no other solution than to get rid of the undesirable guest if they were not to founder in turn. But when a race systematically destroys the conditions in which my own race can live, I am no longer indifferent to who they are. In this case I say: I am one of those who, when they receive a blow on the left cheek, give two or three blows in return!

According to *Kangura*, the Tutsi has already sinned in the past and can only go on doing so. He wishes to enslave the Hutu, to massacre him. He must be forestalled:

> From the 16th century up to 1959, the Hutu masses endured four hundred years of domination, exploitation and menial tasks imposed on them by the Tutsi minority ... and we know that they attacked with the intention to massacre and exterminate 4.5 million Hutu, and especially those who have been to school, as was done in Burundi, but God prevented them. The threat has not been averted however. The enemy is still there, amongst us, and is just waiting for the right moment to wipe us out. So, Hutu, wherever you are, be firm and vigilant, take the measures needed to dissuade them from committing a further aggression.

Anticipating the grisly scenes that were to mark the genocide, the most awful crimes were attributed to the Tutsi: 'They seized a Hutu, cut off his genital organs and had them taken to his wife when they did not ask him to eat them. He who cursed the Tutsi did not wash his hands because they are always so notable for their wickedness, fine words, arrogance and guile that God's curse will always be upon them, for God does not tolerate the wicked.'

An International Enemy, using the same Weapons: Guile, Money and Women

Hitler ascribes the following words to a rabbi: 'To all intents and purposes we are already today the masters of a whole series of states, we control them financially, economically and also politically.' According to Hitler,

> the entire Zionist state would be no more than a kind of university for their international skulduggery. They would run everything from there and, in addition, Jews would have to be granted immunity as citizens of the Palestinian state. (Laughter) And besides, they naturally retain our civic rights. But in this way they only achieve one thing: if one day you were to catch a Jew red-handed, he would then no longer be a German Jew, but a citizen of Palestine. (Laughter) ... Wheeling and dealing when it was a question of their ideals, they were even ready to sacrifice their family. We know that one gentleman, who was recently here, Sigmund Fraenkel, wrote in the *Neueste* that it was absolutely unfair to take the Jews to task for their materialistic outlook. You only have to look at the Jews' intimate and joyful family life. That intimate family life did not for one moment prevent their own patriarch Abraham from acting as his own wife's procurer for the Pharaoh of Egypt with the sole aim of thereby deriving gain. (Laughter) Such was the patriarch and ancestor whose sons grew in the image of their father and were never averse to doing business and, it is all too clear, are still not averse to same. Already two and a half centuries before Jesus Christ, they were everywhere and were beginning to be feared. They were already big with words, they were already merchants, and many Roman writings tell us that, even at that time, they traded in everything, from shoelaces to girls (That's right).

According to *Kangura* the Tutsi loves power and seems ready to sacrifice everything for it. He is said to have two infallible weapons:

When the Tutsi were still on the throne, they governed by two things: women and cows. The Tutsi lust after blood and power and want to impose their rule over the Rwandan people by gun and rifle. The Tutsi have used two weapons which they claim are effective against the Hutu: money and Tutsi women. It is from guile or self-interest that a Tutsi maintains relations with the people who form the majority. When a Tutsi wants to get something from a Hutu, he is ready to make every sacrifice and uses every means including money, his sisters or his wife.

There are many other striking similarities, notwithstanding the distance in time and space. Thus, reference is often made to certain branches of learning, in particular history, medicine and genetics. Only truncated and sometimes invented passages are quoted and commented on without the slightest concern for scientific accuracy. But this enables the speaker to place himself on the side of historical but also scientific truth, so as to suggest that no further discussion is possible. It will be noted that the future victims are never spoken to; they are referred to without any thought of their point of view; they are judged and the verdict is soon proclaimed.

During the Genocide, Silence and Denial

When genocide reaches the slaughtering phase, as programmed, the borders are closed and the killers move into action with terrible efficiency. Men, women, children, babies, old people, the sick, prisoners, rich or poor, everyone without any distinction save the fact of their having been born a Jew or a Tutsi. One speaks of an operation, of cleansing, of cleaning up. The method is radical, the solution is intended to be final. It is not done in secret, despite the code names; everyone knows but no one seems able or willing to react, at least not in time. The genocide unfolds in a situation of war, but the victims of genocide are by no means the victims of war, they are victims solely of their birth (Armenians, Jews, Tutsi). It is even more important to win the war of extermination of the 'enemy' than to win the ongoing military war. Thus, for instance, during the genocide of the Jews, when the news from the front was very bad and the German troops were in difficulty, no deportation train ever failed to meet its schedule, and the whole system for the extermination of the Jews always 'operated smoothly'. In Rwanda, astounding as it may seem, it was considered to be more important to kill Tutsi than to take up arms against the Rwandan Patriotic Front. The logistics of genocide did not suffer in any way from the difficulties bound up with military combat.

It is not until much later that the outside world seems to realize what atrocities are unfolding before its eyes. But that does not mean an end to denial. It is too hard to accept reality, we make believe that it isn't real, as though from one day to the next it might turn out to be just a bad dream. And the psychological processes involved are very complex and frequently unconscious. In the case in point, geographical and cultural distance made denial easier and the world continued to turn more or less normally.

In the Wake of Genocide, the Impossibility of Justice, Negationism

Once the genocidal forces have been defeated, the victims expect to have everyone's compassion. They are soon disillusioned, as they come to realize that they are stopping the world from continuing in the usual way. They find that they trigger different kinds of reaction. In some cases they are asked to be quiet; their story is unbearable to their intended listeners. Often, they are suspected of exaggerating, of harbouring resentment and of thinking only of vengeance. In such cases, it becomes necessary to protect their would-be killers who might otherwise suffer from what may be assumed to be the victims' feelings towards them.

The Near-impossibility but Absolute Necessity of Justice

Human justice cannot, it is true, be equal to the crime of genocide, but in spite of everything it remains absolutely necessary. It forms part of the writing of the history of genocide, it rehabilitates the victim as a human being and separates the killer from the crime. The office-holders of genocidal regimes take to their heels rather quickly and have many rich friends who will protect them, come what may. Despite some international cooperation, quite a large number of criminals long elude justice. The survivors and their families have no choice but to accept this unacceptable fact or to take things into their own hands. No praise can be too great for Simon Wiesenthal, Serge Klarsfeld and their fellow activists for having shown the way. Today, their actions have become a source of light and inspiration to those among the Rwandan Tutsi and their friends who are trying to bring the perpetrators of the genocide to trial. Many of them have found refuge in the Western countries and in some African countries with which they had forged bonds of friendship. Rwandan victims and their families may, however, find hope in the fact that there have been two trials in Belgium and six accused persons had been convicted. Since then, in Belgium and France, the *Collectifs des Parties Civiles pour le Rwanda* (CPCR) have come into being. These associations of victims seeking to institute criminal indemnification proceedings against the perpetrators of the genocide, following the example of Wiesenthal and others, have set themselves the goal of bringing before the French courts those of them who have found refuge in France and in Belgium. The road is long and full of obstacles, but it is lighted by the example of the fight against antisemitism in the aftermath of the Shoah.

A Negationism helped along by Negrophobia

It is worth recalling here some of the comments made about this genocide that was occurring just when the fiftieth anniversary of the Normandy landings was being commemorated: 'Interethnic massacres', 'an ancestral war between two rival tribes, who have hated and fought each other since the beginning of time'. While the genocide was in progress, it was denied by some and misrepresented by others. Immediately afterwards, when the survivors and their families were still trying to find words to describe what they had been through, the virtually intact genocidal machinery continued to turn in the so-called refugee camps in Zaire and Tanzania, and also elsewhere in the world. Denial thrived and was drawn on to rewrite history. Executioners became victims, victims became executioners. European politicians, former friends of the genocide regime, invented the theory of 'double genocide'; the media, NGOs, selected witnesses came forward to rewrite the brand new history of this tropical genocide. From all over the world, TV cameras, NGOs and government advisers jockeyed for space in the camps in Zaire and Tanzania, neglecting at the same time the victims of the genocide. The rebel force of the Rwandan Patriotic Front, which unaided had just routed the regime in place, thereby putting an end to the genocide, was accused of being at its origin. Since then, every year without exception, negationist works are published and distributed and favourably received in our Northern democracies. The victims and their families, together with those who understand the dangers of this negationism, try to fight it, but they do not have enough weapons, they are not equal to the task. The Tutsi of Rwanda who are seeking to get back onto their feet are faced with several challenges. These include day-to-day survival after losing everything or almost everything, coming to terms with what they have lived through, court proceedings, negationism, reconciliation, etc. Not enough is being done in the way of conceptualization, they do not yet have a frame of reference to provide them with the beginnings of answers to all these challenges. And they are powerless to defend themselves against professional journalists writing in national newspapers. They do not have the weapons to respond effectively to the manipulators of public opinion who manage to impose themselves in publishing houses and radio and television studios. They need the support and cooperation of those who have gained experience fighting antisemitism and safeguarding the memory of the Shoah. This is an absolute necessity.

CONCLUDING REMARKS

Efforts to contain antisemitism can be a source of inspiration to those fighting negrophobia, and provide them with suitable tools. The fact is that, while there are several sides to negrophobia, those who are trying to fight it do not yet share a single paradigm. We may wager that if the Tutsi of Rwanda had not been African blacks, what is called the international community would have reacted differently. If Western attitudes were not marked by negrophobia, the case of the Tutsi of Rwanda, as well as what is happening or is in danger of happening in Côte d'Ivoire, or what is unfolding in Darfur, former Zaire and elsewhere in Africa would not go unnoticed, would not be completely absent from the Western media or from the speeches of our politicians. If we do not fight negrophobia we run the risk of allowing the poison of hatred to spread, and seeing extremists come to the fore and trigger explosions whose consequences are incalculable.

Since the genocide of the Tutsi of Rwanda, there have been a number of initiatives on the part of Jewish communities throughout the world, expressions of solidarity, offers of assistance, support in coming to terms with the tragedy of a people. Armenians, Jews and Tutsi have come together to learn from one another, exchange ideas and organize programmes of action (exchanges and field visits, associations, symposia, conferences, seminars, etc). The combat against antisemitism can and must not only offer a model for efforts to counter negrophobia, but it must also be directed against an antisemitism which is still all too present among many blacks (African or non-African). The apostles of antisemitism are still around and their preachings are based largely on ignorance. Once that action has been taken against antisemitism in certain black communities, it may be expected that not only will many blacks no longer be influenced by antisemitic remarks, but also they will discover a paradigm to counter negrophobia. For just as antisemitism does not concern the Jews alone, so negrophobia is not a matter that affects only blacks but is the business of all human beings as members of the human community.

NOTES

1. Stephen Smith, *Négrologie, pourquoi l'Afrique meurt* [Negrology: Why Africa is Dying] (Paris: Calmann-Lévy, 2003).
2. HEVEL is an association of Armenians, Jews, Tutsis and other black Africans based in Paris. It shares the common experiences of genocide, and its first conference in November 2005 addressed 'Armenian, Jew, Tutsi – Three Peoples Confronting Denial'.
3. All the following quotations regarding the Tutsi are taken from *Kangura*, the mouthpiece of the Habyalimana government. This newspaper published words of hate that were subsequently reproduced and discussed at length on the radio, which had a very large audience in Rwanda at the time.
4. All the following quotations are taken from a speech given by Hitler on 13 August 1920, at a public meeting in the main hall of the Hofbrauhaus. The author of this article found the document at the Contemporary Jewish Documentation Centre/Shoah Memorial and has been translated.

25 Containing Antisemitism: Lessons for Tolerance from Northern Ireland

RICHARD ENGLISH

At first sight, it is the differences which are most striking between the late twentieth-century Northern Ireland conflict and the global challenge of containing antisemitism. There was nothing, for example, in twentieth-century Irish history to approach the programmatic mid-century assault on the Jews; and the Israel-centred conflict of the late-twentieth century has been a far more internationalized and internationally dangerous struggle than was the Ulster conflict.

Nor have all problems yet been solved in Northern Ireland, despite the comparative absence now of fatal political violence, and the ongoing pattern of post-war political engagement. The two communities in Northern Ireland – broadly, Protestant unionist versus Catholic nationalist – remain deeply polarized, with the dominant political party on each side (Ian Paisley's Democratic Unionist Party and Gerry Adams' Sinn Fein) each enjoying only single-community backing (Protestant for Paisley, and Catholic for Adams).

But I think that there are indeed some lessons which might humbly be proposed as being of potential value in relation to the containment of antisemitism, and I want briefly to outline four of them.

First, it seems to me that one central feature of the Northern Ireland problem – and one important element of its peace-process solution – lay with the issue of recognition. Traditionally, Irish nationalism failed to recognize the legitimacy and validity of Ulster unionists' desire to remain within the United Kingdom state, and to acknowledge the legitimacy of their self-identity as British people. Nationalists effectively treated unionists as suffering from mass false consciousness: they were Irish people who just did not know it yet;

they would come to their senses eventually and realize that Irish nationalism had been right all along; until then, they could simply be ignored or dismissed. As one prominent Sinn Feiner put it to me regarding Irish republican attitudes towards Ulster unionists, 'In a way we made them a non-people.' Similarly, for many years Ulster unionists tended to underestimate the degree of disaffection and disadvantage which was characteristic of nationalists who lived within Northern Ireland. The Northern Irish state was therefore constructed in the image of the majority unionist community, its symbols and power overwhelmingly reflecting the British preferences of unionist but not of nationalist people.

Now there remains something of a problem here even yet, and much more could be done in the north of Ireland to ensure that each side acknowledges and respects the validity of the other. But there has also been a huge change on both sides, with Irish nationalists recognizing that Northern Ireland will continue to exist within the United Kingdom as long as a majority of people there want it to do so, and with unionists having adjusted Northern Ireland (its governmental structures, its symbols, its police force) in order to make the state one which recognizes the legitimacy also of Irish nationalists' identity and aspirations within the north.

So formal agreements (whether the 1985 Anglo-Irish Agreement between the UK and Republic of Ireland, or the 1998 Good Friday Agreement reached after multi-party talks in Northern Ireland), have stressed the dual legitimacy of both nationalist and unionist identity, aspiration, loyalty, culture and grievance.

This surely has a relevance to our problem with antisemitism. For at the heart of that problem is a refusal to recognize the legitimacy of Jewish existence, whether in the form of the rights of individual Jews, the existence of a Jewish state, or the validity of Jewish identities, grievances and aspirations. And, clearly, there is an imperative also in areas in which the conflict has been most sharp, to acknowledge the identities, grievances and so on of those among whom the poison of antisemitism has at times gained ground. It is not that structures or cultures of legitimacy and recognition will entirely remove the evil of antisemitism. They will not. But they may be able to restrict the power which antisemitism has at times gained, and this must be our goal. We will never eradicate entirely the existence of antisemitic views: but we can limit the degree to which such views become what might be termed forces of major political weight. We can help to marginalize them by stressing – on all sides – the validity of competing identities, aspirations and grievances. Mutual recognition, rather than stubborn solipsism, must be the way forward.

Second, the Northern Ireland experience points to the vital importance of trust, if one is lastingly to build mutual tolerance in practice. This has been made painfully clear in two senses, I think, in Northern Ireland. First, there were key relationships in the building of the peace process which relied on the creation of meaningful and lasting trust between former adversaries or competitors: between rival nationalists such as John Hume and Gerry Adams; between rival prime ministers such as Britain's John Major and the Republic of Ireland's Albert Reynolds; between certain Protestant clergy and Irish republicans, who engaged in dialogue with one another; between Catholic priest Alec Reid and Sinn Fein leader Gerry Adams; between British civil servants and Irish republicans; and between Irish civil servants and Ulster loyalists.

These personal relationships of trust helped to sustain the peace process as a process, and to encourage at least some dilution of the intolerant prejudice which had so long flourished in Ulster. But there is also a second lesson regarding trust, and it is that Northern Ireland's ongoing problems lie now in the remaining lack of trust between the two political communities, Protestant and Catholic. Broadly speaking, neither side trusts the other to act in good faith; so compromises, deals and structures are all more difficult to reach and sustain, amid this world of doubt and anxiety.

I think that there is no neat solution to this problem. But I also think that there is a broad lesson, and one of relevance to containing antisemitism: any genuine and lasting relationship of honest trust between former adversaries contributes towards the possibility of establishing mutual tolerance. This is vitally important, for in the darkest and most pessimistic times it allows for the possibility of at least some forward movement. Bloodshed might have returned, political prospects might seem dire: but even in such circumstances it remains true that to build relations of trust – between individuals, between groups, between community leaders or rank and file members – might establish foundations on which more can be constructed in propitious times. In other words, the *process* of forward-moving tolerance building can be sustained even in bleakest times.

Third, I think that the question of history is vital, and that there is more to be done than has been done in this area at the moment. What I mean is this. History has tended to be used, all too often, in sectarian or partial ways – and this is true in Northern Ireland as in

the world of antisemitism. In many cases, both popular and professional history have been deployed simply as a weapon against one's
enemies: history-telling has been a telling of our grievances as against
their crimes. As such, it merely convinces each side of its own unar-
guable righteousness, and it means that we accept our history as true
but reject theirs as propagandist. Now in Northern Ireland there has
been a generation of scholars whose work has slowly begun to
change this pattern: by explaining what the other community's world
and world-view are, and by establishing, beyond reasonable doubt,
the ground upon which agreed aspects of the past can be established.
Normally, such views undermine simplistic good-versus-evil schemes
of explanation. It is not that there is no right and wrong to be established: as the David Irving episode showed, historians can establish
that terrible things happened, that they were planned in evil ways,
and that they existed in reality beyond any reasonable doubt. But at
a broader level, it seems to me that we need to be better than we have
been – in Northern Ireland and also perhaps in the struggle against
antisemitism – at telling the historical stories of those to whom we
are *not* related, and at explaining why other cultures than our own
have made sense of their past as they have. From such deeper understanding grow the possibilities of compromise.

Fourth, we need to concentrate on the mechanisms of power. In
Northern Ireland the end of paramilitary warfare did not come about
because a generation of formerly immoral men and women became
suddenly compassionate and moral. It basically came about because of
certain realities of political possibility and power. If IRA violence was
clearly not achieving what its practitioners had expected, then the IRA
would turn to other means of establishing political change. Similarly,
it seems to me that there is a range of practical, power-related areas of
activity which might yield the best results in the struggle against antisemitism. We should use all such resources for all that they are worth.
The capacity of states to limit hate crime, to restrict the expression or
organization of antisemitic politics, should be resolutely pursued in all
available cases. The intellectual and moral force of human rights law
and argument should be drawn upon as well; and it should be noted
that, in Europe at least, human rights groups remain far more likely to
agitate on behalf of, for example, Palestinian causes than they do on
behalf of Jewish ones – yet why? And we need to utilize all of the
means of power unleashed by technological innovation (immediate
and permanent electronic media dissemination of information, for
example) in order to publicize and undermine all antisemitic trends

and actions. It is through practical attention to legal, state-centred, or ideological mechanisms of practical power that we will do the most effective work in our effort to build tolerance. In Northern Ireland, noble-minded attempts at reconciliation could coalesce with practical questions of power politics or legal argument. They must coalesce also in the struggle against antisemitism.

26 Holocaust and Antisemitism Studies in China

XU XIN

HISTORICAL BACKGROUND

In order to address the issue of Holocaust and antisemitism studies in China, it seems to me that there is a necessity to examine briefly the background, specially the early awareness of the Holocaust by Chinese, as China is far away from Europe and had very few direct contacts with Jews in history.

EARLY AWARENESS

Generally speaking, the Chinese public knew very little about the Holocaust because there were far fewer reports in China about what was happening to European Jewry than in Western countries between 1933 and 1945 as the Chinese were facing the invasion of Imperial Japan. Their country was in great trouble and they had too much to worry about. However, it does not mean that Chinese, especially Chinese intellectuals, were totally ignorant about the situation. A few events are worth our attention regarding the subject.

Chinese intellectual circles were aware of the persecution against the Jews shortly after the Nazis came to power in Germany. For instance, a protest against Nazi Germany's persecution of Jews was organized on 13 May 1933 in Shanghai by the China League for Civil Rights Protection, a non-governmental organization of Chinese intellectuals and social activists headed by Song Qingling, wife of Dr Sun Yat-sen (Dr Sun was considered as the founder of the Republic of China and a supporter of the Zionist movement[1]), after the news that Germany burned books reached China.[2] A statement issued by Song says: 'Organized persecutions against the Jews by the German government and Fascist Party and antisemitic brutes are symbols of the regression of human beings and their culture to the Middle Ages and the darkest days of the Imperial Czars.'³ This is the first recorded protest against the Nazis in China.

Secondly, from the day that Hitler came to power in Germany in 1933, the Chinese, especially those who lived in cities such as Shanghai, Tianjin or Hong Kong where Jewish communities had existed for many decades, became aware of the ill treatment of German Jews. They learned chiefly through the arrival of persecuted Jews from Germany and other European countries. Quite a few Jews who wished to escape antisemitic persecution in Germany came to Shanghai for a safe haven. The very first groups of those Jews were professionals, such as doctors, lawyers, engineers, architects, editors, journalists, musicians, scientists and professors. They brought with them stories of the horrors committed by the Nazis. From 1937–40 when the persecution worsened, more than 20,000 Jewish refugees from Central Europe sought a haven in Shanghai. Chinese newspapers began to describe them as refugees for the first time and informed Chinese readers that they were persecuted Jews who were forced to escape from their original countries.

In general, Chinese people as well as the Chinese government were very sympathetic to Jewish refugees and took action to assist those helpless Jews in China. For instance, Jews in Shanghai were well treated by Chinese people. Many of them owned shops side by side and survived the war. Some members of the Chinese government spoke of helping the Jews in Europe. Sun Fo, son of Dr Sun Yat-sen and Chairman of the Chinese legislative body, proposed to set up a settlement in Southwest China as a replacement for those who were suffering in German-occupied countries in 1939. Newly-discovered documents show that his proposal was officially approved by the Chinese administrative council and government.⁴ Though the resolution was not implemented due to the complicated situation of the Second World War, it is strong evidence that the Chinese government and people did not stand by in silence and do nothing.

Sun Fo's proposal makes it very clear that at least he and the Chinese government were fully aware of the sufferings of the Jews in Europe. As for the necessity for the settlement, Sun cited in his proposal that:

> Lately, due to the increase of the power of European Fascism, the Jewish people have been tyrannized still worse. Germany is

the worst country among all. Since the annexation of Austria to the Reich by Adolph Hitler, persecution of Austria Jews is aggravated. The Nazis started a massive persecution against Jews on the excuse of the attempt on the life of Secretary of the Legation von Rath in Paris. The brutality is unprecedented.[5]

The significance and importance of that action stands out even more if one takes into consideration the situation of China at the time. In 1939 when the persecution of the Jews in Germany was intensified, half of the territory of China was under occupation by Imperial Japan. In 1937, after the occupation of the then capital of China, a massacre took place, later to be recorded as the 'Rape of Nanjing' which still today hangs heavy on the Chinese collective memory.

It is perhaps worth mentioning that the Chinese communists, who were small in number at the time, also denounced fascism. They considered the Jewish people as a component of the oriental oppressed nations. In October 1941, a gathering on anti-fascism was held in Yan'an, where the headquarters of the Communist Party of China at that time was located. Ye Hua, a German Jewess who had married Xiao San, a well-known Chinese communist writer and journalist, was invited to attend it as a Jewish representative. Both she and Israel Epstein, another Jew supporting the Chinese in the war, were elected as members of an Executive Committee of the Anti-Fascist League after the gathering.[6]

However, one has to keep in mind that the attention given to the issue by the Chinese was not widespread. Only a limited number of Chinese were aware of the Holocaust and were able to show their concern.[7]

POST-WAR PERIOD

News of the horrible consequences of the Holocaust reached China at an early time, almost as soon as the Second World War was over in Europe, because of the presence of Jewish refugees in China. They were eager to learn about the fate of their beloved ones in Europe, and received information through the Jewish network. Lists of those who had died in concentration camps and elsewhere were posted on Chinese streets in Shanghai. Unfortunately, except among a limited number of Chinese, it did not draw substantial public attention to the genocide of the Jews. The reason for that was not that the Chinese were not sympathetic or did not care, but that the sufferings of the

Chinese themselves were too great. Their attention was almost total-ly focused on their own fate. After all, the absolute number of the death toll of the Chinese in the Second World War, if not anything else, was much greater than that of the Jews.[8]

The earliest awareness of the public about the Holocaust during the post-war period was perhaps the publication of the Chinese ver-sion of *The Diary of Anne Frank*. Many hundred thousand copies were sold. It was through the *Diary* that most Chinese learned for the first time about the Final Solution and the atrocities committed by Nazi Germany.

The Holocaust had barely been raised after the Chinese Communists took over China in 1949. This does not mean that the Communists entirely dismissed the issue. Rather they followed the Soviet Union's approach to the Holocaust and viewed the destruction of the Jews as merely a small part of racist fascism's murder of millions of European civilians. Since fascism was considered the ultimate form of capitalism, capitalism had been blamed as the root of the mass killing. According to this perception, nothing was different or special about what had happened to the Jews.

As Communist China was (and is) a highly politicized country, politics and ideology play a decisive role in all fields, including aca-demia and education. The ultra-leftist policies adopted in Chinese social and academic circles since the 1950s made it almost impossi-ble for Chinese scholars to conduct serious studies and academic research on the Holocaust. On top of that, the discussion on estab-lishing formal relations between China and Israel got nowhere in the early 1950s, though Israel was the first country in the Middle East to recognize the People's Republic of China, in January 1950. China adopted an anti-Israel foreign policy in the mid-1950s after estab-lishing diplomatic relations with three Arab countries (Egypt, Syria and Yemen). The abnormal relations between China and Israel made the study of the Holocaust impossible. Thus Chinese academia remained silent about the Holocaust for a couple of decades. Even the trial of Adolf Eichmann in the early 1960s did not break the silence[9] as China became more and more isolated and stood on the Arab side in foreign policies and Middle East affairs. Israel was sel-dom reported by Chinese media.

One of the major consequences of this abnormal situation is that very few, if any, Chinese publications mention the Holocaust. It was not even in Chinese textbooks about the Second World War.

CHANGED SITUATION SINCE THE 1970s

Following Nixon's visit to China in 1972, China came to realize that total isolation was harmful and dangerous.[10] Approaching and making friends with the West became policy. As a result, books and movies about the West were introduced to Chinese and strict control over academic activities was relaxed. Hence, a few Western books which mention the Holocaust were translated into Chinese and circulated among Chinese readers. Among them were *The Rise and Fall of the Third Reich* by William Shirer[11] and *The Winds of War* by Herman Wouk.[12] Those books dealing chiefly with the Second World War and Nazi Germany gave Chinese readers, especially a younger generation like myself who were brought up in New China and had learned very little about the outside world when they were in their teens, a chance to learn about the antisemitic policy of the Nazis and Adolf Hitler. Those books were so popular that college students had to read them in turn, that is, as soon as one student had finished the book, another would begin it. Since then the horror and genocide of the European Jews began to appear fairly frequently in many other translated books. Chinese scholars began to pay some due attention to the issue.

MASS AWARENESS

A marked change occurred in relations between China and Israel in the late 1980s and early 1990s when the two countries had open contact in the United Nations and finally established full diplomatic relations. Chinese attitudes toward Israel began to change dramatically. A good number of Jewish-related activities took place around that time, which helped the Chinese public to learn a great deal about the Holocaust. Some of the activities were:

Genocide, a documentary film about the Holocaust produced by the Simon Wiesenthal Centre, was aired on Chinese TV in 1991 and was viewed by millions of Chinese.

The exhibition: Courage to Remember: The Holocaust 1933–45, also presented by the Simon Wiesenthal Centre, was held in a few Chinese cities such as Shanghai, Beijing and Nanjing from 1991 to 1993. In Nanjing the exhibition received a great deal of attention as it was deliberately held at the Memorial Hall of the Nanjing Massacre and very much reported by the media of the city including China Central TV. According to data collected by the Memorial Hall, it attracted as many as 80,000 viewers in the seven-week period that the exhibition was on display.

The awareness of the Holocaust by the Chinese public has been further strengthened by other events. One is a TV documentary entitled *Sanctuary Shanghai: Jewish Refugees in Shanghai,* which was produced by the Shanghai TV Station and aired on Chinese television in 1998. The background of the topic shows the persecution of the Jews in Europe. Another is Chinese President Jiang Zemin's visit to Israel in 2000. His visit to Yad Vashem, the Holocaust Memorial Museum in Jerusalem, was widely reported by Chinese TV. Because it was aired during prime time, tens of millions of Chinese watched his visit and learned about the Holocaust. No doubt the film *Schindler's List* reached a large audience in China too.[13] It is certainly not an exaggeration to say that it was in the 1990s that the grim revelations of Nazi atrocities were widely exposed in China.

ACADEMIC STUDIES OF THE HOLOCAUST

From the late 1980s, Chinese scholars began to pay attention to the Holocaust. Books on the Second World War written by the Chinese started to include pages on the Holocaust. 'On the Antisemitic Policies of Hitler' by Zhang Qianhong, a scholar at Henan University, is perhaps the first academic essay in Chinese focusing solely on the issue of the Holocaust. It was written in 1990 and published in *A Series of Jewish Culture* in 1992.[14] Though its emphasis is on Hitler's policy without tracing the deep roots of Hitler's antisemitism, the article, nevertheless, gives a fairly good analysis of the issue. The author points out that Hitler adopted a policy based on racism (as an ideology), anti-Marxism (as a political cause), Aryanization (as an economic reason), and ambition to control Europe (as an international objective). Zhang also brings up in her article a 'three-phase' theory in her analysis of the Holocaust, that is, from 1933–39, legal persecutions; from 1939–41, mass expulsion and segregation; and from 1941–45, the 'Final Solution'. The article ends with a brief discussion of the consequences of the Holocaust and its impact on the establishment of the State of Israel. The article may not include many new insights for foreign scholars in the field. It, nevertheless, is one of the first efforts made by Chinese scholars in Holocaust studies.

The beginning of Jewish studies by Chinese scholars in the late 1980s and early 1990s accelerated after the normalization of diplomatic relations between China and Israel in 1992. The major sign of such developments is that Jewish studies took a big step forward and became very popular in Chinese universities. Besides conferences, exhibitions and courses, a large number of books[15] and articles on various Jewish and Israeli subjects appear in the language. Among these publications were the first Chinese version of the *Encyclopedia Judaica* (published in 1993),[16] the Chinese version of *A History of Zionism* by Walter Laqueur,[17] *Jewish People, Jewish Thought: The Jewish Experience in History* by Robert M. Seltzer,[18] and *Israel: A Mysterious Country* by Yang Mansu,[19] to name just a few. Generally speaking, these books aim to cover almost every aspect of Jewish and Israeli life, from the people, their history, politics, geography, economy and culture to foreign relations and military achievements as there had been only a few books dealing with the subject in Chinese. Since Jewish studies is a new subject in Chinese academic circles, both scholars and the general public are much in need of basic information rather than academic insights. Because almost all Jewish-related books published in Chinese in those days mention the Holocaust, the advancement of Jewish studies in China actually promotes the study of the Holocaust in the country.

In 1995, two books on a single subject – the Holocaust – were published in Chinese, which marked a turning point for Holocaust studies in China. They are Yang Mansu's *Catastrophe for Jews: Records of the Holocaust*[20] and Zhu Jianjing's *The Death of Six Million Jews in Europe.*[21] The publications provided Chinese readers with a much fuller and more concrete picture of the Holocaust than any previous books. While both present a narrative description, not a strictly academic analysis, of the Holocaust, this author believes that they play an important role in informing Chinese about the Holocaust. In general, there are many similarities between these two books. Both describe the history of the Holocaust chapter by chapter. Both try to analyse Nazi policies towards the Jews at different stages. Both give accounts of the hunting of Nazi criminals after the war. Both warn their readers that no one should ever forget or deny the Holocaust and everyone should do their best to prevent the Holocaust from happening again.

Nevertheless, Yang's book deserves a bit more of our attention. It was well written and became very popular. As a result it has been published in different editions and more than 100,000 copies were sold within a couple of years of its first appearance in 1995. The author had spent a lot of time collecting information and received assistance from various people including well-known scholars from Israel and the USA. His personal visit to Yad Vashem before he wrote the book, and the many materials provided to him by scholars in the field, certainly helped a great deal with the success of the book. Its primary aim was to make available to the Chinese public knowledge that was previously to be had in the outside world. It traces the roots of Hitler's antisemitism to Martin Luther, who formalized German traditions in the Reformation period. He points out that antisemitism is part of the heritage of the German nation.[22] The conclusion presents many issues faced by post-war nations including Holocaust denial.

The present author's book, *Anti-Semitism: How and Why*,[23] which examines the issue of antisemitism from a historical perspective, looks more closely at the cause of the Holocaust. Regarding the root of the Nazi's antisemitic policy, it not only cites the German's long tradition of antisemitism, the Christian tradition, the church's role in generating the antisemitic concept among Germans, but also points out the fact that antisemitism became a popular policy accepted by almost all political parties in modern Germany. This perhaps could help the Chinese to understand why very few Germans stood up to condemn Hitler's policies against Jews.

When dealing with the process of the Holocaust, it addresses the following issues: the rise and growth of racist ideology and Nazi-style hatred of the Jews; the discriminatory racist legislation under which the Jews were excluded from human society in Germany; the process, instituted against the Jews during the war, of oppression, terrorization, starvation, imprisonment in ghettos, deportation, and the decision for the total destruction of the Jews of Europe. The book also explores the post-war influences of the Holocaust on ideological and political concepts, and on the positions and policies of the various religions and their institutions; the way in which the world regards the Jews and the Jews regard themselves in the post-war period; the treatment of the Holocaust in historiography; and the repeated attempts to deny the Holocaust or to distort its meaning and the responsibility of its perpetrators. Perhaps the book is unique in focusing on an analysis of antisemitism, relating the Holocaust to the antisemitic history of Europe, an issue the Chinese are less familiar with, and thus provides a much broader background for Chinese readers to understand the issues involved.

In 2000, Pan Guang, a Chinese scholar of Jewish history in Shanghai, published 'Nazi Holocaust and Its Impact on Jewish People and Jewish Civilization' in *World History*,[24] a well-known Chinese journal for world history studies. It perhaps marks the beginning of the deepening of Holocaust studies in China. Besides the account of the Holocaust, Pan provides his readers at the beginning of his article with a background description of the revival of antisemitism in Europe at the end of the nineteenth century and the beginning of the twentieth century. The article emphasizes the impact of the Holocaust on the Jewish people and Jewish civilization. He summarizes this as follows. The Holocaust:

1) destroyed the main Jewish communities in Europe and terminated the Europe-centred era in the history of Jewish civilization;
2) strengthened Jewish identity among Jewish people, caused a reappearance of Zionist aspirations and laid the foundation for re-establishment of a Jewish state;
3) resulted in a tendency to sympathize with and rescue the Jews, on a global scale, and created a favourable external environment for the revitalization of the Jewish nation; and
4) had a great influence on Jewish thought, literature and art, and left everlasting teaching materials for Jewish self-education and increased the cohesion of the Jewish nation.

Clearly, Pan's article shows that the study of the Holocaust in China has started to deepen and he offers more insights to Chinese readers.

HOLOCAUST EDUCATION

Holocaust education is another aspect deserving our attention as it is an integral part of Holocaust studies.

Nanjing University, one of the best-known Chinese higher education institutions, has been playing a leading role in Holocaust education in China. Under the leadership of the Centre for Jewish Studies at the University, a 'learning Jewish culture' project was launched in 1992 to promote the study of Jewish subjects among Chinese college students. Though at the very beginning the issue of the Holocaust occupied only a very small portion of the regular courses on Jewish culture, students' interest in learning more about the Holocaust continues to grow. In eight years, more than 1,000 students who took Jewish culture courses at Nanjing University learned about the Holocaust. In 2000, the Centre started to offer an entire course on the Holocaust, entitled 'The Holocaust through Videos', to its students. Over seventy students took it for credits. The syllabus was prepared jointly by this author and Dr Peter Black, a senior researcher and museum historian at the United States Holocaust Memorial

Museum, when I served as a research fellow at the Museum in 1998. A combination of lectures and videos, the course covers not only the roots of the Holocaust, the process and details of persecutions and atrocities, and the consequences of the Holocaust, but also its universal lessons, the human rights issues involved, its message to the Chinese, and how to prevent it from happening again.

The Holocaust education project at Nanjing University brought some unexpected results. For instance, Gong Jin, a graduate student from the English Department, who took the Jewish culture course, decided to write her MA dissertation on the Holocaust. She chose the works of Elie Wiesel, Nobel Prize winner for Peace and a Holocaust survivor, as her subject of study.[25] Her research goes beyond the facts of the Holocaust, focusing on its influences on those who have survived. She pointed out that 'How to return to life after experiencing the immense evil of the Holocaust' is a post-Holocaust question faced by both Jews and non-Jews. After she finished her paper, she commented that 'the fate of the Jews is connected with non-Jews just like the study of the Jewish culture is not of concern to Jews only'.[26]

UNIQUENESS OF HOLOCAUST STUDIES IN CHINA

Holocaust studies have a distinctiveness in China. They are closely linked to Judaic studies in the country, first appearing as a part of Judaic studies. With the advancement of Judaic studies, many scholars realized that the Holocaust is an issue directly linked with the Jewish people since the Second World War. Without a proper perceptive on the Holocaust, we would have difficulty in understanding the establishment of the State of Israel. Most scholars who have either written articles or books on the Holocaust or translated books about the Holocaust have been involved in Jewish studies in China. Yang Mansu, Pan Guang and myself, to name just a few, are all leading figures in the field of Judaic studies in China today. If we could summarize the development of Holocaust studies in China, we would see where they are going: Judaic studies leads to the study of antisemitism. The study of antisemitism leads to Holocaust studies. With the deepening of Judaic studies, Holocaust studies will surely go deeper in China.

Secondly, Holocaust studies become a valuable reference to the Chinese. They provide a positive reference for Chinese to look into their own victimology. We cannot say that the interest in Holocaust studies in China stems from the attempt by the Chinese – as a tactical measure – to highlight their own sufferings in the Second World War. However, Holocaust studies certainly help the Chinese to better commemorate the massacre.

Thirdly, Holocaust studies help to highlight human rights issues in China. What Hitler did is considered a crime against humanity. It raises a number of questions. For instance, how could a group of human beings (the Nazis) do such evil things to another group of human beings (the Jews)? Why did the rest of the world stand by in silence when the Holocaust took place? What is human nature? Where did the sense of human rights go during the Second World War? Those questions and many more were raised and discussed at the Holocaust course at Nanjing University. The study of the Holocaust obviously helps to encourage more human rights discussions among the Chinese themselves.

Finally, Holocaust studies provide many useful lessons for the Chinese to combat attempts to deny the Nanjing massacre. Like Holocaust denial in the West, there are historians who attack the authenticity and objectivity of evidence and testimony regarding these events.

CONCLUSION

Looking back, Holocaust studies in China have made a great deal of progress since they started about ten years ago. The awareness of the Holocaust by the Chinese is far reaching. Interest in the issue among scholars and young people is growing. More and more scholars are involved in Holocaust studies. However, compared to the study of the Holocaust in many other countries, Holocaust studies in China are in their infancy. There is a lack of a national organization or a national programme for Holocaust education in China. Textbooks, especially those for elementary and secondary school students, mention almost nothing about the Holocaust. Moreover, no attempts are being made to change that situation in the near future. There is no Holocaust museum in China so far. Though some thought has been given to the possibility of running a workshop or seminar on the Holocaust for instructors at Chinese colleges, action is needed. The vast majority of the Chinese still have difficulties in comprehending the Holocaust. Many issues concerning the Holocaust such as questions about the guilt of the German people, complicity and collaboration of the countries under German occupation, the failure of non-Jews to attempt to save their Jewish neighbours etc, are rarely touched upon by Chinese scholars. Therefore, there is still a long way to go and much to be done. It is certainly my wish that, with the advancement of Judaic studies in China, more and more Chinese scholars will engage with the topic and deepen their study of the Holocaust. It is imperative for Chinese scholars to upgrade their research to meet international standards and produce fruitful results of value to their colleagues in Holocaust studies the world over.

NOTES

1. Sun wrote in his letter to N.E.B. Ezra, Secretary of the Shanghai Jewish Community on 24 April 1902: 'All lovers of Democracy cannot help but support the movement to restore your wonderful and historic nation, which has contributed so much to the civilization of the world and which rightfully deserves an honorable place in the family of nations.' *The Selected Works of Sun Yat-sen* (Beijing: People's Publishing House, 1985), vol. 5, pp.256–7. See also *Israel's Messenger*, a Jewish publication in Shanghai, 4 November 1972.
2. Some other members of The League are Cai Yuanpei, Yang Xingfo, Lu Xun and Lin Yutang. They went to the German Consulate in Shanghai and protested against Nazi atrocities. See *Israel's Messenger*, 2 June 1933, p.7.
3. Song Qingling, 'Denounce Atrocities against Jewish People in Germany', *Struggle for A New China* (Beijing: People's Publishing House, 1952), pp.49–50.
4. 'Chungking National Government Programme for the Placement of the Jews in China', *Republican Archives*, No.3, 1993, pp.17–21.
5. For details of the proposal, please refer to Xu Xin, 'Sun Fo's Plan to Establish a Jewish Settlement in China during World War II Revealed', *Points East*, 16, 1 (March 2001), pp.1, 7–8.
6. *Liberation Daily*, 16 Oct. 1941.
7. There were from time to time a few articles appearing in various Chinese magazines and newspapers reporting or commenting the persecutions during the Second World War.
8. It is estimated that more than 30 million Chinese died during the War.
9. The book about hunting Eichmann and other Nazis by Simon Wiesenthal was finally translated into Chinese and published in 1991 by Beiyue Art and Letters Press.
10. China had faced a military threat from the Soviet Union since 1968.
11 First published by Beijing by Sanlian Shudian in 1974. There exist many editions by various publishers in China.
12. First published by the People's Literature Publishing House in 1975. There exist many editions by different translators.
13. At the same time, quite a few novels such as *The Holocaust* were translated into Chinese and movies such as *Life is Beautiful* were shown in China.
14. Zhu Weilie and Jin Yingzhong (eds), *Chinese Judaic Studies in 1990s* (Shanghai: Sanlian Shudian, 1992).
15. More than sixty books had been published in Chinese by 1994. For details refer to Xu Xin and Eyal Propper (eds), *Catalog of the Chinese Books about Israel and Jewish Culture* (Nanjing: Centre for Jewish Studies, Nanjing University, 1994).
16. Xu Xin and Lin Jiyao (eds), *Encyclopedia Judaica* (Shanghai: People's Publishing House, 1993).
17. Walter Laqueur, *A History of Zionism* (Shanghai: Sanlian Shudian, 1992).
18. Robert M. Seltzer, *Jewish People, Jewish Thought: The Jewish Experience in History* (Shanghai: Sanlian Shudian, 1994).
19. Yang Mansu, *Israel: A Mysterious Country* (Beijing: World Knowledge Publishing House, 1992).
20. Yang Mansu, *Catastrophe for Jews: Records of the Holocaust* (Beijing: China Social Sciences Publishing House, 1995).

21. Zhu Jianjing, *The Death of Six Million Jews in Europe* (Shanghai: People's Publishing House, 1995).
22. Yang, *Catastrophe for Jews*, p.3.
23. Xu Xin, *Anti-Semitism: How and Why* (Shanghai: Sanlian Shudian, 1996).
24. Pan Guang, 'Nazi Holocaust and Its Impact on Jewish People and Jewish Civilization', *World History*, 2 (2000), pp.12–22.
25. The thesis is entitled 'The Choice of Existence in the Post-Holocaust Era as Seen through Three Early Novels of Elie Wiesel'.
26. Gong Jin, 'Learning Jewish Culture at Nanjing University', *China/Judaic Connection*, 9, 2 (Summer 2000), p.6.

27 Touch the Nerve: A Personal Journey

CHRISTIAN WEBER

When, after an atheistic upbringing in East Berlin, I started searching for God, the Protestant church appeared to me as the most open-minded. I met there the first ecological groups, gays and lesbians, even punks. At that time I also met my first Nazis.

Following my conversion to the evangelical church, my studies took me to South America. In El Salvador, a country where gunmen assassinated young nuns, where Archbishop Romero was shot during a Mass held in San Salvador, I understood why Christians could join the armed forces, and I abandoned my commitment to unconditional pacifism. I approve of the use of arms whenever there is a duty to act in a situation that equals the liberation of Auschwitz – or the prevention of a new Auschwitz.

Back in Germany, I continued my studies. With outrage I realized how strong the neo-Nazi scene had become. At the time, the outlawing of extreme right parties was not yet on the agenda. I was horrified to watch young Nazis on TV, being applauded for setting fire to a home for immigrants in Rostock-Lichtenhagen, and the police arriving long after the event.

In Potsdam, I was the spokesman for Amnesty International, and I helped victims of extreme-right violence. My studies were over then, and I was eager to begin work at last at a real place. My first rectorate was situated in Greifenhein, a town deep in the country of Brandenburg to which my predecessor, a divorced parson, had been transferred for disciplinary reasons. I felt like I had come to the end of the world when I looked out from my window at that landscape ruined by surface mining.

Young right-wing extremists started coming to the events I organized, to the films or discussions. They came flaunting their symbols, their shaven heads, and all their paraphernalia. The young churchgoers were usually leftists, so of course they took exception. I became aware that I could not merely tolerate the Nazis; I was sceptical about a social work approach to the problem and was not willing to believe that it could be addressed by way of empathy, without confrontation.

I asked myself how it was that the young extremists had adopted such opinions. Why was everybody just looking on without doing anything? Knowing from my own experience how healthy confrontation with reality can be, I decided to try a new approach.

The test was our next meeting. I confronted the young Nazis with all those distinctive signs they were showing off, trying to deconstruct their identity. At the time, most Nazis were skinheads, and this was where I started:

> You know, I don't have anything against your haircuts, I have been to Tibet, there local monks have shaven heads, too. But they had lots of love for strangers like me. You are just filled with hatred. Hatred against people who are my friends, Jews, Arabs, blacks, homosexuals, punks, leftists; hatred against an open democratic society. Nor do I have any particular problem with your clothes. The boots are from England, the jacket is from America. And on top of it all, your trousers – you wear jeans, invented by a Jew, Levis. Your outfit is really kind of open-minded. But I don't like what you actually do with your boots, the way you use them to hurt people. Why are you like that?

They answered: 'We don't know any blacks or Jews. And we don't talk to punks, we just fight whenever we meet them. They are asocial elements.'

I pointed out to them that they had so much in common with punks, alcohol, violent concerts, street fights. Wouldn't they like to speak at least once with a punk, or a black man?

I invited leftist youth to work together with me on that, but they considered it a waste of time. I said: 'The Nazis are a minority, but a very violent one. We have to become active.'

I could understand that those committed leftist young people were not enthusiastic about that, but some of them were ready to try. A team of two young Nazis and two young anti-fascists prepared our first event. The first subject we agreed on was 'The German Wehrmacht'. There was even agreement when some young leftists acknowledged courage on the part of their soldier grandfathers, and the young Nazis glorified them. At the time, I had been to see the exhibition on the myth of the – ostensibly 'clean' – Wehrmacht, which was impressive. Those young Nazis would not want to hear about German soldiers being implicated in massacres. For later events, I invited academics whom, of course, did not adopt my own style of confrontation. They could not deal with situations where Nazis just denied certain facts, they just would not talk with them any longer. And the Nazis themselves were unable to cope with it, and left the room.

The sixtieth anniversary of the Kristallnacht pogrom fell on 9 November 1998, but at this time the German media were busy celebrating the fall of the Berlin Wall nine years before. I could not shake off the feeling that something was out of balance. The beginning of the Holocaust was an important date to remember. I realized that an event such as the destruction of the synagogues in Germany had not yet been processed in its symbolism by the collective memory. In destroying the temples of a religion that was meant to free mankind, the foundations of its own civilization were destroyed. That religion had been revolutionary from the beginning, with the message that man must not be reduced to slavery, that man equals God. It is written in the Torah. Christianity is not conscious enough of Judaism's contribution to social liberty. We tend to forget about the Old Testament's command, 'Love your neighbour as yourself.'

On 9 November 1938, a dull crowd became active, not realizing the consequences; their symbolic actions would turn into their destiny, driving them to destroy the very foundations of humanity. I think that, in that dark chapter of German history, the burning of books and Kristallnacht were two aspects of the same phenomenon, they were attempts by a people to annihilate its own cultural roots.

In the meantime I had decided to involve historic witnesses in my educational work, people from the surrounding areas. They recounted how Jews had been treated in the villages. Unlike the urban academics, those local people were not rejected by the young Nazis. The Nazis did not immediately stop listening when confronted with unpleasant truths.

I discovered one major reason for their attitudes in those discussions. Their grandparents had told them stories utterly different from the ones I had been told, exemplified in the following account by a Wehrmacht soldier's grandson. His grandfather used to say, 'It makes me sick to see all that vermin on the streets. Had we known that Germany would become like that, we would have battled harder – and won!'

The responsibility of the grandparents' generation being so evident, I had to involve them in my work as well. But first I invited victims, Jews. The right-wing extremists were not allowed to attend. At *Bayrischer Rundfunk* (Broadcasting Corporation of Bavaria), I had met Max Mannheimer, a concentration camp survivor who had presided over the Dachau Camp Committee. I wanted witnesses to tell the story of their exclusion – how did it start, how had they experienced it? Most of the victims had been surprised by the course of events.

I never invited a representative of neo-Nazi parties to my discussion forums on the upcoming elections. I wanted to show how politicians of the established parties refer to the subject of right-wing extremism. At the time, the extreme right DVU party had a lot of support in Brandenburg. I think that school curricula should include the subject of neo-Nazism, as violent minorities have grown out of the mainstream of society over and over again.

Over time, the press had become aware of my activities. A journalist from *Spiegel Online* approached me, suggesting a meeting with Israeli journalists who wanted to meet the young people I was working with. I had not sought any such confrontation before, but I agreed now as the initiative had come from the Israelis themselves.

From then on, I wanted to focus on educational work. Every year I invited the Israeli journalists so that they could see what was changing. I have continuous contact with certain youth. The young Holocaust denier has left the Nazi scene; but he has troubles with his daughter who is fascinated by Nazi ideology. I often invite his family to join my events.

I have documented that work with the help of a photographer friend of mine. Together we composed a very successful exhibition with portraits of young people from the region. But the problem is still far from being solved.

I have initiated projects in Israel, realizing only then what consequences there were for antisemitism because of the Middle East conflict. I encountered this problem again later, in Berlin, where the local Arab youth culture was marked by antisemitism. I was convinced back then that there should be a mutual exchange between the young Arabs and Jewish culture. There were moments revealing something about the specific customs of those faiths. Once I had invited a Jewish cantor, and when he realized that it was time to pray, he excused himself, but without leaving the room, just stepping aside like for a phone call, putting on his Talith, praying, all in such an utterly normal and concentrated manner. The Arab boys were fascinated!

As parson for the Berlin district of Stadtmitte (City Centre), my work today consists essentially of coordinating and organizing travels, meetings, conferences and developing future perspectives for social work with young people. Even if there was a particular conflict, I would be there to mediate.

I had a special interest in activities commemorating Kristallnacht on 9 November. For the first time ever on that date, I set up a meeting in a Protestant community with a Jewish cantor.

An important focus in my work is to maintain contact with Eastern Europe. Right-wing extremism in Poland operates via football clubs. A common graffiti shows a Star of David hanging on the gallows, and the initials of the rival club; 'Jew' is a common term of abuse. The city of Lódz has a particular problem with its past. One third of its population had been Jewish; today there is barely anyone Jewish left. I took part in a public event against antisemitic graffiti: we did not secretly erase them, but enlisted the support of prominent actors and intellectuals. The aim was to make it clear that we did not want any of that here.

Three or four times a year I travel to Poland, where Jewish tradition is in danger. For example, in the last of Poznan's Jewish communities, only Leopold Sokolowski can read from the Torah anymore.

We have to come to terms with German-Polish history in its relations to Judaism. We must remember that the biggest Jewish cemeteries are situated in Poland. One of the projects brings together Israelis, Germans and Poles, so that they can work jointly on the subject of the Holocaust. An exemplary project under the auspices of Yad Vashem brought together young people from Israel, Poland and Germany.

Right-wing extremism in Russia has more to do with nationalism and racism. One of the centres is in Saint Petersburg, of all places – a city that had earned a reputation for its tolerance, for the co-existence of cultures; a city where many Jews used to live, which contained Russia's biggest mosque. I went to Saint Petersburg to support friends in their local fight against right-wing extremism. 'Memorial' is the name of their group, and they have learnt to live with daily threats, one of their activists already having been killed by right-wing assassins.

I have always searched for people doing similar work to me. I have also found such people among priests of the Russian Orthodox church, which does not have a real tradition of working with young

people. It was the priests who had taken the initiative. A major conference brought together all the lone fighters engaged in social work
for youth. I met a priest who cooperated with the Jewish community. I try to gather allies wherever I can. Daily efforts need of course a
local context, but networks confer strength and courage.

My day-to-day work has taught me that it takes major efforts to
change hardened structures. One can dedicate one's work to individuals, but that is often more of a psychotherapy, since not everyone
can be reached in this way. And if we cannot reach every young person individually, we need more educational work and debate in the
public sphere.

And as often as possible – as long as it is still possible – we should
invite historic witnesses to come and meet with young people.

Young right-wing extremists must be taken out of the isolation
that they have chosen. Society must re-integrate them, and I am confident that it will.

Why? Because change is always possible. That is a theological and
sociological fact. God created all men equal in his own image. Every
single man carries a potential inside of himself that has to be
revealed. This is where we have to become active.

But if we do not touch the nerve, if we do not denounce or provoke, the social body is in great danger. It won't help to dissimulate,
hoping that wounds will heal all alone. History has proven that it just
never happens that way.

28 When It's Not Enough to Know: The European Experience

GERT WEISSKIRCHEN

As the generation of survivors steadily dwindles, it becomes ever more important to educate the young about the Holocaust. Recent surveys show that a growing number of young people consider National Socialism and the Nazis' persecution of the Jews to be things of the past, while there is an increasing tendency to think that the Holocaust has little significance for their present time or has even become irrelevant. According to one recent survey conducted by TNS Sofres Paris in seven countries,[1] less and less is known about the Holocaust. Experts therefore stress the importance of programmes linking together the past, the present and the future.[2] In the OSCE region, there are various approaches to teaching the history of the Holocaust. In some countries, it is a compulsory part of the school curriculum; in others, it is not a systematic concern. Countries where the Holocaust is already being taught need to update their approaches, and countries that are completely avoiding the subject today should establish appropriate curricula.[3]

However, when rethinking current approaches to Holocaust education, in terms of both the subject matter and methodology, we must be aware of the limited effects of educational strategies. Education is no universal remedy against contemporary forms of antisemitism, as noted in an excellent report by the Office for Democratic Institutions and Human Rights (ODIHR) on the current state of Holocaust education and programmes to combat antisemitism in the OSCE region.[4] There would be a sharper awareness of historical and contemporary forms of antisemitism if a clear distinction were made between antisemitism and the various forms of racism. The programmes in question must address the paradox that individuals belonging to marginalized groups and who for that reason are discriminated against may at the same time be antisemites. This is a fact that blurs the line between victim and perpetrator. History students should be confronted with difficult decisions in everyday situations, so that they can find parallels in their own experience.[5]

We should never lose sight of the specificity of antisemitism, whose history includes 2,000 years of persecution, culminating in the Shoah. Education seeks primarily to draw universal lessons from cases of discrimination, genocide and other crimes against humanity. Holocaust education aims particularly to present the historical material in such a way as to guard against its decontextualization. One may refer here to the recent use in Germany of the expression *Bombenholocaust* (Holocaust by bombs), coined by the extreme right-wing National Democratic Party to describe the bombing of Dresden by Allied Forces during the Second World War.[6] Such expressions must be considered even more dangerous than blunt Holocaust denial – disturbing though that is[7] – as they seek to deceive memory and to destabilize our common adherence to those fundamental values on which our post-war societies have been built.

For several years we have been faced with the risk that contemporary manifestations of antisemitism may fall outside our established frames of reference thereby skewing our ethical judgements. Academics speak of so-called 'secondary antisemitism', which consists of placing all responsibility for antisemitism on its victims. It is thus widely held that the Jews have exploited the Holocaust for their own ends, that Israel treats the Palestinians just as the Nazis treated the Jews, and that the Jews themselves are to blame for the existing antisemitism.[8] Moreover, conspiracy theories, as well as simplistic views on the state of the world, are often congruent with antisemitically structured thinking.[9] Research on such patterns is complicated by its potential to bolster – rather than combat – antisemitic stereotypes.[10] The fact of making it clear that there is no conspiracy to subject the world to some 'Jewish' design can encourage antisemites to disguise the evil intent that underlies their prejudices. What is diabolical about antisemitism is that it reduces the ever more ungraspable complexity of social reality to a question of 'the Jews' and blames them for all the conflicts that have arisen in the process of modernization, making them 'scapegoats'. Elucidations of antisemitism can thus serve the wrong ends. The risk of that happening should not, however, lead us to conclude that such explanations should not be attempted. On the contrary, if prejudice is not exposed, it may gain a permanent foothold.

The European Monitoring Centre on Racism and Xenophobia (EUMC), in collaboration with ODIHR, has developed a comprehensive definition of antisemitism that more effectively addresses these stereotypes and clichés.[11] I use this as a basis for my work as Personal Representative of the Chairman-in-Office of the OSCE on Combating Antisemitism.

The training of educators and student leaders is an integral aspect of both the revision of school curricula on the Holocaust, and the design of new educational tools for combating antisemitism. Since teachers inevitably mirror society and thus bring phenomena such as secondary antisemitism into the classroom, this is a problem that must be tackled openly. There is no such thing as an easy solution, and yet we must find a solution. We need to take a more open approach to education. It is not restricted to schools, but also extends into the public sphere, including the media. And we must consider the antisemitic propaganda contained in extremist literature in Arabic and Turkish, which has been gradually finding its way into mosques and private schools in the OSCE region.[12]

Teachers find it increasingly difficult to teach the Holocaust to pupils belonging to immigrant families, that is, pupils whose frame of historical reference is not based on where they are currently living, as has been recognized by the Education on Antisemitism Task Force.[13] While this is no reason to omit Holocaust education as such, it requires a particular sensitivity to the different cultural backgrounds of pupils.

Another important aspect in teaching the Holocaust is to avoid presenting Jewish history as a history of victimization. School books and curricula in most countries urgently need revision; they need to include information about the place of Jews in the national history, as well as in the great Jewish centres, including the United States and Israel. The guidelines of the Leo Baeck Institute in Frankfurt might offer a model for such revisions.[14]

I recommend that the following points be taken into account in any educational work on antisemitism:

1. Holocaust education is of crucial importance for understanding today's world. It should entail visits to concentration camp memorial sites, support for educational activities at those sites, and comparative work on contemporary genocides.

2. Teachers should have opportunities to discuss the problems they encounter in teaching the Holocaust or antisemitism.

Conferences on best practices for educators are needed at both national and international level.

3. Successful educational programmes call for dialogue, especially between groups directly affected by intolerance and discrimination.

4. The education authorities should work with NGOs to produce appropriate elementary and high school teaching materials, which should be made available to teachers.

5. The Organization for Security and Cooperation in Europe (OSCE) and its member states should develop curricula to ensure a deeper understanding of the history, traditions and culture of the Jewish people, as well as their contributions to society in the broader sense.

6. There is a need for educational materials that tell the story of the State of Israel and set its creation in the context of European history. An intensified academic exchange between OSCE member states and Israel could serve that purpose.

7. Calls for the boycotting of Israel, related intimidation and anti-semitism on university campuses endanger academic freedom and must be condemned. Dialogue is central to education, which must accordingly promote intercultural mediation.

8. Antisemitism in the Islamic world is partly due to the non-integration of Muslims with other groups. Dedicated programmes are needed that would underline the respective achievements of Muslim, Christian-European and Jewish civilization, and contribute to mutual acceptance and understanding.

9. OSCE member states should be encouraged to review school books and other materials to ensure their neutrality in respect of subjects like the Holocaust, the history of the Jewish people and descriptions of the modern State of Israel. Ways should be found of promoting similar efforts in OSCE associate member countries.

10. All OSCE member states should be invited to participate in an ODIHR police training programme on hate crimes.

11. The OSCE should call on the parliaments of its member states to set up committees to review laws and education on the subject of hate crimes.

To sum up, emphasis should be placed on the following points:

1. Improved training for teachers, modernized teaching materials.

2. Curricula that include significant education against antisemitism.
3. More consideration for the multicultural backgrounds of pupils and their families.
4. Holocaust education should not allow issues related to the current situation in the Middle East to confuse the debate.
5. As teachers are also susceptible to prejudice, their continuing education has its own particular importance.
6. Uncertainty may arise in discussion of the Holocaust and comparisons with other genocides.

WHAT CAN BE DONE?

The quality of educators is crucial. Some of them may hesitate to teach the Holocaust in their class; they have often had to study the subject by themselves, and feelings of shame and anxiety are not so rare. They need to have opportunities for exchanges with teachers who are experienced in the field of Holocaust education, especially such teachers from Israel. Moreover, the related curriculum content needs to be reviewed. Successful material should be disseminated, particularly through conferences of teachers.

But over and above the efforts made in schools, society as a whole should offer possibilities for discussion. There should be places where people can be encouraged to learn about related topics and such places should be interconnected. The annual commemoration of the liberation of Auschwitz could be accompanied by thematic activities designed to highlight the complexity of the Holocaust. Every young person should visit once in his school career the Berlin Memorial to the Murdered Jews of Europe. Young Europeans and Israelis should get to know each other through international meetings. Concentration camps and other historic sites of extermination and sites of resistance against Nazi rule are all places for commemoration and learning; they should where necessary be restored and made accessible.

There are numerous examples of *good practices* that should be promoted throughout the OSCE region. Since 2001, a programme on Holocaust education in the Russian Federation has been supported by the Swedish Embassy and the Holocaust Educational Trust. Teaching material has been translated into Russian and visits have been organized for young people to commemorate the victims of the Holocaust. Similar initiatives exist in countries such as Britain, France, Germany and Poland. A broad comparative study should analyse their potential to fight antisemitism and suggest improvements for their future. Efforts should be made to identify how local experiences in fighting antisemitism could be used at national level, in order to strengthen weak educational strategies. Knowledge-oriented strategies alone do not suffice. While historical knowledge is necessary for the development of political awareness, individual consciousness is decisive for the fight against antisemitism. We must help to foster a positive emotional climate in respect to the Jewish people. Individual and cultural exchange is the key that will open the door to a common future.

NOTES

1. 'Thinking about the Holocaust 60 Years later. A Multinational Public-Opinion Survey' (TNS Sofres Paris, 2005).
2. Education on anti-Semitism Task Force, 'Results of the European Workshop: Education on anti-Semitism' (Berlin, 18–20 April 2004), p.10.
3. Ibid., p.7.
4. ODIHR: Education on the Holocaust and on anti-Semitism: An Overview and Analysis of Educational Approaches (June 2005) http://www.osce.org/odihr/documents.html.
5. Education on anti-Semitism Task Force, 'Results of the European Workshop: Education on anti-Semitism', p.8.
6. Jörg Schurig/dpa, 'Bombenholocaust von Dresden', *Der Stern*, 21 Jan. 2005.
7. Deborah Lipstadt, *Denying the Holocaust: The Growing Assault on Truth and Memory* (London: The Free Press/Macmillan, 1993).
8. Aribert Heyder, Julia Iser and Peter Schmidt, 'Israelkritik oder Antisemitismus? Meinungsbildung zwischen Öffentlichkeit, Medien und Tabus', in Wilhelm Heitmeyer *et al.*, *Deutsche Zustände 3* (Frankfurt am Main: Suhrkamp, 2004), pp.144–65; Henryk M. Broder: 'Ein moderner Antisemit: Möllemanns Aussagen verraten ihn selbst', In Tobias Kaufmann and Manja Orlowski (eds), '*Ich würde mich auch wehren...*' *Antisemitismus und Israel-Kritik – Bestandsaufnahme nach Möllemann* (Potsdam: Weber, 2004), pp.27–9; Yves Pallade, 'Medialer Sekundärantisemitismus und das Versagen gesellschaftlicher Eliten', in Klaus Faber (ed.), *Altneuer Antisemitismus* (Potsdam: Verlag für Berlin-Brandenburg, forthcoming).
9. Tobias Jaecker: *Antisemitische Verschwörungstheorien nach dem 11. September* (Münster: Lit, 2004).
10. Susanna Harms, 'Mit Shoa Education gegen aktuellen Antisemitismus?', Interview with Gottfried Kößler, in *Vor Antisemitismus ist man nur noch auf dem Monde sicher. Antisemitismus und Antiamerikanismus in Deutschland* (Leipzig: Klett, 2004), p.104; Education on anti-Semitism Task Force, 'Results of the European Workshop: Education on anti-Semitism', p.5.
11. EUMC: Working definition of 'antisemitism'.
12. Claudia Dantschke, 'Islamistischer Antisemitismus', in *Vor Antisemitismus ist man nur noch auf dem Monde sicher*.
13. Education on anti-Semitism Task Force, 'Results of the European Workshop: Education on anti-Semitism', p.9.
14. Ibid., p.6.

29 Reflections on Simon Wiesenthal and the Concept of Genocide[1]

STEVEN JACOBS

The ongoing debate, not only among survivors of the Holocaust/Shoah but also among members of the academic/scholarly community as to whether the Holocaust/Shoah is 'unique', 'unprecedented', *sui generis* or subsumed under the larger category of 'genocide', remains a contentious one. Many survivors themselves – as well as their offspring – fear that such academic debate within the emerging field of genocide studies will, somehow, lessen their own messages, devalue their own experiences, and make the event itself meaningful only in relativistic terms. Many, but not all. Readers of this essay, most likely, are familiar with Elie Wiesel, among others, addressing the genocidal tragedies of Bosnia, Rwanda and Darfur.

One such commanding voice, suggesting the linkage between that which ended in 1945 and that which remains civilization's enduring shame, was that of Simon Wiesenthal. In 1999, in his Foreword to Israel Charny's *Encyclopedia of Genocide,* he re-affirmed for his readers that which had been his concern for half a century:

> For many, many years it has been my opinion that in a humane, in a political, and in an educational sense, we Jews failed to stress the point that we were persecuted and suffered in concentration camps together with people from 18 other nations, during the Nazi reign.
>
> Right after the war, I dreamed about the formation of a brotherhood of victims that could also be a fighting body against any new – or old – forms of National Socialism.
>
> In the 1950s I appealed to all to not always talk about the six million Jews who had been murdered and ignore the others ... No one was prepared to listen.[2]

Despite being criticized among his fellow survivors, Wiesenthal maintained his position regarding this linkage and refused to allow his own journey to be the *only* story with which to confront the world. Indeed, his willingness to lend his name in 1977 to the Los Angeles centre which so proudly bears it was conditional – by his own admission – upon its willingness not only to address the horrendous suffering of the victims of the Holocaust/Shoah but the millions of non-Jewish victims who suffered and died as well. 'It simply does not suffice to stress just the uniqueness of our Holocaust and to think about the future, about those who have been and will remain our friends', he wrote in that same Foreword. And while, sadly, I cannot know whether or not he would agree and/or give his assent to my own critique of the present state of anti-genocidal work in the three areas of prevention, intervention and punishment, I remain reasonably confident that the present call, by the son of a fellow survivor, for an activism in support of all persecuted groups, is one of which he would have approved. I begin, then, with the following vignette.

A CHEESE SANDWICH?

Philip Gourevitch in his now justly-famous and important book, *We Wish to Inform You that Tomorrow We Will be Killed With Our Families: Stories from Rwanda*, tells of the following encounter:

> Listening to him, I was reminded of a conversation I had with an American military intelligence officer who was having a supper of Jack Daniel's and Coca-Cola at a Kigali bar.
> 'I hear you're interested in genocide,' the American said. 'Do you know what genocide is?'
> I asked him to tell me.
> 'A cheese sandwich,' he said. 'Write it down. Genocide is a cheese sandwich.'
> I asked him how he figured that.
> 'What does anyone care about a cheese sandwich?' he said. 'Genocide, genocide, genocide. Cheese sandwich, cheese sandwich, cheese sandwich. Who gives a shit. Crimes against humanity. Where's humanity? You? Me? Did you see a crime committed against you? Hey, just a million Rwandans. Did you ever hear about the Genocide Convention?'
> I said I had.

'That convention,' the American at the bar said, 'makes a nice wrapping for a cheese sandwich.'[3]

The triple issue of prevention, intervention and punishment of genocide continues to be addressed by conferences of the learned all over the world. For example, the International Association of Genocide Scholars met at its own bi-annual gathering in early June, 2005, in Boca Raton, Florida, to debate issues of global human import and tragedy – fully six months *after* the International Commission of Inquiry on Darfur presented its report to the United Nations Secretary-General (Geneva, 25 January 2005), and, as recounted by Warren Hoge of the *New York Times*, 'found a pattern of mass killings and forced displacement of civilians *that did not constitute genocide but that represented crimes of similar gravity* that should be sent to the International Criminal Court for prosecution'.[4] Try sharing that distinction with the victims! Indeed, genocide may be a cheese sandwich after all!

Why, then, after the too-long-denied Armenian Genocide by the Turks, after the Holocaust/Shoah of the Jews by the Nazis and their minions, after the genocide of the Tutsi by the Hutu, after the genocide of the Bosnians by the Serbs, Croats and Muslims, now, in the murderous day-to-day reality of the Sudanese, is it so incredibly difficult to get the seemingly 'good people' of this planet to universally proclaim 'This human tragedy is, *in truth and in fact*, an intolerable genocide, and we and our countries and our governments and our militaries will no longer allow this crime to continue to perpetrate itself upon our species?' The late Leo Kuper, one of the true doyens of the now-burgeoning field of 'genocide studies', wrote more than a decade ago:

> in the modern age it is harder to locate the intention to commit genocide at the societal level because of the anonymous and amorphous structural forces that dictate the character of our world. And there can be no doubt that *the present structure of international relations facilitates the crime of genocide* by the primacy accorded to national self-interest, the protection extended to offending governments, and superpower rivalry and destructive intervention in the internal affairs of divided and other vulnerable societies. But how then are we to modify and transform these anonymous and amorphous worldwide structural forces and to create a new world order in time to respond to the many genocidal emergencies?[5]

How, indeed, to turn our world into an anti-genocidal world with out fomenting armed conflict, worldwide and physically destructive revolutions, and the overturning or overthrowing of all non-democratic regimes presently in existence today remains the central question. I have here, decidedly, used the phrase 'all *non-democratic* regimes' because of the pioneering work and insights of R.J. Rummel, who has patiently and carefully shown through the scrupulous examination of massive amounts of data that genocide as a tangible expression of human behaviour has been and is practised far more by non-democratic regimes than by democratic ones.[6]

TASK NUMBER ONE: PREVENTION

Any discussion, no matter how creative or innovative regarding the prevention, intervention and punishment of genocide, must begin with prevention: how can we ensure that the tragedies of the past do not become the realities of the present or the foundations of the future?

Clearly, those who so thoroughly believe in, and are committed to, the preventive value of education begin here: educational planning globally must start today at all levels so that those in positions of social, economic, governmental and military control tomorrow have the memories of yesterday as part of their own knowledge database when they assume decision-making positions of power. This is, ideally – but, hopefully, not idealistically – the first revolution: re-thinking curricula at all levels from toddlers to graduate schools, from public to private institutions and everything in between, not only in history but in all of the interdisciplinary educational modalities upon which genocide education draws.

Thus, no longer Holocaust education alone, but Holocaust *and* genocide education. And not only within Jewish communities and state-mandated educational systems, but universally. Thus, for example, education about the Holocaust should not be an end, but a beginning, to efforts to confront genocide. Similarly, study of the Armenian genocide should not be limited to the Armenian community, but as with all other relevant genocides, should become a part of universal education. This does not mean the subsuming of Holocaust education into some amorphous, generalized genocide education; rather it means studying the Holocaust or any other genocide in its individual specificity, and then applying those lessons globally.

Secondly, wherever people are seriously committed to fighting genocide, there must also be a serious examination of the past, good and bad, across the board, not limited to talk about the European Holocaust of the Jews. Then again, such studies should not be confined to the direct perpetrators of genocidal acts, but extend to all the social and societal influences that played and play a role in genocide: governmental, social, political, religious, educational institutions and the like. How to focus the microscope on oneself, one's community (however defined), one's nation-state, in addition to the external focus on others, becomes the challenge for the best and brightest of our committed educators.

Part of this overall educational endeavour, additionally, must involve the further development of Genocide Early Warning Systems and their implantation within the very centres of government responsible for their implementation. Such systems are predicated on the commitment of humanity to humanity, and on a belief that the destruction of one group is the potential destruction of all groups. However, those who have already done the initial work of conceptualizing such systems – most especially Israel's Israel Charny, Britain's Kumar Rupesinghe, and the United States' Franklin Littell – have thus far been unsuccessful in translating their work into governmental realities, despite then President Clinton's call in 1999 for the establishment of a National Genocide Warning Center in the United States. Equally, we who seemingly care, not only in the United States but elsewhere, have not manifested the political will to demand – yes, demand! – of those in power the fullest implementation of these historic strategies. Equally, even those organizations fully committed to and concerned with human rights – Amnesty International, Human Rights Watch, Survival International, Red Cross International – have not so far included such systems among their highest priorities. Hence, the call for a second revolution: joining in increasing numbers these organizations and advocating, in the strongest possible manner, 'upping the ante' by calling for Genocide Early Warning Systems throughout the world.

TASK NUMBER TWO: INTERVENTION

It is 2007, and we are still globally under the sway of the historic signing in 1648 of the Treaty of Westphalia which affirmed the sovereignty and territorial integrity of what we continue to define as the *inviolable* nation-state. Genocidal intrusions into one's neighbouring state call forth united or singular military intervention; genocidal destruction within the borders of one's own nation-state remains, seemingly, beyond the scope of military intervention, governmental sanction, or humanitarian aid. To be sure, each external response is fraught with its own set of problems and difficulties which must be addressed.

Military intervention must make sense, over and above nation-state sovereignty, because the potentially violent spill-over effect is ever-present. But only united military action has its own potential to defuse escalating armed conflict and prevent it from descending into imperialist and territorial ambition. Saul Mendlovitz and John Fousek call for a UN 'Constabulary' to address intervention into genocide.[7] John Heidenrich calls for an 'international legion of volunteers' in place throughout the world that would react to any genocidal act.[8] The European Union is already positioning itself for the setting up of a military rapid reaction force, consisting of nine such troops of 1,500 soldiers to be deployed at short notice to conflicts around the world, with Britain, France, Italy and Spain already committed and the expectation that other EU nations will follow suit.[9] With regard to this latter option, it may very well prove to be a model for the African continent, the Middle East and other potential 'hot spots'. Anti-genocide military – and other – interventions mandate nation-states unity and trump individual nation-states' sovereignty. Slowly and painfully, nation-states and their leaderships are beginning to accept this, and the educated anti-genocide citizenries must be there to remind all of them of it.

Parenthetically, Vratislav Pechota makes a most astute observation about military involvements in genocide:

> The defence of superior orders poses an especially difficult question. It rests on the demands of discipline in the bureaucratic and military hierarchies of the states. A soldier's dilemma in the question of obedience (on the one hand, he may be liable to be shot by a court-martial if he disobeys an order and, on the other, to be hanged by a judge and jury if he obeys it) has not been satisfactorily resolved in the Genocide Convention. Until the principle that superior orders do not free an accused of responsibility for an international crime is transformed into national law and spelled out in terms that leave no doubt of the duty to refuse to obey an order to perform a criminal act, it may be impossible to enforce in practice the principle of strict criminal liability embraced by the Convention.[10]

Governmental interventions include such things as economic sanctions, monetary and payment freezes, and trade embargoes, as well as collective actions. In the face of genocidal behaviour by one sovereign state, sanctions by many states should quickly be reflected in economic and other downturns which will force any leadership desirous of staying in power and avoiding revolutionary displacement or political coup to desist immediately from genocidal activities.

TASK NUMBER THREE: PUNISHMENT

To be sure, the guilty must be made to pay, at the level of both those who give the orders and those who carry them out, those who devised the plans for genocide and those who implemented the plans and did the deeds. Full commitment to the over-arching sanctity of international law supersedes that of sovereign nation-state law, and marks a commitment to an international community which sets no one nation-state above that of another. *Realpolitik*, however, reveals that such has not been the case historically, nor is it now. The International Criminal Court, the International Criminal Tribunal for Rwanda, and the International Criminal Tribunal for the former Yugoslavia – especially the latter two, understood by many to be legacies of the International Military Tribunal held at Nuremberg at the close of the Second World War – all testify to this growing desire for a new international judicial system; one, however, that is perceived by some – and not only the powerful – as directly antithetical to America's best and future long-term interests. Indeed, writing specifically about the International Criminal Court, David Wippman discusses pointedly what he terms 'the effect of US nonparticipation'.[11] US reluctance to sign the ICC accords in Rome and the forty-year reluctance to ratify the Genocide Convention, even after President Truman's endorsement of it, testify to an uncomfortable and little-spoken truth: the United States is committed to anti-genocide activities when both the perpetrators and the victims (and, perhaps, even the bystanders) are not Americans, but the aphorism that 'might makes right' permits no reversal and hardens this nation's refusal to consider itself potentially guilty of any genocidal crimes in the past (for example, African-Americans or Indigenous Americans bringing their cases before the ICC) or its military or civilian constituencies potentially guilty of such crimes. It is also true that there is a risk of the politicization of international justice; witness Israel and the security fence. These are valid concerns, even if they come from the world of *realpolitik*. Ironically, too, the US Federal Government declares a week-long Holocaust Remembrance and Observance, which has presented no stumbling blocks whatsoever in its post-Second World War relationship with Germany, but finds a similar affirmation of the Armenian Genocide difficult because of its relationship with Turkey (which has officially denied responsibility for that event, in opposition to the opinions of the overwhelming number of scholars who have studied the issue) and its representatives' own pressure not to do so. '*They* deserve to be brought to the bar of international justice; *we* do not!' The willingness of all sovereign nation-states to surrender, if only partially, their sovereignty for the greater good of our common humanity remains the moot point. Unfortunately, the history of the United Nations and the history of the relations between its member states continues to reveal not the failed vision of Raphael Lemkin (1900–59) and others after the Second World War who fought so diligently to make the United Nations Convention on the Punishment and Prevention of the Crime of Genocide a living reality, but the failed implementation of those for whom tribal politics (read and understood as nation-state sovereignty over all other values) matters far more than living and dying human beings.

CONCLUSION: TODAY AND TOMORROW

After the International Commission of Inquiry on Darfur released its Report (25 January 2005), Doug Saunders wrote an Op-Ed piece which appeared in the Toronto *Globe and Mail* entitled 'The "Genocide Test" – A Mass Killer's Best Friend', and concluded:

> Under the UN charter, genocide is the only permissible legal excuse, aside from the invasion of another country, for using military force to intervene in another country's affairs ... Genocide is based on racist logic: Dividing the single, homogenous species of homo sapiens into arbitrary groups, and eliminating one of them. The problem is that any law designed to stop such acts must itself subscribe to this logic. Mass murder is far easier to define, and does not force us into ugly moral corners. Perhaps it, and not this almost arbitrary concept, should be the crime of crimes.[12]

'Genocide', 'mass murder', 'ethnic cleansing': regardless of the correct or incorrect terminologies applied, we are not talking about theoretical discussions of intellectual concepts or constructs. We are talking about the brutal behaviours inflicted upon one group of usually powerless victims by those with the power to implement their designs and achieve their goals – the obliteration, extermination and annihilation of others. Creative solutions abound to prevent genocide from becoming a current or future reality, to intervene militarily, governmentally and humanitarianly, and to punish the guilty at all levels of guilt. What is lacking is the global will to shout 'Enough is enough! The genocide of one is the genocide of all!'

US President and military hero Dwight David Eisenhower (1890–1969) is said to have remarked, 'One day, the people will demand of their leaders peace, and we had best step aside and let them have it.' Likewise, until the people demand an end to genocide, present and future genocides will remain always possible. Simon Wiesenthal must still be wondering about our reluctance to join together after the Holocaust to prevent any recurrence of such crimes against humanity.

NOTES

1. Originally presented, but here substantially reworked, at the 35th Annual Scholars Conference on the Holocaust and the Churches, St Joseph's University, Philadelphia, PA, 5–8 March 2005, under the title 'Genocide: Prevention, Intervention, Punishment – An Unholy Trinity?'
2. Simon Wiesenthal, 'Foreword: Why Is It Important to Learn about the Holocaust and the Genocides of All Peoples?' in Israel W. Charny (ed.), *Encyclopedia of Genocide* (Santa Barbara: ABC-CLIO, 1999), p.lix.
3. Philip Gourevitch, *We Wish to Inform You that Tomorrow We Will be Killed With Our Families: Stories from Rwanda* (New York: Picador, 1999), pp.170–1.
4. Warren Hoge, 'U.N. Finds Crimes, Not Genocide in Darfur', 1 Feb. 2005, www.nytimes.com; emphasis added.
5. Leo Kuper, 'Reflections on the Prevention of Genocide,' in Helen Fein (ed.), *Genocide Watch* (New Haven, CT: Yale University Press, 1992), p.138; emphasis added.
6. R.J. Rummel (retired, University of Hawaii), *Death by Government* (New Brunswick, NJ: Transaction Books, 1997); *Statistics of Democide: Genocide and Mass Murder Since 1900* (Berlin: Lit Verlag, 1999); *Power Kills: Democracy as a Method of Nonviolence* (New Brunswick, NJ: Transaction Publishers, 2003).
7. Saul Mendlovitz and John Fousek, 'A UN Constabulary to Enforce Law on Genocide and Crimes Against Humanity', in Neal Riemer (ed.), *Protection Against Genocide: Mission Impossible* (Westport, CT: Greenwood Publishers, 2000), pp.105–22.
8. John Heidenrich, *How to Prevent Genocide: A Guide for Policy Makers, Scholars, and the Concerned Citizen* (Westport, CT: Praeger, 2001)), pp.233–50.
9. BBC News, 'EU approves rapid reaction force', 23 Nov. 2004, http://newsvote.bbc.co.uk.
10. Vratislav Pechota, 'Establishing Criminal Responsibility and Jurisdiction for Genocide', in Helen Fein (ed.), *Genocide Watch* (New Haven, CT: Yale University Press, 1992), pp.199–200.
11. David Wippman, 'Can an International Criminal Court Prevent and Punish Genocide?' in Neal Riemer (ed.), *Protection Against Genocide: Mission Impossible?* (Westport, CT: Praeger, 2000), pp.100–1.
12. Doug Sanders, 'The "Genocide Test" – A Mass Killer's Best Friend', 5 Feb. 2005, www.globeandmail.com.

30 The Historiography of Antisemitism in the Shadow of the Holocaust

DINA PORAT

In the minds of many of the public, Simon Wiesenthal was perhaps the most significant figure in the last half-century in the struggle against antisemitism. Not only was he identified with bringing Nazi war criminals to justice, or with identifying and denouncing current antisemitism, but he also published a book, *Every Day a Remembrance Day*, which was a calendar of antisemitism throughout the ages. In that book Wiesenthal clearly drew upon the efforts of researchers and scholars, many in the field of Jewish studies, who have essentially created and institutionalized the scholarly study of antisemitism. Yet the question arises: is the study of antisemitism an integral part of Jewish studies? Or, more importantly, should the subject of antisemitism be a fundamental part of Jewish studies, and if so, what impact and what import does that study have?

Indeed, a number of scholars and researchers have addressed, each in his own way, and all very cautiously, the idea that research on antisemitism and efforts to define it and to understand its driving forces, especially in the aftermath of the Holocaust, contradict not only Zionist aspirations, but even more so Jewish traditions and values, and particularly Jewish studies and the academic status of such studies. Leon Poliakov, Uriel Tal, Ismar Schorsch, Gershom Scholem, Abba Kovner, Efraim E. Urbach and others have expressed their opinions on this issue, either in agreement or in dispute with one another and with other scholars and thinkers. They have done so in written historiography and in their presentations of the results of research to the public at large, as well as by way of establishing museums and delivering public lectures. Let us try and present their views and their differences, and then ask: do they have a message for researchers and historians of antisemitism?

In the foreword to the second volume of his monumental *History of Antisemitism*, published in English in 1974, Leon Poliakov defines the historian and researcher of antisemitism as 'a denouncer', and outlines a number of arguments to sustain this blunt definition: first, this historian is constantly calling into question the values of the non-Jewish surrounding society, pinpointing flaws and criticizing behaviours. If one bears in mind that persecution of Jews and of other minorities has always been pursued in the name of the most revered values, such as religion, the unity of a nation, uniqueness of culture and reverence for the past, then Western Christian societies must indeed be repeatedly arraigned before history's court of justice, in order 'to require an accounting from Christianity', in François Mauriac's words, quoted by Poliakov.[1] True, says Poliakov, but denouncing is a non-academic act, although he himself devoted decades of his life to the history of antisemitism. The professional precautions that he, the historian, takes, and the equal treatment he endeavours to give to all the parties involved cannot change the fact that he is a denouncer and a prosecutor, even when he is fully right. Pursuing his own logic, Poliakov cannot avoid asking whether Jews and the nature of Judaism have made their own contribution to the promotion of antisemitic attitudes and acts, and if so, how, where and when? As he questions events, the historian might also become an accuser, or at least a sharp critic, of his own people. Then again, he may become what Poliakov calls an 'apologist', who constantly tries to prove the righteousness of the Jews, and to portray them as the carriers of moral values.[2] And apologetics is a non-academic activity just as much as denunciation is.

Poliakov's second argument concerns the relations between the historian and his subject matter – the antisemite. These relations are, needless to say, indirect ones. The very concern about the motives of antisemites, he writes, is in fact a continuing return to the role of the righteous victim, which serves, for its part, to heighten the temptation of the antisemite to act out the role of victimizer, thus creating a perpetual vicious circle. Moreover, such concern is an obstacle in the way of the achievement by Jews of a normal national life (because they are constantly preoccupied with the idea of their own uniqueness), and prevents them from appreciating the progress made by other nations in achieving democracy and pluralism (because Jews keep looking for the anti-democratic forces in society that are most often identified with, or even the same as, the antisemitic ones).[3]

Is it possible, Poliakov wonders, that the very fact of recalling past events over and over again by the historian reanimates animosities and hostilities that were, even temporarily, dormant? Can the very pinpointing of the continuance of antisemitic expressions be an encouragement to this very continuity? And if indeed that is so, could it be assumed that the writings of a historian in favour of the Jews might lead to the same results as the writings that attack them? By pointing at the core of antisemitism and at its continuity, says Poliakov, the historian promotes it and contributes to its ongoing existence, because at the same time he transfers the ideas of former antisemites to future ones. And so he does all the more by the very attention and prominence given to present antisemites and extremists.[4] Let us try and explain the seeming contradiction between Poliakov's first argument, that antisemitism originates in the faults of society and the misuse of its values, and his second argument concerning the possibly negative role played by the historian: reading Poliakov's research one may suggest that he was basically of the opinion that the core of antisemitic phenomena continues to exist, and that external changes in its expressions continue to occur, in any case – with and without the historian and his conclusions. And that the role played by historians, if indeed antisemites are inspired by their work, is, even if negative, a minor one.

Poliakov's third argument is one of self-criticism: is any researcher capable of coping with a phenomenon 2000 years old, recorded in almost every human group, of arriving at universal definitions and of writing a serious comprehensive history of it? Let us elaborate on Poliakov's question, and assume that antisemitism does not stem from the deeds and the character of the Jew, but is rather a reflection of the maladies of many societies, and of the status they allocate to human rights; and let us bear in mind Jean-Paul Sartre's famous ending of his *Reflexions sur La Question Juive*: 'It is necessary to show *everyone* that the fate of the Jew could be his own fate'[5] – the inevitable conclusion is, then, that the researcher of antisemitism should indeed be an expert knowledgeable in the history and culture of *every* society. If his knowledge is limited to one country or region, or even to some of them and their languages and cultures, then his scope of analysis and conclusion, and his ability to theorize, is necessarily limited as well.

*　　*　　*

In a lecture entitled 'Jewish History as a demon', delivered at Tel Aviv University in 1999, Moshe Idel, the historian of Jewish mysticism, presented an innovative interpretation of Gershom Scholem's 'Reflections on Hochmat Israel' (the Wissenschaft des Judentums and its scholars). In this well-known attack, first published in 1945 after the Second World War, Scholem, the founder of studies in Jewish mysticism, emphatically called for a different Jewish historiography for the post-war era: one free of self-idealizing, sentimental and lachrymose elements, truthfully depicting all aspects of everyday life and all kinds of Jews including even the criminals among them, and not only the spiritual-theological-martyrological aspects. On the issue of concern to us here, he called for a sober and unprejudiced view of the complicated and problematic Jewish–Gentile relations, avoiding tears on the one hand and arrogance on the other. His attack was directed against any historiography dictated by ideology, whether enlightened assimilation, orthodox religious belief or modern Zionism.[6] Moshe Idel claimed that proper attention had not yet been given to this demand that historians, writing in the aftermath of the Holocaust, should look evil in the eye, and face the real demon that is the actual force operating in Jewish history.

As mentioned, Scholem wrote his 'Reflections on Hochmat Israel' in 1945 in Israel, after the Holocaust in which he had lost one of his brothers in Buchenwald and many other relatives elsewhere. In 1946 Scholem travelled to Europe to look for the remnants of Jewish libraries and archives. For half a year he dug out whatever he could find and sent it to Jerusalem. According to the testimony of his now-deceased widow Fania, he returned home broken, in a state of utter despair as to the chances of the Jewish people to recover: he met the survivors in the Displaced Persons camps, heard their recounting of the suffering they had undergone, and was convinced that the best members of the nation were lost and those left were but powerless ashes. This is a harsh judgment. Had he stayed longer, as other emissaries of the Yishuv did, he would no doubt have changed his mind as they did, when they later witnessed the unbelievable recovery of the survivors. Fania described in detail his trip and return, his mourning that put him out of action for about a year, and how, closeted at home on his bed, he mingled private and national sorrow into one pessimistic view.[7]

After having recovered, so goes Idel's interpretation, Scholem was looking for a historiography adequate to the recent events, one that would look for their roots in occurrences in former centuries. He thought that until then the real demonic forces were left out of the picture created by Jewish historians, because they could not face the conclusions: first, they could not admit that evil is the force that controls the world because admitting the rule of evil means that the Jewish people is in a hopeless situation, one of continuing failure, since there is no remedy for demons; secondly, historians, trained to look for the reasons behind the events, were indeed trying after the Holocaust to trace even irrational forces, but these forces seemed inexplicable in 1945, as they are perhaps even to this very day. Naturally, following the Holocaust, the importance of antisemitism as a subject for research increased. Yet, so Scholem claimed, according to Idel, Jewish historians who knew full well that their history had been dictated throughout the ages by demons, or in other words, evil irrational forces, did not dare write it clearly.[8] Such writing, one may add, could have implied that the immense tragedy has, God forbid, some chance of being repeated.

What kind of demon did Scholem have in mind in Idel's interpretation? Does the demon necessarily rule Gentiles only, and turn them against Jews? Is there a possibility for a demon to motivate Jews, or are they immune? Scholem, true to his own demand not to practise self-idealization, wrote indeed not only about external destructive forces on that occasion. He spoke as well about 'the irrational sting and the demonic passion' that are, in his opinion, the inner essence of Jewish history. He even called Jewish history itself 'this horrifying giant ... loaded with explosive energy'.[9] However, when time passed and Scholem recovered and returned to his desk to study Jewish mysticism, he did not go back to advocating that the Jewish historians should put the evil demons at the core of their work. Rabbi Meir Berlin (later Bar-Ilan, after whom the Bar Ilan University is named), who was among the few who frequented his home during Scholem's year of mourning, tried to encourage him by predicting that the Jewish people would overcome, as it always has, and rebuild itself – and perhaps succeeded in convincing Scholem.[10]

* * *

This issue, of how to write about Jewish history and how to present to the public the suffering caused by antisemitism, became a controversy when Beit Hatefutzot, the Diaspora museum, was being built in Tel Aviv University. It was meant to be a comprehensive exhibition, in fact *the* exhibition, of the history and culture of the Jewish people. The museum, whose doors were opened in 1978, proved immediately to be a huge success. It is still today considered an essential part of any visit to Israel. But severe criticism was not slow in coming. It was alleged, first, that it is too Zionist: it begins with the destruction of the Second Temple, and ends with the return to the Land of Israel, as if this were the only logical inevitable end of the story of the Diaspora; and secondly, that it is too religious and does not allow enough space for the secular modern brands of Judaism, especially not for non-Zionists, among them communists, Bundists, assimilationists and others. One of the most severely criticized and debated issues was the proper balance between Jewish culture, traditions and creativity and antisemitism, its effects and results.

Both Ismar Schorsch, Chancellor of the Jewish Theological Seminary in New York, and Uriel Tal, the Tel Aviv University scholar, severely criticized the amount of antisemitism in the exhibition. The section called 'Among the Nations', which shows the 2000 years of Jewish history in the Diaspora, as well as the martyrological column that cuts through the three floors of the house, seemed to them a grave mistake.[11] The column is made of barbed wire and metal surrounding a pale light of fire, symbolizing external oppression closing around internal life and hope, but at the same time radiating a sombre dark atmosphere. It was criticized by Christian visitors as well. They were insulted by the wording on the adjacent wall that stated Hitler's rise to power on a date (January 1933, of course), counted 'according to the Christian Era'. The wording was thus said to indicate that Christianity was responsible for the centuries-long antisemitism that had made Hitler's 'Final Solution' possible, and that Hitler had in fact continued and materialized Christian notions.[12] Tal and Schorsch saw the problem from an internal Jewish perspective. It was their opinion that the in-house museum historians, who gave the museum its framework and were assisted in their work by the nearby Tel Aviv University Department of Jewish History scholars and researchers, had produced an impressive achievement; and yet the result was an excessively strong emphasis on antisemitism down through the centuries.

'To my mind', said Tal in 1993, when the museum celebrated five years of activity, 'it is impossible that a column of fire will accompany us with such vigour, that one can hardly enlist the strength to oppose it, without a column of life and of affirmation, or a column of water, that would perhaps be able to extinguish the fire one day. It seems to me, that the best of Jewish tradition ... teaches us not to cry too much for the dead, and not to exercise Kiddush Hashem [martyrs' death] when it is not an absolute necessity. Culture develops not only in the shadow of destruction, but also in the light.'[13] This was not the first time Tal expressed this opinion. He later repeatedly tried to convince colleagues and students that the study of antisemitism is an obstacle to the normalization of the nation, claiming that the full weight of antisemitism in Jewish history is destructive for one's self-esteem, and that the study of antisemitism and the Holocaust is bound to be at the expense of research on Judaism and its contribution to the world.

Nevertheless, Tal's opinion fitted in well with the basic Zionist assumptions upon which the museum was built, and complemented them, namely that (a) antisemitism is a result of the Diaspora situation, therefore (b) there is no point in struggling against it and no possibility of countering it, and (c) there remains only one solution, which is to get away from it by living in a Jewish state. Still, (d) it is an insult to Zionism to consider antisemitism, a negative external pressure, to be its main motivation, because Zionism is thus divested of its positive internal contents and motivations; (e) all the above notwithstanding, it is Zionism's duty to struggle against antisemitism as part of its obligation to defend Jews or at least support their attempts to defend themselves, elsewhere, and to strive together with them for normality and national achievements.[14]

Schorsch was indeed more direct: he felt that despite the thematic division of the exhibition into many sections presenting family and communal life, religion and Jewish culture and creativity in all their splendour, from the ocean of rabbinical literature to Nobel prize-winners; and despite the fact that only one section ('Among the Nations') is devoted to history, the basic tone is still one of persecution; and that the martyrological column is indeed the only memorial to the Holocaust in the house, but too conspicuous a one.

He especially did not like the 'Scrolls of Fire'. This text, presented to the public in May 1978, on the thirtieth Independence Day of the state, as part of the inauguration of Beit Hatefutzot, is composed of fifty-two chapters: a chapter for each week of the Jewish year, each describing suffering, expulsion, pogroms and killings, from ancient times through the Middle Ages until the 1940s. And though the last chapters are dedicated to national redemption and to the establishment of the State of Israel, Schorsch regarded the Scrolls as a failure. He saw them as an attempt to create a modern version of the Scroll of Lamentations, Megilat Eicha, which laments the destruction of the Second Temple, and to call it after Megilat Ha-esh, 'The Scroll of Fire', written by Chaim-Nachman Bialik, the national poet laureate, lamenting that same national disaster. Yet the ancient scrolls lead, he emphasized, in the opposite direction: the Scroll of Fasting lists the days when fasting is forbidden, because of victories achieved during the times of the Second Temple, and Judaic tradition combines several mourning days in one so as to have fewer of them. On the 9th of Av the destruction of the two temples is jointly lamented (and three other national catastrophes as well). The late Prime Minister Menachem Begin suggested in 1982 that Holocaust Memorial Day should be moved to the 9th of Av as well, so that the six destructions would be lamented together, in the spirit of Judaism. His idea was opposed in the Knesset wall to wall on the grounds of the uniqueness of the Holocaust. He won only the support of the more extreme Orthodox, who anyhow commemorate the Holocaust on another traditional mourning day, the 10th of Tevet, day of the general Kaddish (Mourner's prayer), because they reject the notion of the Holocaust's uniqueness.

One may say that what the author of the Scrolls, the poet and partisan Abba Kovner, suggested is that the circular dimension of time, one that repeats itself in the cycle of every year and brings past events into the present, is more important then the linear dimension of time, one that leads from the past to the future. Schorsch objected: 'The idea, to dedicate each Shabbath to another persecution, is far too much. One cannot deal every day and every week only with the negative side of the Jewish experience … a cultural entity cannot live only on expulsion and forced conversion', he protested. 'I reject Abba Kovner's way.'[15]

Abba Kovner was a founder and commander of the underground in the ghetto of Vilna, and of Jewish partisans units in the forests of Lithuania, a leader of survivors leaving Europe, a well-known poet and public figure. He was not a historian, yet as a moral authority of exceptional stature he exercised deep influence on other historians of the Holocaust, such as his friends Yehuda Bauer and Israel Gutman (the three of them were members of the Hakibbutz Ha'artzi kibbutzim). He was the spiritual father of Beit Hatefutzot and the author of the 'Scrolls of Fire'. To illustrate his point, that Abba Kovner's way was all wrong, Schorsch reminded his listeners, the members of the museum's curatorion who convened in Tel Aviv in 1991, of the way Kovner used to describe his return to liberated Vilna from the forests. Sitting on the pavement next to his empty home, in a city empty of its many former Jews, he considered suicide, for there was nothing left of the Jerusalem of Lithuania. A Christian neighbour, who recognized him, was surprised to see a living Jew and tried to make him leave, telling him that he was hated and unwanted. Her openly expressed hate helped Kovner to realize that he must go on living, though in another place.[16] This is the wrong attitude to life and to Judaism, said Schorsch, because it is based on the negative, and not on the positive reasons to live and create.

In that respect he followed the footsteps of his admired teacher, Salo Baron, who devoted his lifelong work to fighting ideas like Kovner's, trying to reach the correct historical balance that would show the long peaceful and creative periods in the history of the Jewish people as well, and not only the 'lachrymose' side of that history. It is therefore surprising that Schorsch, in his own research on Jewish reactions to German antisemitism in Second Reich Germany, reached conclusions similar to Kovner. He started off by stating that 'To fight antisemitism ... inevitably required a public affirmation of Jewish identity', and ended by admitting the 'extent to which this transformation [from a fragmented Jewish community to a revitalized one] was due to antisemitism'.[17] This is the case of the Beit Hatefutzot as well – an identity-building museum, standing in the first Hebrew city, on the campus of an Israeli university, showing Jewish–Gentile relations as a necessarily negative outcome of the exile, that would be cured only by the existence of a Jewish state.

Still, the debate goes beyond Zionism–Diaspora relations, for both Tal and Schorsch point at a contradiction between the study of anti-semitism and the display of its results to the public, and Jewish tradition and studies. This tradition, which tries to minimize days of mourning, as the Scroll of Fasting teaches, is rather an affirmation of life, a guide for overcoming both personal and national mourning. This is exactly what Rabbi Berlin told Scholem, that Judaism believes, as the Torah says, '*Vechai bahem*' ('And he shall live by them ...') and as the Talmud adds, '*Velo shey amut bahem*' ('He shall not die because of them ...'): that life and light, and not demons who lurk in the dark, are at its core.

Kovner defended his work: 'I have a friend, a historian and an important thinker', he said, referring to Tal, 'who reacted again to what I say, [again, because it was an ongoing public debate] presuming that nothing has been built so far out of the negative. This is not true. This is not true!' Zionism was born out of the negation of the Diaspora, he said, and suffering was always turned into power: 'I did not [write the Scrolls of Fire] out of the love of suffering or out of hatred of the persecutors ... I wanted to expose the sources of power that generations of Jews demonstrated in their dire distress, to find and refind the meaning of life in the Jewish experience', and to understand how in every generation stubborn Jews turned mourning into a means to live, and Davka (which means 'especially', but with the added connotation of 'in spite of') to live.[18]

Having heard Efraim Elimelech Urbach's attack on the isolated nation ideal, one of 'a nation that dwells alone', Kovner still continued to defend his thesis. 'We have been brought here', that is, back to the Land of Israel, said Urbach, one of the pillars of Jewish studies in the Hebrew University, 'We have been brought here not by fate, but rather by destiny.' Kovner did not accept this assumption. 'We only wish this to be true', he wrote to himself: 'the truth is that few of us came here because of destiny. The avant-garde did, but most of the others, the vast majority, were brought by fate', that is to say, because of antisemites. Bialik's observation on, and reproach to, the people who 'will not wake up until awakened by the whip' and would not get up until forced to by disaster, as Bialik wrote following the terrible 1904 pogrom in Kishinev, is far deeper than Urbach's idealistic viewpoint, wrote Kovner.[19]

Here in fact, much as Scholem did, Kovner calls upon the scholars to admit that antisemitism was the decisive factor behind individual and national turning points, which perhaps would not have occurred in better times, and asks them not to embellish reality. This is what he wrote to himself. But when Kovner was awarded an Honoris Causa by Tel Aviv University, he ended his key-note speech with the following: 'when I walk in the morning in the fields of Ein-Hahoresh [his kibbutz], or stand here [on the Beit-Hatefutzot hill] and look over to the location in which Tel Aviv began, my eyes see that which is in front of me [the future] – and my mind remembers that which is behind me [the past], I feel a strengthening faith, that we are here not because of the slings of fate, but because of destiny', echoing Urbach's words.[20] In other words, what he wrote to himself about the real weight of antisemitism was not fit to be said in public, certainly not on a festive well-attended occasion.

Kovner went one more step in developing his 'strength out of suffering' theory: if the past is but a tool to gain strength from, then the historian does not have to invest the time and effort needed in order to reconstruct the past 'as it really was' – *wie es eigentlich gewesen*, as the German historian Leopold von Ranke, father of modern historiography, put it. Kovner, who had undergone the ghetto and the partisans' forests, had looked Scholem's demons in the eye many a time and reached an opposite decision: times of atrocities cannot be understood by those who did not witness them, no matter how hard the historian tries. Therefore Kovner advocated that historiography be written not as an obligation to look for an objective truth, if there is one at all, but as an expression of a human and Jewish wish for a subjective past that future generations would be able to live with and be proud of.[21]

On another occasion, in a speech he delivered in a gathering in Israeli President Yizhak Navon's residence he defined even more clearly the mission of the Jewish historian: 'I am interested in the past not for past's sake, but as material for the building of future Jewish life and collective consciousness'.[22] He enlarged the concept of a Jewish historian – each Jew is an actor on the stage of Jewish history, and a writer and a researcher, with a national mission: 'To keep silent and let horror fade away with the yesterday, to let legend come out of the fog, and to let illusion turn into consolation'.[23] This is as opposed as possible to Scholem's (or Ranke's) demand for a cruelly accurate historiography, devoid of emotions and ideologies. When in 1984 Kovner was commissioned by George Klein, the New York philanthropist, to submit a plan for a Holocaust Memorial Museum in New York, he tried to visualize his ideas by creating a life-size model of a Jewish *shtetl* in Eastern Europe with all its institutes and inhabitants. At the end of the tour the visitor would see their images fade away, without saying a word about the Holocaust, thus emphasizing the treasures of Jewish life, not the manner of their destruction.[24]

The argument went on, and Tal strengthened his case, though this time indirectly, when, in a series of essays he wrote on Albert Einstein, he pointed out that Einstein had readily admitted, as early as the 1920s, that antisemitism was a major factor in his acknowledgement first of his Jewish identity and then of his support of the Zionist movement.[25] Einstein suffered some virulent antisemitic attacks after having returned to Germany during the First World War, and was called a traitor and a defeatist for being a Zionist and a pacifist. Among the leaders of the attacks were two German physicists, Johanes Stark and Phillip Lenard, who later tried to develop an 'Aryan' physics instead of Einstein's 'Jewish' one. Nevertheless, says Tal, Einstein saw the political reality between the two world wars as a global struggle between optimism and pessimism: political antisemitism is an expression of the pessimist perception of human nature, while Judaism and Zionism must be built on optimistic ground, on a belief in the ability of individuals and nations to live together. In a series of letters to major figures Einstein analysed the causes of antisemitism, and charged Jewish, and especially Zionist, intellectuals, with a task: to pay adequate attention to the internal damage caused by antisemitism to the self-image of the Jew and to see it as their mission to repair that damage. 'The best among my fellow Jews lost their confidence', he laments, because antisemitism in the modern age of emancipation and many ideologies is more effective in tearing the Jewish identity to pieces than it was when Jews still had a crystallized identity.[26]

Einstein had his own view on the origins of antisemitism: the antisemite is frightened by the contradiction between the weakness of a small dispersed minority, and the intellectual vitality and achievements of the Jewish individual, who is always critical and spiritually independent, never readily convinced by dogmas. Here Einstein pinpointed the essence of antisemitism, which is the discrepancy between image and reality: the antisemite, convinced that the Jew is omnipotent, does not know, said Einstein, that this modern independent Jew is constantly hurt by the attacks of the antisemite, and that he is dependent on the Gentiles surrounding him for reassurance. 'Before we could fight antisemitism efficiently,' says Einstein, 'we must first and foremost educate ourselves, change our slave mentality, acquire more dignity and more independence.'[27] By referring to Einstein's letters and suggestions, Tal could re-emphasize that efforts should be invested in what he considered the right direction, as advocated by so important a figure: looking inwards, building identity and strengthening confidence, thereby avoiding undue attention to antisemites and their destructive role.

* * *

What do these great minds tell researchers on antisemitism? Do they regard this research as scientific, and themselves as scientists? It is quite clear that they are ambivalent about their own feelings in this regard, that they have their doubts and even anxieties as to the results of the study of antisemitism, and that their most profound reservations concern the weight that antisemitism should be allowed to have in Jewish public life. Hence it is clear that they assigned great importance to the role the historian and the intellectual play in public life, and to their ability to shape national awareness. So, did they in fact recommend that historiography be written for the sake of the past or for the sake of the future, for research or for one's national self-image? Naturally, the number of scholars who have dealt with this issue is limited, because it means taking a critical look at one's own and one's colleagues' work and its implications.

Let us briefly consider them once again. Poliakov, who dedicated his whole professional life to this study, had grave doubts as to whether he contributed to, or worsened, the situation of his fellow Jews. His own personal situation exemplified part of the problem: A Jewish historian who had left Russia in 1920, he lived in Paris which had become his second home but where he nevertheless always felt a stranger, continually finding fault with his adopted country, thereby constantly ruining his chances of integrating.

Did Scholem in fact have in mind two different demons that, despite the differences between them, complement and affect each other: the external evil one that aims at the destruction of the Jewish people, and the internal one that fills Jewish history with mystic energies and sparkles? Whatever the answer, he did not repeat his demands in later years, and his 1961 lecture in London on the same topic was much milder.[28]

Tal and Schorsch were unequivocal in their call on scholars to invest their efforts in the treasures of Jewish culture. But both invested no less, and perhaps a lot more, in nineteenth and early twentieth-century German antisemitism, and their books on the roots of antisemitism in the Second Reich (Tal) and its impact on a Jewish identity that was forged under the pressure of hostility (Schorsch) are still a model. So are Tal's essays on the cultural roots and the political messianism of the Nazi movement, and Schorsch's on German antisemitism in post-Second World War historiography.[29] Perhaps both first wrote, and then contemplated the impact of their work.

Who but Albert Einstein could afford to say that the achievements of Jewish individuals frighten the antisemite? His achievements certainly commanded awe in friend and foe alike. Still, he fully understood the feeling of enslavement, of dependence, of the loss of self-dignity. He believed in the redemptive power of Zionism, but refused when offered presidency of the State in 1952 when Chaim Weizmann, the first to take office, passed away. The letters he exchanged with Weizmann show his doubts: would great numbers of assimilated Jews be readily affected by the works of Zionist intellectuals and scholars and thereby regain their self-respect, or would verbal and concrete expressions of antisemitism win out?[30]

Kovner knew full well that his ideas to introduce the Scrolls of Fire and the martyrological column in the Diaspora museum as a source of strength, or a fading *shtetl* in an American museum, are difficult to understand. And that the visitors are liable to take the exhibition at its face value, without delving into the meanings and implications it held for Kovner. He maintained that the past is too heavy on us, and either legend, silence or illusion are the best ways to deal with it. Still, it should be noted that Kovner himself never kept silent, and the past with all its demons and evil forces was ever present in his work, in many forms.

The Diaspora museum in-house historians who worked with Kovner, such as Elie Ben-Gal, and the faculty members of the Department of Jewish history, strongly disagree with Schorsch to this very day. They do not accept his charge that the exhibition to which they devoted their professional skills is steeped in the negative side of the Jewish experience, and are convinced that most visitors are given an opportunity to be proud of an extraordinarily rich heritage. Perhaps, so members of the curatorion said, most of whom did not agree with Schorsch either, perhaps his and Baron's way of thinking is a wishful one. Jewish history cannot be changed, and a martyro-logical column stands in almost every home in Israel and in the Diaspora, with light and hope in its midst.[31] Still, is it possible that the builders of the place meant to convey one message, and actually con-veyed another? That they could not break themselves loose from the dark sides of Jewish history, even if they wanted to or planned to?

And finally: is it possible that these eminent thinkers are telling us, for our own good, not to engage in research on antisemitism? It must have been clear to them, as it is to any scholar and researcher, that every issue and phenomenon under the sun is and should be a subject for study. It seems therefore that their warning is directed not at research on antisemitism as such, but rather at the possible lack of balance between engagement in Jewish studies, and the increased presentation of the results of the study of antisemitism to academic circles, and all the more so to the public in general.

Such a lack of balance has been more frequently addressed in the years following the period dealt with in our discussion, the 1980s and 1990s. The recent flourishing, first and foremost among American Jews but in other communities as well, of chairs, forums, departments, institutes and centres, all dedicated to the study of the Holocaust might have pointed to a growing national or at least com-munal problem, had it not been paralleled by the rise of the study of genocide, xenophobia, racism, discrimination and deprivation of individual or minorities' rights in most of the Western world, espe-cially in the1990s. The question of balance is therefore broader now than it was in the first decades following the Second World War, and not restricted to the Jewish public. Moreover, the proportions and balances cannot be changed by decisions taken in scholars' conferences or even by their writings: they are rather a result of long-range, national and international processes, not to be directed or determined by external scrutiny.

So are self-images. On the one hand, it seems that some orthodox Jews have used traditional sources to justify a very strong sense of superiority over Gentiles. Some Jews of other strong ideological convictions, whether Zionists, communists or Bundists, also had their share of high self-esteem and moral superiority, and many Jews, though secular, are deeply aware of the uniqueness of their ancient heritage. On the other, extreme ups and downs in the national mood could perhaps be at least partially explained as related to the infiltration of antisemitic dual notions, both admiration and fear of Jews, into the Jewish and Israeli system.

We have seen here the role of the study of antisemitism in the Jewish academic and national life, vis-à-vis the study of Judaism, and how a number of scholars have related to this issue, both professionally and emotionally. It is this emotional dimension, directly connected to the modern building of an individual and national self-image (and not to the objective and neutral research desired by historians and scholars), which prevents us from reaching definitive answers.

NOTES

1. Leon Poliakov, introduction to *Histoire de L'Anti-Sémitism* (Paris: Calmann-Levy, 1961). Poliakov does not state the source of Mauriac's phrase.
2. Leon Poliakov, introduction to *The History of Antisemitism* (London: Routledge and Kegan Paul, 1974), Vol.II, pp.vii–viii.
3. Ibid., p.ix.
4. Ibid., p.ix.
5. Jean-Paul Sartre, *Réflexions sur la Question Juive* (Paris: Paul Morihien, 1946), p.198.
6. Gerschom Scholem, 'Reflections on "Hochmat Israel"', *Lu'ach Ha'aretz* (Ha'aretz newspaper Almanach), 1944/5, pp.94–112 (Hebrew). Reprinted in Scholem, *D'Varim B'go* [*Explications and Implications: Writings on Jewish Heritage and Renaissance*] (Tel Aviv: Am Oved, 1976), vol. II, pp.385–403 (Hebrew).
7. See her description in Gerschom Scholem, *Shabbetai Zevi and the Shabbetaian Movement during his Lifetime* (Tel Aviv: Am Oved, 1987), pp.28–9 (Hebrew).
8. Scholem, 'Reflections on "Hochmat Israel"', p.111. I would like to thank Professor Moshe Idel for referring me to his articles 'The Role of the Symbol in Gershom Scholem's Thinking', *Jewish Studies*, 38 (1998), pp.43–72; and '"That wondrous, Occult Power": some Reflections on Modern Perceptions of Jewish History', *Studia Judaica*, 7 (1998), pp.57–70.
9. Scholem, 'Reflections on "Hochmat Israel"', p.105.
10. I would like to thank my friend and colleague Professor Avraham Shapira (Pachi) for referring me to Fania Scholem's recollections.
11. See Ismar Schorsch in the 1 July 1991 protocol of the Beit Hatefutzot curatorion; and 'Uriel Tal speaking in Beit Hatefutzot', Tel Aviv 1984, unpaginated (Hebrew).

12. Ella Bar-Illan, in a conversation with me on 17 August 1998. She was in charge of the youth education in the museum in its first years.
13. 'Uriel Tal speaking in Beit Hatefutzot'.
14. Especially to his colleagues and students in the Department of Jewish History in Tel Aviv university. Regarding Zionist assumptions, see Dennis Sharvit, 'The Zionist Ideology and Antisemitism', *Kivunim*, 5, 42 (Dec. 1993), pp.43–6.
15. See Ismar Schorsch in the 1 July 1991 protocol of the Beit Hatefutzot curatorion.
16. Kovner described this incident at the New York 1975 conference on the Holocaust. See Yaffa Eliach, 'The Poet and Partisan Abba Kovner in the International conference on the Holocaust – a Generation After', *Hado'ar*, 21 (11.4.1975).
17. His view was best expressed in his monumental *Social and Religious History of the Jews* (New York: Columbia University Press, 1937). Ismar Schorsch, *From Text to Context: The Turn to History in Modern Judaism* (Waltham, MA: Brandeis University, 1994), Chap.19, and *Jewish Reactions to German Antisemitism, 1870–1914* (New York: Columbia University Press, 1972), pp.1 and 204.
18. Kovner spoke on 27 December 1981 in the Hakibbutz Ha'artzi House. See his files in his private archive in Ein-Hachoresh. See also *Abba Kovner – Seventy years, 14.3.1918–14.3.1988* (Tel Aviv: Moreshet and Sifriat Poalim, 1988), a collection gathered by his friends, pp.46–7 (Hebrew).
19. A handwritten undated page, Kovner's files. He referred to Chaim-Nachman Bialik's poem 'Achen Hatzir Ha'am' (The People is indeed Dry as Hay), see *Bialik's Complete Poems* (Tel Aviv: Dvir, 1950), p.67. See Urbach in 'The Ways and Meanings of Zionism Today', lecture at the opening session of the 29th Zionist Congress, 1978 in: *Bitfutzot Hagola*, 85/6 (Summer 1978), pp.3–12 and especially p.11.
20. On the Tel Aviv 1980 Honoris Causa ceremony. Published in Abba Kovner, *On The Narrow Bridge* (Tel Aviv: Sifriat Poalim, 1981), p.10 (Hebrew).
21. His testimony to Shlomo Kless, 17 December 1982, the Hebrew University Testimonies Archive, 36 (170).
22. See the full text in the Givat Haviva archive, D.2.598.
23. *Abba Kovner – Seventy years, 14.3.1918–14.3.1988*, pp.49–50.
24. See detailed plans for such a museum in Kovner's files.
25. See Uriel Tal, 'Reason, Judaism and Zionism in Albert Einstein's Thought', in idem, *Myth and Reason in Contemporary Jewry* (Tel Aviv: Sifriat Poalim and Tel Aviv University, 1987), pp.32–4 (Hebrew), and Uriel Tal, 'Jewish and Universal Social Ethics in the Life and Thought of Albert Einstein', in G. Holton and Y. Elkana (eds.), *Albert Einstein, Historical and Cultural Perspectives* (Princeton, NJ: Princeton University Press, 1982).
26. Tal, 'Reason, Judaism and Zionism', pp.34–5.
27. Ibid., cited by Tal from Albert Einstein, *About Zionism: Speeches and Letters*, translated by Leon Simon (London: Soncino Press, 1930), p.23; see also Albert Einstein, *Ideas and Opinions* (New York: Wings Books, 1954).
28. 'Hochmat Israel – Once and Today', *Deot*, 4 (May 1961). English translation 'The Science of Judaism – Then and Now', in Gerschom Scholem, *The Messianic Idea in Judaism and Other Essays on Jewish Spirituality* (New York: Schocken, 1971), pp.304–13.
29. See *Bibliography*, compiled by Moshe-Segal Moldavi, for the Department of Jewish History, Tel Aviv University, 1985, following Tal's death. For Schorsch see Note 17.
30. Einstein, *About Zionism: Speeches and Letters*, pp.37–8; Hanoch Gotfreund, 'Einstein's Jewish Soul', *Kivunim Hadashim* (New Directions) 14, June 2006, pp.91–102, esp. 93–95 (in Hebrew).
31. See the 1 July 1991 protocol of the Beit Hatefutzot curatorion, especially the words of Ephraim Hazan and Pnina Talmon.

31 Antisemitism: Mutations of a Virus

CHIEF RABBI JONATHAN SACKS

> Not one alone rose against us to destroy us: in every generation they rise against us and seek our destruction. But the Holy One, blessed be He, saves us from their hands. (The Haggadah reading for Passover eve)

The first mention in the Torah of Jews as a people is a prelude to persecution. 'A new king, who did not know of Joseph, came to power over Egypt. He said to his people, "Look, the people of the children of Israel [*am bnei Yisrael*] have become too numerous for us. We must deal wisely with them ..."' Wisdom in this case means forced labour, followed by enslavement, then the planned murder of every male child. It is the first but not the last attempted genocide in the pages of the Bible. The festival of Purim records a second failed attempt, this time by Haman who persuades the Persian king to issue a decree 'to destroy, kill and annihilate all the Jews – young and old, women and little children – on a single day'.

Ironically, the first two references to Israel outside the Bible are obituaries for the Jewish people. The Meneptah stele from Egypt in the thirteenth century BCE states: 'Israel is laid waste, her seed is no more.' The Mesha stele, a basalt slab dating from the ninth century BCE, stands today in the Louvre in Paris. In its inscription, Mesha, king of Moab thanks his deity Chemosh for his victories in war. It includes the following lines: 'As for Omri, king of Israel, he humbled Moab for many years, for Chemosh was angry with his land. And his son followed him and he also said, "I will humble Moab". In my time he spoke thus, but I have triumphed over him and over his house, while *Israel has perished forever*.' At times it is hard to know which is the greater wonder of history: Jewish survival, or the attempts of others to ensure Israel did not survive.

The historian Robert Wistrich calls antisemitism 'the longest hatred', and in a way it is, though it has taken too many forms for it to be described as a single phenomenon with one name. The Greek and Latin writers of classical antiquity were often hostile to Jews, accusing them of clannishness, strange customs and superstitions. Horace condemns them for trying to make converts. Apion criticizes them for failing to worship the same gods as the Alexandrians. Seneca held that they rested on the seventh day because they were lazy. The worst of the pre-Christian polemicists was the Egyptian priest Manetho (third century BCE) who described the Hebrews as a race of lepers who had been thrown out of Egypt. Many of these calumnies survived to be taken up and adapted in later centuries. That has been the fate of anti-Jewish myths: they may be dormant but they never die. Yet it would be wrong to describe reactions to Jews in antiquity as universally hostile. There is evidence to suggest that Alexander the Great thought highly of them and rewarded them for their loyalty. Aristotle spoke well of them, as did his successor Theophrastus. Besides, the ancient world was not known for its love of foreigners, whoever they might be.

Something new enters the world with Christianity and with the early decision, following the Council of Jerusalem, that it would become, not a religion directed towards Jews but one that sought adherents among the gentiles. A series of fateful judgements was incorporated into Christianity's early texts and developed by the Church fathers: among them that Christianity was 'the new Israel', that God had rejected the 'old' Israel, and that Jews had been guilty of wilful blindness and worse in rejecting the Christian messiah. The proposal of Marcion – that Christianity should be separated completely from Judaism, with the New Testament as its only scripture – failed. From then on, Christianity was locked into an adversarial relationship with Judaism, glaringly apparent in the New Testament and the work of Christian thinkers from the second to the fourth centuries, among them Justin Martyr, Origen, Melito, Tertullian, Eusebius, Gregory of Nyssa and St John Chrysostom. This *Adversus Judaeos* tradition, often savage in its rhetoric, left a deep mark on the development of Christianity, a fact that became immensely consequential when – with the conversion of the Roman emperor Constantine in 313 – Christianity became a world power, which it was to remain for almost 1,500 years.

Hostility deepened into massacre with the First Crusade (1096), during which, on their way to Holy Land, Christians massacred Jewish communities in northern France and Germany. It was at this time that the line, 'Pour out Thy wrath against the nations that do not know Thee...' first began to appear in the Haggadah, the one note of Jewish protest against the Christian slaughter of Jews in the name of God. From then on, the religious anti-Judaism of the Church began to take on a more irrational, demonic character. During the Middle Ages, Jews were accused of ritual murder, poisoning wells, desecrating the host, causing the Black Death and colluding with the Devil. There were periodic forced conversions, public disputations, book burnings, show trials, burnings at the stake, mob attacks and massacres. In the years following the Black Death alone (1347–50), some two hundred Jewish communities were destroyed. Jews were expelled from Brittany in 1239–40, Anjou and Maine in 1289, England in 1290, France at various periods from 1182 to 1394, and from regions of Germany throughout the fifteenth century. In Spain, where they had experienced a rare Golden Age, an onslaught took place in 1391, during which synagogues and homes were burned, businesses looted and many Jews murdered. From then on, Spanish Jews faced increasing hostility until their expulsion in 1492. Nor did the tragedy end there. Still to come were Luther's tirade against Jews ('their synagogues should be set on fire ... their homes should likewise be broken down and destroyed ... they should be deprived of their prayerbooks and Talmuds'), the invention of the ghetto (Rome 1555, by edict of Pope Paul IV) and the Chmielnicki pogroms (1648–58) during which as many as 100,000 Jews died. The experience of Jews in Christian Europe is one of the tragedies of humanity.

Nor was their experience under Islam an especially happy one. Again, there seems to have been an expectation on the part of the first Muslims that Jews would willingly embrace the new faith which, like Christianity, claimed to include and supersede earlier revelations. When this did not happen, reprisals were harsh. Islam began with a massacre of Jews in Medina and, like Christianity, incorporated sharply anti-Jewish sentiments into its sacred texts. There were times, especially in its early period of expansion, when tolerance prevailed, though within limits. Jews were given *dhimmi* status as second-class citizens, which meant that they had to pay special taxes and wear distinctive clothing (the yellow star Jews were forced to wear in Nazi Europe had its origins in medieval Baghdad). They were banned from government service and from building new houses of worship, and were subject to periodic public humiliations. At times, extreme

Islamic sects made life intolerable. In 1066 the Jewish community of Granada was attacked and three thousand were killed. In 1090 the community was assaulted again by an Islamic sect known as the Almoravids, and during the next century it suffered an onslaught from a new group, the Almohads.

There is no doubt, however, that as a whole Jews fared better during the Middle Ages under Muslim than under Christian rule. What, however, was remarkable was the way in which Christian myths which had no salience in Islamic terms were later adopted by Islam to fuel new and essentially alien forms of anti-Jewish hostility. Of these, the most striking is the Blood Libel. First propounded in Norwich in 1144 and then copied throughout Europe, this accused Jews of killing Christian children to drink or use their blood for ritual purposes. Officially rejected by the Vatican, the myth persisted well into the twentieth century. From the perspective of Judaism, the myth is absurd: the consumption of blood is categorically forbidden. Within Christianity it makes sense: that is what the wine of communion represents. Rooted in Christian theology, the Blood Libel none the less spread to Islam, where it appeared in Aleppo (1811, 1853), Beirut (1824), Antioch (1826), Hamma (1829), Tripoli (1834), Dayr al-Qamar (1847), Damanhur (1877) and Damascus (most famously in 1840, but also in 1848 and 1890). In 1983 the Syrian Defence Minister Mustafa Tlas wrote a book, *The Matzo of Zion*, to prove that the libel was true ('The Jew can kill you and take your blood in order to make his Zionist bread'), and in 1991 the Syrian delegate to the United Nations Human Rights Commission urged its members to read the book, the better to understand the nature of 'Zionist racism'.

These are devastating chapters in the history of the human spirit. It was no wonder, therefore, that Jews vested immense – in some cases almost messianic – hopes in the Enlightenment, which promised the defeat of prejudice in the name of reason, and a new dawn of tolerance. It did not happen. Early on, there were ominous signs. In the 1750s, Voltaire, the great advocate of liberty, described Jews as 'an ignorant and barbarous people, who have long united the most sordid avarice with the most detestable superstitition', though he was gracious enough to add, 'Still, we ought not to burn them'. In 1789, as the French National Assembly proclaimed its Declaration of the Rights of Man, anti-Jewish riots broke out in Alsace.

The great philosophers of modernity did not distinguish themselves by their generosity of imagination. Immanuel Kant spoke of

Jews as 'the vampires of society' and called for the 'euthanasia' of Judaism. Fichte argued against giving civil rights to Jews. Hegel took Judaism as his model of a slave morality. Schopenhauer spoke of Jews as 'no better than cattle'. Nietzsche blamed Judaism for the 'falsification' of values. The great logician Gottlob Frege wrote in 1924 that he regarded it as a 'misfortune that there are so many Jews in Germany'. Martin Heidegger, the greatest German philosopher of the twentieth century, was an enthusiastic member of the Nazi Party who never subsequently apologized for his admiration of Hitler or his betrayal of Jewish colleagues. I have seen no adequate account – though this may be my ignorance of the literature – of how it was that philosophy, which carried with it the highest hopes of an age of reason, utterly failed to confront antisemitism. Even Jean-Paul Sartre's *Réflexions sur la Question Juive*, written after the war in 1946, is a deeply flawed work, attributing no independent dignity to Jewish existence (his argument was that Jews do not create anti-semitism; antisemitism creates Jews).

Reviewing this history, it is clear that antisemitism is not a unitary phenomenon, a coherent belief or ideology. Jews have been hated because they were rich and because they were poor; because they were capitalists and because they were communists; because they believed in tradition and because they were rootless cosmopolitans; because they kept to themselves and because they penetrated every-where. Antisemitism is not a belief but a virus. The human body has an immensely sophisticated immune system which develops defences against viruses. It is penetrated, however, because viruses mutate. Antisemitism mutates.

In pre-Christian times it took the relatively simple form of hostil-ity to strangers, a *dis*like of the *un*like. In the early Christian centuries it became a religious phenomenon: anti-Judaism. In the Middle Ages it was transmuted into a series of myths whose common theme was that Jews were the cause of all bad things. Following the Enlightenment, religious or mythical justifications were no longer acceptable to secular public discourse, and thus racial antisemitism was born (the word 'antisemitism' itself was only coined in 1879, by the German journalist Wilhelm Marr). The prestige given to preju-dice by sacred texts was replaced by the new guarantor of truth: sci-ence. A pseudo-science of race was created, designed to prove that Jews were an inferior species. Other quasi-scientific disciplines were enlisted: an anthropology that identified 'old' with 'primitive'; a Darwinian reading of history that saw 'natural selection' as the ruthless elimination of the weak by the strong; and a scientific approach to society (social engineering), including eugenics and other medical ideas, to construct the thought that society could be improved by the surgical removal of 'flawed' individuals and groups. If philosophy failed Jews, so did science: there were all too few protests at these insanities. Inevitably, racial antisemitism was a more deadly form than any of its predecessors, because whereas religious convictions can be renounced, races can only be exterminated.

It is difficult to know what to say in the face of such evil, for evil it is, regardless of the sanctity or high ideals or pseudo-scientific concepts in which it has been clothed. Heaven alone knows whether Jews have been better or worse than other people, but no people who have ever lived have deserved such hate, such persecution. Nor has it ended.

An autobiographical note: I grew up in Christian Britain and went to Christian schools (in those days, Jewish day schools were rare). I experienced nothing but kindness from my teachers and friends. Those days left an enduring impression on me. They taught me admiration for a faith that was not and will never be my own. They showed me that deep and abiding tolerance is possible and has surpassing beauty. They helped me form friendships in later life with Christian leaders and others from other faiths – Muslim, Hindu, Sikh, Buddhist, Jain, Zoroastrian and Bahai – which I cherish. As a child, when I came to the passage in the Haggadah which speaks of hatred through the ages – 'Not one alone rose against us to destroy us' – I felt intuitively that those words referred to an age that had passed. That may have been the experience of my parents' generation but it was not mine. As I grew older, that conviction grew. The Holocaust, I believed, had taught humanity the words, 'Never again'.

I was wrong. Antisemitism in a new and virulent form – now focusing on collective Jewish existence in Israel while also attacking individual Jews and Jewish buildings in the Diaspora – has appeared again. With astonishing speed and ease, it has circumvented the immune systems built up by the West during the course of more than half a century of Holocaust education, interfaith dialogue and anti-racist legislation. How did it happen?

Viruses are effective when they persuade the body's immune system that they are part of the body itself. Viruses mutate so as to appear to host cells not as enemies but friends. So great was the impact of the Holocaust that it rendered certain evils taboo: racism, 'ethnic cleansing', crimes against humanity and attempted genocide.

The only way antisemitism could penetrate such defences was to turn them against Jews. Starting with the infamous 1975 United Nations resolution equating Zionism with racism, it reached a culmination in the United Nations Conference against Racism in Durban in September 2001, in which the State of Israel – the sole democracy in the Middle East – was uniquely accused of each of these evils in turn.

The attempt failed, but the language and narrative were established as acceptable forms of discourse in the public domain. A new myth, as powerful as any of its medieval precursors, was born in which the existence of a Jewish state, however small, became the cause of all international disorder, from the destruction of the World Trade Center less than a week after the Durban conference to the 'clash of civilizations' that threatened the twenty-first century's prospects of peace. Thus racial antisemitism mutated into mythological anti-Zionism with the further rider that all Jews are Zionists and thus legitimate targets of violence. Into this new mould, all the old fantasies of hate, from the Blood Libel to the late nineteenth-century forgery, the *Protocols of the Elders of Zion*, were poured and sprang again into life.

One date links medieval, modern and post-modern hostility: Pesach (the Passover) itself. Pesach was the favoured time for Blood Libels, for it was said and apparently believed, at least by the masses, that Jews needed blood to make *matzot*. It was the date chosen by the Nazis for the extermination of the Warsaw ghetto in 1943 (the Nazis deliberately chose Jewish holy days for their most brutal murders: this became known as the 'Goebbels calendar'). It was the day selected by anti-Israel terrorists in 2002 for the suicide bombing in Netanya in which 29 people were killed and hundreds injured as they prepared to celebrate the seder (the Passover supper and Haggadah reading). There is something about the biblical festival of freedom that outrages those who believe – sometimes in the name of God, sometimes in the name of ethically advanced civilization – that freedom must, by definition, exclude Jews.

Why does antisemitism exist? There has been an almost endless set of speculations. Some have seen it in psychological terms: displaced fear, externalization of inner conflict, projected guilt, the creation of a scapegoat. Others have given it a socio-political explanation: Jews were a group who could conveniently be blamed for economic resentments, social unrest, class conflict or destabilizing change. Yet others view it through the prism of culture and identity: Jews were the stereotyped outsiders against whom a group could define itself. There have been voices within the Jewish tradition that see hostility as inevitable: 'Esau hates Jacob', or 'From Sinai, hate [*sinah*] descended into the world'. Yet others, noting the concentration of antisemitism among the very faiths – Christianity and Islam – that trace their descent to Abrahamic monotheism, favour a Freudian explanation in terms of the myth of Oedipus: we seek to kill those who gave us birth. It would be strange indeed if so complex a phenomenon did not give rise to multiple explanations.

My own view, though it does not essentially conflict with any of these hypotheses, is that Jews were hated because they were different. To be sure, every people, race and faith is different. None, however, has insisted with such tenacity on the right to be different, the duty to be different. Alone among the peoples of the Alexandrian and Roman empires, Jews rose up in rebellion – never on political grounds, but simply in defence of their right to practise their faith. Almost alone in Christian Europe, they refused to convert (some did; the majority did not) despite the immense pressures that were placed upon them, sometimes at the cost of life itself. In post-Enlightenment Europe they remained distinctive. They acculturated, integrated, but did not disappear. In the contemporary Middle East, the State of Israel remains an island of Jewish life in an Islamic sea. Jews were different. That, we recall, was Haman's reason for advocating genocide: 'There is a certain people, dispersed and scattered among the peoples ... whose customs are different from those of all other people' (Esther 3:8). It is one thing to be different and an empire, a civilization, a world power; quite another to be different and a minority, whether in one's own land or in dispersion. Jewish existence raises, and always has, in its most acute form the problem of difference.

There is something unusual, even unique, about the faith of Judaism. It was the world's first monotheism. Abraham, Moses and the prophets were the first to believe in a single God, creator of heaven and earth, whose authority transcended all earthly powers. Integral to Jewish faith is the proposition that God made (with Noah after the Flood) a covenant with all mankind. It is this covenant, with its insistence on the rule of justice and the sanctity of life, which is the earliest intimation of what today are known as codes of universal human rights (the Torah itself speaks of commands and prohibitions rather than rights). Yet Judaism itself – the way of Torah – is not, and was never seen as, a universal code. Instead, through a series of covenants with the patriarchs, and later the Israelites at Mount Sinai, it was the code of a particular people – one people, not all. From this arises the well known but still remarkable fact that Judaism does not see itself as the only path to God. Malkitzedek, Jethro and the daughter of Pharaoh who rescued Moses are just three of the figures who, outside the covenant of Torah, none the less come to know and fear God. 'The saintly among the nations of the world', said the sages, 'have a share in the world to come.' The seeming paradox can be stated simply: *the God of Israel is the God of all humanity, but the religion of Israel is not, and is not intended to be, the religion of all humanity.* This is a phenomenon in need of explanation. To understand it is to reach a theological conclusion about antisemitism. It is also a vital clue in deciphering the place of Pesach in the worldview of Judaism.

The Torah is about one people, Israel, its faith, history and land. Yet it does not begin with one people. It opens instead with humanity as a whole: Adam and Eve, Cain and Abel, Noah and the Flood. Each represents a universal message. The story of Adam and Eve tells us that, in Rabbi Akiva's words, 'Beloved is mankind for it was created in the image [of God].' The story of Cain tells us of the universal danger of sibling rivalry, violence and murder. Noah, after the Flood, represents all humanity in covenant with God. These are the universals of the human condition. There then follows a narrative that marks the transition from the universal (Noah) to the particular (Abraham): the story of Babel. It begins with a dramatic statement: 'The entire world had one language with uniform words.' Babel – a reference to the great city states of Mesopotamia – is a symbol of empire, a single civilization imposed by force on a mass of individuals. Today, historians of the ancient world call this type of civilization 'cosmological', meaning that it projected its hierarchy on the heavens. It believed that its social structure mirrored the cosmos. The Torah tells us, without immediately explaining why, that there is something fundamentally wrong with this kind of order. God confuses the speech of Babel's builders and then, in the next chapter, calls on Abraham to make a lonely journey into an unknown future. From then on until the end of days there will be no universal language, culture or civilization. There will indeed be a universal moral code, the code of Noah, but no universal religion.

It is difficult to overestimate the originality and power of this idea. Having made mankind in His image and made a covenant with all humanity, God turns to one individual, one extended family, one people, and asks it to be different, *thereby teaching mankind the dignity of difference.* The word *kadosh*, 'holy', in the Torah means just that: different, distinctive, set apart. What is wrong with universal civilizations, the echoes of Babel through the ages, is that they sacrifice the individual to the collective. They make men serve the state instead of making the state serve mankind. They impose an artificial unity on a divinely created diversity. Our humanity exists not despite but precisely because of our individual uniqueness. As the Mishnah puts it in one of rabbinic Judaism's most profound teachings, 'When a human being makes many coins in the same mint, they all come out the same. God makes every person in the same image – His image – but they are all different.' Judaism is a particular covenant with the universal God, because it is only in and through our particularity that we are fully human, and it is only through the institutions of particularity – families, communities, languages and traditions, each with its own local character – that we protect and sustain our humanity.

If Babel is the Bible's first symbol of empire, Egypt is its second. The Egyptians – so the Torah tells us and so we know from independent sources – feared and despised strangers. At one time they had been conquered by them – the Hyksos. It is no wonder therefore that they had negative feelings about the *Ivrim*, 'Hebrews'. The Torah uses a strong word, *to'evah* ('abomination', 'taboo') to describe the Egyptian attitude to nomadic shepherd peoples.[1] The opening chapters of the book of Exodus tell an eminently realistic story about the slow slide from discrimination to persecution to enslavement. The Hebrews were different and thus a threat and therefore to be subject to progressive dehumanization, a pattern that Jews experienced more than once in their subsequent history. The Torah leaves us in no doubt whatsoever as to the lesson Israel was to learn from this formative experience, stating it no less than thirty-six times: you shall love the stranger, because you know how it feels to be a stranger. You shall protect and respect one who is different, for you, more than any other people on earth, know what it is to be different.

To be a Jew, therefore, from the days of Abraham and Sarah to today, is to carry the burden and dignity of difference. Jews never built an empire. They never sought to become a world power, imposing their culture on others. Though the prophets foresaw the day when all mankind would worship the One God, they never foresaw a time when the nations would adopt Israel's covenant, the Torah. The task of the people of the covenant – set out in God's first call to Abraham – is to be true to its own faith while contributing to the good of others: 'through you shall all the nations of earth be blessed'. Abraham fights and prays on behalf of the people of the cities of the plain, though their faith is not his. The biblical *ger toshav*, the non-Jew living within Israel's jurisdiction, has equal rights merely by adopting the universal (Noahide) code, not by embracing the covenant of Israel. Judaism accepts converts; it does not seek them. In charging Israel to be the exemplar of the dignity of difference, therefore, God posed two challenges: one to Israel, the other to the nations of the world. For Israel, the question has always been: do we have the courage to be different? For the nations it has been: do we make space for difference? The failure of the first leads to assimilation; of the second, to antisemitism.

Jews were persecuted because they were different. Under the Alexandrian and Roman empires they resisted Hellenization. Under medieval Christianity and Islam they refused conversion. Under nineteenth-century European nationalism they remained a distinctive group. During each of these five civilizations they sought no special rights except the right to be themselves, true to the faith of their ancestors. At each stage, some Jews defected. Most stayed loyal. Their vision was simple, best expressed in the words of the prophet Micah:

> Every man will sit under his own vine and his own fig tree,
> And no one will make them afraid,
> For the Lord Almighty has spoken.
> All the nations will walk, each in the name of its god;
> We will walk in the name of the Lord our God for ever and ever.[2]

I know of no spiritual vision truer to the nature of this created world, with its multiplicity of faiths, languages and cultures; none more generous in its understanding of the myriad forms of the human quest for God; none more vigilant in defence of the particular, the local, the relationships in which our humanity is expressed through covenants of love rather than the coercive force of power. Antisemitism – the paradigm case of the hatred of difference – is more than an assault against Jews. It is a flawed understanding, catastrophic in its consequences, of what it is to be human.

If I am right, three conclusions follow: one for Jews, a second for antisemites, a third for humanity as a whole.

For Jews, the response to antisemitism must be to fight it but never to internalize it or accept it on its own terms. Racial antisemitism, the product of a late nineteenth-century Europe that saw itself as the summit of civilization, eventually cost the lives of six million Jews. But it left another, less visible scar. One of the mistakes made by good, honourable and reflective Jews was to believe that since Jews were the objects of antisemitism, they were also its cause. They argued that since Jews were hated because they were different, they should try, as far as possible, not to be different. Some converted; others assimilated; yet others reformulated Judaism to eliminate as far as possible all that made Jews and Judaism distinctive. When these things failed – as they did, not only in nineteenth-century France, Germany and Austria but also in fifteenth-century Spain – some internalized the failure. Thus was born the tortured psychology known as Jewish self-hatred: the result of Jews ceasing to define themselves as a nation loved by God and instead seeing themselves as the people hated by gentiles. It was a tragic error. Antisemitism is not caused by Jews; they are merely its targets. We now know that there can be antisemitism in countries where there are no Jews at all. Hatred is something that can happen to us, but it is not who we are. It can never be the basis of an identity.

One episode, told by a rabbinical colleague, has long lingered in my mind. It took place in Russia in the early 1990s, following the collapse of communism. For the first time in seventy years, Jews were free openly to live as Jews, but at the same time antisemitic attitudes, long suppressed, also came to the surface. A British rabbi had gone there to help with the reconstruction of Jewish life, and was one day visited by a young lady in distress. 'All my life', she said, 'I hid the fact that I was a Jew and no one ever commented on my Jewishness. Now, though, when I walk past, my neighbours mutter *Zhid* [Jew]. What shall I do?' The rabbi replied, 'If you had not told me you were Jewish, I would never have known. But with my hat and beard, no one could miss the fact that I am a Jew. Yet, in all the months I have been here, no one has shouted *Zhid* at me. Why do you think that is?' The girl was silent for a moment and then said, 'Because they know that if they shout *Zhid* at me, I will take it as an insult, but if they shout *Zhid* at you, you will take it as a compliment.' That is a deep insight. Beyond eternal vigilance, the best way for Jews to combat antisemitism is to wear their identity with pride.

To antisemites, we must say this: we will never return hate with hate. To be a Jew is to work for peace and justice; revenge belongs to God, not us. Yet there is a truth that must also be spoken, namely that antisemitism is a profound psychological dysfunction, a disease masquerading as a cure. When bad things happen to a person or group, there are two questions it can ask: 'How can I put it right?' or 'Who did this to me?' Asking the first defines me as a subject, a moral agent, a responsible self. Asking the second identifies me as an object, a victim; and a victim can feel only resentment and rage.

There is an immense appeal to the culture of victimhood. It wins sympathy and the suspension of moral judgement. Its cost, however, is higher still, for defining oneself as a victim – antisemites always do – involves the systematic denial of responsibility. Dostoevsky once wrote in *The Brothers Karamazov* that 'If God does not exist, all is permitted.' That is untrue. But if *responsibility* does not exist, then all is permitted; and few phenomena have relieved more people of more responsibility than the mythical belief that there exists a group responsible for all the evils in the world, and the simultaneous knowledge, at some other level of consciousness, that it is in fact so vulnerable that it can be attacked with impunity.

It is no accident that throughout history, and no less so today, antisemitism has been the weapon of choice of tyrants, dictators, holders of non-democratic power and rulers of totalitarian states. It appeals because it deflects public unrest at hunger, poverty, ignorance, disease, economic inequalities, bribery, corruption and denial of human rights. It redirects indignation from its proper object to a mythical enemy charged with supernatural powers to control the world. That is why those who care for freedom, democracy and the rule of law must never cease to remind us that in the long run antisemitism harms those who practise it no less than those against whom it is practised. The culture of victimhood, so fashionable today, never liberates but only perpetuates the condition of the victim.

To humanity, the argument must be simple and direct. Antisemitism – the hatred of difference – is an assault not only on Jews but on the human condition as such. Life is sacred because each person – even genetically identical twins – is different, therefore irreplaceable and non-substitutable. Every language, culture and civilization (provided that it satisfies the minimum conditions of a universal moral code) has its own integrity and because each is different, each adds something unique to the collective heritage of mankind. Cultural diversity is as essential to our social ecology as is biodiversity to our natural ecology. A world without room for Jews is one that has no room for difference, and a world that lacks space for difference lacks space for humanity itself.

NOTES

1. Genesis 43:32, 46:34.
2. Micah 4: 4–5.

Notes on Contributors

Steven K. Baum is a psychologist in private practice in Albuquerque.

Michael Berenbaum, former Director, US Holocaust Memorial Museum, Washington, DC; Director, Sigi Ziering Institute: Exploring the Ethical and Religious Implications of the Holocaust; and Professor of Theology, University of Judaism, Los Angeles.

Phyllis Chesler is the author of 13 books and thousands of articles. She may be reached through her website www.phyllis-chesler.com.

Rabbi Abraham Cooper, Associate Dean of the Simon Wiesenthal Centre, Los Angeles.

Irwin Cotler, Member of the Canadian Parliament and Professor of Law, McGill University, Montreal.

Ronald Eissens, Director, Magenta Foundation, Amsterdam.

Morad El-Hattab El-Ibrahimi, philosopher, Paris, Laureate of Lucien Caroubi Prize for Literature, for Peace and Tolerance.

Richard English, Professor of Politics, Queen's University, Belfast.

Michael Fineberg, formerly at UNESCO, currently with the United Nations, New York.

Ian Hancock, Nowlin Regents' Professor of Liberal Arts, University of Texas at Austin; Director, Romani Archives and Documentation Center; Representative to the UN for the International Romani Union; Member, International Romani Parliament (Vienna).

Hannah Heer, producer/director of the documentary film *The Art of Remembrance*, on Simon Wiesenthal's life, New York.

Rabbi Marvin Hier, Dean and Founder, Simon Wiesenthal Centre, Los Angeles.

HM Hussein bin Talal al Hashemi, late monarch of the Hashemite Kingdom of Jordan.

Steven Jacobs, Aaron Aronov Endowed Chair of Judaic Studies, Associate Professor of Religious Studies, University of Alabama, and Secretary-Treasurer of the International Association of Genocide Scholars.

Lord Janner of Braunstone is President of the Holocaust Educational Trust and a prominent leader of the British Jewish community.

Günther Jikeli, Director, International Study Group Education and Research on Antisemitism (IIBSA), London, Berlin; founding member of the Kreuzberger Initiative gegen Antisemitismus (KIGA), Berlin.

Rachid Kaci, President of La Droite Libre, Paris.

Yaakov Kirschen, syndicated cartoonist, Jerusalem.

Beate and Serge Klarsfeld, founders of Les Fils et Filles des Déportés Juifs de France.

Paulinka Wiesenthal Kreisberg, psychologist and Simon Wiesenthal's only child, Tel Aviv.

Franklin H. Littell, Distinguished Professor of Holocaust and Genocide Studies, Richard Stockton College of New Jersey, and Emeritus Professor in the Department of Religion, Temple University.

Hubert G. Locke, Professor of Public Affairs, Dean Emeritus, and Marguerite Corbally Professor of Public Service, University of Washington Seattle; co-founder with Franklin Littell of the Annual Scholars' Conference on the Holocaust and the Churches.

Giovanni De Martis, Chair, Italian Historical Association Olokaustos, Venice.

Koichiro Matsuura, Director-General, UNESCO, Paris.

Martin Mendelsohn, Simon Wiesenthal's lawyer, Washington, DC.

Assumpta Mugiraneza, Rwandan genocide survivor, author, Paris.

Goetz Nordbruch, independent researcher, Berlin.

Richard Odier, President, Simon Wiesenthal Centre, France, and Treasurer, Verbe et Lumière-Vigilance, Paris.

John Pawlikowski, President, International Council of Christians and Jews, Professor of Ethics, Catholic Theological Union, Chicago.

Shimon Peres, Vice-Premier of the State of Israel.

Dina Porat, Professor and Head, Stephen Roth Institute for Antisemitism Studies, Tel Aviv University.

Jerrold M. Post, MD, Director, Political Psychology Programme, George Washington University, Washington, DC.

Basharat (Bashy) Tahir Quraishy, President, ENAR (European Network Against Racism – Brussels).

Pilar Rahola, former Spanish MP and syndicated columnist, Barcelona.

Mary Robinson, former President of Ireland, former United Nations High Commissioner for Human Rights, President of Realizing Rights: The Ethical Globalization Initiative.

Martin Rosen, Simon Wiesenthal's legal advisor, close friend and founder of the Wiesenthal Foundation: Jewish Documentation Center, New York.

John K. Roth, Professor of Philosophy, Claremont McKenna College, California.

Baron David de Rothschild, President, French Foundation for the Memory of the Shoah.

Baron Eric de Rothschild, President, French Memorial to the Shoah.

Chief Rabbi Jonathan Sacks, Chief Rabbi of the United Hebrew Congregations of the Commonwealth, London.

Shimon Samuels, Director for International Relations, Simon Wiesenthal Centre, Paris.

Nicolas Sarkozy, President of France.

Geoffrey Short, Professor of Sociology, Hertford, United Kingdom.

Simone Veil, President Emerita of the Foundation for the Memory of the Shoah, Paris and former President of the European Parliament.

Christian Weber, evangelical youth pastor, Berlin.

Gert Weisskirchen, German Bundestag Member, OSCE Rapporteur on Antisemitism, Berlin.

Mark Weitzman, Director of the Task Force on Hate, Simon Wiesenthal Centre, New York.

Paul Weller, Professor of Inter-Religious Relations, University of Derby, United Kingdom.

George Whyte, President, Whyte Foundation, United Kingdom.

Robert S. Wistrich, Director, Vidal Sassoon Institute on Antisemitism, Neuberger Professor of Modern Jewish History, Hebrew University of Jerusalem.

Xu Xin, Director, Institute of Jewish Studies, Nanjing University, China.

Efraïm Zuroff, Israel Director and Chief Nazi Investigator of the Simon Wiesenthal Centre, Jerusalem.

Index